THE
CONTENT
TRAP

BHARAT
ANAND

RANDOM HOUSE
NEW YORK

THE

CONTENT

TRAP

A STRATEGIST'S

GUIDE TO

DIGITAL CHANGE

Published in the United States by Random House, an imprint and division of Penguin Random House LLC, New York.

RANDOM HOUSE and the HOUSE colophon are registered trademarks of Penguin Random House LLC.

Grateful acknowledgment is made to *The Economist* for permission to reprint the following advertisements on p. 198: "My husband doesn't understand me." Creatives: Gideon Todes & Mike Harris, Agency: AMVBBDO. © The Economist Newspaper Limited, London; "In opinion polls, 100% of Economist readers had one." Creatives: Mike Durban & Tony Strong, Agency: AMVBBDO. © The Economist Newspaper Limited, London; "Is your indecision final?" Creative: Tim Riley, Agency: AMVBBDO. © The Economist Newspaper Limited, London; "What exactly is the benefit of the doubt?" Creatives: Ben Kay & Paul Blackley, Agency: AMVBBDO. © The Economist Newspaper Limited, London; "Would you like to sit next to you at dinner?" Creatives: David Abbott & Ron Brown, Agency: AMVBBDO. © The Economist Newspaper Limited, London. Reprinted by permission of *The Economist*.

LIBRARY OF CONGRESS CATALOGING-IN-PUBLICATION DATA
Names: Anand, Bharat Narendra, author.
Title: The content trap : a strategist's guide to digital change / Bharat Anand.
Description: First Edition. | New York : Random House, 2016. | Includes index.
Identifiers: LCCN 2016019174| ISBN 9780812995381 (hardback) | ISBN 9780812995398 (ebook)
Subjects: LCSH: Entrepreneurship. | Mass media—Economic aspects. | Telecommunication—Economic aspects. | BISAC: BUSINESS & ECONOMICS / Industries / Media & Communications Industries. | BUSINESS & ECONOMICS / Entrepreneurship. | BUSINESS & ECONOMICS / Motivational.
Classification: LCC HB615 .A6825 2016 | DDC 302.23068/4—dc23 LC record available at https://lccn.loc.gov/2016019174

Printed in the United States of America on acid-free paper

randomhousebooks.com

9 8 7 6 5 4 3 2 1

FIRST EDITION

Book design by Simon M. Sullivan

In compliance with Harvard Business School's Policy on Conflicts of Interest adopted in 2012, the author has disclosed all paid and unpaid activities relevant to this book in the appropriate notes.

To my parents,
for starting me down this path
and Anju and Rhea,
for walking with me on it

PREFACE

I loved music growing up. I was enchanted by my mother's voice when she sang—and for many years I indulged in singing too. I also read books, newspapers, and magazines, and watched Bollywood movies and even commercials (which in India were often perversely memorable). In Mumbai, India's media capital, music and the arts were everywhere. And they were an obsession in our family.

So when the Internet came along, years later, I was fascinated by its impact on all these things—the things we hear, watch, and read. It would eventually touch much else besides—cars and taxis, hotels and airlines, banking and fashion. But it impacted certain things first, threatening to destroy them. First was music, then newspapers, then books, movies, TV, and education. These remain the businesses at the bleeding edge of technology—businesses that are being turned upside down. These are the laboratories of change where destruction and reinvention are happening simultaneously. These are the canaries in the coal mine.

Like nearly everyone else tracking these worlds, I wondered how to make sense of it all. Then I noticed something curious. It became commonplace, even fashionable, to try to predict what was going to happen next. What is the future of TV or newspapers? Where will the next innovative ideas come from? What is the next Big Thing?

It's exhilarating to try to predict the future. It's also draining. And the predictions are almost always wrong. This sort of thing, I came to realize, cannot be worth very much. That's what led me and one of my colleagues at Harvard Business School, Felix Oberholzer-Gee, to create a program on digital strategies nearly a decade ago. Rather than making predictions, we tried to make sense of the ground we stood on.

We taught this program for many years. As we did so, I noticed something else happening in the world of experts. New ideas were being tossed around every day, new theories and prescriptions crafted seemingly every week. Many were fascinating. But for anyone trying to keep up, it was no less exhausting than trying to keep up with the predictors. Hypertargeting.

Personalization. Core competence. Focus. Accelerators. Incubators. Networks. Platforms. Bundling. Disruption. Every time you blinked, it seemed a new concept emerged, and a new term was being coined.

And this was the next thing I came to realize. The real challenge is not trying to understand these theories—that's the easy part. The real challenge is to understand where these ideas are relevant, to see how they connect, and to know when they are limited—when *not* to use them.

Those who attended our program—entrepreneurs and managers, editors and artists, lawyers, analysts, and investors—were each experiencing a world of rapid change. They were trying to keep up, figure out when to act, and what to do. They were trying to make sense of what was going on. Above all, they yearned for clarity.

That's how I came to write this book.

This book is about digital change, and how to navigate it. It's about change that has been happening for twenty years now, and an attempt to make sense of it. It's about what's happening today, while recognizing that tomorrow will be mercilessly different. But to get things right, we cannot solely focus on the "here and now," or start by obsessing about tomorrow. Quite the opposite. To make sense of what's happening today, we almost need to forget what's happening today. We need to take a step back, and make sense of what's already happened. We need to get off the bullet train, even if only for a moment, to learn where it's going. We need to understand the game being played before we can know how to win it.

Many of the theories addressed in this book have been written about before, somewhere. But in trying to understand the limits of each and connecting the dots between them, in trying to identify the common mistakes we make in each case, and the right solutions, I came to realize that navigating digital change is all about having a certain mindset.

It's a mindset that I came to see in people who have managed or led digital change successfully. They are humble in recognizing what they can't control, yet primed to take advantage of what they can. They don't claim to know every answer, but are confident about asking the right questions. They are unafraid to go against the grain, to try something different. Throughout, they are able to see the forest *and* the trees.

And that is, ultimately, the central message of this book. Getting things right requires understanding how small things are tied to big ones. More concretely, it requires three things: seeing how what we do is increasingly linked to *what others do;* looking beyond *where we play* to bring related but invisible opportunities into focus; and recognizing how what we do is impacted by *where we are*.

It requires recognizing these connections—then respecting, creating, and leveraging them as well. Do so, and you'll avoid a danger that plagues many who fail, and is deceptively hard to avoid: what I call the Content Trap.

My argument is evidence- and case-based. I will draw on research studies conducted in multiple domains—economics, marketing, and strategy—and on the experiences of various organizations. In researching this book, I traveled around the world to talk to key players navigating the digital challenges businesses everywhere face. The stories here include the accounts of researchers, managers, entrepreneurs, analysts; what they've gotten right, what they've gotten wrong. What have they figured out that has eluded so many others?

Along the way, this book became a personal journey. Three years ago at Harvard Business School, we began creating our own vision of a digital future—in education. We began reimagining our own classroom, and what it should look like. I was drawn into this effort with a few inspired colleagues, and then asked to lead it. As I did so, I found that my thinking on these matters both drew on and fed the ideas in this book. Certain features of our digital classroom are a product of this book—and the book, in turn, is in part a product of our experiences creating our digital classroom. As this journey continued, I was no longer just an observer of digital efforts; I became a participant as well.

This book centers on digital transformations we've seen in the worlds of music, newspapers, books, TV, film, advertising, and education. These are often described as *information goods*—things that rely, ultimately, on moving information, bits and bytes. But I hope the lessons gleaned apply far beyond those domains. There is reason to believe that will be so. After all, everyone today—a businessperson, an educator, a politician, a student, an artist, an entrepreneur—can reach and interact with others directly. In other words, everyone is a media company today.

CONTENTS

Part III: Context—Functional Connections

Part IV: Everyone's a Media Company

INTRODUCTION

1. MANAGING FIRES

The Yellowstone Fires of 1988

July 22, 1988. Targhee National Forest, Idaho. After several hours of cutting timber, a woodcutter gets together with three buddies for a break and a smoke—and drops a still-burning cigarette into the grass. He doesn't notice the small fire that ensues. Within hours the flames spread, soon engulfing five hundred acres of forest. The "North Fork Fire," as it came to be called, would ultimately spread eastward into Yellowstone National Park, whose boundary lay a mere four hundred yards away.

Yellowstone is the world's oldest national park and encompasses 2.2 million acres in the northwestern states of Wyoming, Idaho, and Montana. Within three weeks the North Fork fire consumed 53,000 acres of parkland, making it the biggest fire in Yellowstone's 116-year history. And the fires weren't over. On August 15 a spark from a horseshoe ignited brush in Montana's Gallatin National Forest, giving rise to the Hellroaring Fire, which also quickly spread to Yellowstone. On August 20, a day that became known in Yellowstone as Black Saturday, wind gusts of up to 80 miles an hour whipped the fires into a frenzy. Flames climbed three hundred feet above the forest, trees "snapped like toothpicks," and new gusts were generated by the fires themselves. Two new fires were started by trees falling on power lines. In less than eight hours the size of the Yellowstone fires doubled.

By the time it was over, nearly a month later, these two fires had burned more than 450,000 acres—or 20 percent of the entire area of Yellowstone.

If the fires' triggers were unremarkable, the response to fighting them was anything but. Already in the weeks leading up to these fires, National Park Service managers let several blazes burn, reasoning that they did not appear to threaten people or property. Before they knew it, the fires were out of control.

Yellowstone's superintendent, Robert Barbee, came under harsh criticism. Locals raised a banner calling the fires a "Barbee-que." Ecologist Don Despain was in for even harsher words. An environmental scientist who had made a career of studying fire and its effects in Yellowstone, Despain seemed almost to celebrate the fires in his eagerness to examine their effects. "Burn, Baby, Burn," screamed the headline of a *Denver Post* article documenting Despain's reaction to fires near Yellowstone's Wolf Lake.

Soon after, the *Denver Post* account broke into the national news media, which was scathing in its criticism of what it saw as rangers' negligence. Recently formed CNN aired hourly footage of the fires around the clock. "There are a lot of angry people who believe that the National Park Service is responsible and has let the fires burn too freely for too long," NBC News anchor Tom Brokaw would later report. The dramatic images fueled emotions everywhere.

I had just graduated from college and was becoming a dedicated viewer of cable news. I found the images of the fires, and the little being done to stop them, arresting. Like millions of Americans, I could not understand the tragedy. Why would anyone let fires burn? How could it be that they weren't fought on the day they arose?

As the public later learned, there were fervent disagreements among neighboring park and forest supervisors about how to manage the fires. John Burns, the supervisor of Targhee National Forest, had always gotten along well with his Yellowstone counterpart, Barbee. But they saw things very differently now. After the early fires had spread that summer, Burns let Barbee know that "Targhee would not accept any lightning-ignited fires that had started in Yellowstone and had purposely been let burn," citing the burning conditions and the risks they posed. Brian Stout, the supervisor of the Bridger-Teton National Forest, took a different stance. The Mink Creek Fire, started by lightning on July 11, was threatening to swamp Bridger-Teton and the southeastern region of Yellowstone. Stout, preoccupied by fighting another blaze, decided to let it burn.

When Barbee did decide, in mid-July, to muster Yellowstone's resources to aggressively fight several major fires, he encountered protests from some Yellowstone employees who favored letting natural processes run their course. When he decided to use bulldozers to etch lines that might prevent the fires from advancing, he was derided by environmental groups that feared that the gashes in the earth would last longer than fire scars. Nothing came easy.

On September 10 the park closed to the public—the first closure in its history. As if nature had been waiting for a sign of defeat from man, the year's first snowfall hit the ground the next day and the fires began to subside. Yellowstone residents sang "Jingle Bells" in September. But the damage had been done, and would last for decades, perhaps centuries.

Three months after the first fires had started in Yellowstone, the damage to America's foremost national park was devastating. More than 1.3 million acres of the greater Yellowstone ecosystem, and 36 percent of the park, had burned. Visitors encountered black mountainsides. More than 2 million tons of particulate and 4.4 million tons of carbon monoxide had been released into the air. In some places it was so dark during the day that photography was all but impossible. The air pollution eventually extended all the way to the East Coast and as far south as Texas.

From Forest Fires to Digital Fires

The management of Yellowstone's 1988 fires had several notable features. First was the sheer bad luck of the cigarette butt and horseshoe spark—we can call them *benign triggers*. Second was *passive management response*— the apparent indifference of park supervisors, in part traceable to the distressingly inaccurate predictions of fire experts. As late as August 1, for example, they remained optimistic, arguing that the combination of rain (typical for the region in August), weak winds, and young lodgepole pines would contain the flames. Despain said, "The fires will slow down considerably before the end of August if we don't have rain. If we do have rain, the fires will cover far short of what we've mapped out. We don't predict a whole lot more than we've already got."

Third was the intense *managerial disagreement and conflict* over the appropriate course of action. Supervisors in Yellowstone, Targhee, Bridger-Teton, and the Shoshone National Forest differed on how and how quickly to suppress the fires. So did the heads of the U.S. Forest Service and the National Park Service. State politicians and senators had their own, often passionate, views.

All of which led to the devastating impact that the fires were predicted to have on the Greater Yellowstone ecosystem. Forests would need to be reseeded. Tree death would result in animal death, since elk and other wildlife were deprived of the sweet inner tree bark and the moss and sagebrush they depended on for food. The same would happen to grizzly bears, deprived of the seeds in whitebark pinecones. Insect infestations would increase. Dead trees would serve as fuel for future fires, increasing the park's vulnerability. Soil erosion would increase, filling rivers with silt, and killing fish. And visitors to the park would decrease, possibly in dramatic numbers.

The Yellowstone fires of 1988 seem a lesson in management—in what *not* to do. And they hold hugely important lessons for managing future fires not just in Yellowstone but in other parks. They also contain lessons for managers in faraway arenas like media and entertainment, which have been experiencing "digital fires" for more than two decades.

Consider *benign triggers*. Three friends, all early employees of PayPal, try to find video clips of certain events online, leading them to create a video-sharing site—YouTube—that jump-starts the digital video-sharing industry. Another group of three friends creates a service that lets people easily share MP3 music files with others—Napster, the biggest disruption ever to the music industry. A college sophomore writes a computer program that lets his classmates choose the "hotter" person in a given pairing of students—eventually leading to Facebook. A young MBA graduate working at a hedge fund creates short educational videos to help his cousin with sixth-grade math and posts them on YouTube—resulting in Khan Academy and eventually precipitating the biggest changes in education in three hundred years.

Each of these events—isolated, idiosyncratic, modest at the outset—had a colossal impact. And the pattern can be seen elsewhere. A market trader allegedly slapped by a policewoman sets himself on fire, resulting in the Arab Spring. An eighty-year-old man goes on a hunger strike, leading the Indian parliament to pass its first major anticorruption bill in decades. A single person, through actions that might be hardly characterized as novel or unprecedented—after all, street fights and hunger strikes have been common in these countries for decades—sparks a vast change in politics and society unimaginable even a decade earlier; a small trigger has a large impact.

The second feature, *passive management response*, is also pervasive in the media. Netflix, started in 1997, was inspired by a forty-dollar late fee paid by founder Reed Hastings for a Blockbuster rental. Blockbuster chose not to react. At the time it seemed a rational response: after all, six years later Blockbuster's revenues exceeded $5 billion—more than ten times as much as Netflix's. By the time management decided to react to Netflix, it was too late. Blockbuster declared bankruptcy in 2010.

Newspapers waited years before aggressively moving online. In nearly every case their early digital efforts involved halfhearted moves and low resource commitments. Book publishers embraced e-books only in reaction to Amazon's aggressive move into digital waters, although the transition had been in the cards for years. Recording studios reacted to digital formats only after peer-to-peer services threatened to pull the carpet from under them entirely. Television channels and cable operators continue to hold on to the worlds of their past—cable subscriptions, bundled offerings, and ever-increasing prices—even as broadband video offerings and à la carte alternatives proliferate. Having a problem stare you in the face is often not enough to trigger a response, it appears.

Managerial disagreement and conflict is routinely seen as well. Few issues have sparked as much debate as the digital transition. When and how to react? How to organize? Whether to self-cannibalize? These questions continue to catalyze intense feelings and discussion. Look at any media organization and you're apt to see a manager second-guessed, an editor fired, a board member criticized. Return the following year and you may see their successors suffer the same fate.

Combine these features in content businesses, and the result is analogous to what happened in Yellowstone: a devastating impact to the landscape. By the time the recording industry understood what digital formats, MP3 players, and peer-to-peer services were doing to its business, it was too late. From 2004 to 2014 unit sales of CDs and digital singles—music "content"—declined by roughly 50 percent. This was a harbinger of things to come in other parts of the media and entertainment worlds. Newspaper readership declined continuously during the decade, with profits declining even more sharply. Book and music retailers dropped like flies. People stopped paying for television. Movie theaters closed. The decimation of the "cultural industries," a process that began with the birth of the World Wide Web in the early 1990s, is now well on its way to completion.

. . . Or Is It? The *Real* Lessons from the Yellowstone Fires

Digital fires have a lot in common with forest fires like the ones that burned Yellowstone during the summer of 1988—except for one problem. The description above of the causes, management, and impact of the Yellowstone fires is not just dramatic, it is wrong.

The real causes of the fires, and the real lessons from them, were quite different.

Triggers—and Their Irrelevance

A cigarette butt and horseshoe sparks were unusual triggers for a major fire, much less the fire of the century; lightning is a far more common cause.* But what *really* led to the devastation that summer wasn't the triggers—it was the factors that caused the fires to spread. After all, fires had been triggered thousands of times before. But that summer was the driest in the 112-year recorded history of the park. A drought was afflicting the West for a second consecutive year. By the end of May, the forests and rangelands were drying out with uncharacteristic speed.

Dryness—not any trigger—caused the Yellowstone fires to spread.

The Logic of "Letting It Burn"

The notion that Park Service rangers were complacent, negligent, or incompetent was as much a myth as the idea that a careless woodcutter or a horseshoe's spark was to blame. The rangers' response to the fires was intentional and rational, the result of policy that was decades in the making.

See a fire, and your natural instinct is to put it out. That was Yellowstone's instinct as far back as 1886, when U.S. Army captain Moses Harris led troops into the park to suppress fires that had been rampant for months. Never mind that it was snow, not man, that eventually snuffed out many of those fires; Harris became a hero and fire suppression became park doctrine.

The strategy evolved into a highly systematic response: coordinated team efforts, fire lookouts for early detection, and rapid response. Public campgrounds, which originated at Yellowstone, were actually aimed at fire prevention; they created separate areas for tourists in order to prevent campfires from spreading and to more easily determine their location if they arose.

But over the next few decades, views on fire would gradually change.

---

* Indeed, lightning was behind most of the other major fires in Yellowstone that summer, including the Storm Creek Fire, the Shoshone Fire, the Fan Fire, the Red Fire, the Mist Fire, the Clover Fire, the Mink Fire, and the Falls Fire.

Different scientists, environmental researchers, and rangers would find themselves tackling a series of different problems, and reach surprising conclusions in each case. Some, like noted Park Service supervisor Aldo Leopold in the 1930s, in their efforts to restore devastated prairies, would find that seeding native plants had the unintended consequence of weeds also prospering. Fire might solve the problem. Others, called in to figure out a solution to reducing the unsustainably large elk herd in parks, would find that most efforts were either costly or controversial. Fire could be a cheap and natural solution. Ecologists trying to diversify and renew park vegetation confronted a problem of their own: Existing forests had grown too dense, and too high. Fire could be a solution.

By the 1960s views on fire had changed. The shift in views culminated with the writings of Leopold's son, wildlife biologist A. Starker Leopold of the University of California, Berkeley. Tasked initially with advising the federal government about reducing Yellowstone's elk herd, he and other scientists noted that the best solution to problems as diverse as the need for reducing animal populations, clearing habitat, reintroducing native species, or even eliminating exotic ones, was to create conditions that were as close as possible to primitive America. That would require management, and "of the various methods of manipulating vegetation, the controlled use of fire is the most natural and much the cheapest and easiest to apply."

Starker Leopold's report became the decisive driver of the National Park Service's new fire policy. It came during a period when others like Chapman, Despain, and Barbee were forming similar views. By the time Robert Barbee took over as superintendent of Yellowstone in 1971, the "let it burn" policy had taken firm hold in the Park Service. Over the next fifteen years Yellowstone managed fires that way and saw a remarkable turnaround. From 1972 to 1987, 235 fires in Yellowstone were started by lightning and allowed to burn to varying degrees. Only 34,000 acres in all were destroyed.

So in 1988, Barbee let it burn.

Why Disagreements Are Natural: The Role of Context

Disagreements about how to manage the 1988 fires were intense. Some advocated immediate combat, others supported natural burn. To the untrained observer, this was troubling, but it shouldn't have been. The reason it was troubling in fact reflects our own biases in decision making: we tend to search for a universally right solution rather than recognizing that what the right decision is should reflect the context.

Halve the size of a forest, for example, and a natural fire policy becomes far less attractive—even a small fire might destroy the entire forest. Consider a fire in a single home in a populated city, and a "let it burn" approach would be criminal. Encounter a fire in Yellowstone in the midst of a scorching July after one-quarter of the park has burned and, like the rangers there did, you'd fight it with everything you have. Encounter the same-sized fire in spring and letting it burn might be precisely right.

Why do we recoil at the idea of letting fires burn? Because our frame of reference is how fires impact us, destroying buildings and property and bringing nothing good. By extension, we believe fires can bring no good anywhere. But walk in the shoes of park rangers and you'll reach a very different conclusion.

This simple idea—that the right decision is often closely tied to its context—has profound implications for management. We will return to it later.

The 1988 fires were supposed to destroy Yellowstone—its flora, fauna, wildlife. Park officials put up signs to tell visitors to expect only meadows for years to come. Only, the signs turned out to be wrong.

The near-term devastation of the park contained the seeds (literally) of future growth. The slow decay of pine, spruce, and fir trees nourished the park's volcanic soil, adding nutrients and limiting erosion, helping to provide homes for birds and insects and cover for other animals. The fires burned the protective resin coating on the serotinous lodgepole pinecones, "sending an explosion of seeds to the forest floor," exactly as researchers had predicted decades earlier. New, genetically diverse aspen were able to grow without competition from taller trees. Rare flora and fauna not seen in Yellowstone for decades began to flourish; some estimated that certain germinated plants may have been lying in wait for three centuries before the fires. By 2004, "15-foot-high lodgepoles, well spaced and uncrowded, rose naturally from the ash."

Nor did park visitors disappear. Annual visits increased every year after the fires, amounting to more than three and a half million people by 2015—60 percent more than in 1988. Most visitors had no idea that there had been fires in 1988.

The park wasn't destroyed. As one ranger summarized, it was "reborn, rebuilt, and rejuvenated."

2. THE CONTENT TRAP

"Too much light often blinds gentlemen of this sort. They cannot see the forest for the trees."
—Christoph Martin Wieland, *Musarion,* Canto II (1768)

Few assets are as precious to Yellowstone's rangers as the park's "content": the stirring flora and fauna spread across its millions of acres. Yet those assets were allowed to burn, and by those who cared the most about them.

On the face of it, it's a strange narrative. But it contains enormous lessons for businesses confronting digital fires—economic conflagrations induced by digital technologies.

Few assets are as precious to billions of people around the world as the content they consume every day—books, songs, programs, newspapers, movies. It's perfectly natural, then, that all businesses, entrepreneurs, and creatively inclined people would try hard to nurture and produce "the best" content. It's perfectly natural that they would focus on any trigger that appeared to undermine its value or any spark that might enhance it. It's perfectly natural that they would try to preserve the value of content in the face of inexorable decline. And it's perfectly natural that they would search for solutions by looking to others who also produce or manage content.

These are seemingly rational and sensible behaviors that turn out to be flawed. This is what I call the Content Trap.

In what follows, I will describe the Content Trap's main features. The rest of the book will take us more deeply into the mistakes we make in falling into it, and how we can overcome them. But first, let's look at where digital wildfires come from.

The Source of Digital Wildfires

Today users can interact with others at near-zero cost. That is the essence of digital technologies, be they file-sharing services, social networks, microblogs, news feeds, video uploading, instant messaging, app sharing, viral advertising, or educational platforms.

What this means is that anyone can supply and distribute content today. This is often lauded as the "democratization of media." But it creates a colossal problem for any organization: the proliferation of alternatives and product clutter.

Today more than 300,000 books are released every year by traditional U.S. publishers—and more than one million are released by nontraditional ones, many as self-published books. Television networks now include more than 900 channels, up from barely a dozen forty years ago. Nearly one million musicians release songs every year, a dramatic increase from just twenty years ago. When it comes to digital content the numbers are even more extraordinary. Nearly 72 hours of video are uploaded to YouTube, three million pieces of content shared by Facebook users, and 230,000 new photos posted on Instagram—*every minute*. More than 90 million websites are built every year. And perhaps the most sobering statistic: five exabytes (or 5 billion billion bytes) of data could store all the words ever spoken by humans between the birth of the world and 2003. In 2011, five exabytes of content were created every two days.

Compete in a world of four broadcast channels and you know what you're up against. Compete against 900 channels, millions of short-form videos, and the rerelease of an entire library of video archives—including your own—and it's a strategic and marketing nightmare even to make consumers aware of what you're producing.

Let's call this "the problem of getting noticed."

The near-zero cost of propagation also means it's extremely difficult to control content once it's produced. Digital rights are messy to establish. Content often enters the mainstream before it's formally released—songs and movies are routinely available on file-sharing sites a week before recording or film studios bring them to the public. And a single individual or infringement can have multiplier effects, as Napster, Gnutella, and Bit-Torrent exemplify. All this creates a second problem: not being able to charge for products, once they're offered.

Let's call it "the problem of getting paid."

Considered in isolation, each of these problems is hard enough to tackle. Together, they are lethal, threatening to destroy the business of content—in effect, setting "content on fire" in digital worlds.

The Content Trap and the Business of Connections

The Content Trap is a mindset that afflicts nearly every organization struggling to confront the problems of getting noticed and getting paid, from media to finance to education, and whether they're producing stories or designing phones. It has three main expressions, similar to the three main errors we saw at Yellowstone:

1. First is the obsession with isolated triggers rather than recognizing the conditions that make them spread. This is akin to believing that product features in isolation drive success or failure rather than what causes users to share and connect. This is an error of misplaced focus, a result of confusing cause and effect.
2. Second is the effort to preserve content at all costs—rather than seizing the opportunities around it. This is an error of drawing product boundaries too narrowly.
3. Third is the relentless search for best practices, the belief that there's one "right approach" to confront digital fires—rather than understanding that the right way to fight fires depends on the context in which they burn. This is an error that mistakes strategy for universal solutions.

These three errors are prevalent in nearly every digital domain. And they have something in common. They cause us to see things discretely, in isolation, rather than as connected parts of a whole. They cause us to miss—in Yellowstone's case, literally—the forest for the trees. They cause us to miss what's actually most important—"connections."

Connections, I will argue in this book, are at the heart of what shapes any digitally touched business today and will for the foreseeable future. Being able to recognize, leverage, and manage connections separates companies that succeed from those that fail.

Just as there are three expressions of the Content Trap, there are three types of connections central to our story: connections between users, connections between products, and connections across an organization's activities. Individually and together, they can lead us out of the Content Trap, and explain success and failure in a strikingly large array of examples.

Let's call this the Connections Triad (Figure 1).

User Connections—or, why to focus not on an event's triggers but on why it spreads

The first part of the Triad is to focus on the triggers—the spark—rather than on the enabling conditions that turn that spark into a fire. It's think-

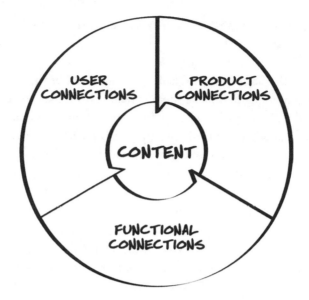

Figure 1: The Connections Triad

ing that a cigarette butt was the reason behind the Yellowstone fires. We view triggers like these to be at the heart of success or failure in business, too. In content worlds, we focus on the actions, tastes, or behaviors of consumers in isolation rather than on what connects them; we focus on making the "best" content rather than on what makes users share; we focus on the creative spark of genius and how to nurture it, or on a particular threat and how to suppress it. But in nearly every case, what's thought of as a side effect of a product's success is the real cause.

Digital wildfires—the propagation of success or failure in digital businesses—come from close connections between individuals, more than the quality of content or any individual action behind it. Allow people to communicate and share and a benign trigger can propagate with stirring speed. Shut off the connections and the same trigger is uneventful. The piracy of media products, for instance, is not a new phenomenon; it has existed for decades. What's changed is the ability to share and spread content.

In 1984 Apple introduced the Macintosh, a personal computer far superior in its ease of use, experience, and stability to any rival product at the time. A decade later the Macintosh had less than 10 percent of market share—and the figure was declining rapidly. Apple struggled not because it somehow failed to make a great product but because it failed to leverage user connections. The primary benefit users derived from a PC was not quality, ease of use, or stability; it was the ability to share files with friends and colleagues—the ability to connect.

User connections—the focus of Part I of this book—explain how an instant messaging company in China grew to become one of the most valuable Internet firms in the world. They explain why a Scandinavian newspaper company has been perhaps the most successful paper in the Western world at making the digital transition. They explain why *The New York Times*'s 2013 paywall experiment generated hundreds of millions of dollars in annual revenue whereas the *Times*'s earlier paywall effort mustered only a minuscule fraction of that. They explain why the unbundling of cable channels—something nearly everyone yearns for—is not only resisted by cable channels but is something viewers might come to regret. And they explain why some of the most successful organizations in digital advertising have experienced success not by trying to predict viral triggers but by predicting how and when those fires will spread.

Product Connections—or, how hurt can actually help

The second version of the Content Trap is to preserve the burning tree at all cost. In digital worlds, it's focusing on a piece of content that may be destroyed, even if it's your entire business. But smart strategy requires looking at tomorrow's benefit rather than today's hurt. It requires focusing not on the death or disruption of content but on the opportunities that lie beneath it. Many apparent threats can be embraced for large payoffs.

Music piracy was supposed to destroy the industry. Instead it created new opportunities to capture value. In Part II, I will examine how it did so—and how destruction in one class of music products created more value in adjacent arenas.

That's just one example of product connections; they are ubiquitous in media and entertainment. I'll show how the success of a single program on India's Star TV network generated a massive across-the-board market share increase and transformed the country's TV dynamics. I'll explore why sports programs command prices that are far higher than could be justified by their ratings. I'll describe how some of the most impressive successes in media businesses come not from trying to predict hits or bestsellers—that's a fool's errand—but from piggybacking on them once they arise. I'll examine both sides of the "synergy" debate—why efforts to systematically create synergies often fail, whereas efforts to leverage them after the fact can work. And I'll detail how an entrepreneur who assembled an array of services for athletes that involved seemingly routine things became the most powerful person in sports. In each case, success came not by increasing the focus on a single product but from managing product portfolios.

Recognize product connections and you'll see new opportunities. You'll see why embracing hurt to one product can help other parts of the product portfolio, or in the future. Accepting or even embracing piracy, reducing product quality, pricing a product low or free—organizations that take these kinds of counterintuitive steps increasingly meet with success rather than doom.

As organizations increasingly narrow their focus on their core products, they tend to exert greater efforts to create content, to define their businesses in terms of content, or to prop up the price of content. These efforts are natural—but they increasingly end up on the wrong side of success. A narrow product lens causes one to miss the connections across products and as a result the large-value opportunities that reside elsewhere.

Functional Connections—or, why differences are not just natural but desirable

The third form of the Content Trap comes from assuming that there's one right way of dealing with fire—fight it, or let it burn. A dominant tendency in content businesses confronting digital worlds is to search for a magic bullet, for the one right approach to preserving value and fighting disruption. "Mimic your competitors," "learn from others," "embrace best practices"—virtually all business advice today has drilled these notions into people's heads.

But these prescriptions don't always work. The reason sounds simple: Context matters. Yet we ignore it.

As we've said, managing fires in dry conditions is very different from managing them in wet ones, even in the same park. Managing fires in a small forest is very different from managing them in a large park—even under the same conditions. And managing fires in a city is very different from managing them in an uninhabited park. State the differences this way and it seems obvious that actions appropriate in one setting might be entirely inappropriate in another. Yet all too often context is treated like background noise when we consider our decisions and actions.

Virtually every book publisher today looks to rivals to see how and how quickly they are transitioning to an e-book world. Virtually every TV network looks to others as it tries to figure out its broadband strategy. Virtually every newspaper looks to *The New York Times* to see what it can mimic. Chances are, such efforts will fail miserably.

In addition to the external context that a business finds itself in, there's an internal context that any business itself creates—the set of all the other decisions it makes.

How should we price our digital product? What should the design of our mobile app be? How should we organize our digital and traditional businesses? Frame questions this way and the tendency is to look for an isolated policy or decision by others rather than to recognize the forest of other decisions that are tied to it. The "right price" for your digital product depends on your marketing choices—whether you are trying to get new users to sample, or trying to engage existing committed ones. Your mobile design must match your content strategy, and vice versa. Whether you separate your digital business from the parent depends on whether you see their products as complementary or not. Each of these discrete functional decisions is intimately tied to many others, creating "functional connections."

The most successful organizations see the entire map of functional links to understand the context within which each decision is made. They don't look elsewhere for answers, but find their own. This is a fundamental principle of strategy. Strategic success doesn't just benefit from being different from others. It *requires* it. If you aren't different in business, you'll die.

Business strategy is about two questions: where should you play, and how will you win. Finding the right answers requires making your product right, knowing your consumers, and understanding how these are changing in your market. But, increasingly, I will argue, that's not enough. Understanding your landscape requires thinking not just about products and consumers—as is the trend—but also about the connections among them. Understanding how to win requires looking not to other organizations for answers—another trend—but to the connections among all the activities inside your own.

3. A NOTE TO THE READER

The Content Trap is both pervasive and insidious. In the rest of this book, I will explore a broad range of scenarios where it arises, but also how particular companies have found their way around it. Through the lessons gained from these cases and research studies, we'll see how strategic thinking can refine our choices and opportunities in a digitally connected world.

One reason why the Content Trap is dangerous is precisely because conventional wisdom and expert opinion can lure us into it.

Companies invariably clamor for creative genius and superior quality as the triggers they need. They are advised to focus and singularly specialize on the products they already have. They are told to base their decisions on the best practices of others. Focusing on content—making it better, charging for it, learning from others—is not inherently unreasonable. But miss the role of connections—user, product, or functional ones—and that focus will fail. Focus on content alone rather than connections and you won't fight digital fires using the crucial lessons of the Yellowstone fires.

Beyond this, there are three buckets of advice we most often encounter when it comes to "digital change." They have come to be built around certain premises: change as threatening, listening to your customer, and the value of forecasting. This book diverges from the usual view on these matters, as follows.

Change as Threatening

Connections can help businesses, not just harm them. Media observers have historically and repeatedly thought that new technologies would destroy incumbents. That was the predicted effect of radio on music sales, piracy on the music industry, videocassette recorders on advertising revenue, digital video recorders on TV advertising, live streaming on cable viewing, and "over-the-top" (or, direct-to-consumer) video offerings on cable business, among other things. In each case the actual effects were quite different from the predictions—often exactly the opposite. Seemingly negative connections turned out to be positive.

We see negative connections all too easily, thinking in terms of "threats," "substitutes," "disruption," and similar terms. The reason for this, in large part, is that we are not trained to look for positive connections. Indeed, each of those terms tends to move managers in the wrong direction. We shy away from embracing technologies, we resign ourselves to our inevitable fate, or we mimic others positioned to disrupt.

Listening to Your Customer

The lens of connections offers a new perspective on an old question: What does it take to be customer-centric? The traditional message for organizations is a threefold cliché: "Cater to every user," "narrow your focus," and "say yes to your customer" to best deliver value. Drawing out the idea of connections will yield prescriptions that diverge from these.

- "Cater to every user": I will argue that *managing user portfolios* is likely to be far more fruitful. This insight follows from understanding user connections.
- "Narrow your focus": I will argue that user centricity often requires broadening your horizons, and even *diversifying your product portfolio*. This insight follows from understanding product connections.
- "Saying yes" to your customer: Understanding functional connections invariably requires *saying no* instead.

The Value of Prediction

By the time you read this book, some of its examples will be outdated. That is the nature of media and entertainment today—technologies change more rapidly than anyone can anticipate. Listen to any digital entrepreneur, pick up any report on the media, go to any entertainment conference, and you'll hear about the technologies of tomorrow and how they will shape media and entertainment. And nearly all the predictions will be wrong.

I will not make predictions in this book. I will offer a perspective on certain forces driving digital businesses and how those forces shape strategy and decision making. My hope is that the perspective will be useful to entrepreneurs, managers, artists, and industry observers even as industries continue to change and regardless of the technologies triggering the changes.

In other words, this book is not about the next cigarette butt or horse-shoe spark but what happens when they *will* occur. Predicting triggers is a futile exercise. Managing them once they arise is not. Hits and duds are familiar triggers, and each has spillovers into other products. But they're regularly unpredictable (indeed, one of the axioms of media businesses is that "we don't know" what will work). And that's where management often goes wrong. Efforts are made to systematize synergistic connections in advance—which one can't know—rather than to exploit them after they arise. These are mistakes of arrogance—rooted in not understanding the limits of what we can predict.

Could the Yellowstone fires have been prevented? One view says yes, if fire suppression had started from day one. Others argue that that misses the point: Not even the most sophisticated analysts could have predicted that the fires would get so breathtakingly out of control. Even the most hardened skeptics later acknowledged that once the mid-July fires sparked, you "could have had the entire United States Army in here and it wouldn't have made any difference." Nature, not managers, was by then in control.

We are not accustomed to managing without control. But we'd better get used to it. It affects strategy—knowing whether to intervene. It affects timing—knowing when to intervene. It affects process—knowing how to intervene. Managing without control is not about immutable laws of nature but about knowing the power—and limits—of discretion, judgment, and will.

And in each case we can do better by understanding connections.

PART I

CLASSIFIEDS—
USER CONNECTIONS

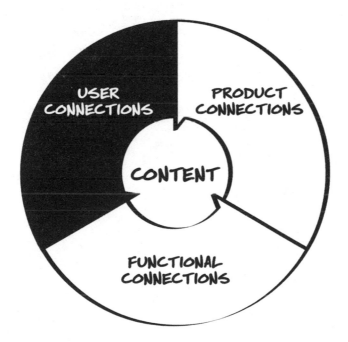

1
A TALE OF TWO GEOGRAPHIES

SCANDINAVIAN WARRIORS

Norwegian winters start early. November 12, 2001, was another frigid arctic day in Oslo, with temperatures below zero. Inside the modest redbrick headquarters of the Scandinavian media publisher Schibsted, there was a distinct chill as well. Schibsted's board was convening to determine the future of CEO Kjell Aamot.

During the previous two years the company's main newspapers, *Aftenposten* and *VG,* had seen revenue declines as Web competitors siphoned off readers and advertisers. Schibsted's own online operations, started more than six years earlier, were growing but had little to show for themselves—investments far outpaced returns. And the recent bursting of the Internet bubble had seen Schibsted's stock crash and then languish. Aamot later summarized the situation with customary candor:

> Everything was going wrong. We saw major loss-making initiatives all over the place—seven years of losses. When the bubble burst, we had a loss of approximately $200 million in Norwegian kroners and that was a huge loss for us. That was absolutely my responsibility. The board of directors very much felt we should close down some activities. Most members were of the opinion that I should resign.

Ultimately, it was only the support of Schibsted's main shareholder, Tinius Nagell-Erichsen, that allowed Aamot to continue. But the crisis shook the company's senior managers, resulting in greater pressure to clarify their Internet strategy.

As a print-media firm struggling to reckon with the threat of the Internet, Schibsted was not alone. Hundreds of newspapers around the world were engulfed in a digital wildfire. That year *The New York Times* announced cuts of up to 9 percent of its workforce; between 2001 and 2006 it lost more than half its market value, and by 2012 the loss was more than

75 percent. *The Washington Post* shed 23 percent of its newsroom, and similar cuts occurred at *The Boston Globe*. Articles with titles such as "Who Killed the Newspaper?" (*The Economist,* 2006) and "Mourning Old Media's Decline" (*The New York Times,* 2008) cropped up everywhere.

But as these events continued to unfold, something strange was happening back in Oslo. Starting in 2003, Schibsted began to make money on its online operations. A little at first—and then more and more. By 2006 the publisher's online operations accounted for 35 percent of operating profits. In a stunning reversal of events, Schibsted had, first shakily but then unmistakably, turned around. *The Economist* noted that while 2005 had been "miserable" for most newspaper companies in the Western world, Schibsted's performance was "a rare exception," making it one of the only newspapers to have turned online into a profitable business. In 2011 Schibsted declared operating profits on its online businesses of roughly $220 million—nearly 60 percent that of the entire group.

CHINESE VIRTUAL GIANTS

Six thousand miles southeast of Oslo lies Shenzhen, one of China's fastest-growing cities. Three decades ago it was a farming and fishing village with a few thousand people. Today it is an eleven-million-person metropolis. Most of its growth was triggered by the creation of a Special Economic Zone in 1979. Shenzhen is now a manufacturing hub, the financial center of southern China, and the home of companies with globally recognized brands, like Huawei and ZTE. Despite this engineered growth, the most famous company headquartered there arose from home-grown entrepreneurs Pony Ma and Zhang Zidong.

In 1998 these two young computer science graduates of Shenzhen University started a company to take advantage of China's Internet boom. Tencent began operations uneventfully, engaging in service work for local telecom operators and paging centers. Like many other local start-ups, its main approach to product development was to copy from the West.

It did so well: Its first product, the free instant messaging (IM) service OICQ, was a near-perfect replica of AOL's ICQ (an acronym for "I Seek You"). In addition to an easy-to-navigate communications platform, OICQ offered useful add-on features such as chat rooms and a mobile service. Within three years the service, renamed QQ, was the leading IM provider in China, with more than 50 million users. The entry of copycat providers did nothing to slow it down.

Instant messaging is a business that's very hard to monetize. Many have tried—and failed. And Tencent launched at the same time as hundreds of other Chinese start-ups. But while most of those ventures struggled, Tencent's offerings grew from instant messaging and its associated iconic penguin mascot to an impressively broad suite: a social networking site, a news portal, a mobile platform, single- and multi-player games, and a microblogging service. Its most recent product, WeChat, was a mobile app that combined voice chat (similar to Skype), photo sharing (similar to Instagram), social network features (similar to Facebook), e-commerce capabilities (similar to Amazon), group messaging, and walkie-talkie features into a single offering—for free. By 2015 Tencent's products and services were used by more than a billion Chinese, who accessed them through mobile phones, personal computers, and Internet cafés.

Like many e-commerce sites, Tencent gave consumers the ability to purchase clothes, pets, guns, and food, but with one important caveat: All Tencent's products were virtual goods existing only in the online world and purchased predominantly with the firm's virtual currency—"Q coins." Against this make-believe backdrop, Tencent's financial strength was hardly imaginary. In 2015 revenue neared $16 billion—similar to Facebook's and more than three times as much as LinkedIn's and Twitter's combined. In April 2015 the firm's market capitalization passed $200 billion, making it the fourth most valuable Internet firm in the world, behind Google, Facebook, and Alibaba.

How does a Scandinavian newspaper company find lucrative revenue streams online when everyone else is struggling? How did Tencent overcome the brutal odds of starting as a free IM product and then translate its advantage there into numerous product categories over the next fifteen years? How does it get users to pay for products that exist only in an imaginary world? And what generalizable lessons can we draw from these examples?

On the face of it, the stories of Schibsted and Tencent could not be more different. One firm resides in a Western developed economy, the other in an Eastern emerging market. One exemplifies traditional media, the other was a digital start-up. One is run by executives with more than thirty years of experience in media, the other by thirty-somethings who've never known anything but the Internet. But the stories are inextricably linked.

The link isn't the superior quality of products or the ability to innovate and bring new offerings to market first. The link is the ability to *recognize and manage connections across users*. This principle—user connections—is a critical concept for media, technology, and Internet organizations. But few get it right.

To unpack the concept, let's start by returning to newspapers.

2

THE *REAL* PROBLEM
WITH NEWSPAPERS

Newspapers seem to be a dying breed. The common reason given is clear: "Readers are migrating online!" And why wouldn't they? Online news is mostly free. It is accessible anytime, anywhere. It is updated frequently. It can be personalized. It is interactive and searchable. It's hard to think of another product where the digital version seems so vastly superior. Clearly, these factors are the reason for the havoc wreaked on the news industry.

Except that they aren't. The real story is different.

Figure 2 shows the steady decline over time in U.S. newspaper readership by household.

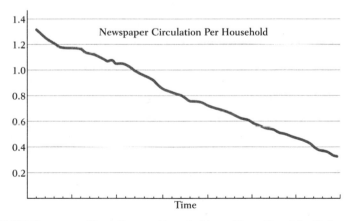

Figure 2: U.S. Newspaper Circulation per Household over Time. (Google's chief economist, Hal Varian, constructed these data from Newspaper Association of America circulation figures for all U.S. newspapers.)

The decline is sobering and perhaps unsurprising in light of the Internet. But now consider the same data again with dates filled in (Figure 3).

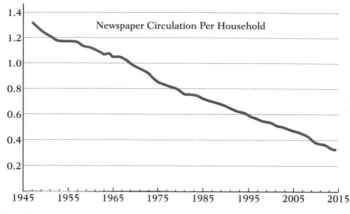

Figure 3: U.S. Newspaper Circulation per Household over Time. (Data for 1947–2007 are from Varian; data for 2008–2014 constructed by author.)

The drop in readership can't be pinned on digital alternatives; it's been under way for sixty years.

It began with the introduction of radio—and free news bulletins—during the 1950s, continued with the launch of television broadcast networks in the 1960s, and then persisted with the introduction of cable TV and 24/7 news channels during the 1980s. But the central point remains the same: The impact of the Internet on newspaper readership is empirically indistinguishable from the factors that came before.

The real reasons for the newspaper problem lie elsewhere.

One factor is the cost structure of a typical newspaper. Most of a newspaper's costs are what economists call "fixed costs"—borne regardless of the number of readers. These are the costs of staff journalists, printing facilities, and administrative and distribution overhead—all the things needed to write, print, and deliver the paper to your door. Fixed costs are terrific during periods of growth—increase your readership by a few thousand and revenue goes up while fixed costs remain the same, so you can spread these costs over more users. For the same reason, they are devastating during periods of decline—lose just 3 percent of your readers and the revenue drop goes directly to your bottom line.

At first glance, fixed costs offer an explanation for why newspapers have suffered during the Internet era—but do they really? Although *per-household* readership declined during the 1950s, '60s, and '70s, *overall* population grew; then when population growth slowed beginning in the 1980s, so did aggregate newspaper readership. Even then, things weren't so bad: Many newspapers increased their prices, offsetting the decline in readership. For the top twenty-five newspapers, prices increased by an average of 50 percent in real terms during the past two decades, causing circulation revenues to increase between 1994 and 2012, even as readership fell. So fixed costs aren't the culprit; it must be something else.

That brings us to a subtler but far more important problem, one that has to do with connections, not content or cost structure. It relates to how newspapers structure advertising.

Most newspapers contain two kinds of advertising: retail ads (the near-full-page ads for Macy's on page three of *The New York Times*) and classifieds (the car ads, job listings, and real estate ads tucked away in the back sections). While retail advertising increased slightly between 1994 and 2008, classified advertising fell by 20 percent. The differences were even starker since the year 2000, when newspaper revenues reached their peak. From 2000 to 2010, fully 74 percent of classified advertising revenue disappeared from U.S. newspapers—nearly double the decrease in retail advertising, which was 39 percent (see Figure 4).

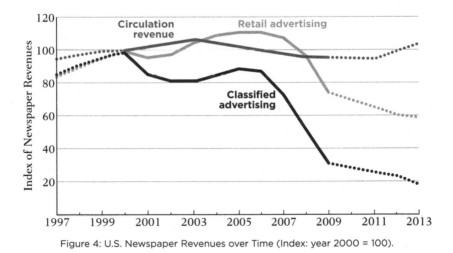

Figure 4: U.S. Newspaper Revenues over Time (Index: year 2000 = 100).

The decline in classified advertising isn't, by itself, surprising. It's the *difference* in revenue declines between classifieds, retail advertising, and news circulation that's striking. All three were vulnerable to the same threats from online offerings: real-time updating, better searchability, greater variety, richer media formats, anytime-and-anywhere access, lower prices. Yet classifieds declined much more sharply. The table below summarizes this puzzle:

TABLE 1. THE ONLINE THREAT FOR DIFFERENT PARTS OF A NEWSPAPER		
	News	Classifieds
Real-time updating	yes	yes
Easier to search	yes	yes
Greater variety	yes	yes
Video format	yes	yes
Anytime-anywhere access	yes	yes
Lower prices	yes	yes
Revenue declines	small	massive

Why would classified revenue alone go into free fall whereas circulation revenues did not? The answer lies in user behavior.

A reader goes to the news site that offers the *best* news for her. But a classifieds "buyer" goes to where the *most* listings are. In the first case, the purchase decision is based on content quality and features. In the second, it is based first and foremost on the number of advertisers listing their wares.

This simple difference has profound implications. While the economics of news depends on attracting readers one by one, the economics of classifieds is about connections between buyers and sellers. These come from "positive feedback loops," or as they're often referred to, a "network effect": The more listings you have, the more buyers you attract, who in turn attract more listings. So while the decision to read print versus online news is made one reader at a time, the decision to go to a print versus an online classifieds site is determined by the choices of many.

As a result, engage in a news battle and you are competing tooth and nail for every new reader in the market—no matter how big you are. Engage in a classifieds battle and positive feedback loops generate greater and greater market shares for the leader, such that it eventually wins the entire market.

This means that Google, CNN.com, news blogs, and all the rest weren't the real problem for newspapers. In fact readers are migrating to online news very slowly. Average weekly print readership for *The New York Times* declined by 7 percent from 1994 to 2006 (the first thirteen years of the Internet era)—an average of just 0.5 percent a year. Incorporating figures from 2008 to 2011, a period including the worst recession in eighty years, raises the figure to roughly 1.5 percent. In other words, just one or two of every 100 print readers of the *Times* defected every year during the Internet era. Other major papers had similar results.

The real culprits were sites such as Monster.com, Craigslist, and Trader Online. Although the Internet changed many things for news—production and distribution costs, ease of search and access, and price—the feedback loop for classifieds was unaltered. Feedback loops—in particular, the winner-take-all effect of classifieds—were the reason most towns in America had only one paper: it wasn't that only one outlet in every town knew how to produce the news. And they were the reason that once classifieds started moving online, they moved very rapidly.

Go to any conference on the future of news and you'll hear calls for greater subsidies for news organizations because of the increasingly fierce digital threat. Understand the classifieds dynamic, however, and you'll see that the real problem is that newspapers were *always* subsidized—until recently. The Internet didn't kill news; it destroyed the classifieds subsidy. Where news organizations went wrong was not in failing to deliver faster, cheaper, better news online—to believe that is to fall into the Content Trap—but in failing to protect the classifieds subsidy or to profitably manage its migration online. Papers were beaten to the punch in capturing user connections in the digital arena.

Miss that connection, as most newspapers did, and no matter how robust or creative your online news strategy, you would be trying to solve the wrong problem. Recognize that connection, as some companies did—a story we'll return to shortly—and the payoff can be spectacular.

3

NETWORKS

A BRIEF HISTORY

Feedback loops in classifieds exemplify one of the most important ideas in digital business—network effects.

The concept was first described (though not by that name) in a 1974 article by Bell Labs researcher Jeffrey Rohlfs with the somewhat opaque title "A Theory of Interdependent Demand for a Communications Service." Rohlfs was interested in the market for video communications services. But, as Professor Richard Schmalensee, of the Massachusetts Institute of Technology, recently pointed out, he was really describing Facebook—thirty-five years before its creation.

Network effects are all about user connections. They are perhaps the biggest reason why technology firms seem to behave so differently from more traditional companies—why they are obsessed with "free" models, fast growth, and rapid prototyping.

The idea is best understood by contrasting a networked with a non-networked product. Think about buying a dress, a shirt, or a car—a non-networked product. You'd decide on the basis of features such as price, quality, color, store location, and service. But your decision about a networked product would depend not only on those features but also on how many others have bought it (Figure 5). The more users of a networked product, the greater its value to you. Examples include instant messaging services, social networks like Facebook and video chat apps like FaceTime, language (think about the growing popularity of English as the world becomes more global), and fashion (though with *too* many users, a brand loses its cool). Conversely, a networked product with few users has little value: Consider the first person to own a phone or a fax machine.

To understand how profound the consequences of these differences are, look no further than Apple—and its checkered history.

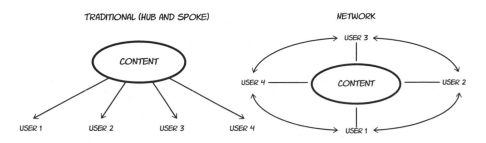

Figure 5: Traditional Versus Networked Products

DIRECT VERSUS INDIRECT NETWORKS: AND, WHEN STEVE JOBS FAILED

Ask anyone about Apple's unprecedented successes—its "i-triumphs"—of the past decade and you'll hear about superb products, beautiful designs, and cool marketing. The same formula is generally considered key in media markets and many other businesses, from cars to clothes and hotels.

But Apple had followed this formula for the better part of two decades in its battle with Microsoft for global leadership in personal computers—and lost.

Starting with the 1984 launch of the Mac, Apple went head-to-head against PCs running Microsoft's operating system. Macs were consistently regarded as easier to use, more stable, and cooler than machines from IBM, Hewlett-Packard, and Dell. Apple introduced its famed graphical user interface (imitated from Xerox) several years before Microsoft's version. And its advertising was memorable: its 1984 "Big Brother" Super Bowl commercial aired only once during the game, and never since, but remains one of the most-watched television ads in history.

Yet, for two decades after the introduction of the Macintosh, Apple's world market share in personal computers steadily declined, reaching just 1.9 percent in 2004. Everyone else used Microsoft. Why?

A user's willingness to buy a personal computer depends primarily on two things: How easy is it to communicate and share information with others—friends, family, coworkers? And what is the range and quality of compatible software applications? Without those connections, a computer is virtually useless. Other features surely mattered—price, design, color, and marketing—but none so much as how many other people use that type of computer.

When personal computers first came out, Microsoft's advantage exemplified two types of network effects that benefit early leaders in a market. First are "direct" user-to-user networks: For every new user, the value of a PC was greater than a Mac because the number of *existing* PC users was higher—allowing new PC users to communicate with more people. Second are feedback loops between users and application developers: As more users chose PCs, the value of the platform for developers increased, because they could spread the fixed cost of development over a larger user base. And more applications, in turn, attracted more users—resulting in powerful "indirect" or "cross-side" network effects.

Direct network effects arise from connections between similar users. To identify them, simply ask: Does the product's value to a buyer increase as more people buy and use it? Indirect network effects result from connections between different types of users or suppliers—in this case, customers and app developers. To identify them, ask: Does the value to one type of user increase as the number of suppliers or other types of users rises (see Figure 6)?

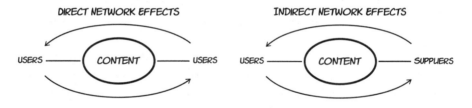

Figure 6: Direct Versus Indirect Network Effects

Indirect networks can be as powerful as direct ones, as shown by classified ads. And consider eBay's advantage in the market for collectible goods: The more potential buyers for a particular product on eBay, the more likely a seller will post her item there rather than elsewhere, which in turn increases the depth and selection for users on the site.

Either direct or indirect network effects alone can explain why companies win big. Microsoft had both. In the face of such an overwhelming advantage, Steve Jobs—otherwise considered to be one of the greatest product designers of the last century—could win only 3 percent market share.

The Apple versus Microsoft battle didn't shape only the personal computer industry; it influenced the very study of network effects. Rohlfs's early work on "interdependent demands"—positive user connections—was followed by an explosion of interest in the area. Carl Shapiro and Michael Katz, two Princeton assistant professors studying the economics of technology during the early 1980s, were early and important contributors to the field. Shapiro recently told me, "Personal computers were just beginning to take off. This was a new platform war, coming on the heels of platform battles like VHS versus Betamax. A lot of network issues go back all the way to telephones. But now we were seeing new dimensions of platform competition."

Shapiro's and others' research in industrial organizations influenced the Department of Justice's efforts to write antitrust policies for networked markets, and they created a new language, too. Terms like *compatibility, dynamics,* and *openness* began appearing in articles. And successes in digital media businesses have necessitated more-recent changes in language. *Product quality* and *creative marketing* have given way to terms like *networks, communities,* and *conversation.*

The language for success in media, as in technology, is less and less about content and more and more about connections.

A NETWORK PRIMER: OR, FOUR THINGS YOU REALLY NEED TO KNOW

Network effects (or "network externalities," as they're sometimes called) are about connections between users. They are rampant in digital markets, as *communication, sharing,* and *social* have come to define success. As businesses continue to learn more about them, they would do well to keep four things in mind.

1. Product quality need not win.

Imagine two companies competing head-to-head but with radically different approaches. One focuses on creating great products, cool designs, and easy-to-use offerings. The other churns out seemingly clunky, bug-filled products and relies on rapid imitation rather than original innovation. The second approach doesn't sound like it could win. But it can.

This was effectively the difference between Apple's and Microsoft's approaches in the PC wars. It's not that Microsoft executives aimed to be quality or innovation laggards; it's just that their priorities lay elsewhere. As early as 1994 Bill Gates summarized his strategy in the simple observation, "We look for opportunities with network externalities."

Once Microsoft had attained market share leadership, its sales efforts to end users were virtually zero; its existing customer base served, in effect, as its sales force for new customers. Indeed, Apple versus Microsoft is partly a story of differences in ongoing effort and bang for the buck. Offer a product without a network advantage and you have to spend disproportionate effort and cost improving product features. Offer a networked product and once you're ahead you can more or less sit back and count your cash, as more users come on board even with no improvement in product features.

In networked markets, the strength of network effects can overwhelm attractive product features. Craigslist beat rivals, and VHS won out over Betamax, not because those companies had superior products but because they had larger network shares early on. Social videogames like Zynga's FarmVille and CityVille or, more recently, Mojang's Minecraft are not notable for high-quality graphics, 3-D functionality, or riveting gaming experiences—their features are bleak compared with Electronic Arts' Madden NFL and Blizzard Entertainment's World of Warcraft. But each of the Zynga games commanded more than ten million viewers within a few months of launch—a feat that took EA and Blizzard years; and Minecraft became the second-bestselling videogame of all time. Success came in each case not from making these games perfect but from making them networked.

It's striking how many digital media managers still think in terms of product appeal to individual customers rather than in terms of managing and exploiting connections. This is even more surprising in view of the fact that media consumption has always been inherently social.

In 2006 sociologists Matthew Salganik and Duncan Watts ran a remarkable online laboratory experiment to assess how people's tastes in music are influenced by others. Participants listened to, rated, and could download forty-eight songs. They were also told at the start how many others had already downloaded each song. Popularity, it turns out, affected taste: The more popular a song, the more likely someone was to download it.

In itself, that didn't establish a causal effect of popularity on taste: After all, it could simply be that the participants had similar tastes. So the researchers altered the experiment. For one group of participants, they inverted the popularity rankings that participants were shown: the song rated forty-eighth by others was shown to participants as having been ranked first in the list, and vice versa; the song rated forty-seventh was shown as ranking second, and so on. The results were dramatic. The least-popular songs were now listened to and downloaded far more often—and only because people *thought* they were popular. Even more interestingly, they were downloaded more often than the songs that were actually popular. The effects persisted over long periods, too.

Listeners' intrinsic tastes had been overwhelmed by social effects. Salganik and Watts had demonstrated, in a different context, what Apple had learned from its battle with Microsoft: It's not just content but user connections that matter.

Scott Cook is hardly a technology neophyte. He cofounded tax software giant Intuit more than thirty years ago, when Silicon Valley entrepreneurship was just getting started. When it comes to business and technology, he's seen it all—or so he thought until he had a ringside seat at an early battle for e-commerce supremacy.

By the late 1990s, when eBay was the unquestioned market leader in online auctions, Yahoo! and Amazon decided to go after it with auction services of their own. Yahoo! was the Internet giant of the era, with its home page drawing the most traffic on the Web, and that's where it promoted the new and impressively designed site Yahoo! Auctions. Amazon was the largest e-commerce player, and its auction service would let buyers and sellers transact for free (in contrast, eBay charged commissions). Cook sat on the board of both eBay and Amazon. He told me about the events:

> [Amazon CEO] Jeff Bezos called me and [venture capitalist] John Doerr and flew in to Aspen to have dinner with us. He described how he was going to launch Amazon Auctions. He wanted me to know this because he was sure I would drop being on the eBay board—eBay was clearly going to be history. And that's probably what would happen in any other industry where the largest competitors in the world copied your product, made it technically better, promoted it aggressively, and made it free. What happened here? It was as if Amazon and Yahoo! had done nothing.

Yahoo! Auctions ultimately closed. Amazon's original auction failed. The company later recreated it as Marketplace, which worked well, but its free-standing auction business never caught on. Cook reflected on what he'd seen: "This was all because of network effects. I have come to the conclusion that network effects are the most profound idea I have encountered in my entire career."

The belief that success comes from great products and superior content is not limited to the media world. Cook recalls the early days of the Internet: "If you attended personal computing technology conferences in 1994 and 1995, the new focus was the Web. And one of the universally held beliefs was that content is king." Industry observers foresaw that the Web would reduce the cost of global distribution to zero and that content owners would rule the Internet, because their assets were scarce. But as Cook went on to note,

> This appears to have been 180 degrees wrong. The big money, the giant breakthroughs, the huge audiences, are pretty universally from the firms that started with no content and largely avoided creating it. Yahoo was ridiculed by people who said, "Wait a minute—you're going to have people come to your website only to send them to another website? What a stupid idea." Yet Yahoo became more successful than any content-owning site. And then Google, Facebook, and others came along.

Cook is describing the Content Trap. He's hardly shy about his views:

> Content has been a curse. It causes you to think you can make what's going to delight customers. It causes you to ignore user contributions. It causes you to focus on your own content rather than on how to get the best content in the world—content anyone can make.

2. Networks protect you from mistakes.

One of the biggest challenges organizations face is keeping up with new technologies, competitive pressure, and rapidly changing trends. Conventional wisdom says to innovate faster. Network effects turn that prescription on its head.

Network effects, as we've seen, are what allow you to win in these markets. They also make it hard for rivals on the losing end of a networked battle to turn things around. In 2010 Google introduced the social network Google+, aimed at competing with Facebook. Reviewers hailed its group video chat service, privacy features, and subsequent innovations like location sharing and full-screen HD. But it lacked an installed base of users. One reviewer noted that "I kept running into the same problem—there was no one in this sandbox but me." Over the next two years, confronting this new and formidable head-on competitor, Facebook nearly doubled its active users—attracting far more new users than Google+ did, and distancing itself even further in the battle for social network supremacy.

In smartphone operating systems, Microsoft's Windows 8 is often favorably compared to Apple's iOS and Google's Android. But the absence of a developer network severely muted the impact of Microsoft's innovative efforts (it was the same lesson Apple had learned two decades earlier). Despite every effort, Microsoft's smartphone share grew from 2 percent in 2012 to a mere 2.7 percent in 2015.

For the same reason, network effects have a better chance than continuous innovation does of protecting you from competitive pressures and organizational mistakes. Few firms have faced as many challenges from upstarts and rivals as Microsoft did during the past decade. Market leadership in mobile devices and operating systems, social networks, search, e-commerce, advertising—all were captured by others. Microsoft's new products received lukewarm reviews at best. The firm went through many restructurings. All that could have left it in tatters—yet in 2016 it remained one of the most valuable companies in the world. *That* is the power of networks. No one has been able to dislodge Microsoft's network strength in operating systems and applications. Conversely, from 2002 to 2016, Apple created more than $500 billion in market value, more than any other company in history—but its worldwide market share in personal computers grew from 3 percent to just 7 percent. Observers have called Windows the "single most profound business in the world."

We are often led to believe that Internet companies succeed by inspiring creative freedom or nurturing open, nonhierarchical cultures (not to mention all the free food). But network strength is more often responsible. Here's Scott Cook again:

> Traditionally, the important question in product innovation was whether a company could systematically churn out good products. But for everything we talk about the innovative ability of successful Internet companies, very few companies have been successful serial disruptors; most have just done it once. Most still rely very heavily, and intentionally, on acquisitions. Network effects are what give them higher margins, deter competitors, and dramatically lower the cost of goods. Network effects are what give them a seemingly durable advantage.

None of this is to say that winners in networked markets can afford to be complacent. In fact, they need paranoia to survive and succeed—because when you win in a networked market, you win big; but if you lose, you fall equally hard. Most newspapers didn't just cede incremental share in classifieds, they lost it entirely. In marketplaces, eBay once enjoyed more than 80 percent market share in China. Once its share declined against Alibaba, it went into free fall—dropping to under 5 percent within a few years, forcing an exit.

3. Networks can be created.

Consider the intrinsic technology properties of networked products, or the word-of-mouth benefits that arise from seemingly unpredictable acts of sharing by interested individuals. It's tempting to view these user connections as "acts of nature" over which managers have little control. But that's not the case.

By 2002 Amazon had spent more than five years creating a formidable advantage in e-commerce. That came not only from a user-friendly platform and recommendation engine—both features were adopted by other entrants—but from its warehousing and logistics operation. By building distribution centers across the country, investing in algorithms to optimize pick-time in the centers, and hiring operational wizards from Walmart and other competitors, Amazon could get products to customers anywhere in the United States faster and cheaper than anyone else. Then, just when it appeared to be distancing itself from its rivals, Amazon did something that seemed incomprehensible: It opened its fulfillment and warehousing network to any third-party retailer that wanted to participate.

Why would a company work so hard to create a competitive advantage only to give it away? The answer speaks to Amazon's sophisticated understanding of network effects. Create a fabulous warehousing network and, ultimately, so can others. Your competitive advantage will vanish. Create a retailing platform where anyone can sell to your customers and you've carved out an entirely different competitive position. Amazon wanted indirect network effects that would give it control over the *entire* e-commerce market, not just the market for its own products.

Through its Marketplace, Amazon had shifted strategy from selling products to owning a platform. A similar "content versus platform" choice confronts many organizations today. Newspapers struggle with the choice between using in-house journalists to produce content and aggregating content produced by others. Netflix and Amazon are seeking a balance between aggregating television shows and movies made by others and producing their own exclusive content. The radio network PRX shifted focus from running a radio station to running a radio exchange—independent producers anywhere can upload programs to the PRX platform, and stations anywhere can download them.

In 2007 Facebook introduced Facebook Platform, transforming its strategy from a product reliant on internally developed features to a platform that offered anyone's apps; the following year, it introduced Connect, further extending this platform strategy by allowing users on third-party websites to connect with Facebook friends and post updates to their Facebook profiles. In 2008 Apple launched the App Store for its smartphone, transforming its strategy from a device running mostly Apple apps to one running anyone's apps.

Marketplace, Platform and Connect, and the App Store weren't desperate acts by companies struggling to survive; they were strategic choices made by companies leading in their digital markets. The gains of shifting from a product to a platform approach have been dramatic. From 2004 to 2008 Amazon's e-commerce sales grew by 25 percent to 30 percent a year—nearly double the rate of the previous two years. From 2007 to 2015 Facebook's active user base grew from fifty million to more than a billion—twice the rate before Platform and Connect. Within a week of Apple's launch of the App Store, iPhone users downloaded more than ten million apps. The lesson is clear: Superior products are great, but strategies that exploit connections are better.

For years, hotels grew by building new properties. Airbnb chose a different route—focused on connecting those who needed rooms with others who already had them. Uber did the same with cars. (There, too, when it restricted its service to "Uber Black" cars that relied on commercially licensed drivers with high-end cars, growth was steady; once it opened its platform to any driver-partner, growth was exponential.) The contrast between "product versus platform" strategies was plainly, though somewhat garishly, summarized in a recent tweet from an Airbnb executive: "Marriott wants to add 30,000 rooms this year. We will add that in the next two weeks."

The point is that networks aren't just a law of technology; they can be created. Pokémon trading cards were endearing when they were introduced, in 1996, but their real value to users lay in trading them. Phone carriers, retail banks, and airlines compete on products and services that appeal to users individually, but they also have "friends and family" programs to appeal to groups of users. When *The Washington Post*'s WaPo Labs first introduced its personalized digital news reader, Trove, it got little traction; after it made one slight adjustment—optimizing for Facebook—its user base exploded, growing by more than ten million in a matter of months.

In all these cases, firms are creating connections.

4. Networks aren't the same as scale.

Apple's experience with personal computers, and the experience of newspapers with classifieds, speaks to a challenge many organizations face: not seeing networks when they are present. But a second challenge can be equally confounding: Once managers are exposed to the idea of network effects, they start seeing them everywhere, even when they don't exist.

Witness Groupon's attempt to build a global business. For years the company's founders claimed that it benefited from network effects and would enjoy a winner-take-all dynamic. The more users Groupon had, the likelier merchants were to offer deals, and vice versa—indirect network effects. And because some deals would not be honored unless enough people bought them, there were direct network effects, too. The firm's early success—Groupon was one of the fastest-growing Internet companies ever—proved it.

But the network story was a myth. Merchants could just as easily offer deals on multiple sites. And the number of people required to activate a deal was small enough that nearly every deal was activated—the social feature was inconsequential. There were no meaningful network effects at work, only the benefits of scale: As Groupon expanded, it employed a large sales force and marketing efforts that smaller players couldn't match. But scale doesn't, in itself, generate exponential growth or winner-take-all outcomes. Within nine months of its November 2011 IPO, Groupon's stock lost 75 percent of its market value. It has recovered little ground since.

The problem is not uncommon: confusing the benefits of scale with those of networks. Scale benefits come from fixed costs, network benefits from communication. Get ahead in a market with network effects and chances are you win everything. Rely on scale benefits to compete and chances are that others can, too, as long as they can incur the same fixed costs.

Content businesses everywhere tend to define themselves by their content. This is the trap. The power of content is increasingly overwhelmed by the power of user connections, of which network effects are perhaps the most potent form. To see the payoff they've had for one content business, let's go back to Scandinavia.

4
SCHIBSTED

I first visited Schibsted in November 2006. Sverre Munck, then the head of its international operations, sat down with me at the start of the day. Munck has an upbeat, curious temperament and a racing mind. Take the conversation anywhere and he'll run with you. But a few minutes into Schibsted's story, he stopped.

> Let me digress for a moment about the economics of newspapers: They constitute natural monopolies. They have a network effect, in the sense that if you want to buy or sell something, you want to do that where everybody else buys and sells. So classified ads tend to migrate to the newspaper with the most readers. And if it gets the most classifieds, it gets the most revenue, the best journalists, and the best product—and thus more readers. It's a virtuous circle.

Network effects? Virtuous circles? Natural monopolies? For a moment I thought I was talking to someone who has a Ph.D. in economics. (In fact, Munck does.) He and his colleagues at Schibsted saw the opportunities afforded by networks and marketplaces as early as 1995.

To this day, it's rare to hear a newspaper executive describe their business the way Munck did. But merely seeing connections would not have been enough. Schibsted had to take advantage of them. And things did not start out well.

EARLY EFFORTS

Aftenposten is Schibsted's premier newspaper in Norway. For much of its recent history it commanded the lion's share of the print classifieds market. From 1995 to 1999 it used a subsidiary to create an online classifieds business—but with a single part-time employee. The ads posted on the site were PDF copies from the print paper, much like other papers were doing at the time. The pricing structure made it even more difficult to attract ads for the site: Internet ad prices were bundled with print, such that if you bought an ad in the paper, you got a copy on the website for free.

Terje Seljeseth was an IT manager in *Aftenposten* at the time. He recalled: "One didn't need a technical background to see it was not the right way to run the business." The problem was amplified by the incentives structures in place. As Robert Steen, then vice president for international classifieds and search, explained, "If a salesperson generates two thousand kroner for a print ad and twenty kroner for an Internet ad, he won't spend one second selling advertising on the Internet. And that was exactly the case."

Shortsightedness, cannibalization concerns, and poor governance are big enough hurdles when launching a digital business. Things are far worse when your competitors leverage network effects that can quickly destroy your core. By 1999, Steen recalls, "[w]e were years behind the pure-play classifieds players—Job Line [for jobs], StepStone [cars], and Tinde [real estate]. Our initiative had failed completely. How could we respond?"

TAKE 2

For the first five years *Aftenposten* ran its online classifieds operation in partnership with the five other major subscription newspapers in Norway. The rationale was sound: There was little geographic conflict between the papers, and each was the market leader in its region. There were opportunities for cost sharing, too, such as creating a technical platform for a classifieds site. This kind of partnership was not unusual: Across the Atlantic, hundreds of newspapers in the United States would embark on a similar effort with Yahoo! a few years later.

Getting managers in one newspaper to agree on things is hard enough. Getting agreement across five different papers is nearly impossible. Steen recalls, "With five equal owners, and each having their own advertising director, everyone just wanted to have their say and their decisions. It was a disaster. It brought our online cooperation nowhere." The U.S. effort would experience similar conflict, with similarly unproductive results.

But when things got worse, *Aftenposten* saw opportunity.

In 1999 Seljeseth took the reins of the online classifieds project. Investing more aggressively was a necessity. But *Aftenposten* needed more than that to compete with players who'd had a head start. So it leveraged its print brand—not by directly transferring it online, but by first creating an entirely new offline brand that could later be leveraged online. Part of the rationale was to leverage the trust readers had in their newspapers. Another goal was to shift what had been a local classifieds business into a national one. Car and job listings, for instance, had appeal beyond their local markets. But to create a national brand, the company still needed its partnership with the other regional papers. Steen explained:

> The first thing was not to establish an online classifieds solution. The first thing was to take all the newspapers in different geographical areas in Norway and rebrand their classified sections under a common brand, Finn. Finn was not meant to be merely an Internet brand; it was meant to be perceived by readers as "belonging to my newspaper, which has been there for one hundred and fifty years and has built up trust over that time." A lot of Internet services then were considered not very trustworthy. There were scams, quick money, white-collar crime. This was a way to establish brand value in a short period of time, and to do so nationally. If you went to the paper in Stavnager to look for a job, you saw the same online brand—Finn—that you were familiar with in Oslo.

Of course, the challenge of coordinating decisions across the different papers remained. To address that, Steen explained, "We changed the ownership structure, revising it roughly in proportion to the national classified shares of the individual papers. *Aftenposten* got 62 percent, the other four each got 9 percent." Circumstances helped them reach this agreement: "By this point, the other papers didn't really believe in the Internet. They saw it as a money-losing proposition. So they didn't really care."

The floodgates were now opened. New hires were made, nearly all from outside the paper. People came from real estate brokers, from headhunters, from the auto industry—"people who understood the business and had contacts." Compensation structures were revised: New hires could buy shares in Finn. Cooperation between sales and product development increased. Schibsted's corporate center gave a competitive nudge as well, letting *VG*—Schibsted's tabloid, and the leading daily in Norway—compete in the classifieds arena. *Aftenposten*'s CEO, recognizing that the parent would benefit no matter who won the classifieds battle, encouraged competition with the print division, whose salespeople, Seljeseth said, "hated us by now":

> The ad department in *Aftenposten* argued that there should be no salespeople or marketing people in Finn. We could have people looking after products, IT, and so on. But no sales or marketing. I negotiated that we could hire one salesperson. Then I gave all the other salespersons titles that had nothing to do with sales, but they were sellers.

Aggressive investments, a cleaner governance structure, new hires, and a familiar brand gave Finn new advantages. The new business plan even included a separate section on corporate culture and how it would differ from print's.

Through Finn, Steen told me, Schibsted was creating a new approach that was designed on the one hand to "forget certain behaviors that exist in the traditional business—the mindset of 1,500 people in the print business that 'this is the way we've always done it'"—but at the same time to "borrow all assets that have any value for your new setup, whether that is brand value, customer relationships, or free promotion and marketing." "Forget and borrow" is how they termed it. It was an approach that would define its digital businesses for many years.

Finn launched on March 17, 2000—two days after the dot-com crash. The timing, Steen noted, "couldn't have been worse." But that didn't stop the paid site from gaining momentum, and growing impressively. "Within a year and a half we had the number one position in real estate. Soon after that, in cars. And then we reached number one in jobs. By 2004 we knew we had won the market."

By 2007 Finn had more than 90 percent of market share in the major product categories of online classifieds. In cars, it even boasted 115 percent market share. The reason? The frequency of transactions was so high that owners in Sweden and Germany posted their cars on the Norwegian site, leading to more cars being sold there than there were cars in Norway. High market shares translated to high prices, and Finn commanded some of the world's highest in the classifieds arena: 400 Norwegian kroner (roughly $50) for listing a car, even while its biggest competitor was free. By 2007 Finn was valued higher than its parent, *Aftenposten*.

Seljeseth recently underscored to me the gains from winning in a market characterized by network effects:

The difference between number one and number two is dramatic. When we started, we could see that this could be a profitable business. But 500 million NOK [Norwegian kroner] in five years? Never, I thought. *Aftenposten* had 90 percent to 95 percent of the real estate listings in Norway. Today we are ten to fifteen times bigger than them. Nobody calls *Aftenposten* anymore.

THE SWEDISH EXPANSION

If you stopped the Schibsted story here, the implications for other newspapers would not be particularly uplifting. One might simply conclude that Schibsted had been fortunate to be early in classifieds. Be late to a networked market, however, and it's impossible to break in.

Except that in 2007, Schibsted was not done. For it, the classifieds game was just beginning. Its actions over the next few years proved even more important for the company in understanding the classifieds market and user connections. In many geographies, Schibsted would be late— and it would still win.

The first market where Schibsted tried to replicate Finn's success was Sweden. Rolv-Erik Ryssdal, Schibsted's current CEO, was in charge of Finn in Sweden at the time. As in Norway, the site had the backing of the country's largest newspaper (Schibsted's *Aftonbladet,* which Ryssdal also oversaw), and it looked to create the same relationships with other parties—car dealers, real estate brokers, job listers—that had brought Finn success. But another small site in Sweden was taking a different route to fighting for network leadership. Blocket, a site created by "two guys with a few PCs," wasn't restricting classifieds listings to businesses only—*anyone* could post items for sale, an approach referred to as "consumer to consumer" (C2C). It's an extreme form of connections—list nothing yourself, just offer a platform that lets consumers connect to each other. Ryssdal described to me what happened next:

> We thought Blocket wasn't too strong and we could overtake it. But C2C, it turns out, creates a lot of traffic, because if you buy and sell small stuff, and you sell things more frequently than you can sell a house or a car, you generate a lot of traffic and buzz. And then you can start selling capital goods as well. I underestimated the pace at which Blocket was growing. Six months later it was far ahead.

In the spring of 2003 Ryssdal approached the founders of Blocket in an attempt to buy them. His bid, 85 million Swedish kronor, was turned down. Six months later Ryssdal realized that "the Finn approach in Sweden was a failure. I went back to the Blocket owners with my tail between my legs and asked if we could restart negotiations." The eventual purchase price was more than twice the previous amount. Fortunately for Schibsted, the growth continued: "Today the valuation is thirty times what we paid—more than five billion kroner."

WINNING FROM BEHIND

The lessons from Schibsted's Norwegian experience had been straightforward: Be early and invest aggressively. Or so it appeared: Attempts to re-create the Norwegian formula in Sweden failed. To begin, Schibsted wasn't first. And even a six-month head start can be insurmountable when competing for network effects: eBay had had a similar experience in Japan some years earlier, losing to Yahoo! after launching only a few months later.

Blocket's success underscored the importance not only of being early, but of being free at the beginning. Further, knowing *how* to create network effects was as important as recognizing the imperative to do so. Ryssdal described the virtues of starting with C2C transactions, as Blocket had done, rather than leaning on professional sellers, Finn-style. This seemingly small difference—creating the conditions for user connections to arise naturally and spread virally, versus engineering them top-down—had profound implications:

> We exported the Blocket model to more than twenty countries. Our Finn model has been in successful only in one country—Norway. We thought C2C would travel better, because we know the concept better than anyone else, we've got the software, we know which categories to focus on, and we don't need to know the advertisers in each country. The reason is that C2C is what we refer to as "a people's movement." It spreads virally—word of mouth rather than TV advertising, rural first rather than big cities, etc. In Sweden, it started in the rural areas. The same thing happened when we went into France with Leboncoin: It started in the rural areas. Paris was the last place to be conquered.

In Spain and France, Schibsted was late to the classified game—and still won. In France, the lesson was that you could not only launch free but remain free and still make massive amounts of money. By 2015 Leboncoin was raking in more than $30 million in profits, generating revenue from display and search advertising, professional sellers, and featured listings (sellers paying to have their ads appear at the top)—all without charging consumers. Exporting and refining the strategy paid handsome dividends. As Schibsted moved into emerging markets—sometimes more than two years behind, as in Indonesia—it learned that moving late did not doom it to failure, since existing players' market penetration might be low.

Schibsted also entered late in Portugal, Philippines, and Malaysia—and won in all these markets. As the organization grew, so did its confidence. It entered Finland—"We were late to a very mature market, one of the most broadband-penetrated countries in the world"—and won again. Seljeseth underscored this: "In most European markets we have won as a late mover. In Italy, Spain, and Austria, we were late, in very mature markets, yet we launched, and won."

Along the way, Schibsted created an even newer approach for market entry, what it called "postponing management." The idea was to launch "shotgun" sites in new markets—sites in a new geography and based on Schibsted's C2C platform architecture, but with virtually no new investment, no people on the ground, and no local operations. The platforms were effectively remote-controlled from Sweden. If they attracted buyers and sellers, Schibsted would scale them locally. It was a management model of trial and error that allowed the company to rapidly explore the attractiveness of different markets around the world.

By the end of 2015 Schibsted had classifieds businesses that were sprawled across forty-two countries and held the number one position in the global classifieds market. Its chief competitor was Naspers, a South African media conglomerate that had aggressively invested in global classifieds following Schibsted's lead. (In 2015, the increasingly intense battle for networked leadership led the two companies to merge their classifieds operations in several countries.) Classifieds accounted for 30 percent of Schibsted's revenue and a whopping 85 percent of its market value. By understanding the power of user connections, Schibsted had preserved—actually enhanced—the cash cow that had served its news operations for 150 years. Along the way it had reinvented the company's culture.

Network effects are the most celebrated form of user connections and one of the most studied areas during recent decades. Yet theory lags practice. Carl Shapiro recently told me, "We are still not sure about many questions concerning network effects and their power: What is the real source of network effects? Can they be neutralized? What are their limits?" That's where Schibsted's journey has relevance. In its global expansion, it has pushed the boundaries of nearly every accepted formula for competing in networked markets: It has won even when it was late, remained free even after winning, and recognized that direct user-to-user connections are more viral than business-to-consumer strategies. These lessons haven't just influenced others looking to compete in classifieds or networked businesses; they've influenced the rest of Schibsted—most notably, its newsroom.

NEWS CONNECTIONS

News, unlike classifieds, is not a networked product. Nevertheless, the concept of networks and user connections soon extended into the news divisions of Schibsted and transformed its online news product.

Torry Pedersen and Espen Egil Hansen are not managers you would expect to find in charge of one of the most impressive business transformations of any newspaper in the western world—Pedersen started his career as an editor, Hansen as a photographer. But in 2000 they came together to lead the online division of *VG*.

Early on, Schibsted's meek online experiments in classifieds were mirrored in its newspaper divisions. Print was still a moneymaker, the print newsroom culture was dominant, and the efforts to start an online news operation were pitiable. Hansen told me:

> We started with a very small team—seven or eight journalists and a few programmers—and even lower self-esteem. We were literally sitting underneath the stairway in the newsroom, and they were sort of bullies. Online wasn't considered journalism; it was considered copy-and-paste from the paper. So when we started, Torry and I realized we had to take the team elsewhere. So we literally went to another floor.

Separating digital from traditional by one floor was hardly a bold move. Nor was the separation of new and old businesses particularly novel. Just a few years earlier Harvard Business School's Clayton Christensen had advocated that approach to innovation in his bestselling book, *The Innovator's Dilemma*. What *was* novel was what transpired next at *VG*—a result of instinct, experience, and accident.

During the next year and a half, two events occurred that were entirely outside the managers' control but would change their entire approach and philosophy. The first was the explosion and sinking of the Russian submarine *Kursk*. Hansen said, "For three or four days it was out in the Bering Sea as they tried to save the crew. It was an ongoing story, a huge drama that went on and on—we had to keep updating. It was really a wake-up call for me."

Then came 9/11.

> We were one of the few news sites in the world that managed to stay afloat. We never went down. It was incredibly important for us, because we delivered news throughout, minute by minute. The main reason was our technical team. It had the nerve, the attention, within minutes, *to take everything else off our news site, except four lines of news in the beginning.* So our servers didn't crash. We'd update these four lines of news about the disaster as we received it in real time. This decision about four lines that we made then turned out to be important—we built from there.

Out of these experiences Pedersen and Hansen developed an entirely new approach to journalism—a "three-layer" approach. Said Hansen:

> The first layer is live or near-live: We are telling you things as they are happening. Journalism there is a process. Underneath this first layer we have a sketch of a story—this is what has happened, this is what we know now, with more editing of the story. And finally there is the traditional news story—written in full, edited, and then published.

Coming from a traditional newsroom, the three-layer approach was sacrilege. The layers represented very different philosophies about news production. It wasn't just the difference between a daily news cycle—a culture that defines most newsrooms even today—versus a live news culture; it was the difference between traditional publishing and a wiki approach. The third layer was just like news production at a traditional paper—edit a story, then re-edit, until you're ready to publish. The first layer was exactly the opposite: publish first, even if as a single sentence, and edit later—like Wikipedia entries. A key sentence Hansen brought back to the team: "We will be back with more." "That was a crucial sentence," he says. "I don't know if anyone else did that, at least not from traditional media."

Already these changes were creating a news culture dramatically different from the parent organization's 150-year-old one. But there was more to come. Go to VG's front page today and you'll see certain unusual features: a predominance of pictures rather than text; an absence of "sections"; on the front page, a seamless blending of stories around politics, entertainment, sports, or culture; and, a long—indeed, a very very long—page. In these respects, VG's approach differs to this day from the vast majority of news sites around the world.

The long, "infinite scroll" feeling of the front page was decided mostly by happenstance, and ran counter to expert editorial opinion. Hansen again:

> The long front page happened mostly by accident. We started to produce more, but we didn't have a strong team to edit at that point, so the front page just grew. We would add a new story at the top and just move the rest below it. Torry saw this and got mad—he felt we should prioritize more. So we reduced the length of the front page. But almost immediately, traffic fell. We then started to look into this more, experimented with short and long pages, and it turned out that people really loved the long.
>
> This also gave rise to our visual language and philosophy. With each scroll, we offer something for every reader—culture, politics, sports, travel, technology—rather than "sections" as in a traditional paper. And we put the most important news at the top, but if you scroll down the whole front page, we are basically telling you that you can get the main stories of the past twenty-four hours.

Part of the reason for why one sees "sections" in papers is that they solve a coordination problem specific to print—how to get stories on different topics, worked on by different teams, into the same paper. Sections offered a simple answer for each section editor: Get your team together, create your part of the paper, and we'll put them all together. Online there is no need to coordinate across sections in order to "produce" news.

The economics are different as well. For the print edition, a reader has to buy the entire issue; online, one can choose to read only certain articles. As a result, online news sites are desperate to get readers to the front page, where they stick around longer and ads are worth more. Hansen elaborated: "When we started there were sections, like in the paper. From the beginning, Torry Pedersen said we needed a new approach. In every screen picture, there should be a mix of news, sports, and entertainment. The reason? There's something for every reader on every page."

And then there were the pictures, as Hansen described:

> As a photographer, I have always been interested in perception psychology. So we started with huge pictures. Torry came in screaming, "What the hell is this?" But because it was big, it was effective. When we took it down, our traffic fell. We agreed from then on that things should be both big and small—not like the archive, where everything is the same size. As journalists, we are telling you what is dramatic or important.

The reason most news sites to this day still have few pictures isn't that they aren't effective—they are. The reason is that the format and design of online sites are still shaped by print prejudices. Create a newspaper in the traditional manner and the pictures that accompany news stories are the *last* thing put in, not the first.

Go today to most news sites launched by traditional papers and you'll see a format little changed from ten years ago—a lot of text, few pictures, similar font sizes, relatively short front pages, the print cycle determining the news day, metrics that track monthly unique visitors rather than daily, an edit-then-publish approach, and sections. In all these respects, *VG* chose a radically different approach. Indeed, as traditional news sites remain attached to their print brethren's hip, it's digital-first sites like Twitter and Facebook that most resemble Schibsted. In March 2015 ESPN reorganized its front page in a similar manner. Over the next several months, traffic soared.

"CAN WE HELP READERS HELP EACH OTHER?"

VG's new approach to building and running its news site was in place by 2004. But that December another world event—the tsunami that ravaged

Southeast Asia—ushered in a signature feature of *VG*'s online newsroom. Hansen described what happened:

> We created a simple tool for users to send us pictures or stories. We invited them: Create your stories here. Tell us where you are. The response was incredible—we got stories by the hundreds. I think we were the first news organization in the world with a picture on the ground sent by a telephone. This led us to ask a question we now ask over and over during major events:
>
> "Can we help readers help each other?"

In the years that followed, this question became a focal point of *VG*'s newsroom approach during major crises or events. In 2009 the volcanic ash from the eruptions of Iceland's Eyjafjallajökull ice caps spread from Iceland to Scandinavia, then to the rest of Europe and as far south as Morocco, fueled by the jet stream. More than ninety-five thousand flights were eventually canceled across Europe and as far away as China. Every flight in Norway was canceled, including medical search and rescue helicopters—an unprecedented event. *VG*'s response was not just to publish more content—it was to create an app. By ten o'clock the first night, it had created "Hitchhiker's Central." Hansen explained:

> It wasn't news. It was a tool. It was like a marketplace. "I have a car, I am going to Trondheim, if you want a ride, let me know and we can share the petrol." Or, "I am stuck here, need to get there." We would hide their phone number but still make the connection between readers. That's all we were doing, connecting people.

The result was remarkable:

> It took off. We were connecting people by the thousands, not only in Norway but in the whole of Europe and beyond. There were bus trips organized through this from all the capitals in Europe—Spain, Bulgaria, France, everywhere. We were sending people to weddings, to funerals. We were getting children home. We sent a cat to a cat exhibition in Finland. It was just amazing. And then people started sending pictures to the newsroom to say thank you. "We are on our way to Bulgaria, thank you, *VG*." So two things happened. We got pictures for an ongoing news story that involved basically everyone. And because people sent the pictures with their phones, we had their numbers and could interview them. It strengthened our reputation.

Creating an app for users to upload car pool information is not a natural starting point for a news story about a volcano—unless you ask the question the *VG* newsroom now asks during any major event: "Can we help readers to help each other?" Hansen described its significance:

> That's the question we ask, not just whether there's a story we can tell them. If there's a crisis or breaking news event, we ask that question always. We will say, are you there? Do you have pictures? Click here. So if something is breaking, you will see immediately it's up there. It's just part of how we work now.

The 2009 swine flu epidemic put more wind in the sails of the new approach. The Norwegian government had recommended that every person get a flu shot and had delivered supplies. But it was up to each local community to decide where to administer the shots and who got priority. "This wasn't a centralized approach, and there was a huge demand for information," recalled Hansen. *VG* created a wiki-based map of all the communities in Norway, allowing users to post information on where and when people could get the shot. Again, the results were remarkable: "Within minutes it started to work, and within hours the information was complete. Again, an eye-opener."

"Can we help readers help each other?" may seem an odd question for a news organization to ask. News, you might think, is something that's broadcast; it isn't "social." But the question shifted *VG*'s mindset about what it did—from "being important" to "being relevant," as one editor put it. It changed the way *VG* covered news, and it changed *what VG* covered. And with dramatic results, as Hansen described: "For each large news event, we gained traffic and reached a new peak. These stories are absolutely critical for us."

By 2007 *VG*'s site was drawing in massive numbers of readers—more than any other site in Norway—even though its print market share was less than *Aftenposten*'s. And readers stayed on the site. Measures of engagement—sessions per visitor, pages per session—were twice as high as for most news sites, including *The New York Times*. And nearly everyone started at *VG*'s front page. The high reach—nearly 70 percent of Norwegians went to *VG*'s site each month—meant high advertising rates, ones that by 2007 were as high as those for the front page of the paper. It was an unprecedented achievement for an online news site.

Today Schibsted boasts some the most profitable sites of any traditional media organization in the world. It achieved that not by focusing on creating "better content" but by first recognizing the threat of classifieds—and doing something about it. It achieved that by creating entirely new, nonprint-based approaches to news. It essentially pioneered a master class in avoiding the Content Trap and embracing user connections instead.

5
THE *NEW YORK TIMES* PAYWALL

Network effects connect users by directly linking their purchase decisions: the value to one user from a product depends on the number of other users who've purchased it. But user connections can arise even when that's not the case. Consider pricing strategies: The decision to tailor product prices to the preferences of a certain group often affects the purchase decisions of *other* users. Those connections have nothing to do with network effects, but they are just as important to recognize and manage.

In probably the most anticipated announcement of online charges for media content, *The New York Times* launched its paywall on March 17, 2011. Its prospects, like those of many other papers, appeared grim. Print advertising revenue for the *Times* had dropped by 20 percent after the 2008 recession. The promise that online advertising revenue would compensate for the decline in print had been severely undermined by the rise of ad networks—data-driven Internet firms bent on replacing the relationship-based selling model for advertising inventory with a technology-driven approach. On top of that was a new, near-infinite supply of advertising space online: As advertisers were fond of saying, "any company with a website is a publisher now." And the *Times's* print circulation revenue had experienced double-digit declines since 2009 after showing remarkable resilience during the first fifteen years of the Internet era.

The 2011 paywall was not the first time the *Times* tried to charge for online content. In 2006 it had experimented with another digital subscription, TimesSelect. That project, as one senior manager noted, had been introduced "largely on gut" and "slapped together pretty quickly." In contrast, the effort this time around was hardly rushed: The pricing structure was decided only after months of internal survey research, McKinsey-conducted "conjoint analysis" (a statistically sophisticated approach to testing how much readers were willing to pay), and focus groups. And it was managed differently as well.

Martin Nisenholtz led the digital division at the time the paywall was introduced. He told me,

> This effort was organized differently from almost any past digital effort. To begin with, Arthur Sulzberger [Jr., the publisher of the *Times*] more or less took direct control. The genesis came from him, and he managed the process. But it was not run in a top-down way. Arthur set up a committee that met once a week to get this done. The feeling was that it was such a seminal and important moment for the *Times* that it had to be done in a different way than some other digital decisions.

Denise Warren was a twenty-five-year veteran of the *Times* and, in 2011, one of the senior managers overseeing the paper's digital transition. Reflecting on the mood inside the organization at the time, she said:

> We were coming out of the worst advertising recession any of us had really ever seen. And while digital advertising was, relatively speaking, okay, many of us realized it wouldn't be enough to sustain the franchise. We needed another revenue stream. But, by itself, that wouldn't be enough, either. It had to be purely additive. The stakes were extraordinarily high to get things right.

Sulzberger, Nisenholtz, and Warren were part of a broader digital leadership team for "the paywall project" and they had reason to be optimistic: "People had shown they were willing to pay for our very expensive print product. There was an emerging market for paid apps on mobile devices. And we thought our content was highly differentiated." But numerous observers argued that most readers, habituated over fifteen years to free news online, would not pay for such content.

The paywall project differed from TimesSelect not only in organization and effort but in philosophy, too. Under TimesSelect, certain types of content—notably, the opinion columns—were walled off from readers, while the rest was free. This time the paper chose a different pricing path: Rather than a hard wall, it charged a flat monthly fee to those who read more than twenty articles a month. Effectively, the *Times* was now charging readers for *how much* content they read rather than *what* content they read.

There were other surprises. First, at $7 a week, or $360 a year, the digital subscription was at least twice as expensive as virtually any other subscription on the market. At the same time, the *Times* decided to give existing print subscribers full access to all digital content for free. Second, and unnervingly, within moments of the paywall's launch, numerous observers noticed a design flaw: Not only could readers circumvent the paywall through sites like Facebook and Google, but also through simple URL hacking, cookie deletion, or by accessing the site through multiple devices. Blog posts sprouted up almost instantly to offer ways to work around the paywall restrictions. Third, there was the head-scratching logic of Sunday pricing. Here's one choice presented to readers:

> Sunday print edition + all-digital access: $7.95 per week
> All-digital access: $8.95 per week

In other words, the *Times* was offering a way to get more for less. Economists call this "price arbitrage." Offer products in this way (as companies sometimes do) and the more expensive product—in this case, all-digital access—is unlikely to get takers.

All in all, and despite nearly two years of research and experiments, the *Times*'s experiment seemed poorly thought out. Many observers were critical. Most could not agree about what the *Times* was trying to do. Some argued that the free digital access for print subscribers and the Sunday pricing arbitrage was evidence of an effort to protect print. Others argued the opposite—that the *Times* wanted to accelerate the digital transition since it was offering digital access for less than the print subscription. One issue on which many agreed, however, was that the leakiness of the paywall would haunt the paper. One blogger wrote, "Either the *New York Times* thinks I'm really dumb or they think I'm really smart and are letting me in on the sly. Either way, I don't get how this makes sense."

Connection 1: Digital Buffs and Print Subscribers

Why would you spend two years trying to create a digital product that could serve as a new revenue stream but then turn around and offer it free to your 1.15 million existing print subscribers? If you asked other publishers the same question they would recoil in horror. "Try not to price digital lower than print, or you'll undermine its perceived value," they might say. And "never offer your digital product incrementally for free," for much the same reason.

Several analysts, respected journalists, and bloggers argued that the bundled offering, at its core, reflected the *Times*'s desire to preserve print. Why else would it give the digital product for free only to print readers? What was the *Times* thinking?

The argument that the bundled offer reflected a desire to preserve print is seductive, but it's wrong. To see why, let's start where the *Times* did—by not really even considering a bundled offer. As the *Times*'s senior executives explained:

> The lion's share of the analysis was done in a kind of digital-only way. . . . We were really focused on the website [in trying to create a new revenue stream from digital]. But what kept coming back from our conjoint analysis was that it would be highly cannibalistic for our print users.

On the face of it, this might seem surprising. Why, after all, would the risk of print cannibalization increase if you charged *more* for the digital product than you had before?

To see why, suppose, for simplicity, there are two types of *Times* readers: print subscribers (who had been paying $15 a week) and digital buffs (who had paid nothing). With free online news, not only did digital readers get a great deal but print subscribers did, too, because they could access news online if they wanted to. Charge for digital and you would make it more expensive for print subscribers to get full access—print plus digital—in effect *forcing them to choose* whether to retain their print subscription or migrate to the lower-priced digital offering. This was the alarm bell from the research.

Times executives had not foreseen this risk. But now they had to manage it: how to price digital content and target digital buffs without compromising revenue from print subscribers. Bundling print with all-digital access was one option. But it was an option the *Times* backed into, rather than started with.

In other words, the decision to bundle the print subscription with free digital access was not part of the research—it was a result of it. Miss the connection between digital pricing and its impact on print readers and the *Times* would have experienced a very different outcome.

Charging different prices to different consumers is a classic strategy that economists call "price discrimination." The jargon is hardly elegant, but it captures a simple idea: It pays to separate consumers by charging different prices.

The *Times* faced the core problem of all price discrimination efforts:

Try to target certain customers with the price that's right for them and you risk attracting customers otherwise willing to pay more. Ignore these "connections" across customer groups and your pricing strategy will unravel.

Bundled pricing of print and digital was the *Times*'s solution. Other companies have their own answers. Airlines offer cheaper fares for Saturday night stayovers, effectively linking price to one's cost of time. Retailers have coupons: If everyone used coupons, it would be no different than a straight-out sale. But not everyone bothers, which is why coupons work.

One of the most successful credit card companies of the past two decades is Capital One, founded in 1994 by former consultants Richard Fairbank and Nigel Morris. Its entire strategy was built on price discrimination, starting with its famous "balance transfer" product. The problem credit card issuers face is that they don't want to give cards to everyone. Nor should the annual percentage rate of borrowing, or APR, be the same for customers with different risk profiles. But in 1994 virtually every credit card company offered the same APR—19.8 percent. Fairbank and Morris began offering APR discounts to certain customers. Those who always paid their bills on time—"transactors"—didn't much care about the APR. But neither did likely "defaulters"—since rate adjustments didn't really affect their decisions *not to pay,* either. The result? The people who took advantage of the offer were precisely the customers Capital One wanted: low-risk but price-sensitive customers, termed "revolvers." This creative way of letting customers self-select into a product on the basis of their risk profile paid off handsomely. During its first five years Capital One was one of the fastest-growing and most profitable financial services firms in America, thanks to a simple product that managed pricing spillovers and separated customer groups almost perfectly.

Successful price discrimination strategies come not just from choosing the right price for a target customer but also from ensuring that nontargets don't take advantage of the target price. Recognize these connections across customers and you greatly increase your odds of profitably managing them.

Connection 2: Paid Subscribers Versus Workarounds

Returning to the leakiness of the *Times*'s paywall, we can now see the rationale. In principle, any reader can search and access *Times* articles through Facebook or Google. Similarly, anyone can delete their cookies, replace their URL, read their articles on different devices, or install bookmarks designed to circumvent the paywall. But it's costly to do so—not monetarily, but in terms of annoyance. You have to leave your desktop computer and pick up your tablet, or browse for instructions on how to delete cookies. It might take only a few minutes of discomfort—once you've figured it out—to sidestep the paywall, but that's enough to put many off. Add in people's feelings about fairness and ethics—as Nisenholtz noted, "One shouldn't dismiss the urge that many, many people have to support the *Times*"—and it's no longer surprising that many readers opted to pay $7 a week even though there were ways to access it free.

Leakiness was not a reflection of incompetence or folly on the part of *Times* management. It was a brilliant price discrimination strategy. Nisenholtz put it simply: "This was all incorporated into the paywall design." Warren elaborated:

> We wanted to charge users who were willing to pay, but we wanted to remain open to those who were not. And the reason we wanted to remain open was twofold. First was the advertising revenue we'd otherwise lose from them. Second was that visitors could one day become subscribers. So we went to great lengths to create a "visitor subscriber campaign" that let users know they could access many articles for free every month.

David Perpich was, at the time, executive director of NYTimes.com paid products. He added:

> Some of the workarounds—like through Facebook or Google—were entirely intentional. Others—like the URL strings, or JavaScript plug-ins—were not. But we knew about them all. We just made the decision that they weren't worth fixing. What people forget is that we were launching the paywall as an add-on to our advertising business. So what we were really saying was, "Let's do no harm to our advertising business." In addition—and this is probably far more obvious looking back—the people who will take the time to work around are less likely to subscribe in the first instance. So the subscription charge becomes somewhat of a convenience fee.

The *Times* team saw the potential for a workaround but bet that enough readers saw it as exactly that: something that required work to get around.

The paywall launched with a series of promos, limited-term discounts, and introductory offers. As a result, it took a few months before the real impact could be seen. Paul Smurl, vice president of digital paid products, described three worries of the leadership team heading into the launch: "Would people pay for digital content—how many digital-only subscribers could we convert? What would happen to advertising revenues—to page views, uniques, and reach? And would people trade down from print as they weighed the relative value of the subscription options?"

When the impact could be discerned, it was dramatic. Warren recalled, "We were sort of stunned from day one how successful we were." Paid digital subscribers grew from zero to 676,000 within two years—a relatively small number off an online reader base of thirty million, but enough to bring in new revenue of $81 million in 2013 alone. There was virtually no print cannibalization: Circulation revenue, which had been declining for several years, held steady, then actually grew in 2013 by 1.7 percent. Advertising revenue also held up, thanks in no small part to the leaky paywall and the visitor subscriber campaign.

The near-term success of the paywall did not guarantee future sustainability, of course. But "year three targets of the business plan had been achieved in the first year alone." Smurl summarized the mood at the *Times*: "Sure, there are things that did not go swimmingly. But in general it is pinch-me territory in a lot of respects."

Connection 3: Foodies, Cultural Avant-gardes, and Opinion Junkies— or, Why *The New York Times* Is Like Software

The success of the paywall, at least for now, still raises a central question: What explains the difference in pricing approach and outcomes compared to TimesSelect, the experiment introduced only a few years earlier? After that project was discontinued, in 2008, some observers dismissed the idea that *any* paywall could succeed. TimesSelect had drawn in roughly 250,000 subscribers at about $2.50 a month. The new paywall drew in nearly three times as many while charging more than twice as much!

To understand the difference between the two experiments, it's useful to return to the idea of bundling—but a different kind. Think of *The New York Times* not as a single paper but as a bundle of content types: world news, politics, opinion, sports, metro, culture, arts, travel. One approach—

the TimesSelect model—is to ask what type of content to put behind a paywall. The answer depends on what you think most readers will pay for. But suppose there are different kinds of readers: opinion junkies and sports fans. Opinion junkies devour Brooks, Dowd, and Krugman. Sports fans follow Araton, Rhoden, and Vecsey, along with stories about their local teams. Then there are world news fiends, cultural avant-gardes, community watchers, and foodies. Each group values different types of content differently. What to do in that case?

Here's a deceptively simple analogy borrowed from the world of software. Suppose there are two products for sale—spreadsheets and word processing packages. Suppose also that they are unrelated in use: Customers cannot cut and paste from one to the other; the products are not packaged together; and they need to be installed separately.

Now make three further simplifications. First imagine there are two types of customers: analysts and journalists. Second, say there are equal numbers of each type—in fact, say there is one of each type. Third, the cost of making the products is zero.

Last and most important for our example, here's what customer preferences look like: The analyst is willing to pay $10 for the spreadsheet package but only $2 for word processing (analysts like to make models but can't write). Journalist preferences are the reverse: $10 for word processing, $2 for spreadsheets (they like to write, but stay away from math). The table below captures this information about willingness to pay:

TABLE 2. WILLINGNESS TO PAY: A SIMPLE EXAMPLE		
	Spreadsheet	Word Processing
Analysts	$ 10	$2
Journalists	$2	$10

This brings us to the key question: if you were selling these products, how would you price them?

To begin, consider "fantasy pricing": a world where the company could charge each customer separately for each product (this ideal scenario is termed "perfect price discrimination"). The company would then price spreadsheets at $10 for the analyst (or $9.99, to ensure the sale) and $2 for the journalist, and charge the reverse for the word processing package. What would total revenue be? Twenty-four dollars.

Of course, perfect price discrimination is not only hard, it's illegal. Typically, companies set a price for each product and let customers choose. In that case, the best prices to charge are $10 for each software product. The company now sells two, not four, units—for revenue of $20. Not being able to perfectly price discriminate means that certain sales are forgone. But that's better than lowering prices to ensure that both customers buy both products. And at the heart of the compromise is the fact that the customers have different preferences for the products.

But could you do better? Here's where bundling can help. Price the two products separately and you're leaving money on the table. Price them as a bundle—for $12—and *both* customers will bite; remember, they're willing to pay this amount for both products in total. The best part of the scheme? Revenue has increased to $24—you haven't lost a dime. Bundling allows you to price as if you're in a fantasy world.

By bundling the two products and charging the same price to every customer, you can increase revenue by 25 percent—even though the products are unrelated in use and even though the bundled price is a 40 percent discount off the sum of the individual prices!

Forget Harry Potter—*this* is magic. (It's also what let Microsoft come from behind to win the Office wars.)

The magic behind bundling comes from a simple insight: View customers in terms of their preferences for separate products and they look very different—making it impossible to charge each the full amount of what they're willing to pay. View them in terms of their preferences for the bundle and they look *very similar*—allowing you to charge both the maximum amount they're willing to pay.

In 1976 economists William Adams and Janet Yellen (now chair of the Federal Reserve System) wrote a lucid paper with the dense title "Commodity Bundling and the Burden of Monopoly," in which this logic was first described. Their key insight was that the real value of bundling came not from combining products that were similar but from combining customers with different preferences.

Bundling is effectively a way to price discriminate across customers. Getting it right requires not necessarily knowing each one of your customers, but knowing how their preferences converge or differ. It requires knowing how they are connected.

Let's return to the *Times* example and the various types of readers. Here's a simple and plausible scenario of how their preferences might differ:

TABLE 3. WILLINGNESS TO PAY OF DIFFERENT READERS					
	Opinion	Sports	Culture	Metro	Food
Opinion junkies	$10	$2	$2	$2	$2
Sports fans	$2	$10	$2	$2	$2
Cultural avant-gardes	$2	$2	$10	$2	$2
Community watchers	$2	$2	$2	$10	$2
Foodies	$2	$2	$2	$2	$10

Each type of customer is willing to pay a lot ($10) for his preferred type of content but very little ($2) for anything else.

Now put yourself in the shoes of *Times* executives, and the problem is amplified: You don't know who is what type of reader. Hence the challenge: What content to put behind a paywall?

And this is where the two approaches the *Times* took to structuring a paywall were fundamentally different. TimesSelect reflected a belief that the *Times* knew what content appealed to its readers. The new paywall acknowledged that the paper didn't know. The 2006 experiment started by asking, "What part of our content offering is exclusive?" The 2011 experiment implicitly acknowledged that the answer might differ across readers. So perhaps it's better to set one price for the entire digital bundle of content and let customers choose what to read.

With the first approach, not only might you err in deciding which content to wall off; you'd also be confining your pool of paid subscribers to a narrow type of reader. With the second approach, you need not know which customer is of which type, and you can induce every type of customer to pay.

Managers of the 2006 experiment fell prey to a version of the Content Trap—believing that content determined pricing, rather than reader preferences for it. Managers of the later paywall effort exploited the connections across customer preferences. Seeing these connections not only informed pricing; it opened up big new opportunities.

Connection 4: Sunday Print and All-Digital Access—or, the Rationale Behind "Price Arbitrage"

The theory of bundling can explain why one would offer a digital version to print readers for a low incremental price, perhaps even zero. But what about the *Times*'s pricing of its Sunday product? Effectively, it was *paying* readers to access digital content along with its Sunday print edition. Bizarre!

In fact the Sunday pricing strategy was brilliant. And it too was based on recognizing connections, this time across two very different sets of customers—readers and advertisers.

Draw in more readers and you get more advertising dollars. Draw in fewer and ad revenue drops. Now, the Sunday edition of a newspaper is the thickest and the most attractive for advertisers, drawing in as much as 50 percent of weekly advertising revenue. So although the *Times* made a profit on every copy sold, Sunday circulation was particularly crucial.

Because of this, preserving Sunday print readership was essential—so much so that the *Times* was willing to pay readers $1 to draw them in. The result? Over the next two years Sunday readership stayed roughly even, and Sunday advertising revenues grew; the decision stanched prior-year declines on both fronts.

In recounting the logic behind the "pricing arbitrage," *Times* executives were thrilled—and self-effacing. Smurl noted that although the Sunday circulation figures "definitely helped, we weren't thinking through the Sunday pricing as intelligently as it might seem." Perpich said only, "As amazing as the strategy worked, this part of it was unintentional."

AN EXERCISE IN MANAGING CONNECTIONS

In sum, the *Times*'s paywall strategy had little to do with subsidizing or protecting print. It wasn't intended to cheapen the value of digital. And it wasn't intended to accelerate a transition to the digital world. Instead, it all started from a simple question—can we charge for digital content?—and extended to recognizing and managing the connections across customers that would arise from pricing decisions.

The design and philosophy behind the *Times*'s paywall is a case study in successfully managing customers with different preferences, and recognizing how their decisions were connected. There were connections between print subscribers and digital hard-cores. There were the connections between readers willing to subscribe and ones who never would. There were the connections between opinion junkies and cultural avant-gardes. And there were connections between readers and advertisers.

None of these connections had anything to do with network effects. But they were no less important in affecting user behavior, shaping the design of the paywall, and clarifying the reasons for its success. Perhaps most important, recognizing these connections moved the *Times* away from pricing content—the trap it fell into in 2006—and toward pricing these connections.

Managing the connections between two groups of customers is hard enough. Having to get it right across many different demographics can be downright intimidating. At the end of the day, part of the *Times*'s paywall success was marvelously intentional, the result of careful research. But another part of it—something Smurl and others say "it pains to admit"— was just pure dumb luck.

6

TELEVISION: CONNECTING STREAMS

Few parts of the entertainment sector have seen as dramatic an explosion of digital alternatives as the consumer video market. Today, 300 hours of video are uploaded to YouTube every minute, and four billion videos are watched every day by more than one billion viewers around the world. Upstarts like Netflix, Internet giants like Amazon and Apple, joint ventures like Hulu, and Facebook, Twitter, and Instagram are among the hundreds of parties offering streamed video content—content that is increasingly seen by many as a viable alternative to traditional TV.

What does this mean for the pay TV industry—chiefly, cable operators, who lie at the center of nearly every debate? There are three burning concerns, each with bleak implications.

First, how should cable companies respond to the à la carte options emerging as alternatives to, say, $75 cable bundles? You should have to pay only for what you really want, the argument goes. But for cable operators, that means eroding valuable revenue.

Do nothing in response and they feed into a second concern: the increasing numbers of "cord cutters," or consumers who cancel their cable subscriptions entirely and instead stream video through their computers or mobile devices. This is even worse for cable operators than à la carte, since they lose $75 from each cord cutter, rather than just the revenue from channels à la carte viewers don't select.

Third, and most fundamental, is the question of what to do about streaming in the first place. Fight it or embrace it? Is there a way out? Many aren't optimistic: *The New York Times* soberly concluded, "It appears that cable TV may be in the early stages of a transition that began in the telephone business more than a decade ago when Americans started giving up their land lines and began relying mostly on cellphones. That change took time to gather momentum but then became unstoppable."

The conclusions often drawn—à la carte offerings and cord-cutting are destined to destroy the business of television, and streaming video is a force that just can't be reckoned with—are sobering for the industry. In each case they relate to the power of content—who has it, how to get more of it, or enough of it, at lower prices. It turns out, though, that the real story is quite different. To understand it, you need to recognize the user connections at work and how they are shaping these debates in every case.

WHY HASN'T À LA CARTE PRICING KILLED THE CABLE BUNDLE?

Virtually all cable television viewing in the United States occurs through a few operators. Together, the five largest—Comcast, Time Warner, Charter, Cox, and Cablevision—reach roughly 77 percent of TV households. Each might compete against a satellite or telecommunications company, but they don't compete against one another, thanks to decades-old Federal Communications Commission regulations granting them "local monopoly" because of the hefty capital infrastructure investments required to operate. And each offers take-it-or-leave-it bundles: purchase roughly 150 channels for $75 or so a month, or get nothing.

Because digital technology has increased the number of channels that can be sent through cable pipes, industry insiders argue that viewers are getting a great deal: A basic cable bundle now includes more than 100 channels—many times the number included just two decades ago. Nonsense, consumer groups say: Viewers are forced to pay for 150 channels even though they might watch only 15 or so regularly. And with cable prices rising by a whopping 97 percent in just over a decade, those 150 channels aren't cheap.

Stanford University's Ali Yurukoglu studies the structure of media industries. In a recent conversation, he posed a question that's been asked by nearly every media observer, investor, and entrepreneur over the past decade:

> Music got transformed with digital technology. News got transformed. Books got transformed. Radio got transformed. Video rental got transformed. A lot of people are asking: What's with cable? Why is it offered pretty much the same way as in 1997? Things are getting unbundled elsewhere, moving to à la carte and customization. Why isn't that the case here?

Now, recent events might lead you to think the cable bundle is finally coming apart. In January 2015, Dish Network announced the launch of Sling TV, a streaming service that would deliver a few mainstream channels, including ESPN. A few months earlier, on October 6, 2014, CBS announced its own streaming service, one that would let viewers watch programs without a cable subscription. A day before that, HBO made a similar announcement. "In less than a day," *The Atlantic* noted, "the most critically acclaimed network and the most watched network bet on the future of Internet TV. And just like that, the cable bundle has unraveled more in the last 24 hours than in the previous 24 months."

But, not so fast. Most industry observers weren't betting on the death of cable bundles. Even *The Atlantic* wasn't: In the very same article, it acknowledged that "HBO and CBS à la carte won't blow up cable." *Time* magazine gave an article the sensational title "The Cable Bundle Is Finally Starting to Unravel" only to meekly concede that "the cable bundle isn't going anywhere."

To return to Yurukoglu's question: Why has the cable bundle remained seemingly impregnable? One could argue that cable operators are too big and powerful, or that their stranglehold on live sports keeps them going, or that viewers are too lazy to switch.

But those aren't the real explanations.

To see why, let's return to the basic argument for à la carte, which goes as follows: "Don't force me to pay for what I don't want. Let me decide which channels to receive and I'll pay far less."

Choose only thirty channels, the logic goes, and you'll pay a fraction of your current bill. This is a persuasive argument to the person on the street, but a misguided one.

To see why, let's look at our earlier bundling example, recontextualized for cable TV. Suppose there are two channels offered, ESPN and the Food Network, and two viewer groups with different preferences.

TABLE 4. SPORTS BUFFS VS. FOODIES			
	Value from ESPN	Value from Food Network	Value from Bundle
Sports buff	$10	$2	$12
Foodie	$2	$10	$12

In our analysis of *The New York Times,* we examined à la carte pricing (charging for individual articles) and then explored what bundled pricing (under the paywall) would look like. Here, let's do the reverse: We'll start with bundled pricing—the status quo—and then examine what à la carte would look like.

If viewers had no choice but the bundle, what should the price be? Twelve dollars—just enough to get each viewer to purchase both channels rather than none. Then, each channel would receive $6 per viewer—to compensate for the share of total viewership (50%) that it gets.

What happens if the channels are offered à la carte? Each viewer would purchase only their favorite in that case. On the face of it, they'd be better off—paying less for what they actually want. Except that the channels wouldn't be priced at $6 each, their "average price" when bundled; they'd cost $10 now. And that's only about 15 percent less than the cost of the bundle, even though you're getting only half of it!

This simple example illustrates the flawed logic of the usual argument for à la carte. Give viewers the flexibility to purchase only the channels that they really want and they'd be better off since they pay proportionately less, one might think. But this logic misses a crucial point: Because ESPN and the Food Network would attract only their most loyal viewers in an à la carte world, they wouldn't keep prices the same. They'd be able to increase them without losing their fans—making things *worse* for viewers.

The notion is provocative: Bundles not only increase revenue for cable operators, they also help viewers. And the reason is that by "smoothing prices" across viewers with different preferences—by pricing connections right—bundles provide more to watch at a low incremental cost. That's the same benefit we saw earlier with software pricing and with *The New York Times*. Put another way, if channels were offered one by one, they'd be priced far higher, too, since now you're pricing only to attract your most loyal viewers rather than others who didn't care much.

One often hears the logic for bundled pricing described in terms of subsidies—that by forcing us to purchase channels we don't want and preventing us from purchasing only the ones we really do, some channels are effectively subsidizing others. But this suggests that consumers would never purchase the channels they value less, no matter how low the price. Offer a less-valued channel for an incremental $2, however, as in the example above, and the consumer will purchase it.

Our example makes another important point: which channel is perceived as the "subsidy" differs across viewers. Some would consider that ESPN subsidizes the Food Network, others the reverse. That's the reason bundling works.

View the bundling versus à la carte debate from the perspective of individual consumers and it's easy to see why they would prefer the former. Recognize how user preferences are related—the connections across them—and an entirely different conclusion emerges.

The example above is stylized: two types of viewers, two channels. Let's look at what happens when more types of viewers are added to the example:

TABLE 5. SPORTS BUFFS, FOODIES, COUCH POTATOES, AND INTERNET SURFERS			
	Value from ESPN	Value from Food Network	Value from Bundle
Sports buff	$10	$2	$12
Foodie	$2	$10	$12
Couch potato	$8	$8	$16
Internet surfer	$4	$4	$8

Although the relationship between viewer preferences isn't as simple—preferences aren't just the "opposite" of each other now—the same result obtains. If you offer a bundle, you'll draw in more viewers (everyone but the Internet surfer purchases the bundle for $12). If you offer à la carte, since each channel is priced at $8 now in order to maximize its total revenue you'll not only lose viewers but drive up per-channel prices, too.

Where's the Data?

That's the theory, at least. Viewer preferences are far more complex in reality. And it's not to say that à la carte prices will surely be higher than bundled offers; that wouldn't happen if, for example, bundles merely reflected intransigence on the part of cable providers or inertia on the part of consumers, rather than price discrimination.

So what *would* happen in reality if the cable world were forced to move to à la carte? It's a hard question to answer: Predicting the effect on prices requires knowing viewers' preferences for each channel if offered separately. And therein lies the rub. Since viewers are never given the option of choosing channels à la carte, we have no data on such a scenario. Predicting à la carte outcomes, as a result, would appear to be hard, if not impossible.

That all but halted the debate for a long time; no one could figure out how to get over this empirical hurdle. Then, in 2009, two graduate students in economics—Yurukoglu (while he was at New York University) and Dmitri Byzalov (at Harvard)—each recognized something neat. Even though channels are offered in bundles, viewing decisions are recorded channel by channel (that's the data collected by Nielsen—what we watch, when, and for how long). With this information, you can figure out every viewer's preferences for every channel—finding, in effect, the "demand curve" for each channel. And from there you can figure out how channels would be priced in an à la carte world.

The approach was clever, allowing one to go in reverse: from bundled prices to channel preferences, which in turn allowed predictions about à la carte pricing.

The NYU and Harvard researchers came to more or less the same conclusion. For example, Yurukoglu, working with Gregory Crawford (then at University of Warwick), found that if channels were offered à la carte, with prices fixed at their levels in the bundled world—the "naïve" à la carte analysis—consumers would benefit. But if channels revised their à la carte prices, as they would do in the real world, then the results would be very different. "Programming costs to cable operators [would] increase 103 percent," they wrote, "and prices [would] follow suit." Consumers would be no better off than in a bundled world.

Accounting for advertising revenue and different bargaining positions of upstream channels didn't change the basic result.

Yurukoglu summarized the logic this way:

> A typical channel would have a core niche audience who watch a lot and might be willing to pay a lot. And then there's a large chunk of people who might tune in now and then but who aren't willing to pay that much. When you're selling the bundle, you choose a low price for a lot of viewers. When you sell à la carte, you're tempted to choose a higher price for your really loyal viewers. So you move from pricing a moderate amount to get everybody, to pricing for the tail.

That's not to say everyone loses. Some viewers—those who watch just a few channels, never anything else—would indeed benefit from à la carte. But, as Yurukoglu noted, "the more channels you watch, the worse off you are." And for viewers as a whole, the à la carte benefits of greater flexibility are entirely offset by higher prices.

Cable bundles could well be a thing of the past a few years hence. Exploding broadband video offerings might make it too hard for Hollywood and cable providers to stick to bundles. That wouldn't be surprising. What would be surprising is how many viewers would find that à la carte is not actually what they want.

So be careful what you wish for. And the reason for caution is based not on the content we like but on the need to price connections right.

THE CONTENT TRAP AND DUMB PIPES

If à la carte alternatives might chip away at the profits of content providers and cable companies, cord-cutting seems destined to entirely destroy their business. No other phenomenon has received as much attention from the industry.

The cable industry enjoyed nearly thirty years of uninterrupted growth, ending around the turn of the century. That's when fears about cord-cutting arose—first when national satellite operators like DirecTV and Dish Network began offering viable alternatives to cable, and later when video streaming came along. On the face of it, cord-cutting presents devastating economics for cable operators. ARPU, or average revenue per user, is $75 for a basic cable TV subscription, with an additional $50 for broadband Internet access. Fifteen years ago consumers needed both services. Television was for watching shows, news, and sports, while broadband was for connecting to others and speeding up delivery of files over the Internet. But as broadband entertainment offerings exploded, along with the amount of time people spent on computers, so did the lure of cutting the cord—and saving 60 percent of one's cable bill.

No wonder cable operators have called cord-cutting "the biggest nightmare scenario" the industry has encountered. One business publication noted the trends: sinking cable TV ratings, increasing prices of cable subscriptions, and shifting of advertising monies from TV to digital media. In a dramatic understatement, it concluded that all "this is going to hurt cable TV providers."

Its analysis was wrong.

Craig Moffett has observed the cable industry for more than twenty years. He didn't start out doing so. As an undergraduate at Brown, Moffett majored in painting, becoming an art dealer soon after. Business school changed his trajectory, leading him to Boston Consulting Group, then back to the art world (he founded Sotheby's e-commerce business in 1999) and painting. In 2001 he moved to the Wall Street firm Sanford Bernstein to leverage his consulting expertise in telecommunications, this time as an analyst. He's remained one since. Moffett has always favored hard economics over vague predictions, which has earned him respect: He was the top-ranked cable analyst on Wall Street for nine of the past eleven years—a remarkable stretch.

In 2006 Moffett lead-authored a report that turned the analysis of cord-cutting on its head. Titled "The Dumb Pipe Paradox," it began by describing the conventional wisdom, "a world where video over the Internet has reached its endgame. Cable operators are no longer in the video business. Customers access content via the web. They use their own media center PCs. They pay for only what they want. The cable operators simply provide raw connectivity . . . they're just a dumb pipe." For many investors, he wrote, "this is the 'worst case scenario.'"

Then he proceeded to destroy the conventional argument, offering charts, numbers, and scenarios (wrapped in near-impenetrable economic jargon) to make the case for why the "dumb pipe" scenario might not be so bad.

Had Moffett lost his mind? How could cable operators lose 60 percent of revenue and come out ahead?

Leaving aside the technical aspects of the report, Moffett's thesis was disarmingly simple. It rested on three assumptions. First, although cable revenue in a broadband-only world would decline, so would cable costs—a large, and growing, fraction (one-third) of pay TV revenue went toward acquiring content, but almost none of its broadband revenue did. (The cable company simply charged for access, and customers streamed whatever they wanted.) Second, capital expenditures were far lower for broadband than for pay TV: Broadband had no set-top boxes, network-based projects, or head-end servers (facilities that receive, process, and distribute television signals). As a result, invested capital could be put to work more efficiently. Third, there was room to further increase broadband prices, since in most parts of the country, cable operators remained the only providers of high-speed broadband. (Wireless and DSL providers presented competition in less than 30 percent of the nation.) And prices could be tailored to demand: If consumers using more bandwidth were charged more, revenue would increase still further.

These three arguments—lower costs of acquiring content, lower expenditures on capital, and the potential for price increases and price discrimination—led Moffett to a "dramatically counter-intuitive and starkly anti-consensus" conclusion. The economics of a dumb pipe scenario, he wrote, "are actually *better* than those of the business today."

None of Moffett's assumptions was controversial. His math was simple. And almost everything in his paper is now widely agreed on by industry insiders and observers. But at the time his conclusion was unique. He recalls:

> In retrospect, the analysis probably shouldn't have been surprising. I think the reason it was so counter-consensus was that the notion of a dumb pipe was always immediately rejected without any serious consideration of what it meant. It just sounded like a bad thing, so you could write off cable as a dying old-media dinosaur simply by saying it would become a dumb pipe. The report's real contribution was in saying, You have to consider whether the economics of becoming a dumb pipe are as punitive as the name suggests.
>
> For ten years I had tried to explain that cable companies are not media companies. They don't sell content; they are infrastructure providers. Once you think of them in those terms, it's much easier to imagine that they won't be killed by the emergence of online media. The argument that they will is a bit like saying, We're on the brink of this incredible transition from gas-powered cars to electric cars, so we won't need roads anymore. It's a non sequitur.

It's one thing for content providers to define their business narrowly, in terms of the content they make. It's another for distribution companies to believe their future must be tied to the content they offer. That's an even more extreme and insidious version of the Content Trap. It comes in part from the language we use: Contrast "dumb" pipes with "value-added" services. The reason Moffett's analysis gave cable providers hope was, he noted, that "in part, I gave them the language to talk about something most of them intuitively understood but had trouble articulating. I still hear about this piece with regularity, going on ten years later."

By 2016 some smaller cable companies had voluntarily cut the cord to content, moving away from their pay TV offering to one focused on broadband. And they were breathing easier.

HAS THE WINDOW SHUT?

À la carte offerings and cord-cutting were challenging enough. But they were symptoms of a bigger threat: Netflix. Once the consumer darling in the DVD rental business, by 2007 the company had set its sights on the exploding market for video streaming. On the face of it, this was a ferocious threat to the television business, destined to send incumbents there to the graveyard in much the way Netflix had buried Blockbuster. How do you compete with an offering that has come to define "disruptive technology"? Disruption experts surely didn't have an answer.

It turned out that the industry had not one, nor two, but three strategies in response. First was recognizing the vulnerability in Netflix's content licensing strategy. In 2013 Starz upped its charge for providing content to Netflix tenfold—exposing Netflix's dependence on purchasing branded content from traditional players.

Second was price discrimination. The gains Moffett projected from "usage-based pricing"—charging consumers according to how much bandwidth they used—didn't apply just to individuals. It applied with even greater force to streaming providers—their entire business depended on broadband access. Netflix alone ate up about 35 percent of all Internet bandwidth during prime-time hours—but paid nothing for it.

Third was a plot hatched by one of television's biggest players. In 2009 Time Warner's CEO, Jeff Bewkes, announced the TV Everywhere strategy: Time Warner's cable subscribers would get access to television content on any additional device at no additional cost. It seemed a brilliant move to combat low-priced broadband video offerings like Netflix: By not charging extra for video content, Time Warner hoped to retain pay TV subscribers *and* undercut streaming providers in one go.

Price discrimination and TV-broadband bundling were exactly the strategies that later paid off for *The New York Times* in its paywall. And they yielded early success here: In August 2013 a failed agreement with Starz triggered a nine-month collapse in Netflix's share price from $300 to $58. It seemed that one could develop a strategy to deal with disruptors after all.

Yet, barely three years later, things looked different. Netflix recovered impressively, its market value increasing from $3 billion to $40 billion. Usage-based pricing faced increasing regulatory hurdles. And TV Everywhere never quite got off the ground.

What happened? It's one thing to formulate smart strategy; it's quite another to execute it well, and to do it with focus.

As cable companies experimented with price discrimination, they were halted in their tracks for a variety of reasons. One was poor choices: Time Warner Cable launched some of its early trials of usage-based pricing in Austin, Texas, a major tech hub whose blogosphere soon raised hell. One was pushback from unexpected sources: As backlash from Austin spread to Rochester, New York, local politicians picked up on consumer senti- ment and introduced bills declaring usage-based pricing unconstitutional.

A more basic reason was cable companies' response to the siren call of higher prices rather than to the more reasonable call of differential prices. Instead of dropping prices for low-bandwidth users while raising them for high-bandwidth users, Time Warner Cable raised prices across the board, "starting at the status quo price of $40 per month and charging for usage on top of that," Moffett says. The result was "all stick and no carrot for customers. Usage-based pricing became perceived as 'We're trying to take advantage of everybody.'"

As for TV Everywhere? The industry got seduced by other goodies. For content providers, it was the promise of quick dollars from Netflix in ex- change for "long-tail" content—archived shows that were mostly sitting around unused. That wasn't in itself a bad thing; as Moffett observed, "nobody was going to drop their pay TV subscription because you've li- censed a bunch of old *Beavis and Butthead* episodes to Netflix." But when providers ran out of old content, they started selling more-recent content to sustain the licensing revenue they'd become addicted to. "The crack cocaine of digital licensing turned Netflix from a sheep into a wolf," Mof- fett said.

The seduction also had to do with cable companies' efforts to get bigger on their own turf. When Comcast announced a proposed $45 billion megamerger with Time Warner Cable, in 2014, it invited consumer and regulatory scrutiny that nixed the deal and also "accelerated industry regu- lation by a decade."

It's not that price discrimination and bundling didn't work. They did, and they had. When Rogers, Canada's leading cable company, introduced usage-based pricing, it forced Netflix onto the back foot, prompting changes to its infrastructure and streaming quality that made its growth far more difficult. And the cable companies' pricing approach differed in important respects from AT&T and Verizon's earlier, successful introduc- tion of usage-based pricing in the wireless industry. In television, content and distribution companies alike got distracted: seduced by near-term licensing revenues that made streaming providers stronger in the end, seduced by the lure of higher prices that ultimately created consumer backlash, and seduced by megamergers that were struck down and that made usage-based pricing harder to implement. Seduced by the trees, they had forgotten about the forest.

7
CROWDS

Networks can be used for content creation, not just consumption. *Crowdsourcing, user-generated content,* and *user contribution networks* have become commonplace terms. But what that means for the future of content businesses is a matter of fierce debate. While many observers scoff at the content increasingly emerging from crowds, others believe it will ultimately replace traditionally created material.

Karim Lakhani studies crowds. He's been at it for more than a decade, first at MIT and now at Harvard Business School. A few years ago, after giving a presentation on how some organizations draw on the so-called wisdom of crowds to solve scientific problems—Innocentive's "solver community," for example, comprised more than 500,000 users from nearly every country around the world by 2015—he was approached by an audience member with an invitation to discuss his work further. This was Jeff Davis, NASA's chief medical officer, "the guy who keeps astronauts alive in space," as Lakhani put it.

Lakhani visited Houston to share his research with Davis's team. Then they agreed to experiment with crowdsourcing solutions to a problem NASA had been working on for decades—how best to pack medical kits taken on missions. As Lakhani described,

> The problem is important, because you can't ship up an entire hospital emergency room on a rocket. Your space medical kit is constrained by mass and volume, and it costs roughly $10,000 per kilogram to launch it into space. Then, you need to figure out how the mission characteristics and crew health might lead to various outcomes: Somebody could break an arm, somebody could get food poisoning. You need to create a kit optimized for such events—you want to minimize the chance of evacuation. The joke is that people in space are still covered by OSHA laws, which say that if a sick worker is untreated, you've got to bring them home.

NASA ran a two-week contest to solve the problem, using Topcoder, a platform that routinely hosts online programming competitions for tasks ranging from user interfaces to logo design. The prize was $25,000. More than 400 people participated; some entered multiple solutions, resulting in more than 2,000 submissions of code in all.

NASA used two metrics to score the submissions, Lakhani explained. "The design of any kit would have an associated probability factor for what the evacuation would be—the likelihood that a kit would fail to cover some contingency based on simulated mission data sets. And given mission constraints, the time needed to calculate optimal kit composition was important." The results were startling: The best submissions exceeded the probability factors in NASA's calculations. As for time? The NASA team's algorithm usually took three hours to come up with an answer. The winning submission took thirty seconds.

Bara Reyna, then head of medical hardware on the International Space Station, noted, "To put it very bluntly, we were blown away with the results." The experiment had a lasting impact. NASA funded the creation of the Harvard-NASA Tournament Lab to run similar crowdsourcing experiments. Meanwhile, researchers at Harvard Medical School were intrigued by crowd-based experiments and decided to try one of their own on Topcoder, in immunogenomics. Here, too, the scoring algorithm was objective, taking into account a submission's accuracy in a particular gene-sequencing task and also the time needed to solve the problem. The prize was $6,000.

For the contest, a highly specific immunogenomics problem was reframed as a more general computational science problem. One hundred twenty-two people generated roughly 650 submissions. "The best results were more accurate than both the NIH [National Institutes of Health] solution and the internally developed Harvard solution, and an order of magnitude faster," Lakhani said. "And many of these came from people with no background in medical research. They were coming from mathematics, computer science, and so on."

These weren't experiments relying on crowds to create seemingly simple content—a short video or a text blog. These were problems that had been worked on for years by leading researchers, sometimes over the course of entire careers. Yet crowds performed better. What did it all mean?

One view is that crowds will displace traditional modes of production. By now crowd-reliant models are routine in digital worlds, where they generate opinion (on Twitter and Facebook), create videos (YouTube), evaluate internal projects (Google), expose secrets (WikiLeaks), raise funds (Kickstarter and GoFundMe), and uncover relevant information. This last application was particular relevant to *The Guardian* a few years ago, when its newsroom relied on readers to filter hundreds of thousands of documents on British MPs' expense claims and identify misconduct. In this light, it's hard not to think that crowds represent a powerful model and promising future for content creation, deployed in more and more places and inevitably improving in quality.

But there's a more pessimistic view, holding that although crowd-generated content can be first-rate, that's not usually the case. Lakhani and others note that the value of crowds lies in the ability to tap a diverse range of inputs—the ability to "exploit variance," a feature typically missing from traditional approaches that rely on narrow groups of experts. But critics say that the content on most crowd-based websites remains *on average* substandard. The vast majority is never read or watched. And online vandals and trolls, inevitable by-products of opening up to crowds, further undermine quality. *The Guardian* has termed this the "Age of Rage," while *The Economist* refers sardonically to "User Generated Discontent."

Opposing points of view—but both evaluate the prospects of crowds in terms of the quality of their content, missing the real issue. Often, quality isn't the right yardstick—connections are.

The opportunity, and the challenge, of connecting crowds takes different forms. First is the challenge of creating great content and then getting others to read and share it—often the most salient objective of crowd-based models. "It's about creating a community, messaging between users," Anil Dash told me recently. Dash is one of the most experienced bloggers on the Internet—he's been blogging for seventeen years. "If you view community as a crowd, you're destined to fail."

The *Bleacher Report* may never be as good as ESPN; *The Huffington Post* and BuzzFeed may never be as good as *The New York Times*. But the success of those organizations—by 2011, the *Bleacher Report* was the second-most-visited sports site, after ESPN, while both BuzzFeed and *Huff Po* had passed the *Times* in readership—was always premised on sharing, not on content. Janet Balis is the former publisher of *The Huffington Post*. She described to me the real innovation there: "*Huff Po*'s growth was largely driven by its ability to capitalize on traffic driven through the social dynamics of Facebook and Twitter, and through search. News used to bring people to 'the thing'; now you have to bring 'the thing' to the people. That completely flip-flopped distribution; it was the death of the portal. The model used to be a hub, but now people consume at the spokes."

It's fashionable to think the growth of such sites came from opening content creation to crowds—inviting contributions from anyone and relying on an army of bloggers. That isn't the case. Sharing was the secret. Have your content shared, and it amplifies the incentives for people to contribute in the first place—creating positive connections or feedback loops. Otherwise the crowd will soon fade away.

"People need to believe either that their contributions will make a difference—as with NASA—or that they'll get discovered," Anil Dash told me. "But crowdsourced news reporting tends to be like giving people homework: 'Tell us what happened at the city council meeting.' It turns out, most people don't want to go to those meetings, and they can sniff out very quickly when you're just trying to get them to do your homework for you."

Sharability has costs, too. After the Boston Marathon bombings in 2013, a false rumor that a Brown University student was a suspect spread like wildfire. Harmful triggers can also spread. As with vitriol and vandals, the challenge is not only to create positive connections but also to prevent negative ones.

Focusing merely on contributions at the expense of connections is the first error commonly made in crowdsourcing. There's a second, more basic, one: thinking that merely "opening up" to crowds will generate content.

Wikipedia is perhaps the most studied crowdsourcing organization in the world. "There've been over 6,000 papers written about it," noted software-developer-turned-social-scientist (and now University of Washington professor) Benjamin Mako Hill, whose own Ph.D. dissertation added to the list. Yet, when he embarked on his study of its success, Mako Hill noticed something interesting: Wikipedia wasn't the first effort to create a volunteer-driven online collaborative encyclopedia. Seven similar efforts preceded its 2001 launch. None came remotely close to achieving Wikipedia's success. Whereas Wikipedia would come to comprise more than five million articles, half of the other projects generated fewer than fifty.

Mako Hill has contributed to open-source software since he was twelve. It wasn't just online encyclopedia projects that failed so often, he noted: "The median number of contributors for *any* free and open-source software project is one. We only talk about the large and successful projects like Wikipedia, Linux, or Apache. But the vast majority of these projects never mobilize anybody."

Studying successful open-source projects is useful. But to understand what makes successful projects *really* work, you've got to study failed ones too. "It's the familiar problem of selection bias," Mako Hill noted. It's the reason why studies of successful CEOs can't offer much guidance: The characteristics observed—for example, that successful leaders are inspiring, or data driven—may also be common among CEOs who failed but weren't studied.

So why did Wikipedia work where similar projects failed? Mako Hill offered a few explanations.

First, the crowd needs to be clear on what content is wanted. The common notion that Wikipedia was out to displace the encyclopedia is a myth. Its founders—more than the founders of the failed projects—wanted to *re-create* the encyclopedia, and they were clear about this objective and what it meant: be impartial, cover only important subjects, prohibit original research, and reference everything. Other projects were more expansive and thus less clear. One, titled "Everything2," aspired to be a "flexible web database" and to "find the best way to store and link ideas." When a contributor asked, "What is 'Everything'?" the answer was, " 'Everything' is what you make of it. . . . It's open-ended, open-minded, and waiting for you." Contributors to another project were confused about whether they could include fictional material; as a result, one of the initiators said, "We had piles and piles of shit." Ironically, by being narrow in its goal, Wikipedia drew the most contributors.

Second, you need to make it easy. In contrast to other projects, editing on Wikipedia required little effort; anyone could do it. You didn't need to log in, have an account, or learn HTML. You could "do a drive-by edit and never be involved again," noted one expert. Every other project had significant "barriers to contribution."

Making contributions easy can, of course, have perverse consequences—you attract undesired contributors, resulting in clutter, vandalism, or conflict.

This leads to the third requirement: a mechanism to sort the wheat from the chaff. Because anyone could contribute, Wikipedia needed ways to resolve conflicts, prevent vandals, and remove contributions that didn't merit publishing.

What that mechanism is will depend on who you're trying to attract and what you're trying to achieve. It's a delicate balance. Relax the norms too much and you'll invite vandals and conflict. Make them too demanding—by requiring an account, registration, or invitation, for example—and you'll drive away valuable contributors, as other projects experienced.

The norms on Wikipedia emerged gradually and were tailored to solve specific problems begat by earlier norms. No one had authorship of an article, so it was easy for others to edit. If you disagreed with an edit, you could chat online with the editor to resolve it. Fail to do so—engage in "edit warring," as it came to be called—and you'd have administrators (themselves anointed on the basis of prior contributions) step in. If you automatically and repeatedly reversed the edits of a conflicting party, you'd trigger a flag (called the "3RR," or three automatic reverts rule) that not only drew in other editors but could result in a ban. If you made offensive edits—say, adding words like *poopy*—you'd be automatically deleted, this time by algorithms like ClueBot, which were trained to "learn" in a Bayesian manner from edit patterns of humans. If you tried to insert edits on an article that had been tagged with a verified check mark (indicating that it had already been thoroughly vetted), you wouldn't be able to do so. Even for articles without such tags, many were flagged by active editors anyway so that they could be automatically notified anytime an edit was made.

Imagine a news organization with no hierarchy, no selection process for editors, and nearly no barriers to contribution—and imagine that every contribution is published instantly. You'd expect a product replete with errors, an enterprise destroyed by vandals, and a setting where conflicts are rampant. What's remarkable about Wikipedia isn't that articles sometimes contain errors, but that the errors aren't pervasive enough to undermine the entire enterprise. Somehow it all works.

It's tempting to view Wikipedia as a miracle of crowds—a place where, somehow, vandals restrain themselves, where good drives out bad, and where collective interests magically trump individual ones. That's folklore. Wikipedia works because of the complex system of norms, rules, and algorithms that has emerged over time. The norms aren't much different from those in a traditional content organization. But rather than bestow decisions rights on a few, no editor had veto rights here, and no one "sat at the top" of the organization. The norms themselves were shaped and policed by the collective.

Similar issues apply to online discussion forums and account for why they often fail. It's one thing to open up to comments, but unless they are easy to search, users will get frustrated and won't return. Allow the "wrong" people in, or impose no consequence for inappropriate comments, and the entire process is undermined. Dash noted "the problem of YouTube comments, which are set up as an optimal system for causing others grief." It's a problem of negative connections.

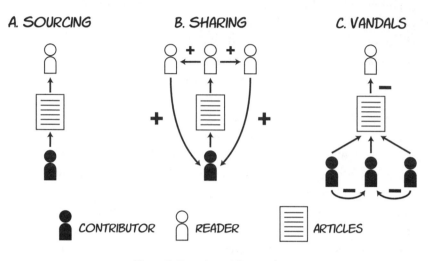

A. SOURCING   B. SHARING   C. VANDALS

CONTRIBUTOR   READER   ARTICLES

Figure 7: Crowds and Connections

It's a problem that companies can do a lot about, but don't. A few years ago Dash wrote a post about policing posts. Some of his prescriptions: Have real people monitor comments. Be explicit about community norms. Require accountable identities, not anonymity. Embrace technologies to identify and stop bad behaviors. Devote effort and money to moderation. These things aren't rocket science, but, as Dash noted, the tendency of most websites is quite the opposite—to do little to moderate. One reason is the belief that moderation flies in the face of openness. But that's flawed logic. After all, Dash wrote, "Businesses that run cruise ships have to buy life preservers. Companies that sell alcohol have to keep it away from kids." The main takeaway of his post is in the title itself: "If Your Website's Full of A*holes, It's Your Fault." He recently elaborated:

> Community moderation is seen as a low-status task, delegated to junior people—typically, interns with low pay, no prestige, very high turnover, and no institutional memory. It's no surprise they fail. Another reason is the metrics companies use. For many years the only metric of success was the number of comments. That's easy to measure, but it values unique users more than engaged ones, and that's the worst way to build a com-

munity. Imagine having a community center that people visit just once. The problem of ensuring successful comments has been solved. Companies just don't want to do what's required.

That's the real lesson about crowds: It's not enough to "open up." "For a long time," Dash continued, "there was this belief about the utopian empowerment of people—where nobody will be in charge and everything will be grand. What inevitably happens is that things get worse and worse until there's a breaking point."

In other words, crowds require management. They require selection, incentives, and curation, just like contributors in any organization do. Most important, you need to connect them.

Interpedia was created at about the same time as Wikipedia. Both were online projects, both were collaborative, both relied on volunteers, and both were intended to create an encyclopedia. But there was one important difference, as Mako Hill notes: "Interpedia's design called for individuals to work together to build an encyclopedia, but to have each article produced individually," whereas Wikipedia's design called for people to edit one another's contributions (see Figure 8). It was a small difference, but an important one—the difference between tapping crowds to *create* content and recognizing the need to *connect* what they do.

Over its lifetime, Interpedia attracted just 400 contributors and produced fewer than 50 articles.

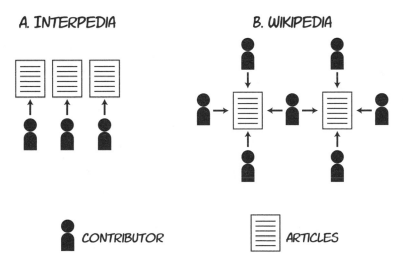

Figure 8: Interpedia versus Wikipedia

––––––––––

The power of *Huff Po,* BuzzFeed, and similar sites is that people *share* their contributions with others. The power of Wikipedia isn't just that anyone can contribute; it's that people can *improve* the contributions of others, while vandalism is curbed. The power of NASA-style crowd-based experiments comes not from the fact that anyone can contribute but that they're designed to *select* the right contributions.

In each case the real power comes not from merely using crowds to *create* content—by itself, that rarely works—but from optimizing connections.

The notion of crowds as a model for *content creation* is just another version of the Content Trap: thinking that if you open up they'll come, or that you'll automatically have a robust content-generating model. It's not enough to allow everyone to create content. You need to make sure you attract the right contributors. You want them to connect and share. You have to create positive feedback connections rather than negative ones. It may be intoxicating to look to crowds as a new way to create content, but without ensuring the right conditions, you'll fall into the same old trap.

8
COST-BASED CONNECTIONS

KINDLING THE PUBLISHERS

Few events shook the book publishing industry as much as the launch of Amazon's Kindle, in 2007. When Jeff Bezos, Amazon's CEO, introduced the product on November 19, he invited representatives from the publishing industry to witness the occasion. Madeline McIntosh, a senior executive at Random House—the world's largest trade publisher (now Penguin Random House, and the publisher of this book)—was among them. She described the reaction:

> Bezos was up on the stage going through all the features of this new device. Our general experience thus far was that e-books had not been a big deal. We were being polite in attending Amazon's event, but not really expecting much. And impressive as the Kindle was with respect to product features and number of titles available, it was an expensive device. It seemed like a fairly specialist product. But the part I cannot forget about the event was when he announced the price—$9.99 for *New York Times* bestsellers. There was definitely a gasp in the audience. We really didn't know what to think.

Publishers suddenly had a lot to worry about. Discounted print prices for bestsellers were $15 to $20 for the end consumer. And Amazon's $9.99 salvo proved even more devastating than it first seemed: The price would apply not just to bestsellers but to a large selection of titles (echoes of Apple's $0.99 songs). The fact that Amazon was willing to take losses in the near term to ensure market success—by choosing to pay publishers the same price as for print books, $12 or $13, it would lose money on every e-book sale—served notice as to what publishers could expect in the future. Once the Kindle's popularity was established, they believed, Amazon would demand different terms.

Headlines were swift and frightening. *Newsweek*'s cover story "Reinventing the Book" called the Kindle "a milestone in a time of transition, when a challenged publishing industry is competing with television, Guitar Hero and time burned on the BlackBerry." David Young, the chairman and CEO of Hachette Book Group USA, captured the mood of publishers when he remarked, "If it's allowed to take hold in the consumer's mind that a book is worth ten bucks, to my mind it's game over for this business." Publishers were already coping with declining margins. How could they survive if book prices dropped by 50 percent?

Contrary to such pronouncements, in fact publishers might be fine in a $9.99 all-e-book world. The reason is that if print were to disappear, a lot of costs would, too. Publishers wouldn't have to pay printers. They wouldn't bear the costs of retailers returning unsold books. All told, the costs of printing, production, and returns average about $3 a book. On top of this, publishers also wouldn't have to store books in a warehouse or ship them anywhere—saving another $2 a book. Retailers wouldn't incur the costs of brick-and-mortar stores—that's another $10 in costs per book, on average. Some new costs might arise from the technology, but those are relatively small compared to the physical cost savings. Add it all up and you realize, remarkably, that existing publisher and retailer profit margins, each about $1 a book, could still be preserved at an e-book price of $10.

One can only marvel at the munificence wrought by e-books on the publishing industry! McIntosh and many other publishers realized this at the time: "If the market were to go completely digital," she told me recently, "it could be extraordinarily good financially, because you could get rid of a lot of cost. There is a lot of good news in digital transformation."

The publishing industry isn't alone when it comes to cost economics like these. Similar savings hold for other types of media content. Digital news costs a fraction of what it takes to produce a newspaper; for example, in 2012 *The New York Times* spent some $600 million on print and production, costs that would disappear in an all-digital world. The cost of making and delivering a digital music file is just over half the cost of making and selling a CD—thanks, once again, to the savings on manufacturing, distribution, and retail stores.

But that leaves us in an apparently confusing place. Where, then, are the cataclysms that digital content was supposed to bring upon traditional media firms? And why, then, did many publishers recoil in horror at the very word *digital*? The answer is not that they couldn't envision an all-e world or even that they didn't want to. The answer has to do, instead, with a feature common to nearly every content business: the fixed costs of making and distributing content.

Why do fixed costs matter? Let's return to our previous analysis, this time with an additional scenario—a world where some books are still sold in print. Imagine that a publisher lost only *some* of its traditional business, say 30 percent, to e-products. Even though print unit sales have dropped by 30 percent, fixed costs for supporting the print infrastructure—the cost of a printing plant, a warehouse, of fulfillment and distribution—remain as high as they were. (Of course, some costs, such as editorial and design, are shared with e-production. But that's not enough to overcome the fixed-cost problem.) The economics of this hybrid world are distressing: You still bear the entire fixed cost of your print enterprise but now on only 70 percent of your volume. The result is a dramatic drop in profitability with even a small reduction in print.

So, e-products impact the profitability of a print sale not because they come at the expense of print, but because of fixed costs, which make it hard to gradually scale down the print infrastructure as e-sales grow. Markus Dohle, the CEO of Penguin Random House, summarized the problem:

> You have fixed costs in many areas of the print value chain—your production department for the print runs, your systems to support your production process, and your distribution centers—so that if your volume in print goes down, your costs per copy go up. We live in a world where, even in fifty years, if print is part of our business even as digital becomes more and more important, we'll have to support two infrastructures going forward.

The challenge that digital technologies pose for content businesses is often attributed to one of three things: cannibalization of traditional products by digital ones; complacency of existing managers who refuse to embrace new technologies; or worsening economics of content in a digital world. While these factors surely don't help any business trying to forge its own digital journey, the preceding economics of publishers highlight a more important, and far more insidious, force at work: fixed cost.

The problem facing book publishers, like so many other content businesses, has little to do with the 50 percent price drop in moving from print to electronic. And it isn't that they can't make money with digital products—the economics of an all-e world are robust. The real problem is figuring out how to get from here to there—and all because the structure of their costs is mostly fixed.

Managing the transition from traditional to digital—managing Dohle's "two infrastructures" world—might appear a bigger problem for incumbents (who already have an existing business) than for entrepreneurial new entrants (who don't have one). That's true, but only for a while—until the entrepreneurial firms "grow up." Start a new business and no legacy infrastructure encumbers you. Expand from your existing business into a new one and it will. Reed Hastings would know. Named one of the top ten CEOs of the past decade by *Inc.* magazine, he seemed to manage Netflix easily—while it was focused on DVD rentals. The day it started managing two formats—DVD rentals and streaming video—is the day big problems and questions arose. How quickly should the core business be wound down? How closely should the new business be integrated with the old? In 2011, following a popular prescription, Hastings tried to separate the two businesses completely—and struggled. From July 2010 to January 2012 Netflix lost 80 percent of its market value.

It's the reason *The New York Times,* despite healthy returns from its paywall, is still not out of the woods. In an all-e world, getting rid of printing, distribution, and warehousing saves more than half a billion dollars a year. But operate in a hybrid world—where print still remains, but at a lower volume—and the question of how to manage those fixed costs continues to bear.

FIXED COSTS AND USER CONNECTIONS

Fixed costs, by definition, don't vary with customer volume. And fixed costs characterize nearly all content businesses. Whether you print 50 copies of a newspaper or 1,000 copies, your printing and production costs are fixed. The cost of producing a TV program is the same regardless of whether it gets 100,000 viewers or one million. And so it is for movies and magazines.

For this reason, fixed costs "connect" users. The profit from serving any single customer in a fixed-cost business is inextricably linked to that of serving every other. This means you can't look at each user gained or lost in isolation—he or she affects profits and losses from all your other users. Lose just three customers out of a hundred in a fixed-cost business and your entire profit might disappear. This is the main problem media firms looking to embrace digital technologies face. It isn't that customers are fleeing traditional content in droves, or that new digital products are far superior to them. It's more often that they bear fixed costs.

Fixed costs create user connections that are different from the other forms of connections we've seen. Connections arising from fixed costs relate to the cost structure of your business; they have nothing to do with customer preferences, pricing, or behavior. But they're no less important to manage.

In *The Vanishing Newspaper,* Philip Meyer predicts that the last reader will leave print in 2043. Thankfully, this is not a bulletproof prediction. Even if it came to pass, however, the value of newspaper firms would fall to zero long before. It wouldn't pay to operate a printing plant, a newsroom, and a sales force if the number of print readers fell below a certain level. Fixed costs create a tipping point for content businesses that are in decline: Lose a (very small) fraction of your customers and you may not want to keep it going.

Similar dynamics operate in other industries where fixed costs are prevalent: Airplanes, hotels, and retail stores immediately come to mind. Air traffic dropped by roughly 6 percent in the year following 9/11. That was enough to send most airlines into the red. When occupancy rates for hotels fall from 90 percent to 80 percent, it's enough to shut them down. Erode retail sales by only a few percentage points and a lot of retailers go bankrupt.

In each case, fixed costs make the dips from small triggers spread like wildfire. That's what requires management.

A LESSON IN MANAGING FIXED COSTS

The problem of managing fixed costs is hardly new. And there's much to learn from businesses that have done it well. Let's look at one of the most successful companies of the past five decades—one that owes its success to the principles of fixed-cost management.

From 1978 to 2015, Walmart shares experienced a cumulative annual growth rate of more than 21 percent—higher than almost any other company during that period. Some of the company's choices are well-known: its decision to first locate in rural areas, not cities; its decision to cluster its stores relatively close together (far closer than competitors like Target); its decision to enter the groceries business in the early 1990s; and its decision to advertise less than any of its competitors.

On the face of it, none of these decisions makes sense. Rural locations should mean fewer customers. Clustering should mean stores cannibalize one another. Entering groceries should lower profits—supermarkets are known for cutthroat competition and razor-thin margins. Less advertising should mean fewer customers.

But view these decisions in light of high fixed costs and a different picture emerges.

Discount retailing is fundamentally a fixed-cost business. Roughly two-thirds of Walmart's costs are its payments to suppliers for their products (referred to as the "cost of goods sold," or COGS)—variable costs. The rest are mostly fixed: the capital expenditures of building stores or renting space, the costs of warehouses, trucks, and IT systems. Conventional wisdom is that Walmart wins by lowering COGS—squeezing out a few extra cents from its suppliers. In fact that's not the case. Winning via COGS is hard—it relies on tough negotiations. The secret of Walmart's success is its ability to manage fixed costs in a uniquely effective way.

Let's revisit some of Walmart's choices. Locating a store in a rural area might present challenges in terms of attracting crowds, but for that reason it discourages competitors, thereby allowing the store to spread its fixed costs across a far less contested customer base. Locating stores close together allows the firm to spread fixed warehousing costs across a larger number of stores. Selling milk and other perishables might mean slim profits on those products, but by drawing customers in more frequently and selling them other products, the store lowers its break-even point. Less advertising might mean fewer new customers, but Walmart can afford not to hold, or market, sales. Sales often serve to get rid of excess inventory, but Walmart's high-fixed-cost IT systems keep inventory at minimal levels.

Walmart's success comes not (only) from a unique culture, from offering value-for-money products, or from its tough negotiators. It comes in large part from managing fixed costs better than its competitors.

Fixed costs are often associated with brick-and-mortar businesses, but they apply to digital companies as well. Take Amazon.

It's tempting to think Amazon's advantage over physical retailers comes from convenience: online ordering from your home. But that brings a disadvantage, too: It takes longer to get the products you buy. When Amazon set up operations, in 1997, delivery took about seven days—around 6 days and 23 hours longer than it would take to drive to the nearest Barnes & Noble. That's longer than most customers will accept.

To reduce delivery times, Amazon began building distribution and warehousing facilities. By 2015 it had more than fifty fulfillment centers, representing billions of dollars in capital expenditures. It had created a massive fixed-cost operation—expensive to build, but advantageous to scale. As Amazon grew, so did its cost advantage. By 2002, for every $50 million in growth, Amazon's per unit costs fell by roughly 30 cents—a substantial advantage in a business where margins are tiny.

For more than a decade, Amazon's approach to managing fixed costs has been curiously similar to Walmart's. In 2002 Amazon launched its version of store clustering with Marketplace, inviting other retailers to use its website and fulfillment centers for a fee. The risk was cannibalization of Amazon's own sales, but the benefit was spreading fixed costs over a greater volume.

From 2001 to 2006 Amazon launched its version of Walmart's IT strategy by increasing its investments in IT servers—it built more than two million across the United States. To spread the massive fixed costs that required, it opened access to its servers and the cloud to anyone who wanted to use them. By 2013 Amazon was one of the top three players in the cloud-computing sector. It had reached that milestone not because cloud computing was its core business, but because it had leveraged fixed investments in servers that made customers' online experiences faster and better than what others could offer.

In 2007 Amazon entered its equivalent of Walmart's groceries—streaming video content. This is a challenging business, involving large payments to Hollywood studios for the rights to redistribute content. But, much like Walmart's "milk," streamed video content was designed to draw more users to Amazon's devices and e-stores, and bring them more frequently. After streaming video was introduced for Prime subscribers, total customer spending increased, in turn allowing Amazon to spread its fixed costs further.

The stories of Walmart and Amazon appear different, but their approaches to managing fixed costs are strikingly similar. Scale fixed costs over larger product volumes. Spread them across more product categories or stores. And find new revenue streams to lower the burden of fixed costs. For any company in a fixed-cost business, success depends on implementing these strategies.

These principles apply to declining markets, too—where most content businesses find themselves today. Managing fixed costs in such settings isn't pleasant. A natural, almost knee-jerk response is cost-cutting (often a euphemism for layoffs). But far more intriguing and effective are other strategies some media organizations are employing.

SHARE YOUR FIXED COSTS: INSOURCING

Book publishers have been experiencing the fixed-cost burden of print infrastructures since e-books exploded, in 2008. The most common advice of consultants and industry experts was to get rid of owned assets and fixed infrastructure—to "variablize" fixed costs by outsourcing printing and distribution.

This was a reasonable prescription. But one publisher, Penguin Random House, went a different way. Rather than variablize its fixed costs, it increased them by doubling down on its print investments. Why? "It's dangerous to run away from print when your business is still eighty percent print," Dohle said. McIntosh added, "The data absolutely shows that digital growth rates have leveled off. It's not that there is a resurgence of physical—physical never went away. Print has remained very strong, even dominant; digital is not seeing the exponential growth rates we saw earlier."

Penguin Random House was essentially betting that the need to deliver the right physical copy of a book in the right store at the right time was not going away anytime soon. By doubling down on print, it put more emphasis on the ability to rapidly resupply retailers. Dohle noted:

> The premium on our ability to respond by shipping titles at short notice is greater than before. Fall short in stock, and retailers—including Amazon— are unhappy. Reprint, redistribute, and replenish faster than others can, and it's not only a high service level; it puts money in retailers' pockets, because of lower inventories, lower returns, books arriving faster, which means higher revenues. It gives us the opportunity to gain market share, because few publishers can manage this well.
>
> The normal reflex of management upon seeing a decline is to ask: How can I get out of my physical infrastructure? How can I variablize costs? How can I manage this problem down? And we have done exactly the opposite. We call it our zigzag: Everybody went zig, we went zag.

Building on a strategy initiated a few years earlier by his predecessor, Dohle took the approach a step further:

> We said, Let's become the outsourcing partners for others—many publishing houses would consider getting rid of their fixed infrastructure and outsourcing their distribution. We said, Let's make a business out of it, provide that service to others with whom we don't compete, add to our top line and bottom lines, and keep the volume stable in our warehouse in order to manage our cost per copy.

Sound familiar? Penguin Random House's "insourcing" mirrored Amazon's Marketplace and fulfillment strategy. Invest heavily in fixed costs to gain an advantage, then spread the burden not only across your business but across other businesses as well. Third-party publisher revenues brought the firm millions of dollars in annual revenue—not a bad outcome for a publisher confronting the long-term decline of its print business.

FIND NEW REVENUES: STAR TV'S *SATYAMEV JAYTE*

In 2012 Star India launched a new TV talk show, *Satyamev Jayte*. For its anchor it chose a gifted Bollywood actor, Aamir Khan. For content, it went the other way, focusing on hard-hitting issues like female feticide, domestic violence, and intolerance, not formulaic entertainment. Nothing like it had ever aired in India. It was designed to be "non-shrill and bipartisan," CEO Uday Shankar told me. "We aired it at a time when serious cynicism appeared to be setting into the urban middle and upper middle class, the great Indian economic dream was coming to a halt, and politics were looking dirtier than ever. Indian media had become tactical, shallow, and disengaged with serious issues. The research for this program was immense, the quality of content was authentic and authoritative, and it was not flippant."

The show was complex to produce—it took nearly two years to produce before it launched. And it was costly, too—because of the time it took to make and because of Khan's fees.

How to make the economics work? "Because of the content, because of Aamir, and because of us," said Shankar, "we were driven by the idea of giving it maximum reach." To do so, Star chose to dub and air the program on several of India's regional language channels. It then did something bolder, choosing to simultaneously air it on the government broadcast channel, Doordarshan. Shankar described the logic:

> Doordarshan was excited, because this kind of content had not been put out in a long time, and I presume it was not even in the position to have that kind of content. Dealing with the government channel, financial matters could have become very complex. We wanted to keep the construct very simple. So we said, You don't have to pay us for anything. We'll offer you the content free. However, all the advertising you sell on the show will be shared fifty-fifty with us.

For years, cable and broadcast TV had been viewed as competitors. Broadcast still had greater reach: roughly 88 percent of all households, compared with 45 percent for cable. Now Star was reaching across the aisle in an effort to increase its top line. Star's "marketing and brand teams weren't necessarily too happy about it since we were putting our content on another platform," Shankar recounted. But the results paid off: substantially more viewers for *Satyamev Jayte* than Star could have gotten on its own, together with a share of Doordarshan's advertising revenue. The reach and impact spilled into social media, too: The program's website, designed to continue the conversation started on TV, generated more than one billion impressions across twelve episodes—as high as any program anywhere in the world.

"It was a clear win-win. Doordarshan got high-quality, marquee content for cheap—it was pure profit for them. We extended our reach, with a very meaningful addition to our profit," Shankar said. "The strategy of extending reach and sampling, and shared marketing, was a way of handling the fixed production costs which we bore entirely."

If you can't reduce costs, increase your revenue. It's a simple formula, but it's hard to make it work.

The Star-Doordarshan arrangement was unusual for television. There, exclusive airing has always been the norm. Hollywood studios, it turns out, had seen the value of a similar approach years earlier. "Co-syndication"—a strategy now common in the movie business—started during the 1990s. With international demand for Hollywood features growing, studios began cutting deals with international distributors to share the up-front production and marketing costs. "Windowing" strategies went back even earlier, when studios realized that rereleasing a movie in multiple formats—first for the U.S. box office, then internationally, then for DVD, and finally through pay and broadcast TV, with each release carefully timed to reduce overlap with the preceding one—could multiply revenues on the same fixed-cost base.

Back in India, *Satyamev Jayte* triggered further business creativity in the Indian TV market. Star subsequently made similar arrangements with Doordarshan for three more programs. Rival networks Sony Entertainment Television and Colors tested the boundaries further, airing prime-time dramas on YouTube for free within thirty minutes of the TV broadcast. Shankar speculated that this was only the beginning: "Technology is disaggregating linear broadcasting, and that will happen more and more. We will need to think of more moves like this, as a way of managing fixed costs and getting additional reach and sampling. We will need to question received wisdom about where to draw our business boundaries."

REDUCE YOUR FIXED COST, SOMEHOW—PLANNED JOURNALISM

Increasing reach and revenue is one approach to managing fixed costs during industry declines. Reducing fixed costs can be even harder, though media organizations are trying everything they can. Just ask the folks running U.S. television networks. Shifting from high-cost scripted dramas to low-cost unscripted reality TV is one trend that's been embraced by broadcast networks. For newspapers, cost reductions are even harder.

Unlike magazines, daily newspapers are outlets for breaking news. And breaking news means chaos: deadlines, last-minute confusion, rushed stories. This increases costs, too: Newsroom resources need to be sufficiently high at the last minute to ensure that content can be produced on time. Economists call this a "peak-load problem." (Peak-load problems are familiar elsewhere, notably in electricity markets, which can experience substantial unpredictable variation in demand across times of the day or month. Plants need enough generating capacity to meet peak-load needs.) The problem is that by meeting peak-load demand, you create excess capacity and added cost during nonpeak periods.

As radio and television entered the news market, the mantle of breaking news shifted away from newspapers. But for the most part, their approach to news production did not. Some papers—like Schibsted's Swedish subsidiary, *Svenska Dagbladet* (SD)—are trying to change that.

SD is the fifth-largest general interest newspaper in Sweden. Like nearly every paper today, it faces the challenge of cutting without producing worse or less content. In 2011 *SD* recognized it "would need to think differently," Schibsted's chairman, Ole Jacob Sunde, told me recently. "The question they asked was, What can we do in a superior way? The answer was, We can't be telling people about what happened—we've got to tell them *why* it happened. But to do so, we need to plan better what we are doing."

Planning for news—commonly thought of as unpredictable events—can seem an oxymoron. How might one possibly do that, in the face of a deadline-oriented twenty-four-hour daily cycle? The debate over it led to "a second observation that was critical," noted Rolf-Erik Ryssdal, Schibsted's CEO. "Most of the time you *could* know well before the previous day what the likely news themes would be. Unless there's an earthquake or a terror attack or something like that, news is very predictable, actually. So instead of leaving everything open, they decided to plan stories two or three days earlier. And then it would be easier to produce the paper."

Sunde recalled the industry reaction to this idea: "Alan Rusbridger, editor in chief of the *Guardian,* did not believe us when he first heard about it. So he had his team actually count which of the stories in a typical paper related to news from the past twenty-four hours. And they were surprised—very, very few were. Seventy percent were known further in advance."

That's what prompted *SD* to shift its approach to news production, moving toward what it called "planned journalism." At its core was dividing their journalistic work, and the newsroom, into two speeds: fast and slow. Schibsted's Sverre Munck said:

> The slow desk was a kind of Zen journalism. News stories were planned one to three weeks ahead, the front page seven to ten days in advance. The other desk was more traditional: fast-paced, right-up-to-the-deadline. Newspapers have always had a slow pace for investigative journalism. Now they've extended that approach to everyday stories. They have two desks, two editors, and two approaches.

The core insight was not just to reduce the number of journalists but to spread their output over time. It was reminiscent of Walmart's strategy to spread warehouse costs across store clusters. Planned journalism resulted not only in fewer journalists but in greater productivity. Journalists could write more and better. Munck spoke of the contrast: "Just-in-time delivery resulted in more mistakes, worse designs, less flexibility, loss of editorial control, higher costs, and staff working late. And the news was still old." In contrast, by planning ahead, "you have more time, you do better research, you do more investigative journalism, you can get all the graphics and rich multimedia that you can't get when a story comes up five minutes before deadline."

The results were impressive.

Before, around 90 percent of the stories waited until an hour before deadline, and then everybody scrambled. It was incredibly inefficient. Today roughly 50 percent of pitches are ready by lunch hour. Journalists are happier—they can go home to their families on time. And costs have been reduced by more than 50 percent.

9

CHINESE CONNECTIONS: TENCENT

And the end of all our exploring
Will be to arrive where we started
And know the place for the first time.

—T. S. Eliot, "Little Gidding"

Let's return to Tencent, in China, and the puzzle we started with: How do you create a $100 billion business from free instant messaging?

Tencent is the most interesting Internet firm you've probably never heard of. Here's one way to view its success:

TABLE 6. FACEBOOK VERSUS TENCENT: A SIMPLE COMPARISON		
Metric	Facebook	Tencent
First product	Social network	Instant messaging
Number of users	Over 1 billion	Over 1 billion
Annual revenues (2015)	Roughly $18 billion	Roughly $16 billion
Market value in April 2015	Over $200 billion	Over $200 billion
Fraction of revenues from advertising	Over 95%	Less than 20%

How do you create a business as valuable as Facebook's while largely eschewing advertising revenue? How do you persuade users to pay for online products and services in a market generally regarded as one of the toughest nuts to crack in this regard?

The answers to these questions lie not in leveraging network effects or understanding price discrimination or managing fixed costs or creating platforms for user content. It lies in *all* these things. Perhaps more than any company, Tencent centers its entire strategy on user connections.

Instant messaging is about the simplest media product you can offer. The content is provided by users themselves (the messages); you simply provide a platform through which they communicate. It's easy to start and even easier to scale once you have users. The reason is that the business of IM is characterized by strong network effects. As the number of users grows, the platform's value to any single user increases since she can communicate with many more others. When IM platforms win, they win big.

The problem with IM is that it's the quintessential free product. And once users are used to getting something free, monetizing it is very hard.

That's where Tencent charted new territory. It gave users personal on-line identities—and then charged for them. It started fairly innocuously. In 1998 more than 95 percent of Chinese households had no access to a personal computer, so had no email address. Tencent gave them their first online identity—typically, a multi-digit number on its platform called QQ.

Eight-digit numbers aren't very memorable by themselves. Generic ID numbers, as a result, quickly gave rise to demand for numbers that could more easily distinguish users from one another. Numbers that were "straight" (for example, 2345678), identical (where all digits were the same), or symmetric (numbers that read the same forward or backward, such as 9888889) quickly became popular, along with numbers that had particular meanings. As they did, they started changing hands in secondary markets for high fees. For example, 89975 (David Beckham's marriage date preceded by the Chinese happy number 8) resold for nearly $1,000 in an auction; 88888, once the number of Tencent's CEO, sold for more than $30,000. Other numbers had value because of their personal significance to users—ones that matched a birthday or a cellphone number, for instance.

As QQ grew, so did the menu of identity options. First Tencent allowed users to augment their ID numbers with cartoon-character-like icons (chosen from a menu of a few hundred options). Next, in 2002, it offered simple visual figurines termed avatars. Called "QQ show," avatars were Tencent's second major product. (The term comes from Sanskrit and literally means "incarnation"—more colloquially, "appearance" or "manifestation.") There were hundreds of varieties, and as more and more users flocked to QQ, they embraced them.

Psychologists and sociologists regard identity as an important anchor for relationships. Identity can be personal (self-image, esteem, individuality) or social (where it reflects one's position vis-à-vis others). Many daily actions—eating at a restaurant, buying a car, wearing clothes—have elements of both: They give us pleasure or contribute to our self-image, *and* they let others know who we are. We signal our relational identity through what we wear (Armani or Abercrombie), where we eat (French or Ethiopian), what we read (Grisham or Gladwell), what we watch (dramas or documentaries), and what we hear (punk rock or funk pop), to name just a few.

It was initially thought that one of the Internet's greatest benefits was anonymity. Users could communicate without others knowing who they were. Expressing opinions, sending customer complaints, or seeding grassroots movements could all be done without fear of reprisal or retribution. But as interpersonal communication and the social Web grew, a funny thing happened: Relational identity became as important online as in the real world.

Tencent's first stroke of genius was in recognizing this early on. As the users on Tencent's IM platform grew in number, so did their desire to differentiate themselves from millions of others.

To allow users to stand out from the pack, Tencent tapped still more alternatives. Users could supplement their avatars with various features—a happier face, a different hairstyle, a more colorful hat, a Gucci bag—for a small charge each, less than $1. In 2003, fewer than 10 percent of Tencent's users bought these identity enhancements. Annual purchases amounted to roughly $5 per person. But given the size of the user base—10 percent of subscribers amounted to more than thirty million users, generating $150 million in aggregate revenue—and given that the cost of creating a virtual Gucci bag was the same as creating an unbranded one (namely, zero), the business of selling virtual figurines was spectacular.

This was price discrimination at its simplest and most powerful. Tencent did not need everyone to purchase a premium avatar. In fact, it didn't *want* everyone to purchase one—if that happened, differentiation would suffer.

In 1974 the future Nobel laureate Michael Spence, then a young economist at Harvard, wrote about the value of signals and how they are conveyed. The power of a signal, he noted—whether it was about identity, ability, or any other personal attribute or action—wasn't inherent in the signal itself; it derived from the fact that it would be costly for others to use the same signal. Thus "smart" students signaled their intelligence through a college degree—not because education necessarily provided special knowledge, but because doing the hard work required was costly enough to provide differentiation. A firm might signal its quality through advertising—not because advertising was necessarily lucrative, but because a low-quality firm could not afford it.

Tencent recognized that virtual goods could be powerful signals. Purchasing an expensive virtual Gucci bag would have the same sort of signaling effect as owning a real one. This simple intuition redefined how Tencent saw its business, and its opportunities to leverage user connections. It was now far more than a communication platform; it was, in essence, selling identities.

By 2003, three years after its founding, Tencent was profitable, enjoying gross margins of more than 65 percent. In June 2004 it became China's first Internet business to go public, on the Hong Kong stock exchange.

FROM NETWORK CONNECTIONS TO CONNECTING NETWORKS

Tencent soon expanded into other spaces, even where other firms had entered first. In 2003 it entered the online gaming business. Although it was two years later than Shanda and Sino, China's leading game developers, Tencent was successful even there.

Tencent's road to victory didn't come from better games. Its advantage, much like Microsoft's twenty years earlier against Apple, came from the strength of its existing network. It cross-promoted its games on its IM platform—a user could launch the game directly from her IM screen rather than be directed to a separate site to play. It bundled its services effectively—its chat service could be used within a game, and a gamer could import her avatars. And it transferred the strength of its network effect in one product to others—with the click of a button, a user could import her social graph from QQ into a Tencent game in order to play with her friends.

Tencent was doing something many companies that compete in winner-take-all markets struggle with: It successfully created connections across different products—IM, games, microblogs—where each relied on connecting users. In effect, it shifted its strength from just one network to a portfolio of connected networks.

To monetize these advantages, Tencent turned again to price discrimination. Borrowing from a trend started by Korean game companies, it offered games free but charged for features that would enhance the playing experience.

Consider one, the pay-to-skip feature. One frustrating thing about playing a game is not being able to progress beyond the initial stages. Often this happens not because a player lacks the ability to improve but because she lacks the time to do so. Against this backdrop, powerful virtual swords or guns are perfect price discrimination tools. Hard-core gamers don't need them, but amateurs—particularly those who can't afford to spend more time but do have the money—jump at the chance.

It's a bit like Disney World's FastPass, only better. Introduced in 1999, new FastPass tickets allowed visitors to bypass long lines at Disney's popular attractions. The benefit was enormous time savings. The problem? At the time, anyone could get a FastPass free (though quantities were limited). And visitors who used their FastPass vouchers to bypass a line merely added to the wait time for others. By contrast, virtual swords were not free and imposed no costly externalities on other participants.

More than a decade ago Ben Colayco started Level Up, a Philippines-based gaming firm that expanded into India and Brazil before Tencent acquired a 49 percent minority stake. Colayco described to me the power of in-game virtual goods and how they've evolved:

> Virtual goods weren't big in the early 2000s. Most games in Asia were pay-to-play PC-based games. That's what Korean games were, and Chinese firms copied the trend, as did we. Pricing was roughly the same for each game, and the fight was about who had the best content.

But then Chinese game developer Shanda changed everything by introducing free games. "It seemed crazy," Colayco recalled. "Everyone said they were out of their mind. On top of that, they were a publicly traded firm, needing cash flow. But the whole industry followed suit within six months."

Free games were great for everybody. Users got to play for as long as they wanted at no charge. Those who wanted an extra kick to their gaming experience could purchase one. Colayco recalled the new "products" the company created:

> We set up events where the monster you're fighting is too strong, and we put potions on sale. We have lotteries: for $1 you get ten potions—you get a chance to buy an item that makes you a lot stronger in the game. We sell items that increase self-expression, enhance user experience and engagement, or boost player recognition—it could be a fancy virtual shirt or a powerful sword. In one case we auctioned off a virtual sword for $30,000.

For the users, it's paying what you want. One gamer could play for an hour and pay $20, with another playing eight hours and paying nothing. We are matching price with willingness to pay.

Like other game developers, Tencent offered all these advantages—and more. In the early 2000s, it had another stroke of brilliance, creating its own virtual currency. Users could pay for the add-on features—euphemistically termed "value add services"—on Tencent's various products using Q Bi, a currency with value only on the Tencent platform. The "exchange rate" was nominally set at 1:1—it took 1 renminbi (RMB, about 15 cents) to acquire 1 Q coin. Users could also get Q coins by playing the game longer or better. Tencent was relying on price discrimination once again, allowing users to substitute time for money.

One curious feature of Q coins was its nonconvertibility: Once bought, Q coins could not be exchanged for RMB. The reason for this strange feature? Recall that the power of connections comes not just from creating them but from owning them. Once you've created a network, you want to ensure that only you benefit. Nonconvertibility ensured that users would stay within Tencent's product suite.

For a simple illustration of this idea, let's turn to Hollywood. *The Diary of a Wimpy Kid* centers on, well, a wimpy kid—Greg—who doesn't get much love from others, including his older brother, Rodrick. Their mother has a seemingly brilliant idea:

MOM: Things between the two of you have really gotten out of hand. You may not realize it now, but having a brother is one of the most important relationships of your life. . . . So you need to get to know each other. You need to spend more time together. So that's why I have come up with a new program to reward you for spending time together. I'm calling it Mom Bucks.
RODRICK's reaction was natural: You're paying us with fake money?
MOM: For every hour that you spend together without fighting, for example, you give Greg a drum lesson, you each earn a Mom Buck—which you can then trade in for one real dollar. So to start you off I'm giving you each five Mom Bucks. Now if you're smart you'll save up your Mom Bucks.
RODRICK: Can I cash out now?
MOM: Rodrick, if you save—
RODRICK: But can I cash out?

MOM: Yes, but—

RODRICK: I want to cash out.

Mom had no choice but to honor the rules. She redeemed Rodrick's five Mom Bucks for the real thing. And Rodrick had just found a gold mine.

Creating funny money—virtual currency or Mom Bucks—can be a good idea. But let users exchange it for real currency and you've lost control over what they can do and when.

Harrah's casino, the biggest in Las Vegas, had a similar experience to Rodrick's mother's. When it first introduced "same day cash" for its customers—giving back to customers at the end of each day a small percentage of the bets they'd made that day, in the hopes of incentivizing a return visit—the program backfired. Casino goers welcomed the cash back, but were no more likely to return to Harrah's than they were to go to another casino. So Harrah's switched to loyalty programs that rewarded return visits only—the equivalent of nonredeemable tokens—and met with considerable success.

The origins of virtual currency can be traced back even earlier, to another, more conventional, gaming platform—Chuck E. Cheese. Its founder, Nolan Bushnell, was no stranger to videogames; he had founded Atari, a pioneer in the electronic entertainment industry. Chuck E. Cheese was an arcade for children. Draw children into the door, it did. But Bushnell found it was harder to bring them back—until he came up with the idea of tokens. These were fake coins that visitors would need to purchase in order to play games. They were nonrefundable. In addition, users could win tickets for superior performance; these were also nonredeemable for cash, but could be exchanged for trivial items like plastic rings. The result? At trip's end most kids found themselves with cups of tokens or tickets they didn't know what to redeem for—drawing them back for a subsequent visit. The result was impressive growth in Chuck E. Cheese sales.

Chuck E. Cheese tokens were foreshadowing online virtual currencies—and their power in drawing customers back.

With its virtual currency, Tencent had figured out a way not only to get users to pay, but to keep them on its platform. But for users, virtual currency has a downside: Sometimes you accumulate funny money when you don't need it. This led to some surprising developments. By the late 2000s Tencent's platform had become so popular in China that a secondary market emerged, where users could exchange their unused Q coins for real products such as clothing, haircuts, and cosmetics—practically creating a parallel economy. Some entrepreneurs even set up virtual sweatshops, where young people were paid to play and earn Q coins that were then sold to others—a practice generously termed "gold farming." China's Central Bank, noting that Q coins had risen sharply in value against the RMB, soon stepped in to restrict the trade of virtual currency for real goods. The virtual-for-real trades had threatened to affect the country's money supply.

From 2003 to 2013 Tencent introduced a dizzying array of products. One was Q Zone, in 2005, a social network and portal that offered users additional opportunities for self-expression and entertainment: They could not only post real-life pictures and blog (as on Facebook and elsewhere) but also create virtual homes equipped with personalized furniture and decorations; they could also stream music (five years before Facebook integrated Spotify). A key to success here, too, was how easily these features connected with other Tencent products. IM could be launched within Q Zone. A user could listen to her friends' playlists. Revisions to a user's avatar would automatically update on her friends' pages. As usual, certain basic features were free, but add-ons—ranging from the personalized furniture and decorations to background music—needed to be purchased. Within a few years Q Zone had more than 150 million active users.

More products were added in similar fashion, including IM groups (for multi-person chats), a chat robot (in case a user had no one to chat with!), Voice QQ (linking a person's user number to her cellphone), a Yahoo-like Web portal, and a Twitter-like microblog (Weibo). Each was introduced late—as many as two to five years behind the early product leader. But each time, Tencent leveraged its advantages—cross-promoting its existing user base, importing its existing network, bundling with its existing products, and monetizing using its virtual currency. It invariably usurped market share leadership within a few years.

QQ Pet, a simple game launched in 2005, is an instructive example. It allowed users to adopt and play with virtual pets, including dogs, cats, and penguins. The virtual pets shared many characteristics with real-world ones: They needed food, drink, and love (which, in the game, was measured in terms of time and activities spent with them). The game grew quickly. The trick, as always, was to keep owners coming back. The game did so cleverly. Pets that weren't cared for looked glum or ill—states that could be reversed by buying virtual remedies. More important, users could meet other pet owners, sharing information or connecting to schedule pet playdates. Pet rankings and "pet love indices" also generated conversation.

The game generated impressive revenue. To get pet food, take pets on vacation, or decorate their rooms, pet owners had to spend money, in the form of Q Bi. Users could purchase one Q Bi for one RMB, using a credit card, through retail outlets, or with a mobile phone account; they could also earn Q Bi through their game activity and skill. Tencent's aggregate revenues from the game exceeded $40 million within two years. And they were highly predictable and controllable: If they were below target at quarter's end, game managers could simply increase the number of pets that were ill.

By 2013 more than 90 percent of Tencent's revenue came from charging users directly, while only 10 percent came from advertising—a direct contrast to Facebook, whose ratio was almost exactly the opposite. The difference had real managerial consequence. While Facebook toiled to find creative ways to advertise—and, as it would discover in many cases, annoy—its users, Tencent faced little conflict of the sort. Advertiser-dependent companies continuously struggle to reduce or manage the inevitable negative connections between their users and advertisers. Tencent's business model allowed it to focus on leveraging positive ones.

It's tempting to dismiss the success of Tencent and the other "Big Three" Chinese Internet companies, Alibaba and Baidu, as the result of a fairly closed domestic Internet market. And all three firms have benefited from that fact. But it doesn't explain their success. Hundreds of other Internet firms inside China, after all, have been trying for years to dislodge them. Neither can Tencent's success be attributed to funky products, unusual Chinese norms, or peculiar features of virtual currency. That narrow lens misses the broader business principles at work—ones involving networks, bundles, platforms, and price discrimination. Those ideas apply everywhere, as many other stories in this chapter confirm.

THE NEXT FRONTIER

By 2011 Tencent was the leading Internet company in China, with a market value of more than $100 billion—making it the third-most-valued Internet company in the world (after Google and Amazon). But for all its success, certain questions remained. Tencent had not become mobile-centric, even as Chinese users were migrating to mobile. It had little success outside China, even though it had tried in India and elsewhere. And its forays into e-commerce remained insubstantial, with Alibaba dominating the local market.

Through its decade-long expansion, Tencent's strategy remained, at its core, about connections among users and communication. Its next act would again leverage this simple idea and threaten to address the nagging questions, in one go. In March 2011 Tencent launched a new product, Weixin, subsequently reincarnated as WeChat, that would propel it to even greater heights.

WeChat was the creation of Allen Zhang, a master's graduate in telecommunications from the prestigious Hauzhong University. Zhang isn't your typical Tencent employee: He lives in Guangzhou, far from the nerve center of company headquarters in Shenzhen and Beijing. Even after his first product, Foxmail, was acquired by Tencent (and renamed QQ mail), he chose not to move. QQ mail had come from behind—more than five years behind—to overtake all incumbent email services in China. Dylan Zhang, one of Tencent's leading technology engineers (and no relation to Allen Zhang), succinctly described why it succeeded: "It was faster, it was more reliable, and it was user friendly." Of course, it helped that QQ mail could leverage Tencent's network; the company's founder, Pony Ma, had promoted it aggressively from early on. But, as Dylan noted, "it wasn't only the network—the product itself was terrific. It had to be, because switching costs are huge for most people who already have an email address."

By 2010, Dylan said, Allen Zhang was "bored." But certain developments in the mobile market had caught his attention. First was a product called Kik, launched that year. Kik was a free mobile short message service. All it required was Wi-Fi, not phone service. As a result, users paid no traffic charges. Copycat products immediately sprang up.

Zhang was back at work again. He assembled a small team (five or six people), emailed Pony Ma, and created a similar product in six weeks. Weixin launched in March 2011. "It wasn't successful," Dylan said. It had little to differentiate it from other free short message services.

But it stirred passions within Tencent. For more than a decade the mobile version of QQ had been managed by a separate team. Its success had relied almost entirely on revenue-sharing arrangements with local telecom carriers (the powerful China Mobile and others), whereby Tencent received 40 percent of carriers' revenues from users for QQ's short message charges. Now free text message products threatened those revenue streams of QQ mobile. It was the classic cannibalization scenario—except it was playing out inside an Internet firm rather than a traditional one.

Zhang was determined to move forward with Weixin. It helped that Ma was, too. Version 2, launched in December 2012, was a different product. Not surprisingly, its core features were powered by user connections. First Ma ensured that the new product could tap into QQ's vast user base through seamless log-in. You could tap into your existing address book. You could leave voice messages for others for free. And you could start a group chat.

Dylan described what he saw as the real reasons for Weixin's success, along with its significance for Tencent:

> It was mobile first, unlike anything we had done at Tencent. The differences in design features from a PC-based product are subtle but important. On a PC you may be online or not. On a mobile phone we have to assume you're always online. So Zhang created a feature that made the pull-up experience much faster: there was no log-in required every time, no passwords. On a mobile device, no one wants to wait ten seconds. So we cached everything to ensure no delay. In addition, group chat was far easier: On mobile QQ you had to form groups, but here you could create a group on the fly, add or delete people on the fly, anyone could add new people to the group, etc. There were location-based services—you could Find People Near You. And the feature Shake—when you shake your phone, it tells you who near you is also shaking their phone. It's a cute feature, and though it's probably not used that much, it brought huge word of mouth.

Tensions between divisions blossomed into full-blown animosity. "They hated WeChat, their guts." But there was no stopping now. Version 3, launched in March 2013, introduced even more features. "Moments," according to Zhang, "was a feature that single-handedly undermined Weibo [Tencent's Twitter-like microblog]: It allowed you to upload your pictures and comment on friends' pictures—except that your comments were private: Only your direct friends could see them. This is a major difference from Weibo and Facebook. Users feel they are in control."

Features continued to be added to WeChat: first, a news service; then QR Code, a feature that allowed users to scan a bar code and purchase a product through Tencent's e-commerce platform with one click. (Some described this as the first real threat to Alibaba.) By 2013 WeChat had more than 300 million users. That December it went international, gaining nearly 100 million users outside China within a year.

Zhang is not known for shouting from the rooftops. But in 2012 he described the nature of WeChat and the principles followed in developing this connected product. Notable were several features centered on three specific user needs: "the need that comes from people's curiosity about others," "the need that comes from your feedback and those of your friends," and "the need that comes from a sense of presence from interacting with others which makes them feel comfortable."

A 2012 article in *TechCrunch* described WeChat as combining the best features of WhatsApp, Skype iMessage, Instagram, and Google's Circles. The description may have been overly effusive, but it pointed to an interesting evolution of Tencent's strategy. The company's past success had come from its ability to leverage network strength from a single product, IM, into a portfolio of products including games, a news service, a social network, and a microblog. WeChat was only the latest example of how the company successfully leveraged user connections in a broad range of ways. Except, now they were all being combined into a single product.

As Tencent has evolved, so has its approach to monetization. Avatars for QQ gave way to revenue sharing for mobile QQ and then to virtual goods and in-game monetization for social games and WeChat. Few companies have their DNA rooted in user connections. Fewer still have the discipline to recognize and create those connections and repeatedly monetize them—all the while maintaining a free basic product.

Perhaps the biggest challenge for companies that win in networked markets is figuring out how to do so again. As Intuit's Scott Cook noted, "For all we talk about the innovative ability of successful Internet companies, very few are able to do it again and again." Companies then tend to shift focus in one of three ways: They become obsessed with creating the "next big thing" that embodies network effects in a new market; they shift focus from user experiences to advertising revenues in the hopes of monetizing their initial success; or they dilute the deep understanding of user behavior that created their success in the first place. Tencent is an outlier in these respects. When it *has* innovated, it's done so masterfully—leveraging existing user connections in new product areas. When it has drawn revenue, it's gotten users to voluntarily pay for the value from connections, rather than relying on advertisements as new revenue streams. And it has refined its understanding of the psychology of connections, over and over again. It's a story that exemplifies the art of managing connections. It's a story with much to teach.

10
CREATE TO CONNECT

Product quality, hypertargeting, user personalization, and customization are today's prescriptions for digital success. And they may be precisely why so many companies find digital transformation hard, misdiagnose threats to their business, and miss opportunities.

These prescriptions tend to lead firms to focus on customers one by one and miss the connections that arise from managing customers as a portfolio. They lead us to believe that content quality is the key to success—when connections are. They lead us to believe that traditional hub-and-spoke marketing still wins—when networks do. They lead us to believe that traditional media is threatened by better and more varied digital content that lures customers in droves—when fixed costs are the real culprit. In each case, they lead us into the Content Trap.

User connections come in different forms: network effects (as in the PC wars or news classifieds), preference connections (as in print-digital usage or broadband-cable viewership), or fixed costs (as in most content businesses). See these connections and exploit them and you'll create the conditions for large success—as Microsoft, eBay, Uber, Airbnb, Schibsted, and Tencent have done. Remarkably, in nearly every case billions of dollars of value were created *without* owning content or a product—simply by leveraging connections. Miss these connections and you'll pay a price—as Apple did for two decades, and as so many content businesses did in reacting to digital threats.

Connections explain why the *New York Times* paywall was effective in 2011 although earlier paywall efforts by the paper had failed. They explain why cable bundles are a force of nature that refuse to go away, and why they might benefit not just cable operators but also viewers. They clarify why digital may not be the real threat for book publishers and cable operators. And they point to why fledgling start-ups such as Tencent have grown in a decade to become among the most valuable firms on the planet.

But managing user connections doesn't come naturally, and there are two reasons for that. First, the center of gravity in organizations tends to be products, not users. The value of newspapers was thought to reside in news; of cable operators, in channels; of PC manufacturers, in ease of use of their devices. But the real value came from classifieds, pipes, and interoperability. Second, the tendency is to treat as the unit of analysis the individual user, rather than connections between them. This trap is even more insidious than the first, arising as it does in organizations that are ostensibly user-centric or aspire to be.

Focus on your relationships with individual customers one by one, or on the content you produce for each of them, and you'll miss the secret of success in a connected world.

Success comes not just from creating content—it comes from Creating to Connect.

PART II

CONCERTS—PRODUCT CONNECTIONS

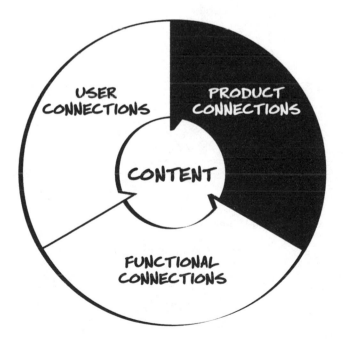

11

JERRY MAGUIRE

It was early 2000. Tiger Woods had recently signed the largest endorsement deal in sports history and was about to embark on the longest winning streak in championship golf in more than fifty years. Michael Jordan had retired after a remarkable NBA career and returned to the sport of basketball as part owner of a team. Wayne Gretzky had been inducted into the Hockey Hall of Fame with the unprecedented distinction of having his jersey number retired league-wide—the only player ever to receive this honor.

Against this backdrop of iconic sporting moments, *Sports Illustrated* had just published its annual rankings of the "Most Powerful Persons in Sports." And right near the very top of the list was Mark McCormack.

Who?

McCormack was virtually unknown to anyone outside the field of sports marketing. Within it, however, he enjoyed near-mythic status. He'd practically invented the industry forty years earlier.

As an undergraduate at the College of William and Mary, McCormack had been an accomplished amateur golfer. But probably the best thing that happened to him was recognizing he could not compete with the pros. The decision came after some blunt self-reflection, as he was wont to undertake: "I had no chance. I didn't have a very good swing, and I wasn't very good." Among McCormack's collegiate peers and friends was Wake Forest's Arnold Palmer. McCormack would follow Palmer's career closely even as he embarked on a law career himself. He saw that someone like Palmer—an accomplished athlete with an appealing personality— had the potential not only to earn money off the course because companies could heighten their images from such endorsements, but also to take the sport to a new level. This simple observation shaped McCormack's subsequent career and revolutionized the field of sports marketing.

In 1960 McCormack founded International Management Group, or IMG, signing Palmer as its first client. "I could make only two guarantees [to Palmer]," he recalled. "First, that if I didn't know something, I would tell him. Second, that when I didn't know something, I would find someone who did know." During the next two years, with IMG's help, Palmer's endorsement income increased from $59,000 to $500,000. The endorsements were not only substantial, they were creative, too: Heinz, for example, paid Palmer $500 per year and all the ketchup he could use. Palmer's success soon brought two more clients to McCormack: Jack Nicklaus and Gary Player. "I didn't realize until much later," said McCormack, "that I was, in fact, making a commitment to quality." Palmer, Nicklaus, and Player dominated golf for the next decade.

McCormack's early success was unprecedented. It was also sobering for him. Reflecting on it, he noted: "With 250 golfers out on the tour, we had gone three for three. It was like winning a lottery. . . . The initial success had been far too phenomenal simply to take it in stride, congratulate ourselves on how smart we were, and wait for lightning to strike again. . . . We weren't going to sit around until another 'Big Three' came along."

Talent management is a risky business that depends on lightning strikes. A large agency might invest in hundreds of relationships with young athletes from an early age, hoping just one might become a star. And once in the limelight, stars may see little reason to stay with their first agent. Other agents descend like wolves to lure them away. Money lures. And, loyalty is "oh, so yesterday."

How costly are such defections for agencies? To start with, the agent loses commissions on future revenue streams that come from both prize money and endorsements. Then there's the reputational hit and the consequences for attracting new talent. There's also the sunk cost of time and money invested in discovering and marketing the star—often a decade-long investment down the drain.

As if *that* weren't enough, there's also the reality that most relationships never even return their investment cost: The odds of a talented twelve-year-old athlete turning into a star are about as good as winning a lottery. As a result, the revenues from stars not only help recover the direct cost that an agency incurs by investing in a long-term relationship with them; they also help recover the cost of investing in everyone else.

That's why they say in the talent management business, "Lose one star, and you're upset. Lose three, and you're in trouble."

In some respects talent representation is even more fragile than other media businesses. Unlike in music or publishing, agencies own no intellectual property; if an athlete walks away, there are no assets to monetize.

And there aren't necessarily benefits to building a large organization, either—individual agents can set up shop on the strength of a single valuable relationship. Remember *Jerry Maguire*?

Against this gloomy business backdrop, IMG defied all the odds. Starting with McCormack's early success, IMG grew its early client stable in golf to become the largest talent representation agency there. Then it expanded into tennis, signing Australians Rod Laver and Margaret Court in 1968. A year later it entered motor sports racing, taking on Jackie Stewart. Over the ensuing decades, it not only extended its representation to track and field, baseball, and football, but ventured into non-sports areas as well, including fashion models, literary authors, and classical musicians. Strikingly, every time it entered a new talent arena, it quickly rose to the top.

The IMG story is impressive and also puzzling. How does an organization like IMG defy, for so long, the underlying fragile economics of the industry in which it competes?

The story of IMG isn't just one of brilliant people skills (though McCormack's instincts were renowned in this regard), or of tough negotiation, or of entrepreneurial innovation. Each of these factors can create the conditions for success, but they're rarely enough to sustain it. No, the secret to understanding IMG's success comes from a simple business principle—managing connections across products. The principle is relevant not just to IMG, but to a broad swath of businesses today. And it's a principle that cuts against the grain of many common tenets we encounter in business today—"unbundling," "product focus," and "core competence."

Understanding product connections requires one to think differently about what makes a successful media business. It sheds light on how upstart TV networks can overcome established ones, accounts for Apple's remarkable turnaround during the past decade, and makes sense of the uncomfortable "war" between Hollywood and Silicon Valley. It reveals why newsrooms' efforts to integrate print and digital operations often bear little fruit. It tells us the *real* reason why media companies love hits. And it offers insight into why companies often expand into seemingly unrelated business areas with surprisingly good results.

Let's start by looking at that most challenged media business of all—music.

12
MUSIC

The story of how digital technologies devastated the recorded music industry is by now familiar. The Internet brought with it the promise that any individual could become a content distributor online. File-sharing technologies started with the peer-to-peer file sharing service Napster in 1999 and were soon followed by Gnutella, eDonkey, and Freenet. Within a few months after the launch of Napster, online sharing of music files was in full bloom. A billion files were posted by users around the world in a single week in 2002.

The decline of CD sales was slow at first, averaging 3 to 5 percent per year in the late 1990s. In 2001, the dam broke: CD sales declined by 5 percent, followed by annual double-digit drops for several years thereafter. Recording studios' profits plummeted; major retailers including Tower Records, HMV, and Virgin Megastores shuttered their stores or went bankrupt.

The impact of these changes would spread and have a devastating effect on the creation of music itself, industry observers predicted. They would reduce incomes for music producers and artists. This in turn would reduce incentives to produce music content—both quantity and quality. More than a decade later, headlines like "The Music Industry Is Dead" and "Who Killed the Music Industry?" were commonplace.

Or so we were told. It turns out, certain basic facts in this story are exactly right. But most of the dire predictions were wrong.

CD sales indeed declined, by more than 80 percent. Studios' profits indeed dropped, often sharply. But along the way, something strange began to happen as well in other parts of the industry. Just as demand for CDs was falling, the price of live concert tickets began increasing, as did concert revenues (see Figure 9). From 1981 to 1996, ticket prices had done little more than keep pace with inflation. But, just as file sharing began to explode in the late 1990s, so did concert prices. Between 1996

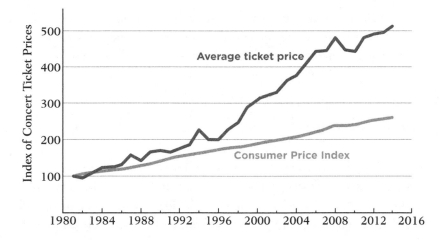

Figure 9: Growth in Concert Ticket Prices, 1980–2014 (Index: 1981 = 100). (This is an updated version of the figure in Krueger 2012. Data for 1980–2003 are from Krueger 2012, data from 2003–2014 are from Pollstar.)

and 2012, they rose at three times the rate of inflation. The average price of a ticket to a show by a major artist, only $13 in 1981, was $71 in 2014.

What about the fact that piracy appeared to be decimating CD sales? Many artists, surprisingly, didn't much care. Neil Young said, "It doesn't affect me, because I look at the Internet as the new radio." Others concurred, noting that illegal music downloads were even good "because it's people trading music." Radiohead's Ed O'Brien even questioned the premise that piracy was killing the music industry: "I don't actually believe it is," he stated matter-of-factly. Lady Gaga announced that she had little problem with people downloading her music for free. Shakira spoke out in support of illegal file sharing: "It's the democratization of music in a way. And music is a gift. That's what it should be, a gift."

Now, it might be tempting to conclude from these pronouncements that artists really always believed that access to music should be free. But, economics played a role, too. When a CD sold for $15, an artist took home only about $1; the recording studio kept the rest. But for a concert priced at $100 a ticket, the artist's share could be $50 or more. And for most artists, more than 70 percent of their income came from concerts, only 10 percent from CDs. (The other 20 percent was mostly from publishing.) The result of all this? More than a decade after file sharing and piracy hit the scene, top artists were earning upwards of $100 million a year—and more than $1 million *per concert*.

In other words, the real reason why artists didn't appear to care about CD declines was that they had never made much money off CDs anyway. And the place where they had—live tours—was now booming.

THE BOWIE EFFECT

Understanding how the music business reinvented itself during the recent decade, and why artist incomes (particularly for those at the very top) actually increased even as piracy and file sharing exploded, requires understanding, among other things, what led to the rise in concert prices in the first place.

Alan Krueger is not the person you'd expect to be studying these issues. He's a labor economist at Princeton, one of the most respected in the profession, and a former chairman of the President's Council of Economic Advisers. A decade ago he turned his focus to the music industry. Part of his interest was academic; as he noted, "many of the forces that are buffeting the U.S. economy can be understood in the context of the music industry." Part of his interest was just plain fun.

Using data on more than 200,000 concerts, Krueger had previously documented the surprising rise in concert prices starting in the mid-1990s. He now went looking for an explanation.

One popular explanation, he noted, was that a few concert promoters had monopolized the business since 1996. That year the Telecommunications Act had relaxed restrictions on radio station ownership, sending Clear Channel Communications on an acquisitions binge of both radio stations (it acquired nearly 1,200 in the process) and concert promoters. But Krueger was not convinced. One problem with the "monopolization" argument, he said, was that Clear Channel's national monopoly didn't confer pricing power at the city or state level—the relevant geographic unit where concert prices are set. Concert promotion had *always* been highly concentrated in cities.

Krueger decided to look further. He examined the concentration of concert promoters in particular geographic areas from 1994 to 2001 and the growth in concert prices in those areas, and found "essentially no correlation." He searched for a relationship between Clear Channel's radio share in a city and its local concert promotion share, but found no correlation there, either. And he noticed that concert prices had increased in

Canada and Europe, which had *not* deregulated radio stations, as the United States had done. Krueger's conclusion? "The industry has gone from having regional monopolies to having a large national firm, but *within cities* competition could possibly have increased."

Economists are nothing if not persistent. Krueger looked for other reasons—only to discard most of them, one by one, as well. Perhaps concert prices had risen only for the most expensive seats in a venue? Not so. High-priced tickets had indeed gone up, but so had the lowest-price tickets in a venue. Increases weren't limited to a few bands, either (although top bands had gained disproportionately). Nor did they reflect an overall trend in the price of entertainment: The price of movies, sporting events, and theater had also all risen, but only by about half as much as concert prices.

And the prices didn't reflect cost increases. Certain important costs, such as the cost of audiovisual equipment, had if anything gone down. Nor were concert promoters pricing higher to squeeze resellers (if that were the case, higher list prices for tickets would come at the expense of the secondary market). Finally, the increases could not be explained by a rise in star quality, a dubious hypothesis that Krueger nonetheless debunked. Using the millimeters of print columns devoted to each artist in *The Rolling Stone Encyclopedia of Rock & Roll* as a proxy for the elusive concept of quality, he found that returns to superstars hadn't changed after 1996. Rather, higher prices had *always* accompanied superstars, both before and after this period.

So, at the end of a long and arduous analysis, Krueger reached this conclusion: David Bowie was right.

In 2002 Bowie had said that the decline in CD sales and the rise of file sharing meant that "music itself is going to become like running water or electricity." As an artist, Bowie advised, "you'd better be prepared to do a lot of touring, because that's really the only unique situation that's going to be left." Bowie's prediction was now being borne out.

THE UPSIDE-DOWN BUSINESS OF COMPLEMENTS

To understand the relation between CDs and concerts, it's useful to first return to one of the central ideas in business strategy: the idea of complements. It's a simple idea, first coined a long time ago, and popularized recently by the economists Adam Brandenburger and Barry Nalebuff. It goes like this: Two products are complements if a user's value from consuming both is greater than the sum of her values from consuming each alone.

In other words, sell two complements together and a consumer will pay more for each than if they were sold individually.

Take hot dogs and ketchup. Each without the other isn't particularly enjoyable. Have them together and you're in grilled nirvana.

One way to think about complements is that the *value* of one product depends on the availability of another—as with hot dogs and ketchup. But complementary relationships can be stated in terms of *price* effects, too: Specifically, the demand for a product goes up when the price of its complement goes down.

What does this all mean for the music business? To start, note that CDs and concerts are complements. The cheaper one of them becomes (and therefore the more it's consumed), the greater the demand for the other. For many years concerts were the cheap complement that boosted CD sales. But as the price of recorded music fell, more fans could afford it—and were then drawn to live concerts.

Before the rise of the Internet, concerts were effectively "advertising" CD sales. After the explosion in file sharing, the relationship effectively reversed: Free recorded music became the advertisement—and, as a result, the ideal complement—for live concerts.

Concert promoters are quite forthright about this reversal. A senior vice president of AEG Live, one of the world's largest presenters of live music events, said, "As the recording business has gotten hit by piracy, the fact that a lot of bands are getting played all over the Internet on sites like Myspace and YouTube that are exposing music—we're the beneficiaries, in all honesty."

SO, WHAT BUSINESS ARE YOU REALLY IN?

Concerts aren't the only complement to recorded music. There are many others. To see where they reside, return to ask the basic question regarding complements. As the price of music declines, which are the music-related products, services, or accessories that might benefit from this price decline? Music complements, it turns out, are many and varied. To start, there were CD burners, blank CDs, and CD players; MP3 players became a leading complement in subsequent years. And then there's broadband access: As demand for file sharing increased (and with it, the loss in content sales for recording studios) so did demand for high-speed Internet (and with it, a dramatic increase in revenues for Internet service providers and cable operators).

Ask a music industry executive about the industry's challenges and you're likely to hear that "young people don't pay for products anymore." It's a common refrain, often used to bemoan why the economics of so many digital businesses have turned south. But it's wrong.

As a recording studio executive, if you define your business in terms of how many CDs you sell, you'll be right to berate the young. Define your business as music and *all its complements*—MP3 players, concerts, merchandising, broadband, and so on—and you'll realize that young people are spending more than ever.

The figure below charts the sales growth of just two music-related complements—concerts and iPods—over the last twenty years. Strikingly, as the sales of CDs declined, those of the complementary products rose by *more* than the decline in recorded music.

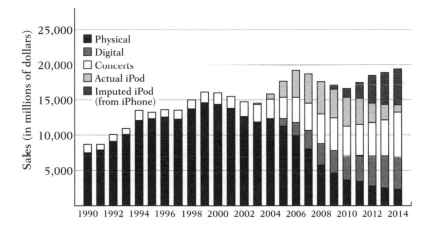

Figure 10: Music Industry: Recordings, Concerts, Digital, and iPod sales, 1990–2014. (Adapted from Oberholzer-Gee and Strumpf, 2010.)

The music industry is far from dead. Quite the contrary. Billions of dollars of value were created within the music industry during the recent decade. It's just that value has been redistributed—from recording studios to artists, from music retailers to technology manufacturers, from CDs to live concerts. The value shifted from recorded music to its complements.

13

APPLE AND COMPLEMENTS

AN INCONVENIENT TRUTH

During the past decade Apple enjoyed one of the greatest turnarounds in corporate history. From a beleaguered position in 2002—a $1 share price, meager profits, and a market share of 3 percent in the PC industry—it grew into the world's most valuable company in 2011. Well documented in the story of its turnaround is Apple's near-eerie knack for regularly producing high-quality products—"insanely great" products, as Steve Jobs once called them. Less well understood is the role of complements in turning around its fortunes.

Ask anyone for the reasons behind Apple's success and chances are that you'll hear reasons like "innovation," "quality," "ease of use," and "design." These are appealing explanations—seemingly self-evident. But they're not sufficient, owing to an inconvenient truth—exemplified in the following table, which documents Apple's market success across three product generations.

TABLE 7. APPLE: PRODUCT PORTFOLIO AND MARKET SHARES			
Product	Quality	Notable features	Apple's Market Share Five Years After Launch
Mac (1984)	Insanely great	Design, cool, brand, plug & play, innovative, ease of use	<10%
iPod (2001)	Insanely great	Design, cool, brand, plug & play, innovative, ease of use	>70%
iPhone (2007)	Insanely great	Design, cool, brand, plug & play, innovative, ease of use	About 30%
iPad (2010)	Insanely great	Design, cool, brand, plug & play, innovative, ease of use	About 30%

Table 7 makes a simple point: "Insanely great" products have more or less been a feature of Apple's corporate history *ever since it was founded,* in 1976. But its performance for its first twenty-five years was not nearly as impressive as what it's achieved during the most recent period.

"Insanely great products" are no guarantee of corporate success. Thinking that they would be is a mistake Apple made during its early history, by focusing on that aspect at the expense of all else. Many media companies have made the mistake, too, convinced that if they produced great content, everything else would take care of itself. The mistake is the Content Trap.

To better understand the reasons for the performance differences across Apple's product generations, we need to take a closer look at history. And the real lesson from Apple's history is this: While the quality of its products can be directly traced to the factors like design, organizational makeup, and vision, the company's fortunes have stemmed in large part from how well—or poorly—it has managed its product complements. To understand this lesson, let's go back to 1984.

NOT GREAT PRODUCTS, BUT GREAT COMPLEMENTS

The Macintosh was generally considered superior to anything the PC industry had produced. It boasted a brilliantly simple graphical user interface, seven years before the PC came up with one. Its "plug-and-play" feature allowed even the most unsophisticated user to feel comfortable. Its design was original and suited to even the most inexperienced user. Yet, remarkably, it never exceeded 15 percent of market share. Why?

One reason, as we've seen, was that Apple's low market share early on consigned it to the wrong end of a network effects battle with PCs. But as important to its demise was Apple's strategy around complements—a "closed" strategy. Hardware without software is useless. Treat the two as separate profit centers and neither has an incentive to price low enough to stimulate the complement's sales. Keep third-party software developers from creating applications to accompany your product, as Apple did, and you're unlikely to succeed. In 1985 the Mac commanded only a small fraction of the applications available on the PC, and this dynamic only worsened over time. It looked to be "game over."

The iPod, introduced in 2002, not only gave the company a new lease on life but, as we now know, also triggered a remarkable resurgence in its fortunes. The device quickly grew to command more than 85 percent of the market share in MP3 players. Again, a common explanation one often hears for this success was Apple's innovation and vision in introducing an MP3 player to the market, engineered to take advantage of increasing interest in digital listening. Except, the iPod wasn't the first such device on the market: RCA's Lyra, Creative Labs' Nomad, and Diamond Multimedia's Rio X, among others, preceded it, and in some cases were more technologically sophisticated than the iPod.

How did a product coming late to market, in an environment where a six-month head start can be crucial, overwhelm its rivals? The reason for the iPod's early success came in large part from the availability of its software complement, iTunes. Buy another MP3 player and you'd have had to go to a separate (and often obscure) site to download music. Buy an iPod and the process was simple: Go to the iTunes Store and peruse more than 200,000 songs. One click and a song was transferred to your device.

Steve Jobs had apparently learned, painfully from the earlier Mac experience, the importance of having software for your hardware: He had spent months negotiating with the major recording studios to ensure that on the day the iPod was launched, it had a song library to ensure its value. The price was right too: 99 cents for a legal download. And the system was open: iTunes software could be installed on a PC, making the iPod compatible with the largest computer platform.

Apple's ability to produce a great product was not the only game changer during the last decade. Its ability to manage complements was.

PRICING COMPLEMENTS RIGHT

iTunes, of course, proved an amazing success in its own right. Between 2002 and 2013, more than ten billion songs were downloaded through the platform, producing an equivalent dollar amount in revenue.

But there was one nagging problem: Apple made almost nothing from iTunes. That's right: roughly zero profits off $10 billion in revenues. And the reason behind these strange economics? Roughly 70 of the 99 cents charged for a song went to the recording studio, with another 20 cents going to credit card processing fees, leaving Apple with about a dime for overhead.

Ask any businessperson how much profit they can generate off a $10 billion revenue base and even the most inexperienced will argue they could do better than Jobs. But that's the wrong way to view iTunes, and its real value for Apple. An unprofitable iTunes business was a deliberate choice.

Think of songs on iTunes as a stand-alone product and you'll charge as much as possible. Think of them as a complement and you'll charge as little as possible. That's because iPods were how Apple made its money. The "bill of materials" (everything needed to manufacture) for a $250 iPod was only about $130, leaving an astounding profit margin. In other words, pricing songs low wasn't a strategy to give away profits to consumers. It was a strategy to make even more profits elsewhere.

Jobs had taken a flawless approach to pricing complements: Make one product (iTunes) easy to use, widely available, and cheap, and thus create dramatic demand for its complement (the iPod). Rival MP3 manufacturers hadn't failed on hardware innovation; they had missed the software boat.

CHEAP COMPLEMENTS ARE GOOD, BUT FREE COMPLEMENTS ARE BETTER

This story of the iPod has another twist. In 2007 Jobs urged the major recording studios to abolish digital rights management, or DRM, to effectively allow users to share their downloaded files with anyone. For years Apple had been seen as the savior of the music industry, with its means of protecting legal digital sales. But now Jobs posted a memo on the Internet titled "Thoughts on Music," where he noted that going "DRM free" would be consumer friendly, encourage competition, and "create a truly interoperable music marketplace."

The memo attracted intense scrutiny, and the reaction from many industry observers was downright puzzlement. Why would Apple, which had so forcefully negotiated terms with recording studios to create a legal downloading offering for consumers, now apparently retreat from that approach? Why would it let users download from *any* site, possibly at the expense of purchasing songs on iTunes?

One view was that Jobs had somehow, like the music artists earlier in their defense of "free," become a spirited consumer advocate overnight.

But let's look at some numbers again—numbers that Jobs himself had plainly written in his memo: "Between 2002 and 2006, customers purchased a total of 90 million iPods and 2 billion songs from the iTunes store. On average, that's 22 songs purchased from the iTunes store for each iPod ever sold."

Twenty-two songs per iPod? The math was striking. By 2010, the numbers hadn't increased much: roughly ten billion songs sold through iTunes, and roughly 300 million iPods sold, for an average of thirty-three songs per iPod. And all this while iPod storage capacity had dramatically increased over time—from roughly 1,000 songs at the time of Job's memo to more than 10,000 five years later.

Although Jobs had put the numbers out for everyone to see, many observers missed the point: The iPod had never been about making it easy to get songs from iTunes. It was about making it easy to get songs from *anywhere*. iTunes was a great complement to hardware, but it was only that. And there was something even better than a cheap complement (that is, a 99-cent song). It was free music.

One industry observer said, "If anything can play on anything, it's a clear win for the consumer electronics device world but a potential disaster for the content companies." Another noted, "In many ways, Apple's business model for the iTunes service is very closely aligned to that of the online pirates they're so desperate to destroy."

Apple had transitioned from a company that churned out great hardware to one that also aggressively stimulated (music) content and software. It had transitioned from one that priced *all* its products high to one unafraid to price its complements low. It had transitioned from one that erected proprietary barriers everywhere to one that knew when to let them fall.

14

FOUR LESSONS ABOUT COMPLEMENTS

1: EXPAND YOUR VISION, NOT NARROW IT

The stories of concerts and iPods illustrate the dramatic role of complements in the music business. They also illustrate the perils of ignoring them. But what leads managers to overlook complements? Why is it that they overlook opportunities in arenas so closely related to their own core products, as with concerts for CDs, or music for MP3 players? How could recording studios eschew the chance to stake a claim on the growing concert business, or early MP3 manufacturers miss the means of converting their first-mover status into winning positions?

A large part of the reason is that for years, we've been telling them to ignore these opportunities.

Over the past several decades, popular management mantras have extolled "focus" and "core competence," beseeching managers to "do what you do best," "avoid the temptation to expand into new arenas," and "make your core products better and price them higher." The idea of complements directly cuts against these prescriptions.

These are fine prescriptions for optimizing market share in your own business. But when your entire industry comes under threat, these prescriptions cause you to adopt an overly narrow lens and define too-restrictive boundaries.

Some complements are obvious: Hot dogs and ketchup, printers and cartridges, razors and blades, right and left shoes. But many are not.

A tire manufacturer offers restaurant guides, eventually becoming so successful in doing so that it creates a worldwide standard for assessing food quality. It's not that making tires somehow translates into skill at recognizing good food; it's that making customers aware of high-quality food in faraway places spurs driving.

Some movie theaters in the United States and Europe are managing to both raise prices and increase moviegoing—without offering better films, more comfortable seats, or cheaper popcorn. How? They're providing childcare service right next door.

Some European e-commerce retailers are enjoying upticks in sales without offering more attractive deals, price promotions, or new products. How? In part by building centers where consumers can pick up their orders on their way home from work, thereby eliminating the risk that when a product is shipped to their doorstep, it will disappear.

Complements often explain the success or failure of innovative products, too. Amazon's Kindle is widely thought to have revolutionized the e-book market because of its product features: portability, elegance, light weight, decent battery life, large e-book selection, sizable storage capacity, and a pleasant reading experience, all for $399. But Sony's LIBRIe reader came a year earlier, boasted each one of these attributes, was priced even lower—and went nowhere.

A big reason for the Kindle's success wasn't the features that improved e-reading, but a key complement that facilitated e-purchasing: wireless connectivity. To download an e-book on prior devices, one had to first connect the e-reader to that computer with a cable, buy the e-book through the computer, and transfer the file. With Amazon's wireless device and free access to its "Whispernet" wireless network, a reader could download an e-book directly onto the Kindle anywhere and at any time, with one click. That's the reason Jeff Bezos, Amazon's CEO, excitedly underscored in his remarks at the Kindle's launch, "This isn't a device, it's a service."

In 2009 Tata Motors, the car division of India's largest business house, launched the Nano—priced at about $2,500, half as much as the world's next-cheapest car. The Nano received enthusiastic reviews from many of the industry's most prestigious trade magazines not just for its low cost but for its design, quality, and road-sturdiness. But the Nano flopped, selling as little as 500 units monthly a year after launch when expected unit sales were 100 times that. Safety concerns, an unappealing brand image, and manufacturing problems all contributed. But more problematic was the lack of complements: The dealer network was sparse, financing and warranty programs were limited, test-drive opportunities were inconvenient, and trade-in options for two- and three-wheeled vehicles—typically owned by consumers likely to buy the Nano—were few. Tata had focused so intensely on making an impressive product that it had neglected to create its complements.

It's good not to define product or business boundaries too narrowly. To do this, ask what complements your customers find useful when they buy from you, not just what features they care about in your product alone (see Figure 11). Growth and innovation often come not from offering better content, but from offering better and cheaper complements. They come from product connections.

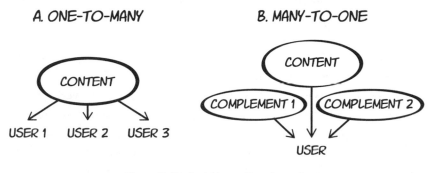

Figure 11: Content Versus Complements

Complements and the Smartphone Wars

Apple introduced its first smartphone in 2007. Like all Apple products, the phone was hailed for its design, innovation, ease of use, and quality. The basic version was $499, nearly five times as much as leading phones and roughly twice as much as Research In Motion's BlackBerry, a leading incumbent. Sales were impressive, and revenue was more than $115 million in the first two quarters after launch alone.

But just when it appeared to have cracked the code for phone quality, Apple did a complete about-face in strategy. In July 2008 it dropped its price by more than half. The reason wasn't that it had discovered its phone wasn't much better than others on the market; rather, Apple had learned *what* made it better.

At its launch, the iPhone was basically a phone with a few added features. It had all of nine applications: Maps, Stocks, Weather, iPod Calculator, Mail, Camera, and a few others. At first glance, the apps weren't what made the iPhone unique; BlackBerry and Nokia phones also had some. But Apple's were accessible by simply touching the screen, and the product was easy to use. Apple's hardware innovation seemed to be driving sales and success once again.

Within a year, however, the consumer research indicated something quite interesting, and quite different. Whereas users of other smartphones spent about 70 percent of their time on plain-vanilla phone service—making calls—exactly the reverse was true of the iPhone. The nine apps alone—the complements to hardware and voice services—were accounting for more than 55 percent of time spent by Apple iPhone users.

In other words, neither phone service nor product design, by itself, was driving interest in the iPhone. Apps were. And with a $500 price for the hardware and a closed-platform app development approach, the product may have struck Jobs as eerily similar to the ill-fated Mac of two decades earlier.

So in July 2008 Apple simultaneously created the "App Store" and dropped the phone's price. It opened up production of the device's primary complements to *anyone*. And it gave them 70 cents on every dollar of app revenue generated. Those moves were not only a sharp contrast to its earlier smartphone strategy; they were moves the company had never dared take during its early Mac history. During the first three days of the App Store's launch, more than ten million apps were downloaded. Within two years more than 50,000 independent developers had contributed to creating some 100,000 iPhone apps.

Nowhere are the effects of complements, or the perils of ignoring them, more apparent than in the contrasting fortunes of BlackBerry and Android phones in recent years. At the time of Apple's entry, BlackBerry had nearly 50 percent market share. Google debuted the Android in 2009, nearly two years after the iPhone and ten years after BlackBerry. Its strategy was to try to beat Apple at its own game—by increasing competition among hardware manufacturers (effectively reducing the price of its phones) and allowing any developer to create apps for the platform, with no restrictions or oversight. BlackBerry chose to remain closed. By June 2013 BlackBerry's share of the smartphone market was less than 1 percent—and Android's was more than 75 percent.

2: DARE TO PRICE LOW—BUT KNOW WHERE TO DO SO

Managing complements requires not only identifying them and increasing their supply; it requires pricing them right. But what's "right"? Apple's pricing of iPod and iTunes violated perhaps the best-known rule in the book for pricing complements—the familiar razor–razor blades model.

"Price the durable cheap, and make profits off the consumable," was the conventional thinking around complements pricing. The rule had worked beautifully for decades—for Gillette and other manufacturers. It had also worked marvelously in other product settings, such as printers and cartridges, or consoles and videogames.

Why did Apple reverse this tried-and-true approach? It had to do with who was on the other side of the table when it came time to splitting profits. For every song downloaded, only one studio held the artist's rights. So Apple's position was a bit like negotiating against a monopolist. But when it came to the $100 in profits that Apple commanded from the iPod, the company was negotiating with dozens of near-commodity component assemblers. The power there rested with Apple.

"Price hardware low, services high" is a rule that's sensible for razors or printers, where a single firm made both products. But it wasn't for Apple, since it didn't. Indeed the real lesson about complements pricing turns out to be this: Price according to where *you* have a competitive advantage, not just based on rules that make sense for others.

3: EXCLUSIVE CONNECTIONS: FROM INDUSTRY COMPLEMENTS TO PRODUCT COMPLEMENTS

Did it matter whether 99-cent iTunes songs or free pirated music was the real complement to iPod sales? Both, after all, yielded similar quality music. Both could be played however long the user wanted. And both made similar contributions to iPod profits. But the two differed in an important respect. iTunes benefited iPod users only; because of its DRM technology called FairPlay, no other MP3 player could access iTunes. Pirated music, on the other hand, aided *every* MP3 manufacturer.

iTunes, in other words, was a proprietary complement; illegal file sharing was an industry-wide one.

Complements are good. Proprietary complements are better. It's for this reason that companies often try to make complements exclusive to their business, particularly early in a product life cycle, when the trajectory of demand and competition is unclear.

It's not that nonexclusive complements hurt your business. It's just that they also help everyone else. Michelin stars for faraway restaurants might increase sales of Michelin tires, but they also help Bridgestone, Goodyear, and Pirelli. But childcare services by theaters and pickup stores for e-commerce products are exclusive to the company offering them.

So why did Apple eschew proprietary complements? It wasn't that Jobs favored an "open ecosystem." It's that he realized iTunes wasn't strong enough to create customer "lock-in."

That's not to say Apple products were suddenly on a level playing field. By the time Jobs embraced DRM-free music, an array of other Apple-exclusive complements had appeared—Nike armbands, iPod-compatible speakers, and a range of proliferating, wide-ranging, even bizarre, accessories tied to the iPod, such as billfold wallets, belts and boxers, beds, and toilet paper holders.

A similar logic led Amazon to quickly change course on its Kindle strategy after its launch. Initially the device could "read" only those books that were available in Amazon's proprietary format, and e-books in that format could be read only on the Kindle. Amazon was trying to make both sides of the business proprietary in the hope that, if successful, it could win on both e-books and hardware. Within a year, however, it had reversed course and opened up its hardware to other e-book formats, signaling its belief that the earlier strategy would not be sustaining.

The idea of exclusive complements also finds application in the ongoing smartphone wars and might inform the question of whether or not multiple platforms can coexist there. Consider, for example, the monthly press releases issued by the competing iOS and Android platforms:

TABLE 8. NUMBER OF APPS ON IOS AND ANDROID PLATFORMS, 2011–15		
Date	Number of Apps on iOS Platform	Number of Apps on Android Platform
January 2011	350,000	180,000
February 2012	500,000	400,000
January 2013	775,000	800,000
June 2014	1,200,000	1,300,000
July 2015	1,500,000	1,600,000

The numbers are impressive and yet somewhat comical; the typical smartphone user has about thirty apps. The millionth app is somewhat irrelevant.

The fuss over apps isn't because the total number of apps matters to the average, or avid, user. What does matter is exclusivity over them. Create one million apps and it might appear like you're creating a powerful ecosystem for your device, but their competitive effects are neutralized if they are available on competing platforms. Create "killer apps" exclusive to your platform, and that is the nightmare scenario for your rivals.

Consider Maps. In 2012 Apple removed Google's acclaimed app from the iPhone, replacing it with one of its own. It did so not because Google's product was bad or unpopular. Quite the reverse: About 25 percent of smartphone users used it actively. The frightening scenario for a product developer (in this case, Apple) is negotiating with a provider of the killer complement (in this case, Google).

View Apple's decision to remove Maps through the lens of software quality and it appears foolish. View it through the lens of complements management and it suddenly appears far less so.

4: ASK NOT WHAT YOUR CORE BUSINESS IS, BUT KNOW WHEN YOU'RE SOMEONE ELSE'S COMPLEMENT

Complements are marvelous when it comes to creating value for your customer. But when it comes to capturing that value, they invariably benefit at your expense. Consider razors and razor blades, printers and cartridges, CDs and concerts: In each case, one product benefits from lowered prices of the other. So it's important not just to know what business you are in—an increasingly popular strategic question—but to know whether you're *someone else's* complement.

"Companies are sufficiently focused on their strategy and not on their complements' strategy, but that's how the game is often played," Yale economist Barry Nalebuff told me recently. "You can have the world's best gas pumps. But if you don't have a convenience store, you just lost to somebody who does. GMAC made more money from GMAC [its auto financing arm] than from selling cars. Railroad companies recognized a decade ago that they were worth more for the fiber rights alongside their tracks than for the railroad themselves."

Many companies often make one of two mistakes: believing foes to be friends, or vice versa.

Believing Foes to Be Friends

In 2003, just as file sharing was exploding, Warner Music figured it had a strategy to fight it: It would seek the names and IP addresses of individuals engaged in illegal downloading and sue. The apparent brilliance of this approach was that the company wouldn't need to go too far to obtain this information—its sister division, leading Internet access provider Time Warner Cable (TWC), had it all.

Or so Warner Music's executives thought. Disconcertingly to them, TWC refused to cooperate. Worse, it filed briefs in support of rival Verizon, which had itself refused to give recording studios the names of customers who might have downloaded music files without authorization. It was like sleeping with the enemy.

View these frictions between sister divisions against the backdrop of Warner Music's efforts to fight piracy, or its familial relationship with TWC, and you'd conclude that personal animosities or politics were in play. View them as a relation between complements and you'd realize it was simple economics at work. TWC executives made the decision to withhold customer information not because they disliked their own colleagues, nor because (as they argued years later in a lawsuit of film producers against file-sharing service BitTorrent) it was impractically costly to retrieve it, but because they had much to gain by doing so. Demand for broadband services had been fueled in part by file sharing: Roughly 30 percent of all broadband traffic was estimated to come from sharing music and movie files. TWC wasn't about to bite the hand that fed it.

Similar tensions surfaced elsewhere. In 2002 Disney then-CEO Michael Eisner and Steve Jobs engaged in a highly publicized spat that came to a boil when Eisner testified before Congress that the "greatest killer app in Silicon Valley is piracy," singling out Apple's "Rip, Mix, Burn" slogan. In 2003 executives at the recording studio BMG were dismayed to learn that their corporate parent, Bertelsmann, had invested in Napster just as they were trying hard to terminate it. It's tempting to attribute conflicts like these to politics and personality, when a large part of these differences resides in the underlying economics of complements: One party's gain came at the expense of the other.

Believing Friends to Be Foes

News aggregators like Google are viewed as the misery of newspapers: They source content, pay nothing for it, and redistribute it for free. And in doing so, they may be conditioning readers to go to aggregators rather than news sites. That's the conventional wisdom. It's zero-sum rhetoric, with each side convinced the other gains at its expense. Look more closely and you'll find complementary relationships at work. After all, aggregators would have no value for readers if news sources disappeared.

One concern is that although news sources and aggregators are complements generally, any single news source is undifferentiated and therefore expendable—and this possibility is greater as entirely online news outlets, blogs, and tweets become viable sources for news. But the data suggests otherwise: Surprisingly, the top sources of news continue to command disproportionate numbers of readers and links on aggregators.

In early 2014 we analyzed the rankings of sources on Google News, examining more than 20,000 randomly selected stories over a month. At first glance, the threat of commoditization appeared real: More than 2,000 news sources were ranked as the top source for *some* story. If news was undifferentiated—so that each source was as likely as any other to be ranked at the top—then the predicted top-rank market share for any single news source would be very small: 1/2,000, or 0.05 percent, to be precise. Adding the market shares of the top thirty outlets in that world and one would predict they'd get a meager 1.5 percent. And that's sobering.

But a closer look offered a very different picture. The most frequently ranked source in Google News overall was *The New York Times,* which achieved that distinction for 642 of the 20,000 stories, giving it a "top-ranked market share" of 3 percent—by itself. The combined share of the top thirty outlets was 35 percent. And the share numbers for specific news genres were even more impressive. For example, *The New York Times* was the top source for nearly 15 percent of political stories. Add the next four high scorers for political news, on the reasonable assumption that a reader might click on any of the top five sources but would rarely go further, and you'll see that at least one of the top ten media outlets was in this group a remarkable 40 percent of the time. Notably, every one of Google's top ten news sources was a "traditional" media outlet. None was a digital upstart or blogger.

Google News, it seems clear, can't do without traditional media. For this reason, the future of newspapers is of great interest not just to the papers' owners but to Google (and more recently Facebook) as well. This understanding helps clarify the behavior of each side in different markets around the world. In some markets, recognizing their collective power, major publishers came together to aggregate their news content online under a single umbrella, for a fee. In others, aggregators are reaching out. China's foremost online news portal, Tencent, has more than one billion readers each month. It seeks out news outlets, striking paid deals for exclusive content, showcasing them in internal conferences, and sometimes offering them educational programs on managing their own digital transition.

Let's see how book publishing has fared. The Kindle's version of 99-cent songs was $9.99 books—a 40 percent discount from the hardcover retail price. It seemed that publishers were destined to follow the same path as recording studios, as Amazon appeared intent on commoditizing the book market to prop up hardware sales. To fight the trend, five major publishers struck deals with Apple, according to which they themselves—not the e-retailer—would determine the retail price, and would retain 70 percent. (Subsequent antitrust investigations of price-fixing have now rendered these agreements obsolete.) Random House, the world's largest trade publisher, held out.

In effect, the five publishers reasoned, "An enemy of an enemy is a friend." That's impeccable logic for managing complements; a decade earlier, Brandenburger and Nalebuff had advised, "Make your complements compete." But *which* competitor to align with? That's where Random House disagreed with the others. "Amazon had been our best customer in digital retailing," a Random House executive told me. "As for Apple, well, we'd all seen what happened in music."

As these stories demonstrate, firms ought to look harder to identify friends and foes. Content businesses continue to learn about the economics of complements the hard way. Figure 12 is a kitchen-napkin diagram of where different players are drawing battle lines. In 2014 Microsoft still generated more than 90 percent of its profits from software (its operating systems and applications); Apple generated a similar percentage from devices; Google and Facebook gained theirs from advertising; Amazon and eBay from e-commerce; and cable providers from infrastructure access.

These examples are striking not just because of the differences in where the core businesses of these digital giants reside. What's also remarkable is how proactive each company has been in enlisting others to help increase its value and then capturing that value—often at their ex-

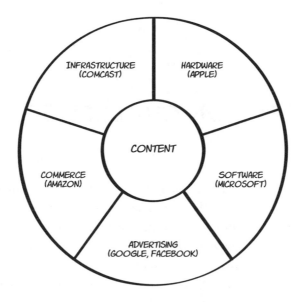

Figure 12: Content Versus Complements: The Battle Among Digital Giants

pense. Ninety-nine-cent and DRM-free music was *a choice* by Apple, free office applications through Docs *a choice* by Google, and $9.99 e-books, self-publishing, and low-cost hardware *a choice* by Amazon. In each case the choice related not only to a strategy for propping up value in the core business but to reducing the price of, or even commoditizing, the complements.

Therein lies perhaps the greatest challenge for content producers: Their future will depend not only on what they make but on how effectively they manage value-creating opportunities in adjacent areas. Otherwise complements will continue to capture value—often at their expense.

15
A DETECTION CHALLENGE

Yes, companies are often slow to recognize the power of complements and product connections when they could be seizing opportunity. But that isn't the only error typically made. Sometimes, they make the opposite mistake—rushing too fast to action when it pays to first get the diagnosis right.

The music industry is a case in point.

Its first error was tunnel vision—believing the future of music lay in preserving the CD. Its second error was confounding cause and effect—believing that CD declines were almost entirely *due to* piracy.

Piracy was the obvious culprit; its rise coincided almost perfectly with the rise of file sharing. (Figure 13 illustrates the decline in CD sales.) The Recording Industry Association of America was convinced of the link, quantifying the impact of piracy as "$12.5 billion of economic losses every year, 71,060 jobs lost, [and] a loss of $2.7 billion in workers' earnings." Congress was also convinced, initiating bipartisan antipiracy legislation. (The Stop Online Piracy Act, introduced in 2011 but never passed, would

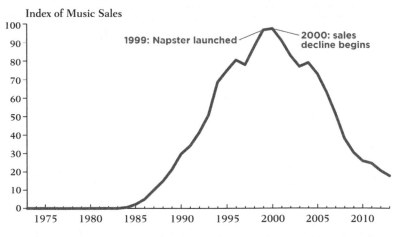

Figure 13: Changes in CD unit sales, 1973–2013 (chart constructed from RIAA data)

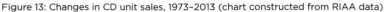

have statutorily barred advertising networks, payment services, search engines, and Internet service providers from engaging with any website involved in digital copyright infringement.)

But completely unrelated factors were also at work that might plausibly explain part of the CD declines, and they had little to do with piracy. CD prices were rising over time. A recession was under way in 2000. And digital formats provided a natural substitute for the CD.

On top of this, there's the problem of calculating "lost revenue" to the industry. Would a teenager who illegally downloaded 3,000 songs have paid for all of them if copyright protection were somehow stronger? Surely not. The point is that not every pirated sale is a lost sale.

So how important were the other factors in explaining CD declines? Here's a variation on Figure 13 that just looks at the role of format changes. It compares the rate of CD declines with the earlier declines of vinyl and cassettes, when each was substituted by newer formats in a natural product replacement cycle. (To more directly compare the different periods, we normalized peak sales for each format to 100 in every case.)

Look only at Figure 13, and your response as an industry executive would be clear: hire as many lawyers as you can to fight piracy. And that's what executives did. Your response as a policy maker would be clear, too: introduce aggressive legislation to stop copyright infringement. And that's what Congress did.

Now look at Figure 14 and evaluate your diagnosis.

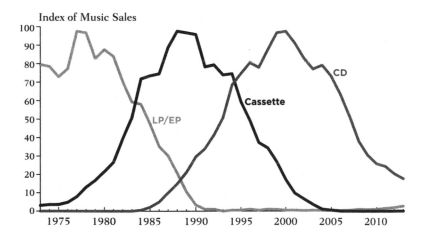

Figure 14: Impact of Format Changes on Music Sales, 1973–2013 (Peak unit sales normalized to 100 for all formats)

Diagnosing the music industry problem is not simply a question of seeing that CD declines are coincident with trends in file sharing. It requires separating cause from effect. The problem with the diagnosis stems from an age-old problem in statistical inference: separating correlation from causation. We see it everywhere. Does TV viewing increase obesity, or are obese individuals more inclined to watch TV? Are Asians innately better at math, or do they work harder at it? Simple correlations would lead you to infer that there's some causal relation between two variables, when in fact there might be none.

The most common approach to uncovering causation between two variables is to look for a third variable that correlates with only one of them—an "instrumental" variable, in the language of economic statisticians. So for music, was there some instrumental variable—some independent factor—that might increase file sharing but that was not directly correlated with CD sales? If so, examining the changes in it, and their follow-on impact on CD sales, would allow one to determine any "causal" effect of piracy on CD sales.

Debating the causal impact of piracy on CD sales nearly became a contact sport among academics during the last decade. The reason is that finding such an instrumental variable wasn't easy, because most plausible factors driving piracy also directly affected CD sales. Access to broadband might be a candidate—it reduces the time to illegally download a song, thereby accelerating file sharing. But it also increases online entertainment options and reduces CD sales for that reason alone. University enrollment might be a candidate, because it gives students access to computing facilities that can be used for downloading. But college students are the customer group least inclined to buy CDs in the first place, so lower CD sales in university areas might simply result from student preferences, not piracy.

In a 2005 study, Felix Oberholzer-Gee (a colleague at Harvard) and Koleman Strumpf (at the University of North Carolina) looked at the impact of German school holidays on file sharing and CD sales in the United States. On first glance, that was a mystifying variable, but in fact the logic was inspired. German schoolkids uploaded more files during vacation, the researchers reasoned, simply because they had time on their hands. And because Germany was an important source of files downloaded in the U.S. market (accounting for 16.5 percent of all U.S. downloads), the researchers could trace the impact of this "supply shock" on CD sales in the United States.

When the researchers examined their data, they found that file sharing did increase in Germany during school holidays. More than that, it increased precisely in tandem with when holidays fell in each region (school holidays varied from geography to geography in Germany). This in turn triggered increases in file sharing in the United States.

As for the final link in this chain of results? The researchers found that the increase in file sharing in the United States that was propagated by this chain of events in Germany had *no* meaningful impact on changes in U.S. CD sales—that is, no causal effect. It's not that they could not detect a statistically significant relation between file sharing and CD sales. They did. And it was precisely zero.

Industry insiders summarily rejected the finding. File sharers embraced it. Oberholzer-Gee told me, "It's one of those instances where you have instantaneously a million friends and a million enemies, and nothing of what you actually did matters. All that matters is the result. People who like the result think that you've done something for humanity. Those on the other side tell you it's the worst study they've ever seen and that you don't understand the business. I have never lived through such antagonistic presentations."

The point, of course, wasn't that the paper had nailed a causal relation between piracy and CD sales, but that it showed how hard it would be to do so. And, like various other studies that would follow, it was forcing one to grapple with the data, introducing objectivity to a debate that had been shaped largely by preconceptions.

Demand declines for a product don't tell you what to do in response. You first have to know *why* the decline occurred. CD declines weren't enough to conclude that the trigger was piracy, just like newspaper readership declines weren't enough to conclude that the Internet was the cause.

Similar challenges confront debates today about pay TV. Industry observers are obsessed about declines in subscriptions after nearly three decades of growth. The culprit seems clear: "over-the-top" (OTT) video packages such as Netflix offer increasing variety at a lower price. Buy into this explanation as a cable operator and you'd focus all your efforts on crushing Netflix. Those efforts might be misplaced.

Just as with music and newspapers, there are many plausible reasons for the drop in pay TV subscriptions.

The declines could come from a "Facebook effect": new forms of entertainment, from Internet and mobile browsing to videogames and time spent on social networks, place increasing pressure on TV viewing time. It could be a "cohort effect": Younger viewers growing up with devices and video offerings (the "cord nevers") never got into the habit of watching TV and never will. It could be an "age effect": Young people can't afford $100 a month for a subscription, but that will change once they're older. It could be a "poverty effect": Hikes in pay TV prices combined with reduced purchasing power, especially among low-income households, after the 2008–09 recession. It could be a "complements effect": The relative appeal of OTT could relate not to differences in content but to differences in service, such as ease of installation, repairs, search interface, and content recommendations. (In 2014 Netflix's net promoter score, an important measure of customer satisfaction, was 54, whereas the average NPS for major cable operators was a negative number.)

Each of these reasons plausibly explains the decline in pay TV subscriptions. But each merits a very different strategic response. See the decline and without identifying what the root cause is, you could easily be barking up the wrong tree.

So, let's return to the story of music—the real story, as we now know it: Piracy did impose price pressures, causing value to shift to concerts and other complements. Format substitution was indeed real, causing demand to shift from CDs to digital formats. Everything else is a myth.

The industry focused almost all its efforts on preventing piracy, hoping that would stem CD declines. That was error one. The overwhelming emphasis was on preserving CDs. That was error two.

It's a sobering tale of fighting digital wildfires, one that brings to mind Yellowstone. Except, not only were the predictions of hurt wrong, as in that case, too—this time, even the trigger was misidentified.

GROUNDHOG DAY: A LESSON IN MEDIA HISTORY

The reaction of recording studios to file-sharing technologies is not the first time we've seen such a response. The history of the media industry is replete with similar stories of misperceived threats that turned out to be quite different. In every case the false belief was that content was under siege. It almost never was.

In the early 1900s, radio stations first began playing commercial music. Recording studios had a simple response: fight it. Free radio surely posed a danger to the business of paid music. Commercial radio eventually survived, thanks in part to a Supreme Court ruling. But over the ensuing decades, studios noticed that record sales hadn't declined; they had actually increased. The reason? Free listening on the radio had turned out to be a marvelous advertisement for albums.

In 1984 MTV made its appearance. Again, recording studios had a simple response: fight it. Free listening, with funky videos to boot, surely posed a danger to the business of paid music. But over the ensuing years, studios noticed that record and cassette sales hadn't declined; they had actually increased. The reason? Music videos had turned out to be a marvelous marketing tool for CDs.

In 1985, VCRs appeared. Movie and TV studios had a simple response: fight it. Free video recording and sharing of movies, accompanied by fast-forwarding through commercials, surely posed a danger to the business of broadcast TV and home movies. In *Universal v. Sony*, a case that went all the way to the Supreme Court, the plaintiffs sought to block VCR sales on the basis of copyright infringement. Studios lost the ruling, but over the ensuing years, noticed their revenues had increased markedly. The reason? VCRs turned out to be a powerful advertising tool for TV shows and movies, drawing in viewers who couldn't watch shows on schedule and creating a new revenue stream for movie studios.

These are not just examples of historical interest. Similar stories continue to play out today.

In 2002, the digital video recorder TiVo first appeared in homes, allowing owners to self-schedule TV viewing and to fast-forward through commercials. Broadcast networks had a simple response: fight it. Fast-forwarding of commercials surely posed a danger to the advertising business of broadcast TV. But over the ensuing decade, advertising revenues for the major networks, surprisingly, barely changed. The reason? DVRs might have enabled commercial-skipping, but ad-avoidance was hardly novel for viewers: They'd *always* been doing so during restroom or kitchen breaks. One of the most careful studies of the impact of DVRs on product sales found "no statistical evidence for a TiVo effect on purchase behavior during the year following the issuance of a DVR."

In 2012, a broadcast network (NBC), for the first time, experimented with live streaming of a major sports event, the Olympics. Until then, the response of TV networks to video streaming had been simple: fight it. A live stream would draw audiences away from prime-time viewing, undermining the advertising revenue stream on which networks survived. But, during the London Olympics, NBC Sports' executives observed that prime-time viewership had actually increased. The reason? Live streaming had only whetted viewer appetite for hearing more from athletes *after* they'd performed. By the end of the Games, NBC announced the streaming experiment resulted in their highest Olympic prime-time ratings on TV, *ever*.

FROM DISRUPTION TO COMPLEMENTS

What's remarkable about these accounts isn't that managers overstate the threat of new technology—it's how often they do so. In every one of these cases, the new technology, device, or product turned out to either have no impact on existing revenue, or to actually increase it. In each case, the perceived threat proved to be far less harmful than at first thought, or often a helpful complement.

We're not good at recognizing connections. When we do, we often mistake positive connections for negative ones. Or we see a negative connection when no connection exists at all. There are at least three reasons for this difficulty.

1. A Problem of Mindset

Experience price pressures, as most content businesses have, and the natural instinct is to increase prices in order to preserve value in the core product. This preservation instinct is natural. But it's often futile. It exemplifies the Content Trap, a consequence of a product or a content-oriented mindset.

Embrace a complements mindset instead—following value where it leads—and you'll find new opportunities.

The irony about complements is that they've always been important in content businesses. Theaters made money from popcorn sales as well as movie tickets. TV networks and newspapers made money from advertising as well as content charges. Artists made money from concerts as well as CDs. Not much has changed in these complementary revenue streams for many years. What's different now is that digital technologies are forcing a rethinking of where the *future* complements are likely to be, and how to proactively manage them.

The idea of complements also highlights another difference in philosophy—between law and economics. To see this, return to piracy, and traditional efforts to deal with it. When media executives witnessed widespread music downloading, their natural instinct was to almost entirely focus on vigorously fighting it rather than recognize other opportunities in play. It stands to reason that legal strategies would be part of the solution. The problem comes when they are viewed as the *only* solution.

The feebleness of legal approaches to combating illegal downloads was becoming clear a decade ago. Around the same time, a scholarly literature on tackling such problems through "market-based strategies" was mushrooming. It had its roots in a celebrated 1983 survey of more than 600 managers in thirty industries by researchers at Yale. The survey had revealed that formal intellectual property protection was largely *irrelevant* to nearly every business (pharmaceuticals was the exception), and it documented a range of strategies employed by firms to protect their innovations. More than a decade later, as digital technologies and the Internet were exploding, the study was repeated by researchers at Carnegie Mellon, with similar results. A 2004 book by economists Michele Boldrin and David Levine was even more provocative, arguing that the very idea of patent protection was incompatible with a dynamically efficient market economy. Other scholars drew attention to the difference between legal and effective property rights, noting that statutory rights did not automatically result in secure ones. The winds in the debate were shifting. Many writing in this area were reasonably sure that content businesses would soon look beyond the toolkit of legal strategies toward more creative solutions to piracy. But shifting mindsets is hard and can take a long time.

2. A Problem of Language

Part of the problem has nothing to do with managers' inadequacies or inability to "get it." It has to do with the language we use.

Ideas such as industry convergence, hypercompetition, and disruption have been the rage in recent years. The implication is nearly always the same: Your business is threatened by new technology, and you'd better do something about it.

Industry disruption is real, and disquieting, for managers who are confronted with it. It strikes with particular severity on industries impacted by new technologies born of the Internet. It's tempting to therefore conclude that it is almost peculiar to today's times. But many of the ideas of recent years—the blurring of industry boundaries, product convergence, and disruption—are neatly captured in a concept conceived by economists more than a century ago: the concept of a *substitute*.

A substitute is just the opposite of a complement; it's any product or service that, when cheaper or more widely available, reduces demand for your core product. On the face of it, it's a seemingly benign definition of competition. But the reason it's insidious is that the definition says nothing about *what* the substitute product is.

Consider Little League baseball. For the longest time, its "competitors" came from traditional arenas—other sports, such as soccer and basketball. Then videogames came along. Today, the high-definition graphics and 3-D functionality of these games might energize a child as much in thirty minutes as going out to play baseball for two hours, while getting one's cleats dirty or shoes muddy. Videogames, in other words, are a substitute for Little League.

Or think about Black & Decker power tools. Natural competitors— "rivals"—include Bosch, Craftsman, and Makita. But that limits the competitive field of vision to companies making similar products, when there are other relevant substitutes for power tools—the handyman (he'll repair things for you), IKEA (its ready-to-assemble furniture needs no power tools), cheap rental furniture (easier to throw away than repair), even glue. You can stretch the list still further and include neckties.

Neckties? How could they be relevant to power tools? Consider that sales of power tools spike on certain days of the year: Father's Day, Christmas, Valentine's Day. That's because the tools have value as gifts—to a father, a spouse, a loved one, or a friend. What makes for a great alternative gift? You see the point.

Define competition solely from the perspective of your product or content and you'll focus on a single class of competitors. Define it from the perspective of your customer—in the case of power tools, the one who actually purchases it as a gift—and you'll see entirely new competitors. Substitutes force you to define competition from the perspective of your customer, rather than from the perspective of the content you offer. That's why they are terrifying.

The rise of digital technologies sparked renewed interest in the concept of substitutes. The language coined was different: *convergence, hypercompetition,* and *disruption*. But the underlying idea was the same—watch out for substitutes.

It's perfectly natural to be frightened by new technology. Competition is everywhere. Disruption is coming. The threats to your business were never greater. Most entrepreneurs, when asked about a cheap or free alternative to their business, would perceive a business-destroying threat, not an opportunity. Managers have been trained to think in terms of negative connections, rather than positive ones.

3. A Problem of Data

The first task in any corporate change effort is to correctly diagnose the problem—the problem of "perception," as strategy scholar Jan Rivkin has termed it. When it comes to distinguishing complements from substitutes, the stakes are especially high, because the strategic implications are so different. Encounter a complement and you should make it as cheap and widely available as you can. Encounter a substitute and you should try to drive up its price and limit its access. Mistake one for the other and your efforts will backfire.

Distinguishing complements from substitutes can be straightforward—hardware and software are clearly complements, for example, since one is useless without the other. But many times the difference isn't obvious at all.

Consider print and digital news. A plausible view is that they're substitutes, with one reducing the value of the other. An equally plausible view is that they're complements: Reading stories in print spurs people to seek out more information about them online, and vice versa.

The difficulty in sorting these conflicting explanations rests with the data we typically rely on. Consider the following example, fairly typical of what a newspaper executive might look at. (The numbers are artificial, but they are drawn from an actual analysis by Stanford economist Matt Gentzkow of print and digital complementarities for *The Washington Post*.)

TABLE 9. DATA ON PRINT VERSUS ONLINE READERSHIP FOR A HYPOTHETICAL NEWSPAPER		
30-Day Period:	Read ABC.com	Didn't Read ABC.com
Read newspaper ABC	900	3,000
Didn't read newspaper ABC	300	3,300

(Adapted from Gentzkow, 2007)

Taken on its own, the lower left box, showing that 300 people read news on the website but not in print, seems to suggest that print and digital news are substitutes. But that interpretation would be wrong if those people were entirely new readers who would never look at print in any case.

Similarly, the upper left box, showing that 900 readers read both print and digital, seems, on its own, to suggest that the two formats are complements. And *that* interpretation could be wrong: It might merely reflect that some people—"news junkies"—read news all the time, regardless of the source.

To know whether print and digital are complements or substitutes, we need to know what readers of one format would have consumed *in its absence*. Would the digital readers in the lower left cell consume print if digital were unavailable, or would they read nothing at all? Not knowing the answer to the questions can lead to wrong inferences. Worse, the data in the table offers no hope of answering the question—we can't ever know what the counterfactual would be. But if you track the same reader's behavior over time, you can solve the problem by seeing how her reading patterns changed after the new format was introduced.

This simple example contains a warning. More data doesn't pay—the right data does. And having the wrong data can be worse than having none at all.

That's the real lesson from the recording industry—what *not* to do. Believing that piracy drove the declines in CD sales led most executives there to focus on one solution—fight it. Some studio executives would acknowledge years later that the industry had lost time fighting piracy rather than creating new business models The single-minded fixation on negative connections had buried the possibility of capitalizing on positive ones.

COMPLEMENTS VERSUS SUBSTITUTES—AND THE ROLE OF MANAGERIAL CHOICE

Textbook descriptions of complements would lead you to believe that complements are either present in your business, or they're not. Hardware and software. Printers and cartridges. Game consoles and games. Gasoline and cars. Razors and blades. Lamps and bulbs. Each without the other is useless. Compete on one of these products and you *must* have the other to provide value. In each case the role of the complement arises from the nature of your product, not from the choices you make.

But restaurant guides aren't necessary for users to purchase tires. In-house childcare isn't needed for theaters to sell tickets. Music lessons aren't needed for someone to buy a musical instrument. Bike lanes aren't needed for cyclists to buy bikes. Mortgages aren't needed to purchase real estate. Carpet cleaners aren't needed to convince people to own a dog. Jelly isn't needed for users to like peanut butter sandwiches (all right, it might be).

These complements aren't *necessary*—but making them available increases customer value from your product. So companies should think hard and creatively about how to offer complements.

Offer print and digital versions of a newspaper that are identical in content and you're essentially telling your readers to treat them as substitutes. Vary the content between the versions—make certain content exclusive to one, or tailored to each—and you might have a pair of complements. Offer print and e-books priced separately and you're telling customers to treat them separately. Bundle them at a discount and the customer might buy both.

Such ideas don't require creative genius. Consider the examples below (Figure 15).

Figure 15. Complements

And here's an example involving the simple T-shirt. Offer two similar T-shirts—like the ones in the picture below—and they're substitutes:

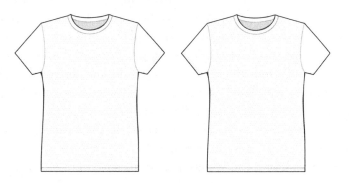

Now add this "content" and you've suddenly turned them into comple-ments.

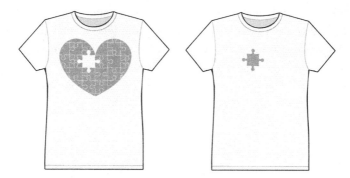

When Digital Helps Traditional: Fantasizing About Football

If you talk to any media executive about digital formats, you'll be met with nervousness: Will the digital product cannibalize the traditional one? That's the mindset of substitution and disruption—of negative connections. But view the new format as an opportunity to carve out a new version or an entirely different product and you might create positive connections.

Ask the NFL. It learned about positive connections the easy way—without doing anything.

Fantasy sports are not new. The first recorded leagues, dating back at least sixty years, were merely groups of friends who got together to post lists of their favorite players and track their performance. Golf lent itself to fantasy sports, since the metrics to track player performance were relatively straightforward. Baseball soon followed, with more metrics to track. By the early 1980s publishers were offering guidebooks to the relevant statistics. By then fantasy football had firmly entered the picture too.

Fantasy sports allow fans to do exactly that—fantasize. In NFL fantasy leagues, anyone can create their own unique team of stars—their "fantasy team"—drawing from all the players in the league. Team performance is based on how each player fares in each week's actual league games. Standardized scoring lets fans compete against one another.

At least that's how fantasy sports started. It was a simple, social game. Throwing the Internet into the mix had explosive results. Analysis could be done in real time and results shared instantaneously; everyone could participate on the same platform. Yahoo! was the first to create an Internet platform to anchor its fantasy league; ESPN soon followed. Algorithms did the work of calculating results. And for a while, many were free.

Participation skyrocketed: By 2015 more than thirty-three million people were in a fantasy league, usually with friends but sometimes with strangers. Some leagues remained free, while others charged $50 or more to participate. By 2015 about 90 percent of the activity centered on the NFL. On the face of it, fantasy sports was a low-stakes, entertaining activity with your friends. But the aggregate revenue impact on the NFL was anything but that.

That's because fantasy players aren't interested just in their local team—they follow nearly every one, because they're drawing their fantasy players from the entire league. They follow not just close games but blowouts, too. They follow not only the best teams, but the worst ones, too—what matters is how individual players in your fantasy team perform, not how the real team does. They track their players' health and injuries on social media. They chat with friends about upcoming games. They buy magazines that guide them about player drafts, and they follow websites and TV shows for in-season advice about upcoming player matchups. They watch replays of key plays. They tune in to broadcast networks with greater frequency and for longer than non–fantasy football fans, spending an average of eight hours a week watching games, versus six hours.

As fantasy interest exploded, so did accessories and complements. Foremost was Red Zone, a TV channel created by the NFL primarily to cater to the fantasy market. It offers a commercial-free highlights package aired continuously on Sunday afternoons and showing every scoring play in every game that day, for a monthly subscription fee of about $5. By 2015 it was offered through all major cable and satellite providers.

And there were other complements. Draft kits helped teams organize their drafts, and "cheat sheets" aggregated player statistics. Mobile applications were extra. Fantasy magazines popped up everywhere. You could even buy insurance for your fantasy players.

The impact of fantasy sports on the NFL itself has been breathtaking (and even a bit controversial). Observers estimate that by 2015, about $11 billion was changing hands annually through fantasy football leagues around the country. The NFL's platform alone draws some three million fans, or one-sixth of the fantasy sports market. On top of the Red Zone channel subscribers, there was the feedback impact on NFL TV viewership itself: Studies indicated that a person's viewership of NFL games increased by roughly 30 percent after he or she joined a fantasy league.

Consider the impact of digital formats on traditional products and the immediate worry is about how large the substitution or cannibalization will be. That comes from assuming that the product offered in digital and traditional formats has to be the same. Think creatively about how to differentiate the digital product from the traditional one—as with the case of NFL and NFL fantasy games—and you'll not only have created a great complement, but quite possibly a veritable gold mine. And that's no fantasy.

16
SPILLOVERS

WHO WANTS TO BE A MILLIONAIRE—IN INDIA

Complements are examples of positive product connections. But connections can arise in other ways. Zee TV, India's leading local network, learned about this the hard way.

In early 2000, nearly a decade after the Indian television market opened up to competition, Zee boasted an impressive fifteen of the top twenty prime-time TV programs and a 70 percent prime-time market share—numbers unheard-of in most markets around the world. A year later its advantage had completely disappeared. Why?

Zee was founded and financed by a veteran Indian entrepreneur and had enjoyed unprecedented success even while battling Star and Sony TV, rivals financed and owned by global multinationals. I visited Zee in October 1999 to understand the reasons for its success. Those were clear to its senior executives: Zee had started early and grown quickly. It was agile. It had a unique content strategy, airing Hindi-language programs right from the start, whereas Star and Sony combined Hindi shows with Hindi-dubbed English programs, such as *Baywatch*.

By 1999, Zee's strategy had paid off handsomely. It was the unquestioned market leader. It continued to move quickly, and learn continuously from viewer feedback: Every week, it received an incredible thirty thousand letters from them. And it was able to hire the best local talent. The organization's confidence was palpable.

The strategies of the three competing networks were not only different, they were intentional. While Zee looked toward preserving its leadership and profits with reasonably low-budget soaps, Star and Sony adopted a swing-for-the-fences approach: Look for a big hit, their senior team advocated—whether from Bollywood, expensive dramas, or cricket. Zee's executives viewed that as an act of desperation. One said, "Competition is heating up, but our overall program strength remains unassailable. Even if our competitors secure two or three top programs, it won't change things that much." It was an entirely reasonable, and evenhanded, response, one that you'd expect from most businesses.

Then in July 2000, something unexpected happened. Star launched the game show *Kaun Banega Crorepati* (*KBC*), a local Hindi version of the popular ABC program *Who Wants to Be a Millionaire*. *KBC* aired four times a week on the flagship channel Star Plus. Anchoring the show was Amitabh Bachchan, once Bollywood's most famous star, now making his first sustained appearance on television after years of declining big-screen popularity. The game prize of one crore rupees (about $230,000 at the time) was an audacious move in an emerging market. The show quickly rose to the top spot in prime-time ratings.

Star executives had expected *KBC* to do well, but not this well. For Zee's part, ceding the top spot to a rival network's program was perhaps inevitable one day. But what happened next stunned everyone.

KBC's regular placement and ratings meant that it very quickly commanded sixteen of the top 100 monthly prime-time slots. But, Star's success didn't stop here. Within a month—and with little immediate change to the rest of its lineup—Star captured nearly 50 of the top 100 prime-time slots. Within six months it had 80. *KBC*'s success had somehow spilled over to the rest of Star's lineup.

Figure 16 depicts this remarkable rise, and reversal of fortune, for Star TV.

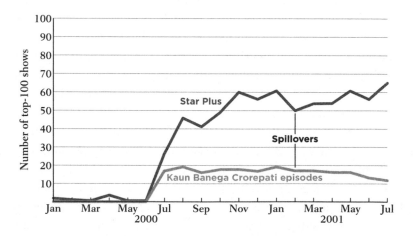

Figure 16: Market Share of Star Plus Channel, 2000–2001

One can understand that a single program brings in impressive profits for a network—that's, after all, what hits do. But how could one program change the fortunes of the *rest* of the network's program lineup? In other words, how does a single product create such a magical portfolio advantage? To understand this dynamic, let's start with some basic facts about TV viewing behavior.

Ask any TV executive, media scholar, or industry consultant about robust patterns in television viewing and the one most commonly mentioned is the following: Once a viewer tunes in to a program, he or she rarely leaves that network for the rest of the viewing session. Put more precisely, the probability that a viewer will watch a program after having watched the previous program on that network averages about 65 percent. This pattern of "sticking around" is long-standing. It wasn't particularly surprising in the 1980s, when it was first systematically measured: At that time it was tedious to switch programs, because viewers would have to get up from the proverbial couch to change channels, and they'd have to look at a printed guide to know what to switch to. What *is* surprising is that, three decades later, after new technologies (electronic program guides and remote controls) have made it easier to switch, relatively high percentages of people still stick around. Of course, there are differences between male and female viewers (men switch more), across times of day, across genres (switching is lower during dramas than sitcoms), and so on. But the basic fact remains: Viewers stick around.

What explains this somewhat bizarre fact? What "connects" the different programs on a network so that once viewers tune in to a program, they stick around to watch the others? There are at least four types of connections at work here. First, there's viewer inertia—referred to ceremoniously within the industry as the "lead-in effect." Tune in to one program and chances are you'll stay with that network during subsequent time slots because you're satisfied, or lazy, or can't find the remote. Second, there's cross-promotion: Networks often use advertising slots in one program to promote subsequent ones, partly at the expense of valuable prime-time commercial advertising revenues. This translates, again, into viewers tuning in to subsequent programs on a network after they've watched one there. Third, there's "program homogeneity": Networks often air similar programs in sequence, family sitcoms after family sitcoms, and so on. Finally, there's brand familiarity: A viewer who likes what a network generally offers is likely to stay tuned in.

It's not surprising that product connections like these exist. What is surprising is how large they are. In 1998, Ron Shachar (a former colleague of mine at Yale) and I sought to understand the magnitude of one of these connections, cross-promotions. At that time, the networks spent roughly one of every six minutes of commercial time on self-promotion. The opportunity cost in forgone commercial ad revenue was significant—larger than in most other industries. So we decided to examine how effective these self-promotions were.

Answering this seemingly simple question wasn't easy. It required precise data *for every viewer* on their viewing choices, combined with data on their exposure to network promotions. (For the first set of data, we relied on Nielsen. To create the second set, we hired an army of research associates who videotaped, watched, and coded every show on television for a period of time and then matched the resulting data with viewing choices to obtain viewer exposure to promos.) And we needed to consider other factors. One was viewer tastes—did someone watch *Seinfeld* because she had been exposed to a *Seinfeld* promo on *Frasier,* or simply because she liked both programs? There were also lead-in effects, differences in preferences among viewers, differences in attributes across shows, and so on.

We inserted more than 150 such factors into our model. We expected the resulting estimates to show that networks were leaving substantial money on the table by airing so many self-promotions in place of paid commercials. We were wrong.

A single exposure to a promotion increased a viewer's likelihood of watching that program by more than 40 percent. Additional exposures further increased viewership until about the fourth promo, after which viewership declined. Even accounting for the large opportunity cost of lost prime-time revenues, self-promotions (by virtue of their increasing ratings for the promoted program and *its* advertising revenues) were very profitable. The networks knew what they were doing—and all without access to the kind of viewer-level data we had.

This was one illustration of the magnitude of program connections. Similarly large effects were seen for other types of connections. Lead-in effects in television viewing, for example, were so dramatic that unknown programs like *Union Square* and *Veronica's Closet* (anyone remember them?) were consistently among the top ten weekly prime-time television programs. And this effect had nearly nothing to do with program content: It was simply because they preceded or followed popular shows like *Friends, Seinfeld,* or *ER* on NBC's Thursday night lineup (see Table 10).

TABLE 10. TOP-RANKED PROGRAMS IN PRIME TIME
FOR THE WEEK OF 1/5/98–1/11/98

Prime Time Ranking	Name of Program	Time Slot	Network	Rating Points
1	ER	Thursday 1/8 – 10:00 p	NBC	21.5/34
2	Seinfeld	Thursday 1/8 – 9:00 p	NBC	20.8/31
3	Veronica's Closet	Thursday 1/8 – 9:30 p	NBC	16.8/25
4	Touched by an Angel (R)	Sunday 1/11 – 8:00 p	CBS	15.8/24
5	Friends	Thursday 1/8 – 8:00 p	NBC	15.7/24
6	Dateline NBC – Monday	Monday 1/5 – 10:00 p	NBC	15.0/25
7	60 Minutes	Sunday 1/11 – 7:00 p	CBS	13.8/22
8	Union Square (R)	Thursday 1/8 – 8:30 p	NBC	12.9/19
9	X Files	Sunday 1/11 – 9:00 p	FOX	12.9/19
10	Frasier	Tuesday 1/6 – 9:00 p	NBC	12.7/19
11	20/20	Friday 1/9 – 10:00 p	ABC	12.3/21
12	Drew Carey Show	Wednesday 1/7 – 9:00 p	ABC	12.1/19
13	King of the Hill	Sunday 1/11 – 8:30 p	FOX	11.9/18
14	Sunday Night Movie – The Fugitive	Sunday 1/11 – 8:30 p	NBC	11.9/18
15	People's Choice Awards	Sunday 1/11 – 9:00 p	CBS	11.9/18
16	Simpsons	Sunday 1/11 – 8:00 p	FOX	11.9/18
17	20/20 – Monday	Monday 1/5 – 9:00 p	ABC	11.7/17
18	FOX NFC Championship – Green Bay at San Francisco	Sunday 1/11 – 7:10 p	FOX	11.7/20
19	Home Improvement	Tuesday 1/6 – 9:00 p	ABC	11.5/17
20	Law and Order	Wednesday 1/7 – 10:00 p	NBC	11.5/20

There are an estimated 98 million television households in the USA. A single ratings point represents 1%, or 980,000 households. Share is the percentage of television sets in use tuned to a specific program. Source: Modified from 1998, Nielsen Media Research

Combine the connections, and the implications are profound: A single program, through its domino effects, could have a disproportionate effect on a network's success.

Years later Uday Shankar, Star's subsequent CEO, described the impact of *KBC* to me: "*KBC* worked as a program because of its unique combination of glamour and greed. But what *really* worked wonders was what we were able to do on the back of it."

Early on Star had made few changes to the rest of its lineup. Yet ratings for its other programs soared. Then Star introduced two slickly produced dramas that also aired four days a week—and then a third show, and a fourth. "It created a gigantic assembly line of very addictive stories," Shankar noted. Bollywood traditionally featured tragedies. The new soaps turned that formula on its head and made household stories glamorous, as "the hapless housewife gave way to the assertive one, and connected really with the emerging aspirations of households." In summary, Shankar noted:

> *KBC* by itself didn't change the fortunes of Star. On the back of it Star ratcheted up its premium content and created a winner-take-all dynamic. *KBC* was really, at its heart, just a tremendous tool to market the rest of our content initiative. *That* is what changed the competitive dynamic forever.

Star had gone from network irrelevance to near-total domination. Zee's fall was equally dramatic. But Star's dramatic turnaround, and Zee's fall from grace, had resulted not from the strength of just one program. Good content was merely the trigger; connections were what made the success spread.

THE IMPLICATIONS OF SPILLOVERS

Spillovers are another type of product connection. But they aren't like software and hardware, or complements like those—where one product without the other is useless. Here they are generated by customer behavior, not product features.

TV spillovers arise from viewers' habits, or because their tastes match a particular network's profile, or, increasingly, because they're overwhelmed by choice. Whatever the cause, the result is the same: Viewers stick to a network once they find a program they like.

Behavioral and informational spillovers are pervasive beyond television, too. They have large implications for many current phenomena and can clarify many puzzles.

The Price of Content

Increases in the price of content are central to the future of TV. Ask any network executive or pay TV operator about the challenge they face and they'll start by pointing to the seemingly outrageous prices required to acquire sports content. These drive up overall programming costs, which increase subscription prices, making pay TV more and more expensive as a product and less and less sustainable as a business.

Figure 17 shows the near-continuous two-decade rise in the price of the National Football League rights, which by 2015 had ballooned to more than $6 billion a year. Why do companies like "hit" programs if they're so costly? Some obvious answers: Hits draw in large numbers of viewers, they offer top-quality content (some may disagree that's the case), they generate enormous revenue, and they are far more profitable than other products.

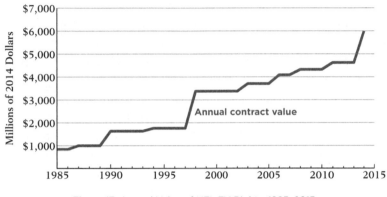

Figure 17: Annual Value of NFL TV Rights, 1985–2015

These explanations are all tautological: By definition, a hit is more popular than other programs and will command greater revenues. More than that, these explanations cannot reconcile one of the most puzzling things about NFL rights: Prices continuously increased for nearly three decades despite the fact that regular-season viewership for the NFL games was roughly the same in 2014 as it was in 1988 (Figure 18).

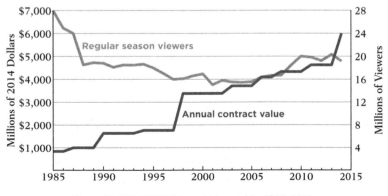

Figure 18: NFL TV Rights and Viewership, 1985–2015

The NFL isn't alone in this respect. NBC is thought to have paid out its entire annual profits in 1997, when renegotiating the rights for just one program, *ER*. ESPN commands more than $6 a subscriber from cable operators—more than three times that of any other channel—even though its ratings are barely higher than the next most popular channel. (And in 2014 ESPN wasn't even the most watched cable network—it came in only third, after USA Network and Disney Channel.) Tiger Woods received as much as 50 percent of all appearance fees for the tournaments he entered in recent years, even after his ranking had declined considerably. Radio stations and platforms often pay out sums approaching their entire profits to popular hosts. And for other professional sports leagues, the divergence between the price of rights and TV ratings is even more dramatic.

The most compelling explanation for the "economics of superstars" came from economist Sherwin Rosen in 1981. Rosen was trying to rationalize why talented individuals, particularly those in the entertainment business, often command payouts that appear disproportionate. He traced the reasons to two features of these markets: "imperfect substitution" between products (we'd rather have one album by our favorite singer than three by a different artist) and "joint consumption" of a product (a single artist can reach thousands or millions of listeners simultaneously—unlike other products, like, say, cars). Take either of these features in isolation and you can rationalize differences in incomes across hits and other products. Put them together and you get superstar effects.

Rosen's theory pointed to factors that create winner-take-all payouts. It also explains why superstar incomes have increased over time—new technologies have made it easier to reach ever-larger audiences at once. But it doesn't explain hits like the NFL, *ER,* or ESPN, where the puzzle is not why they command impressive sums but why those sums far exceed what their popularity or direct profitability would justify—why payouts far exceed demand. Rosen's world was a world where prices match demand; where, ultimately, payouts to superstars simply reflect higher demand for them.

So why *do* sports rights increase despite flat or declining ratings? To understand the dynamic, it's useful to look at how it all started.

In 1993 one of the great negotiations in broadcast TV unfurled, one that would alter the competitive landscape forever. The broadcast rights for NFL games were up for renegotiation, and conditions weren't favorable for the NFL to match its prior deal. Just four years earlier the three major networks (ABC, CBS, and NBC) had paid the NFL roughly $220 million a year each for its three packages—the American Football Conference (AFC) games, the National Football Conference (NFC) games, and *Monday Night Football*. Now each network said that it had suffered losses on the prior deal. NFL owners thought they'd be lucky to match the previous contract sums.

However, the market had changed in one significant respect: a fourth network (Fox Broadcasting Corporation, or FBC) had launched seven years earlier and was gaining traction. On December 7, 1993, Fox senior executives—David Hill, the unrestrainedly free-spirited and iron-willed sports head at Fox, accompanied by Rupert Murdoch of parent company News Corporation—made a presentation to the NFL about why Fox was the right home for its games. And they accompanied it with a $300 million a year offer for broadcast rights to NFC games—40 percent more than the soon-to-expire deal.

In the ensuing flurry of negotiations, NBC locked up the AFC package for $230 million a year. Fox executives reacted swiftly, upping their bid to $395 million. It was all too much for CBS, which bowed out. Fox began assembling a sports division and eventually became the fourth major U.S. broadcast network. It was the first major network to successfully establish itself as a rival to the big three networks in more than fifty years.

High costs for premium content are not surprising, by themselves. What was surprising was the dramatic increase in rights, coming as it did against the backdrop of an increasingly fragile broadcast network business. Using estimates of the direct advertising revenues from NFL games, analysts estimated that Fox would lose roughly $600 million on the four-year deal. Why would a network carefully built around a low-cost model (as Fox had been) give it all away in one go? Why would its parent company, generally averse to corporate extravagance and with a reputation for lean cost management, encourage the offer? The answer wasn't that Fox's content strategy for sports was somehow unique—the NFL games under Fox were exactly the same as they'd been under CBS. It lay in the program connections Fox was looking to create and exploit.

One involved affiliate carriage. Fox, despite its recent growth, had no presence in some markets around the country. The NFL deal, Fox's Hill noted, "forced cable operators to put Fox on the air. It established us in 100% of the markets—even in places like Nebraska, where we couldn't get carriage earlier. That could never have happened without football." Another concerned the lead-in effect. Table 10 shows the NFL's impact on Fox's other Sunday night programs that followed it: Shows including *The Simpsons* and *The X-Files* were catapulted into the prime-time elite. There was also brand impact: Many viewers who had been unaware of the network now looked to it as a viable source of content.

Beyond this, there was Fox's promotional strategy: Draw in millions of NFL viewers and aggressively cross-promote the rest of the lineup. For more than a decade after the NFL bid, even as other networks lost viewers to cable, Fox's ratings held steady.

Look at the value of the NFL as its direct advertising revenues, as most analysts did, and you'd think Fox overpaid. Add up these different program connections and you'd see this clearly wasn't the case. Years later, even rival networks would concede their mistake; at CBS, they would acknowledge that they'd "vastly underestimated the impact of the NFL on *60 Minutes*." (Figure 19 illustrates this impact.)

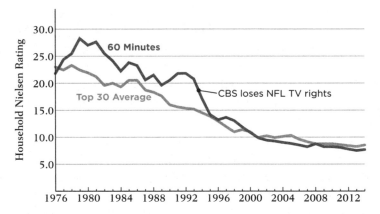

Figure 19: Ratings of *60 Minutes* Over Time. (Household Nielsen Rating represents the percentage of television-owning households in the United States that were tuned into the particular program. Top 30 Average represents the average Household Nielsen Rating of the 30 shows that year with the highest ratings.)

Fox emerged as a viable fourth broadcast network not because it understood sports content better than the other networks. It understood the business of connections better.

Four years later at the negotiating table, CBS reentered the NFL fray, bidding $500 million for AFC broadcast rights. Sean McManus, then president of CBS Sports, said, "We are not going to lose money on this deal, because of the promotional value and all the other things this brings to the network." This time NBC was left out. The NFL's new four-year television deal was valued at $17 billion, making it the largest ever in sports broadcasting. And it occurred during a period when broadcast viewership was shrinking, cable viewership was rising, and alternative forms of entertainment were exploding.

The dynamic of spillovers was also crucial to NBC's deal for *ER*. In 1998, just a few weeks after losing the NFL rights, NBC renegotiated the rights to the show for $12 million per episode—1,200 percent more than its previous price. Although *ER* was the number one show on television, analysts estimated that the deal would erase all NBC's annual profits. But to NBC, the logic behind its decision was clear: *Without* the program and its spillover benefits, the network probably stood to lose its entire profit stream anyway.

The phenomenon of apparently disproportionate investment in hits extends beyond TV. In radio, Howard Stern benefited from the same sort of logic. In 2004, two years after launch and after various efforts to attract listeners had failed, the struggling subscription station Sirius settled on what seemed a last-ditch effort: Stern. He was the most popular radio talk show personality at the time. Even so, Sirius's offer was unprecedented: $500 million for five years—or, as one analyst calculated, more than $2,000 a minute.

During the next three years, Stern drew in listeners—some 3.3 million of them. As for the direct payoff to Sirius? With each subscriber paying about $150 a year, annual revenue skyrocketed to $450 million. The spillover benefits were even more impressive, as Stern drew awareness to the platform and pulled in listeners for Sirius's other programs as well. By 2010, right after its merger with XM radio, Sirius had nearly twenty million subscribers and nearly $3 billion in revenues; it thereafter embarked on a run of hundreds of millions of dollars in annual profits. Stern's cost had more than been worth it.

Sometimes the large sums of money paid out for hits, bestsellers, superstar talent, and celebrities can appear farcical. But not always. Popular assets command dollar payouts that often far exceed their direct popularity, yet simultaneously result in massive benefits for the paying firm as well. They do this because of spillover effects.

To circle back to the start of the discussion: Spillovers were what triggered the increase in the price of sports more than twenty years ago, and they continue to work in its favor to this day. As television audiences fragment across programs and channels, driving down the ratings for most prime-time programs, and as technology has allowed viewers to watch according to their calendar, not the network's, sports programs have been insulated from the pain, largely because they are a "must-see-live" proposition. Watch a drama one hour later and you don't lose much. Watch a sports event an hour later and you might as well have not watched it at all. And that matters, because audience size affects spillovers: The more viewers a program can draw, the larger the magnitude of spillovers that result from it. That's in large part why networks are willing to pay out more and more for sports over time.

Relative scarcity helps, too. Two decades ago networks could choose between a dozen programs capable of attracting ten million viewers. Today only sports programs command those numbers. Add the growing number of downstream bidders as well—cable networks like ESPN and TNT have entered the picture—and it's easy to see why prices are through the roof.

And the connections don't stop there. Beyond program spillovers, consider the complements to sports viewing. High-definition TVs are one: The better the sound and picture quality, the greater the enjoyment from watching sports. Online fantasy sports and gaming are others.

Try to explain the explosion in sports rights, cable fees, and superstar incomes by looking at direct popularity and you'd be hard-pressed to explain the phenomenon. Hits matter not only because of their direct revenue streams but also because of large indirect follow-on streams. They command *apparently* disproportionate sums not because they are popular assets but because of the spillovers they create across products and the complements that increase their value.

In summary, popularity doesn't explain apparent overinvestment in hits; connections do.

17
GETTING NOTICED

A challenge endemic to virtually any business today is when a company has created a new product and is trying to get marketplace traction. This could be a book, magazine, TV program, or movie. It could be a new car model, website, financial product, or line of clothing. In the past, there was a simple answer to the problem of getting noticed: spend more. Increasingly, that doesn't work—since everyone's trying to do the same, the result is cacophony and clutter.

More effective, and increasingly common, are approaches that rely on connections. Rather than spend more, it pays to connect to known products. Such "informational spillovers" are paying off in a range of settings.

FEEDING OFF A TIGER

Few sports personalities have commanded the drawing power of Tiger Woods. From 1998 to 2008, Woods played in roughly seventeen tournaments a year—less than half the number of events on the U.S. PGA tour, and far fewer than his top peers did. The difference in TV ratings between Woods and non-Woods tournaments was astounding: nearly 100 percent.

Appearance fees are another indicator of star power. In 2011, when Woods had the lowest ranking of his career, the Dubai Open invited him to play in the season-opening event. All the stars were there, including Luke Donald, Rory McIlroy, and Lee Westwood, ranked first, second, and third in the world. Event organizers paid out $5 million in appearance fees—and 50 percent was estimated to have gone to Woods.

It is tempting to think that most of the benefits of Tiger's presence ac-

crued to him alone. Not so. For more than a decade, higher ratings benefited the entire sport. During Woods's career, they meant higher advertising
rates for networks and larger corporate sponsorships for the PGA Tour.
Both increases in revenue were funneled back into larger prize money for
events, which benefited every top golfer: The average award grew by about
400 percent during Woods's career. Rival Phil Mickelson, whose own mer-
curial career was often in the shadow of Woods, observed, "There's nobody in the game who has benefited more from Tiger than myself. He
drove the purses up. He drove up the TV ratings. He increased the marketing expectations. He raised endorsement values. Nobody has been able
to capitalize from that as much as I have."

Lesser players benefited, too. Jay Williamson earned more than
$5.5 million in prize money despite never winning a PGA event—largely
because his career coincided with Tiger Woods's. Even when criticizing
Woods's personal indiscretions in a *New York Times* interview, Williamson spoke of the positive spillovers from Woods's career: "I certainly
don't live like a king, but I do have three kids in private school, and that's
probably a direct result of Tiger." Another observer noted, "In 1996, only
nine players on the tour earned $1 million. In 2009, ninety-one golfers
did."

The Woods halo extended to his endorsers, too. In 1996, Nike struck a
five-year, $40 million endorsement deal with Woods, raising many eye-
brows and questions about whether it had overpaid. A 2013 study conducted by three Carnegie Mellon researchers found that the endorsement
increased sales of Nike golf balls by nearly 9.9 million units from 2000 to
2010, drove prices up by roughly 2.5 percent, and increased profits by
$103 million. Put differently, more than half of the $181 million endorsement fees paid over the course of the decade were recovered from U.S.
golf ball sales alone.

The Woods narrative is notable not only as an example of how large the
positive connections from "hits" can be, but also because it reminds us
that spillovers can be negative—and with results that are just as great.
During 2008–09, when Woods was sidelined with a knee injury, TV ratings for the final rounds of events he normally played in dropped 47 percent. In 2009 networks charged 30 percent less for ads during tournaments
Woods did not play in. And researchers calculated that his sponsors
collectively lost more than 2 percent of their market value, or roughly
$10 billion, in the thirteen trading days after the scandal involving him
erupted later that year.

HELP YOURSELF: THE EFFECTS OF BACKWARD SPILLOVERS

In June 2003 Dan Brown's newly released novel, *The Da Vinci Code*, jumped to number one on the *New York Times* bestseller list, staying there for several months. During the next six years, Brown wrote no new books—but still had three more appear on the bestseller lists. The reason for this strange fact? Brown's three previously published, but originally modestly selling, titles—*Angels and Demons, Deception Point,* and *Digital Fortress*—were rereleased by the publisher Pocket Books in the wake of *Da Vinci Code*'s success. Now they quickly rose to the top as well.

Brown's success after *The Da Vinci Code* did not come from new content, but from "backward spillovers," in which today's hit draws attention to yesterday's content. We see them in other markets, too. In an intriguing study of music artists, Ken Hendricks and Alan Sorensen, economists at the University of Texas–Austin and Stanford, respectively, at the time, found that an artist's hit album increased sales of previously released albums by the same artist (also referred to as "catalog" albums), often by very large amounts. Figure 20, reproduced from their article, illustrates these spillovers for two bands, one relatively obscure (alternative rock band Bloodhound Gang) and the other more popular (hard rock band Foo Fighters). In each case, the release of the band's second and third albums (which were hits) increased the sales of their *prior* album, in some cases significantly.

Hendricks and Sorensen examined these spillover effects for more than 300 artists' sales from 1993 to 2002. The results were equally striking in the larger sample. For artists whose second album was their first hit, weekly sales for the first album increased, on average, by more than 100 percent. The researchers also found that increases tended to be far lower for artists who were *already* popular, and they were lower in an artist's home region—suggesting that spillovers worked by increasing awareness of artists among those who didn't know them, rather than by simply persuading all fans to buy more albums. Spillovers played an informational role.

In a subsequent, fascinating part of their analysis, Hendricks and Sorensen used their results to assess the relative importance of spillovers in two scenarios: when consumers hadn't been fully aware of artists, and when they had been. When consumers were "fully informed," hits created substantially fewer spillover sales. This finding underscores the primary role through which spillovers work: They increase consumer awareness of related products.

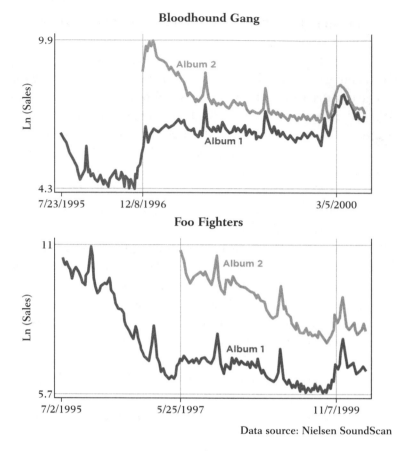

Figure 20 (reproduced from Hendricks and Sorenson, 2009): "Backward spill-overs" for two bands. These graphs show the logarithm of album sales over time (measured in weeks) for the artists' first and second albums. The vertical lines indicate the release dates of albums 2 and 3. The graphs illustrate how the release of a new album tends to cause a sales increase for previous albums by the same artist.

Few incidents better exemplify the importance of informational spill-overs than what occurred in the summer of 2013. "Robert Galbraith" published a new book, *The Cuckoo's Calling*. Despite positive reviews, the book sold only 1,500 print copies worldwide during its first two months. Then, on July 15, 2013, the pseudonymous author's identity was revealed: Galbraith was J. K. Rowling, creator of the Harry Potter series. Sales increased by 156,866 percent in the first day alone, propelling the book to the top of the bestseller lists. In a month they reached 1.1 million copies.

Produce good content and you might receive praise. Publish the same content under a familiar name and the connection will make it a block-buster.

Although Rowling-esque experiments are rare, the strategy of *piggy-backing* on familiar names is widespread. Even the most traditional arenas of big-money marketing—movies and television—are shifting their ap-proach. In 1981 just three of the top-ten-grossing Hollywood movies were sequels or adaptations; in 2011, all ten were. Roughly 20 percent of all major Hollywood studio releases are now sequels or prequels to success-ful first runs. "Investments in franchises" is the flattering explanation. "Lack of creativity" is the less flattering one. The truth is that connections allow newer products to benefit from familiar ones.

Television networks increasingly are adopting a similar, but less publi-cized, strategy—not by the use of sequels per se, but by putting popular actors, or familiar characters, into new shows. *Seinfeld* spawned four shows from its original five characters; *Cheers* had one of the most suc-cessful spin-offs in TV history, *Frasier*. From 2005 to 2012, two-thirds of network programs either included actors from previously successful shows or were remakes of earlier programs (think *Charlie's Angels* and *Hawaii Five-O*, whose remakes were at opposite ends of the success spectrum).

When informational spillovers are taken to the logical extreme, it raises an intriguing possibility: For an extreme version of piggybacking, one reli-ant entirely on spillovers rather than content, you could attach someone else's name to your content. My colleagues and I recently ran an experi-ment to examine the impact of names, interchanging the names of media publishers and seeing what happened.

We asked 700 people to read an article on Greece's financial crisis and its effect on the European Union and to rate it on "editorial quality," "crit-ical insight," and "quality of language." The article combined political analysis and historical allegory, invoking the myth of the Augean stables to describe Greece's predicament.

The quality readers assigned to the article was just over 5, on average, out of 10. Some gave it ratings of 8 or higher; others panned it with a 1 or a 2. Here's the important variable: Readers were randomly assigned one of three websites to read it on (Figures 21a, 21b, and 21c). A third read it on a "white page," with no source. A third read the article on a site made to look like *The Huffington Post* (where the article originally appeared). And a third read it on one that looked like *The Economist*.

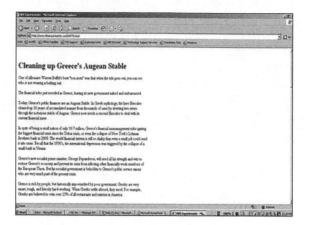

Figure 21a: Article appears on unbranded website

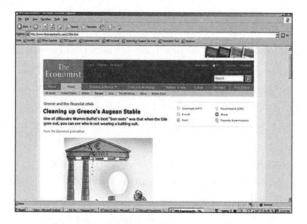

Figure 21b: Article appears on *The Economist*

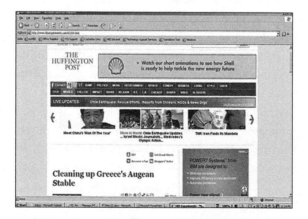

Figure 21c: Article appears on *The Huffington Post*

More than a third of those who read the "unbranded" story gave the article a 4 or worse. And 22 percent of the *"Huffington Post"* readers gave similarly low marks. Less than 10 percent of the *"Economist"* readers did so. The content was identical in every case.

TABLE 11. THE EFFECT OF NAMES ON PERCEIVED EDITORIAL QUALITY: A RANDOMIZED EXPERIMENT			
	Article appears on:		
Reader Rating of Editorial Quality	Unbranded Website	*Economist* Look-alike	*Huffington Post* Look-alike
1–4	34%	10%	23%
5–7	47%	45%	45%
8–10	19%	45%	32%
Average	5.4	6.9	6.1

Piggybacking on others' names is now commonplace in digital arenas, where the challenge of getting noticed is great indeed. It's sometimes used by unscrupulous hackers or lazy "entrepreneurs," as with same-name applications on the App Store. (Amusingly, an app ironically titled "A Beautiful Mess" spawned seven clones within a few weeks—little had its founders realized how apt the name would prove.) It can be a viable strategy for drawing attention to otherwise unnoticed creative talent. A common route for aspiring new musicians, perfectly legal under copyright law, is publishing YouTube "covers"—their versions of popular songs by famous artists. A few years ago an artist named Alex Goot uploaded his first YouTube cover album, honorably titling it *Songs I Wish I Wrote*. It included remakes of Train's "Hey, Soul Sister" and Michael Jackson's "Beat It." By 2015 Goot had uploaded more than fifty more covers on YouTube, and his efforts had paid off. He had his own YouTube channel, which drew in more than 2.3 million subscribers, and he was regularly featured among lists of "Top Ten YouTube artists." And how are these young artists monetizing their efforts? They're relying on concerts, of course.

SPILLOVERS ACROSS FORMATS

How Digital Helps Print

Informational spillovers are relevant not only for promoting content of the same format, but *across* formats, too. Most common is the impact of digital content on print success. For the longest time, news publishers viewed this spillover in negative terms. Put your content on the Web and it will cannibalize your print sales. Improve your digital offering and it will undermine your core product. It's a mindset that Pieter du Toit now believes is profoundly wrong.

Du Toit is the news editor of *Beeld,* one of the largest Afrikaans-language daily newspapers in South Africa. He recently told me how one event in February 2013 "fundamentally changed our entire approach to news—and the spillovers from digital to print. It was due to Oscar."

Oscar Pistorius is a South African Paralympic track champion. A double amputee at eleven months old, he carved out an impressive career, breaking world records in the Paralympic Games and eventually participating in the 2012 London Olympics. But on Valentine's Day in 2013, *Beeld* broke the news that Pistorius had shot and killed his girlfriend, South African model Reeva Steenkamp.

Beeld had been the first to hear of the story that morning. Once it established the credibility of the report, it had to decide: publish first on digital, or wait until the next print cycle? In a sense, there was no choice: It was obvious the story wouldn't stay under wraps for long. But they'd never broken a big story online. "Our website had very much been an afterthought to the print product," du Toit recounted. "It was loaded with print stories from the previous day."

When *Beeld* published the story at eight that morning—on Twitter, no less—"the world came crashing down on us. The exposure it created for us from the very beginning continues still to this day. But the impact went far beyond digital. Print sales jumped 30 percent the first week after Oscar, which was unheard-of." (See Figure 22.) The reason? There was awareness—break a story in digital, and it was logical for people to buy the paper the next day to get deeper coverage: "They want the insight, the firsthand account," du Toit noted. There was brand impact. And there were additional benefits, as *Beeld* became a go-to outlet for leads, whistle-blowers, and sources. Those were the positive spillovers to print that came from being first, and from breaking the story on digital.

Until that event, *Beeld* had been inclined to ask, What are we going to lose by publishing on Twitter? rather than, What are we going to gain? Oscar "changed our mindset and took away our fear," du Toit said.

The positive spillover also affected the culture of the newsroom. *Beeld* reoriented to be digital first, with a dedicated team writing for the Web rather than having the site recycle print stories. It changed its workflow

Net Print Sales

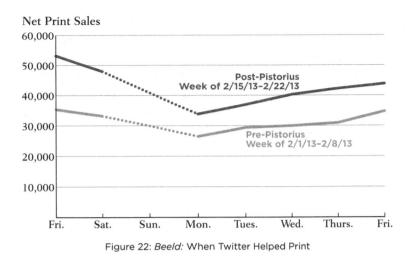

Figure 22: *Beeld:* When Twitter Helped Print

for the day. The newsroom began planning around traffic spikes on the website rather than the once-a-day print product. It updated stories throughout the day rather than writing just once.

Beeld's traditional mindset was familiar: one that saw negative spillovers instead of positive ones, one that had led most content businesses to similarly eschew the question of beneficial connections across the two formats and to obsess about not damaging either. But the mindset is changing, slowly but surely, at papers around the world.

How Print Helps Digital

It's tempting to think that when it comes to driving awareness, digital formats are many times more effective than print. It's also tempting to think that spillover benefits flow only from digital to print. Neither is true. Consider the following example.

Most people are by now aware of E. L. James's erotic romance *Fifty Shades of Grey*. Few know how it became so popular. The book initially came out in a digital format, where it experienced modest success: sales of several thousand copies. Then Anne Messitte of Vintage (the paperback division of Knopf) offered James a contract for a print version—a move that, superficially, made little sense. "The skeptics said that digital already has a lead," Messitte told me. "You won't sell too many in print. And people won't want to be seen with it."

But print has some advantages when it comes to driving awareness. It's easier to be noticed in big-box retailers like Walmart or Costco, in super-markets, and in airports. It's easier to share with others. It's easier to give as a gift. And Vintage carefully choreographed the book's distribution, merchandising, and publicity, getting James onto television shows as the print edition came out. The result of moving to print? Book sales went from several thousand e-copies to ninety million print copies in a year—making it the bestselling paperback of all time, and dramatically increasing e-sales too.

The content hadn't changed. The format had. And in this case, spill-overs ran from print to digital rather than the other way round.

THE PUZZLE OF VERTICAL INTEGRATION

Vertical integration refers to the combination of content and distribution. The idea has long been a lightning rod in the entertainment industry. The recent rush was triggered by vertical combinations between TV studios and broadcast networks—20th Century Fox and Fox Broadcasting Corporation in 1986, ABC and Disney in 1996—and continued with megamergers since: AOL–Time Warner in 2000, Comcast–NBC Universal in 2009. Oddly, just as vertical mergers began finding favor with industry players and their bankers, criticism of them deepened. Why?

Consider the canonical scenario: a distributor or a TV network buys a production studio. The conventional arguments for vertical integration go something like this: When a distributor buys upstream content, it can better control programming costs (if a cable operator bought ESPN, it could avoid continual renegotiations over subscriber charges). It can guarantee access to the producer's hits without engaging in price wars (when Disney bought Pixar, it gained access to its animation films without having to bid for them). And it can share the risk borne by the studio when searching for hits.

Every time you read about a vertical merger in the newspaper, you'll hear one or all of these arguments. But none are valid.

That's because of what economists call "zero-sum transfers." Think about the argument pertaining to access to a studio's hits. There's a nagging problem: Limiting downstream price competition might help the distributor, but it hurts the studio, preventing it from selling a hit for a higher sum. Conversely, guaranteeing shelf space for content that proves a dud comes at the distributor's expense: It could have put material from another studio there for greater profit.

In other words, gains for one party in the transaction are offset by losses to the other. There's no net gain from integrating, after all.

The same criticism applies to arguments about keeping content prices in check. Control the price of content by fiat once the distributor purchases the content producer, and the distributor's gains come directly at the expense of the producer's profits, which suffer. It's another zero-sum transfer.

The flaw in the logic of vertical integration is simple: Transferring money from one pocket to another doesn't increase your cash. Yet it's an argument that most proponents of vertical integration repeatedly miss.

The logic of zero-sum transfers implies that the value of content in a vertically integrated entity should be no different than that in a nonintegrated one. However the relationship is structured—whether producer and distributor are merged into a single entity or contract at arm's length—the content decisions should be the same: Hit programs should always be kept on the air, duds always taken off. Zero-sum logic suggests, then, that vertical integration brings no benefit other than increasing the power and influence of an acquirer. This is the reason for skepticism about integration, for why in practice it is more likely to destroy rather than increase shareholder value.

There are exceptions. Consider a setting where both the content provider and distributor have asomething unique to offer. Then, we might observe what's called the "double markup problem": the content provider marks up the price of its content to capture value from the distributor, who in turn marks it up again when reselling the content to the end user. The result is perverse: Each party, pricing to gain at the expense of *its* immediate buyer, ignores that the end price for consumers is excessively high, reducing both overall demand *and* the profits for each party. Integration can pay off in that case. An integrated firm by charging one markup rather than two, not only expands its profits by increasing demand, it helps consumers too. And that's no longer zero-sum. A recent study of vertical integration in cable television found just this effect: When cable operators acquire regional sports networks, prices fall by around 18%, making everyone better off.

Vertical integration can create value in other cases too—but you need to dig deeper into content quality and what drives it.

Content quality is a mysterious thing. Sometimes you know immediately whether you have a hit or a dud on your hands. But far more often, content quality isn't revealed instantaneously and objectively. Understanding what works and what doesn't takes time. Audiences might get drawn into a program gradually, over a season. Some episodes work better than others. Word of mouth kicks in at unpredictable times. Awareness increases.

And that's where distributors can play a major role. They can give content better time slots. They can heavily promote it. They can keep it on the air rather than kill it at the first sign of trouble—they're invested in it, after all, especially given the profits that can come from long-term success and lucrative syndication rights. In other words, distributors can shape quality. These considerations don't apply to hits or duds—distributors' treatment should not vary according to whether or not they owned them. But they apply to everything else—or, roughly 90 percent of all content.

A study of vertical integration in the broadcast television industry found precisely this. The 1990s were a good time to examine this issue: During the prior decade integration had increased, so that most networks had come to own roughly 50 percent of the programs they aired. The author (a Ph.D. student at Northwestern University) gathered information on all the programs aired on the four major networks during the decade—when they aired, what their ratings were, and, crucially, who owned them. He then examined one aspect of distributors' effect on content success—their decisions about whether to renew programs for another season.

For programs at the extreme ends of quality distribution—the hits and the duds—there was, predictably, no difference in renewal probabilities. For the rest, ownership resulted in higher renewal rates. They weren't dramatically higher—5–10% on average—but there was a real difference.

And that's not accounting for the other ways networks could nurture content they owned—by placing it next to more established programs (see *Veronica's Closet* and *Friends*), or promoting it to viewers drawn there.

If you view vertical integration as a way for a distributor to acquire well-known content or gain access to an established property—often the rationale touted for such deals—you'll probably be disappointed, since it's unclear why the benefits couldn't be obtained at arm's length. If you view it as a means of nurturing lesser-known content and bolstering its odds of success, the picture changes.

The benefits of integration in such cases aren't in acquiring great content—they're in promoting lesser-known content by piggybacking on established content. They come from product connections.

Fifty Shades of Piggybacking

Vertical integration isn't the only form of piggybacking in TV. Channel bundling—when content providers offer all-or-nothing deals to distributors—is another practice whereby providers use popular channels as bargaining chips to gain carriage of lesser-known ones.

One reason cited to support bundling is that popular channels subsidize others. But that logic is backward (and the notion that unprofitable, unpopular channels would survive for long is unconvincing). The reason ESPN was valuable to parent Disney wasn't just its monthly subscription fees but its leverage in getting distributors to carry secondary channels (such as ESPN2, SOAPNet, and the Family Channel) in the hope some would become winners.

Discussions of digital technologies and their effects on the TV market resound with words like *democratization, fragmentation,* and *à la carte*. As digital capabilities become more widespread, you would think it would be pretty easy to establish a new channel. Look at the television market, on the other hand, and you see something quite different: In fact only six companies own the vast majority of all television channels. The reason is not that it's hard for a cable network to get produced; it's hard for a new one to get noticed. That's why content companies are increasingly relying on a portfolio approach, rather than a product-by-product one.

Sometimes, even more desperate measures are required to get new products noticed. News Corporation launched Fox News in 1996, when it was thought that the cable news market was saturated—three 24/7 news networks were already on-air, along with four broadcast networks. Cable operators had no appetite for an unknown news channel. In New York City—the country's largest media market—Time Warner Cable was particularly intransigent in refusing carriage. News Corporation's response was to charge negative prices: Rather than have the operator pay to carry the channel, it offered to "pay to play"—at a cost of $10 for every subscriber. The bet was that once the channel got popular, they could reverse the fee structure.

Content bundling is like taking a stick to the distributor. Pay to play is a carrot.

Fox News didn't stop there in trying to get viewers. It made another piggyback move, this time off major news events: Success came not just from targeting a different set of viewers than the other providers, but also from how it handled such events—the Monica Lewinsky scandal, the presidential elections, and the Iraq War—in its early years. Each time one of these events occurred, Fox would draw in new viewers—and build awareness for how its coverage was different, so that even after the event was over, some viewers stuck around.

This approach is not confined to companies with unproven track records and small marketing budgets. Tencent and Schibsted—hardly digital pushovers—relied on similar piggybacking strategies to promote their new Web properties, recognizing that in a world where 150,000 websites are created every day, it's hard to stand out.

When Tencent decided to launch an online news portal in China, it was five years late to the game: Its rival Sina already had hundreds of millions of viewers. Caitlyn Chen, editor-in-chief of Tencent's Online Media Group, described the difference in approach, one that seemed familiar: "Our focus was on winning the news battle around big events." Some were known in advance—the Beijing Olympics, the soccer World Cup, the Shanghai Expo, the March Congress every year. Others were not—the Japan earthquake, the Gansu school bus accident. "Those are the times you can reach large numbers of new users. If you can draw them in to your coverage during those events, many don't leave—even after the event's gone." Piggybacking on "big events" seems attractive in principle. But how to pull it off? Chen's team would enter into contracts with athletes for exclusive interviews during sporting events; they'd leverage the fact that most everyone in China—athletes, celebrities, businesspersons, and political leaders—had an account on one of Tencent's platforms (its Twitter-type microblog Weibo, its popular IM Qq, or, later, WeChat); they'd cross-promote heavily; they'd assign additional resources during these events; and, for scheduled events, they'd start coverage not just when the event occurred, but weeks before it. The result? Within a short period of time, they'd caught up with Sina, then overtook it.

By piggybacking on the large daily audiences for its core properties ("traffic machines," the company now calls them), Schibsted parlayed its success in online news and classifieds into ancillary digital venture growth. Take Schibsted's Blocket, its leading classifieds site in Sweden. Selling ad space to another large-volume site was traditionally considered the easiest way to generate ad revenue. As online ad prices fell, Schibsted discovered another way. The same ad space was worth far more to a site selling a complementary product. Sverre Munck, head of international classifieds, described the difference to me: "The ad space on Blocket's auto vertical is worth roughly $7 per 1,000 impressions to a site like *Aftonbladet,* our own news portal. The same space is worth far more to a comparison site for secured loans: Every lead they send to a bank is worth six or seven dollars."

On the face of it, the idea was simple: Promote a complement. But getting traction wasn't just a question of reshuffling ad space across sites; it required "intelligent integration."

> Let's say you've clicked five times on a used Volvo, so there's a presumption you want to purchase that car. We'd take the price of the car as presented on the ad, put it into a small calculator with a picture of the car, and provide information in the ad to let the person know what the repayment schedule would be if they bought the car, and where they could get a loan for it. We'd also allow the user to provide information in the ad, for example about the loan size they were looking for, by dragging a simple scale. The conversion rates turned out to be an order of magnitude higher if you got this right.

Intelligent integration isn't merely targeting to the right user—or knowing whom to send the ad to. It requires tailoring the ad copy itself to individual needs. And this requires not only data sharing but experimentation.

"Advertisers had not yet realized the potential of what they could do with a dynamic partnering relationship rather than just a purchased banner ad," Carl-Nicolai Wessmann, the project manager for Group Strategy, told me. "So we ran our own experiments, which showed that conversion rates could increase threefold. Buy a car and there's a loan and insurance. Buy electronics and there are price comparison sites. This led us to rethink the core of what we do in the classifieds space and explore how to create an entirely separate business focusing on related products." The resulting business was called a traffic fund. The fund manager tracked click rates on Schibsted's various sites in real time and worked to optimize the allocation of ad space across them. In return, the fund received 3 percent of resulting revenues from participating companies.

Munck said, "It's now in the interest of our classifieds site—Blocket—to put its ad space to work because the better Blocket integrates with other sites, the more money it gets. The incentive really is for the ones with the ad space to do the best job of making the advertisement effective, rather than merely the best sales job of getting money from the advertiser."

To bring additional discipline to the process—a common concern when cross-promoting your own products—Schibsted explicitly measured the opportunity cost of using ad space for internally promoted ventures rather than selling it to others. Economists call these "shadow prices." Schibsted calculated shadow prices for each ad at each time of year, sometimes each day. Munck elaborated: "For example, January is a low ad-purchasing month. But it's a high-activity month for certain sites, such as weight loss and credit cards—where there's post-holiday traction. Shadow prices allow us to allocate ad space across our sites in a sensible way and to keep track of what we're giving up."

Schibsted's piggybacking strategy had impressive payoff in growing its digital properties. By 2014 Blocket's traffic fund encompassed some thirty new ventures. The aggregate payoff was around $150 million, with a profit margin of 20 to 25 percent. Wessmann noted the simple reasons for this advantage: "We own the leading platforms for classifieds, and we now have the marketing know-how as well in the organization."

The mantra "focus on what you do best" is one of the most common today. But often it's not product focus that wins; it's product connections. Franchises and sequels, covers and same-name apps, vertical integration and bundling, backward spillovers and traffic machines—all are responses to the challenge of getting noticed. The solutions are all similar: Use known products to market unknown ones. If you think great content alone will do the trick, you're likely in for disappointment. You need product connections, too.

SOME VEXING QUESTIONS

Spillovers Versus Synergy

It's tempting to equate product spillovers with synergy. But that would be misguided. Not exploiting connections is one trap. Trying to exploit ones that don't exist is another.

Look at most forms of business synergy and you'll notice certain patterns when they arise. They are ongoing (for example, two products sharing a manufacturing facility or two businesses sharing a sales force). They don't ebb and flow much with market conditions (manufacturing and sales force synergies remain even as demand conditions change). And they require systematic revisions in organizational structure if they're to be well exploited.

Contrast these features with the spillovers and piggybacking strategies we've discussed—be they hit programs, breakout novels, stars that emerge, or newsworthy events. In each case they've exploited connections *after the fact*. The reason is that the occurrence of hits—and therefore opportunities for piggybacking off them—is episodic, the triggers hard or impossible to predict. So connecting is far from straightforward.

The point seems obvious, yet this is where many content businesses' efforts at synergy fail. Product spillovers and piggybacking strategies rest on exploiting connections after the fact, not before they arise. You need to know where the next hit product will come from before you can piggyback off it. The difficulties firms encounter can be traced to their mindset around connections—to thinking of them as being like the synergy between manufacturing plants or sales forces, rather than recognizing their random triggers. Firms create fixed structures designed to exploit synergies, when the structures need to be flexible. They treat content businesses as systematically related, whereas their connections ebb and flow. It's not surprising so many efforts end badly.

Brands Versus Products: Which to Favor?

Product connections suggest a potent prescription for business strategy: Shift the basis of competition from products to portfolios. This is why broadcast networks resist unbundling—having viewers "watch networks" is better for them than having viewers "watch programs." It shifts the locus of competition from individual programs to network brands, making things more predictable and stable.

But connections create one of the most vexing questions for marketers and strategists: Should you promote individual products or your overall brand? With a few exceptions such as Disney—the master at creating a distinct brand identity—most firms, media and otherwise, remain uncertain about the answer. When a consumer products giant such as Coca-Cola acquires an organic food start-up, how aggressively should it let consumers know who the corporate parent is? Overpromote the umbrella brand and you risk alienating customers loyal to the niche product. Underpromote it and you risk missing valuable opportunities to enhance your brand image.

Why are so many organizations enamored with the idea of brand loyalty? One reason is that they're seeking protection from creative fickleness. It's logical to compete for customers by always offering the best content, but that's very challenging: Your odds of winning repeatedly in that game are like a lottery. Engender loyalty to your overall brand, rather than any single piece of content, and you shift how the game is played, creating the possibility not just of individual successes but of sustained success.

Uday Shankar, India's media veteran, has experienced this many times during his career. When he was in newspapers, he saw that "the stories change, the writers change, the reporters change, the headlines change—but many readers still have their favorite newspaper, and they won't change that very easily." When he moved to the local network NDTV, he created a brand around "speed: being there and being first." He gave his team license to report stories "even if quotes weren't well edited, even if there were a few jump cuts, even if the visuals were not strictly in the right sequence—as long as our story was on the air before everyone else's. Breathlessness was our brand cachet," he ruefully recounted. Now at Star TV, Shankar aspires to a different brand identity, to be "the network with a difference." The goal was sparked by Star's groundbreaking show on social justice, *Satyamev Jayte*:

> Despite our intent, our ability to piggyback off *SMJ* [*Satyamev Jayte*] was not as strong as with *KBC*. We're already the number one network, so incremental growth is a bit harder. And we didn't do as good a job creating content engines and connections as we did a decade earlier, between *KBC* and the specials that followed it.

Whether or not Shankar's vision succeeds remains to be seen. But the bet he's making is clear—it's around brand connections, not individual programs. "If we can create a strong network brand, we'd be in a great position, because it would protect us from ambushes by individual programs or channels. Technology is moving to à la carte, and there are many competitors. In this environment, it's even more important to bring a certain brand saliency to Star, so that people immediately have some comfort."

Shankar's not alone, of course. Nearly every manager would like consumers to be brand loyal. But do consumers care?

Answering this question is not easy. Consider two competing scenarios where consumers are loyal to a brand. Under one, viewers choose a product because they know what it's about and like it. In the other, they choose a product even when they *don't* know what it's about—they're guided to it by brand image. (For example, does a customer buy a particular Lexus model because of its particular design and engineering or because of the comfort of knowing it's made by Toyota?) These two competing scenarios are "observationally equivalent," to use a statistician's phrase: They result in the same purchase decision. But in one case, the Toyota brand has little value to the customer, and in the other, it matters a great deal.

This is what makes it hard for companies to be confident about the strength of their brands, where its real value comes from, or whether it even exists. But knowing which explanation is right is central to marketing and strategic efforts around one's brand.

Television can tell us a lot about how to tackle this problem. It's not the first place you'd look for loyalty to umbrella brands, since viewers tend to be loyal to individual programs, and everything digital suggests that this trend will become more important, not less. But network executives (like Shankar) have for a long time tried to brand networks, or "network nights." And there's one appealing aspect of television that allows a solution to the empirical problem described above: Program variety is large, and viewers' tastes are fairly predictable. Young viewers like programs with a young cast, older viewers ones with an older cast. Viewers like to watch cast members whose ethnicity and gender match theirs. And so on. And because networks don't *always* air the same types of programs, it's possible to separate brand loyalty from program loyalty. To see how, consider the time slots when a viewer's habitual network airs programs that *don't* match her preferred ones—and those when a competing network airs ones that do. If she consistently switches networks during these time slots, one can conclude that her loyalty is to the programs. If she stays on her preferred network, it's to the brand.

When we looked at the data, we found that viewers place as much importance on network brands as individual programs when they decide what to watch. About half the time when a viewer could have watched her favorite type of program on a less preferred network, she stayed with her favorite network, or brand.

Why are viewers brand loyal in television? One reason is information. Viewers rarely know what's on the air on every channel at any point in time, a trend that's only getting more pronounced as channels multiply and programs change more frequently. In that case brands serve as conduits of information about what they might expect to see.

In other words, brands provide *informational connections*. Watching a particular program at any given time tells viewers something about what to expect *at other times* from the brand. Of course, there's a chance that by just tuning in to her favorite brand, a viewer might end up with a show she doesn't like. But more often than not, she'll get one she does. And thus, the stronger the informational ties across programs—say, because of a clearer brand image or a more distinct identity—the greater the benefits to brand marketing. The weaker the informational ties—because of widely varying product offerings or because consumers are well informed about each—the less one gains from emphasizing brands over products.

Now let's return to the question of when it makes sense to shift the basis of competition from products to portfolios. It makes sense when there are too many products or when they change too frequently; when clutter overwhelms consumers so that they don't know what to find where; and when brands are distinct enough signposts to help consumers sort through the clutter. It *doesn't* make sense when a portfolio has just a few products, when they are replaced often, when they're very different from one another (when the brand image is diffuse), and when customers are already well informed about the individual products. In those cases, brand marketing won't pay.

Why Do Spillovers Persist with Digital?

Why spillovers across TV programs still matter today seems a mystery. New technologies were supposed to change all this. Why haven't they?

Three decades ago the introduction of the remote control was supposed to end network loyalty. It didn't. More than a decade later, the introduction of electronic program guides was supposed to end network loyalty. It didn't. A decade after that, the introduction of DVRs was supposed to end network loyalty. It didn't.

In each instance, giving viewers more control, more searchability, and more interactivity had almost no effect on network loyalty.

A 2003 study of viewer inertia found, remarkably, that it was as great then as two decades earlier. Technologies had not affected it. Connections are preserved in all these cases not because we as users are *forced* to watch programs in a bundle (as was the case with music CDs) but because we *choose* to do so.

Andrew Rashbass observed a similar phenomenon with regard to magazine consumption when he was chief executive of *The Economist*. When

the Web came along, readers opted for single articles rather than the curated offerings assembled at great expense by media companies. But when
the Kindle and iPad followed, giving readers even more control over what
they read, something strange happened. "Curated packages appeared to
have value again," Rashbass said. "People were now spending more time
reading or watching the content of their choice. And they were willing to
pay more for content."

Why were curated offerings successful with these technologies when
they'd failed with another? Rashbass coined a phrase to explain it—*lean
back* versus *lean forward*.

> When you look at the times tablets are used most, they're when people
> are emotionally and physically in "lean-back" mode—the opposite of the
> accustomed "lean-forward" activity while using a computer. It's no coinci-
> dence that the Kindle was designed to be read with one hand and can be
> read outside.

These aren't rigid distinctions, Rashbass noted: "We engage in lean-
back activities on our PCs, and we email or go on Facebook or Twitter—
lean-forward activities—on our iPads. But that reinforces the point: It's
about the use case, not the device."

It's about the use case, not the device. We don't always use new technologies in the ways product development engineers envisioned. And that's why
spillovers are often preserved, sometimes even reinforced, as new technologies multiply. Lead-in effects on TV persist not because we *can't* switch
channels easily with a remote, but because it's a nuisance to continually do
so. Cross-promotions persist not because we *can't* get information from
electronic program guides, but because ads are also effective in providing
it. Brand loyalty persists not because we *can't* figure out what's good for us,
but because it's often more convenient to rely on brands to do so.

NBC's Olympics coverage serves as an every-four-years reminder of the
persistence of spillover effects. At Beijing in 2008, swimmer Michael
Phelps's dominance created a ratings bonanza. His record-setting eighth
gold-medal swim was NBC's most-watched Saturday night program in
eighteen years, and the resulting bumps for the network's *Today* show and
evening newscast expanded both programs' leads over the competition.
Four years later in London, Phelps's swims commanded even higher ratings. The ratings bump was nice for NBC, but the spillovers were even
nicer. *Today* posted its highest margins of victory for the entire year, and

America's Got Talent made NBC's adult viewership the highest for any entertainment telecast on any major broadcast network in weeks. The network's vigorous promotion of its September prime-time lineup during the Olympics—a full month before those programs aired—paid off, too: That fall its prime-time ratings catapulted it from fourth place to first, a position it had not reached for nearly a decade.

Product connections persist with broadband video offerings too. For one, à la carte offerings don't characterize over-the-top video, subscriptions do. And, when Netflix decided to offer its own original programs for the first time in 2013 (*House of Cards, Orange Is the New Black*), it chose not to offer these programs in conjunction with *other* new programs, but with other episodes of the *same* one. The result gave rise to a new form of product connection, this time with its own cultural vernacular: "binge watching."

The delicious irony in all this is that a better understanding of product connections doesn't require a better understanding of the product or of new technologies. It requires a better understanding of *customers*. Product connections are pervasive in so many arenas because they result from user behavior, not from managerial choices or new technologies forced on users.

18
IMG

We started this section with a puzzle: In the fragile business of talent representation, how do you create an organization that can not only hold on to clients for more than a year but also establish undisputed advantage for four decades? How, indeed, does one explain the success of IMG?

IMG's story is a story of product connections. But it's not just a story of complements, of spillovers, or of piggybacking. Instead, it's a story of *all* these things. And it offers lessons about dealing with a fragile core business when competition is fierce and intellectual property rights are weak or ill-defined—problems confronting nearly every media organization today.

Recall the basic problem confronting IMG, one that's endemic to any media business: It's hard to predict who or where the next star is. Even if you happen to be lucky, it's hard to get stars to stay with you. And once they've left, few if any assets remain.

The natural instinct for any business confronted with a threatened or fragile core is to escape—diversify, and run as far as you can. That's what IMG appeared to do after recognizing that its early success with Palmer, Nicklaus, and Player had come from luck as much as anything else. Starting in the 1960s, IMG began expanding away from its roots in golf talent representation to a host of new areas in that sport: events management (starting with the World Match Play Championship at Wentworth, England, in 1964), golf course design, television production and broadcasting (launching Transworld International Division in 1968), licensing (starting with Wimbledon in 1968), training academies (boosted by its acquisition of Nick Bollettieri's academy in 1984), golf player rankings (devising the Sony World Ranking System), and corporate representation. Similar expansions into new business arenas became the norm for IMG in its other areas of talent representation—tennis, football, classical music, and so on.

Understanding why this approach worked for IMG yet goes wrong for so many other organizations is central to understanding product connections and when they work.

Let's see why.

FLAWED LOGICS FOR DIVERSIFICATION— OR, WHAT IMG WAS NOT

Risk Reduction

IMG-style diversification is often ascribed a reassuring moniker in business: "risk management." Diversifying one's revenue streams can reduce the risk from depending entirely on the fortunes of a single core business, the reasoning goes. It's an alluring argument. It's been made for a long time by business managers. But diversification motivated by risk reduction almost never pays.

The essential logic is flawed. An investor wanting to diversify her risk can do so directly through the stock market rather than relying on each company in her portfolio to do so itself. Diversifying through the financial markets is easier and more efficient than doing so through mergers and acquisitions.

For much of the twentieth century, diversification was a routine element of corporate life, and many of the best-performing firms were large and diversified. By the 1970s the allure began to diminish; many of the benefits of transacting internally within large companies could be had through improved capital and labor markets. In 1994 finance scholars Larry Lang and René Stulz compared the market values of diversified and undiversified companies. They found that, for every year during the previous decade, diversified companies were valued less than more focused counterparts—a phenomenon dubbed the "diversification discount." The researchers were unequivocal: "Our evidence is supportive of the view that diversification is not a successful path to higher performance." The findings were replicated in follow-on studies that used different methods and different measures, and examined different markets. The myth of diversification's power crumbled.

The research inspired by Lang and Stulz showed that diversification *generally* did not work. What about expansions into business arenas closer to home—wouldn't they bring synergistic benefits? "Related" diversification, as this type of diversification was often termed, had at least been documented as less harmful to firms. But IMG's case, and others like it, showed that the logic of related diversification was not without its own problems.

Consider IMG's expansion to golf events. A key driver (*sic!*) of the success of an events business, it turns out, is simply whether or not the top stars—fragile assets over whom it may have little negotiating power—show up. Let's recap our earlier discussion: From 1998 to 2008, Tiger Woods played in roughly half of the PGA events each year. The difference in gate receipts was roughly 2:1—or, 100 percent. Viewed this way, IMG's events business hardly reduced the risk inherent in its dependence on its starts—it increased it: IMG's success there depended in large part on whether its star clients—the fragile assets over whom it had little negotiating power to begin with—would play!

Diversifying too far from the core business, Lang and Stulz had shown, almost never pays. But diversify too close and you might not escape the vagaries of the core.

The "One-Stop Shopping" Logic

A second reason for business expansion is that it lets companies expand their offerings to customers and suppliers, increasing their leverage. Represent corporations in addition to individual talent and you can get better endorsement terms for your star clients. Organize events and you can control player participation. Broadcast sports on television and you can influence the on-air coverage of talent and affect their TV deals. Own training academies and you can determine who participates in them. Offer golf course design opportunities to your clients and you can offer it as a sweetener to retain stars. Control adjacent businesses, in other words, and you will be able to exert more power over your stars.

This is the archetypal "full-service" logic that companies use to justify business expansion. During the 1990s virtually every major financial services acquiring company invoked this logic as it pursued a "financial supermarkets" strategy—combining retail banking, investment banking, corporate banking, asset management, and brokerages under a single roof. Virtually every media megamerger did, too. Viacom's 1999 acquisition of CBS was typical: By combining cable networks that reached younger viewers with a broadcast network that reached older ones, the company could offer one-stop shopping for advertisers seeking to reach viewers of all ages. Analysts were ecstatic about the deal. One noted that "you can literally pick an advertiser's needs and market that advertiser across all the demographic profiles, from Nickelodeon with the youngest consumers to CBS with some of the oldest consumers, and with the Country Music Network, the Nashville Network, MTV and VH1 right in the middle."

Unfortunately, one-stop shopping almost always results in disappointment.

The reason is not that it's hard to create a suite of full-service offerings, but that it's hard to create something that a customer can't access just as easily on his own. Think of a store selling both pizza and milk. By doing so, it offers customers the convenience of purchasing both items in one place. But locate a pizzeria and a grocery store right next to each other and the customer enjoys nearly the same convenience. In that case the full-service store has almost no advantage over two independent, focused ones.

Assembling different businesses under one roof doesn't create additional value for customers when they can assemble these product and service combinations on their own. One-stop shops, in other words, give the *illusion* of creating connections—but they do not.

One of the most hotly debated examples of the one-stop shop logic occurred about a decade ago. It had to do with whether there was value in combining brick-and-mortar stores with online offerings—the so-called "bricks-and-clicks" strategy. As companies like Amazon and Netflix employed a clicks-only strategy against brick-and-mortar incumbents like Barnes & Noble and Blockbuster, many argued that they were doomed. Companies with a bricks-and-clicks approach, they argued, could always offer more than either one alone. Two assets must be better than one, the simple logic went. By now, of course, this argument has been proven spectacularly wrong. The reason wasn't that bricks and clicks don't work but that customers can put them together themselves.

Internet analysts and trade experts are starting to change their tune. One remarked in the context of the battle over consumer video services: "I honestly believe most consumers would like a bricks-and-clicks solution. The reality is, they do have it. It's just two different companies: Netflix and Redbox." While Netflix had become the go-to site for online purchases of DVDs, Redbox had elected to pursue a bricks-only strategy, locating a remarkably large array of video rental vending machines within grocery and retail stores. Similarly, the author of the article noted:

When Barnes & Noble started its online store in 1997, it . . . seemed a giant capable of sweeping aside an online-only company like Amazon with an effortless swat. But that giant had to compete against the world's most highly evolved, easiest-to-use e-commerce Web site.

With rare candor, he went on to write,

I bet that the author of an article titled "Why Barnes & Noble May Crush Amazon," which appeared in *Fortune* magazine in September 1997, now feels no small embarrassment about underestimating Amazon.com's chances at the time.

Actually, I'm certain that the author feels embarrassed: he was I.

CREATING CONNECTIONS AT IMG—OR, THE REAL STORY BEHIND ITS SUCCESS

The real secret of IMG's success came neither from escaping from its core business to reduce risk nor from offering a full suite of services. It came from connections. Offer services one by one and chances are that a single agent can reproduce the benefits you offer by directly accessing those services on talent's behalf. Connect the two businesses to create more value and matching this becomes much harder.

Starting in the 1970s IMG began its full-court press on talent. Young and undiscovered talent offered IMG opportunities to connect its portfolio in a way that no else could match. To start with, there was tournament access: As an events organizer, IMG had discretion over who would receive its "host exemptions" (in golf) or "wild card entries" (in tennis). For emerging talent, more tournaments meant a better shot at higher rankings. There were other benefits, too, from being an IMG client: Being paired with IMG's better-known stars during the first two days of a golf tournament—a straightforward piggybacking strategy—meant greater exposure to television cameras, which might in turn facilitate more lucrative endorsements. Then there were the world golf rankings—a system McCormack devised—and the influence for IMG that came with controlling its algorithms. In 1999, IMG's power drew charges of excess, including from nonclient Lee Westwood. Westwood, on an unmatched run of 11 victories in 34 golf tournaments, had strangely risen only to a world ranking of number 6.

IMG's array of services extended to stars past their prime. One media executive was fond of describing the "S-curve of talent" that confronts any media or entertainment business: "Talent has an arc inherent in its value over time. It takes off or is discovered at some point, then peaks. But it always enters a period of decline as well, which is inevitable, no matter how talented you are. . . . A good manager anticipates that decline just as much as they manage the ascent."

While most companies retreat from their talent once that talent is past its prime, McCormack's insight was to create unique opportunities for them then. It might offer them broadcast booth positions—a scarce, and coveted, asset. It would help them design golf courses and then ensure greater exposure for those courses by having its current stars play events there. And it created playing opportunities for past-their-prime players. Starting in the 1980s, IMG rode the success of the senior golf tour, which had expanded in no small part due to its three celebrated clients Palmer, Nicklaus, and Player. It helped organize events, provided television coverage, and landed corporate sponsorships and endorsements. The winner's purse for the Senior PGA championship grew from $20,000 in 1980 to nearly $500,000 by 2015—a growth rate that outpaced inflation by a factor of nine to one. As prize money increased, IMG benefited, since a good chunk flowed back to its own clients. Playing careers, and golfers' endorsement opportunities, were now being extended for fifteen years.

Creating more value for talent over whom it *did* have some negotiating power allowed IMG to expand the pie for its current stars as well. Agents without access to a business portfolio like IMG's or to its talent stable found it far harder to compete.

But IMG didn't stop there. It also found ways to *directly* expand the pie for its current stars.

One way to do this was to create new opportunities for prize money. But how? Every year the PGA tour runs roughly 35 tournaments. Stars rarely play in more than 25. (Tiger Woods would play roughly 17.) To expand opportunities during the "downtime," IMG conceived of a new event. In 1999 it launched *Showdown at Sherwood*, a one-round made-for-TV golf competition played between IMG star clients (two at the start, and later four) on a golf course designed by former star and current IMG client Jack Nicklaus and aired during prime time. The prize money was nothing to scoff at, either: $1.1 million at the time, about as much as for a four-day major. IMG's vice president of golf later described the strategy:

We are in the business of promoting our golf clients who are in the business of golf course design . . . [but] where IMG really gets sexy is when developers want to access IMG's resources. We design courses, we manage them, we manage the professional athletes that they can access and we can conceptualize and implement a tournament for them, then we license the event and televise it globally.

This was synergy in action: creating new markets and more value, where none existed earlier.

Creating new opportunities extended not only to new events, but to new geographies. In 1997 IMG drew Tiger Woods to participate in its Honda Classic in Thailand, his mother's home country. His payoff wasn't limited to the considerable prize money; it included appearance fees (reportedly $300,000 for showing up) and reverential media coverage.

It's not that Woods didn't command appearance fees from non-IMG-owned events; in 2002 he was guaranteed NZ $3.7 million to play the New Zealand Open. Other events offered similarly fat appearance fees to Woods. But the appearance of being "paid to play" also had its pitfalls. Event organizers of the New Zealand Open, in an attempt to recoup Woods's appearance fees, were forced to double ticket prices in one year, sparking outrage among fans and some golfers, too. By contrast, having a star play in an IMG event brought important advantages: IMG not only controlled the flow of money (and could therefore choose *how* to recoup Woods for his services, whether through appearance fees, endorsements, or other perks) but also could shape the narrative. By playing in various locations around the world, the press release now read, Woods was serving as a global ambassador of the sport, helping jump-start the game in new markets around the world (and, in the case of Thailand, paying tribute to his mother's homeland, too).

It's not just the money, it's the message—what's euphemistically called "brand management." And it pays.

The same approach toward value creation and brand management extended to IMG's training academies. Offer a star a chance to teach kids at an academy, and even if he accepts, the media can be unflattering: "paid to play," the story might go. But by owning the academy, IMG could choose how to share the resulting revenue streams in return. Don't pay the star for showing up; instead, offer reduced commissions on your other revenue. It's not just a better narrative, it's smarter business.

The business of television offered additional benefits to IMG and its stars—again, mostly because of connections. Competition for the rights to broadcast a major tournament is often fierce. IMG had little to differentiate itself from the major networks when competing for events coverage, except for one nice benefit: A considerable portion of the TV rights money paid to the golf tour went back into the tour events as prize money; and approximately 50 percent of this was won by IMG clients. A 10 percent commission to agents on prize money meant that roughly 5 percent of the prize money spawned by TV rights flowed right back into IMG's pockets. A similar benefit accrued when events competed against each other on prize money, regardless of whether IMG owned the event or not.

Controlling the cameras also meant that IMG had discretion over whom to cover and how. (Sound familiar? It's similar to the benefit described earlier for TV networks vertically integrating to purchase studios.) McCormack once spoke of how this worked in practice: In its bid against the BBC for the rights to cover the BMW German Open, IMG won. Why? It could commit to providing great coverage not only of the golf, but of the sponsor's logos around the course, too.

Between 1970 and 2000, IMG represented more than half the top players in golf. As it expanded into tennis, motor racing, fashion modeling, and classical music, it followed the same formula: Start by representing talent, then build and connect a network of businesses. Each time it won handsomely.

The iconic now-retired football superstar Peyton Manning, an IMG client, was once asked about IMG and the benefits it brought. He said, "They were the only ones who could do player representation, marketing, and financial advice." In effect, they were the only game in town.

USER-CENTERED DIVERSIFICATION— AND HOW IT'S DIFFERENT

IMG's is not a story about talent discovery: The odds that a star will emerge from your stable of horses are negligible. It's not a story about expert negotiation: The odds that you will win that battle against a superstar are also meager. Neither is it a story motivated by familiar reasons for diversification. In contrast to "risk-reduction" motives that advocate escaping from a fragile core business, IMG's approach was to more deeply connect with its stars. In contrast to "one-stop shopping" arguments for offering more services for talent, IMG's approach was to offer far more than anyone else could.

IMG's success illustrates the virtue of looking at talent representation in a different way (see Figure 23). First, view stars not in terms of the opportunities you can present them with today, but in terms of what you can offer over their lifetimes. For IMG, creating new opportunities after stars were past their prime (and when IMG had more leverage over them) allowed the firm to better compete for talent during their peak years (when it had less leverage). Second, view each client not only as a unique relationship—every representation must do that—but as connected to others in a broad portfolio. Leveraging its relationships with today's stars to create more value for lesser-known and retired ones allowed IMG to share those spoils with the current stars, and so better compete for them. Third, see new business expansions not as individually interesting opportunities but as part of a broad product portfolio.

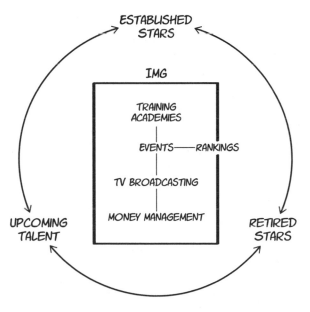

Figure 23: Strategy at IMG

IMG's is a story of recognizing and managing connections. It's a story of creating connections across products, talent, and life cycles, and benefiting from each one.

These examples call up the question: How do you make $1 + 1 = 3$? It might appear a strange question—but it's the only relevant question in portfolio management and corporate strategy. It's the only test any executive or entrepreneur considering a business expansion ought to pay attention to. And it's a question that forces you to look for connections.

For a long time, connections were framed in terms of "product synergy": How related, or synergistic, were two products or businesses that a company owned? Left shoes and right shoes are obviously related. So are tables and chairs, and microwaves and ovens. Portfolio expansion made sense, it was deemed, only for closely related products. Expand into unrelated product areas, said the experts, and you're doomed to fail.

Then, in 1991, C. K. Prahalad and Gary Hamel offered a new twist: Rather than viewing relatedness in terms of products, companies ought to view it in terms of processes, or competencies. Honda's expansion from cars to lawn mowers was sensible not because the products were related but because its expertise in engines and power trains was. This "core competence" logic to diversification was intoxicating, and hundreds of companies embraced it.

Over time the ideas were sharpened—How related was "related"? What constituted a core competence?—but their basic thrust, and defining connections in terms of "products" or "competencies," remained.

Only, here's the catch. The examples described in this chapter suggest that the two perspectives—product and competency relatedness—can ignore productive new expansions. Theaters and childcare are ostensibly "unrelated." So are restaurant guides and tire manufacturing, sports and classical music, and training academies and television broadcasting. But they work—because in combination, they create more value *for users*. This idea of connecting products to increase value for customers, rather than to only exploit product synergies or common competencies, requires a user-based perspective on diversification, not a product- or competency-based one.

IMG's approach might exemplify the mantra "think about your customer." At the same time, IMG's broad business expansion and its tendency to continually diversify runs counter to it. Narrow focus, not broad diversification, is commonly thought of as a defining characteristic of customer-centric companies. So, how to reconcile the two?

There's an appealing logic to keeping a narrow focus. Invariably conflicts arise from trying to serve too many different customers. Serve a broad range of banking clients, for example, and some will plead for online services while others want longer branch hours. Serve a wide range of airline travelers and some will demand great food and service while for others on-time arrivals and departures are more important. "Being everything for everyone" can be a surefire route to mediocrity. Product focus often allows organizations to make choices without compromise.

But the rationale for focus rests, ultimately, on a far deeper point: Diversification should be avoided not because it's harmful per se but because it's hard to manage conflicts that arise in practice. Viewed this way, that's a profoundly different reason not to diversify. It implies that if expanding your business scope is likely to increase value for your users, there's no reason to avoid it. IMG showcases such possibilities, as do the examples described earlier of complements, piggybacking, and platforms.

As for the aforementioned empirical findings about diversification? It turns out that the discovery of a "diversification discount" was never a prescription *not* to expand; the discount was an empirical result that only holds *on average,* not for every single firm. This distinction, it turns out, has often been lost. As consulting firms and academics warned for a long time of the perils of diversification, many diversified companies continued to perform rather well. Indeed, a lively debate ensued for twenty years about whether the diversification discount even existed. Had the data been measured precisely? (No.) Was the causality logic robust? (No—subsequent research showed that diversifying firms were poor performers to begin with.) Was the result generalizable across geographies? (No.) These debates were all part of a spirited back-and-forth between the proponents of diversification and its skeptics. But somewhat lost in the debate was the simple distinction between means and variances—about whether an average effect generalized to every individual firm. Indeed, when looked at more closely, it turns out that the share of diversified firms that systematically outperform their focused counterparts over the long haul is a robust 40 percent—an impressively large figure. Diversification can pay off—if it's done the right way.

19
EXPAND TO PRESERVE

What do you do when cheaper or free alternatives storm your market, threatening to destroy your product's economics? How do you get noticed in a world of increasing clutter? Why is it that in the face of commoditization, the price of certain types of content rises at rates disproportionate to their popularity?

The response is often this: Double down on your efforts to protect your core business from price pressures and customer flight. Spend more to market your product. Focus on growing, acquiring, or investing in content, since "content is king" and valuations will follow it.

These prescriptions reflect a bias toward content, product, and quality, even as the evidence continues to suggest otherwise. They lead firms toward a "citadel" mentality of preserving their core business at all costs, and toward a narrow product focus. This is the mindset of companies that fall into the Content Trap.

The solution to these problems, puzzles, and apparent contradictions lies not in greater focus on making content, preserving it at all costs, or spending more to market it. It lies in recognizing, exploiting, and creating product connections.

The markers of this idea are everywhere. How did a talent agent grow his business into an impressive long-standing organization, competing all the while against firms ten times his size? Why does product quality sometimes bring incredible success, as with Apple, but other times (and also with Apple) meet with resounding failure? Why does apparently secure advantage sometimes end up so fragile and other times brings thirty-year dominance?

In all cases, the answers come back to product connections. The music industry experienced a revival not by propping up prices, fighting pirates, or making better music, but because of the value that migrated toward concerts and other complements. Apple turned itself around not just by making great products—after all, that same principle had yielded it a market share of 3 percent in the personal computer business—but by recognizing and managing the power of complements. Zee TV lost its once-dominant position not through incompetence or bad luck but because of product spillovers. Mark McCormack experienced astonishing success in the fragile arena of talent management not by escaping it, or by somehow figuring out how to identify great talent, but by creating new businesses and markets that connected to it.

Successful companies think more, not less, expansively about the products they offer and the businesses they compete in. IMG, Apple, and Amazon broadened their horizons. Many of today's Internet giants are doing the same. Once you embrace the idea of product connections, the expansion of tire companies into restaurant guides or of theaters into childcare seems not only logical but necessary.

Misunderstanding the logic of connections is one reason companies make wrong decisions. Another reason is the language we use. With terms like *disruption, hypercompetition,* and *substitute* defining digital technologies and their impact on existing businesses, it's no surprise that virtually every incumbent views those technologies as a threat to be shunned. Yet the history of media suggests time and time again that perceived threats are often opportunities. Perceived substitutes may be complements. Perceived negative connections are often positive.

More promising for managers and entrepreneurs is the fact that it's not just forces of nature that dictate success versus failure. It's managerial choice. Most of the time, it's not enough to hope that product connections will be positive or that opportunities are lying around waiting to be grabbed. Managers need to find or fashion them.

Perhaps the really important point in the success stories described above is that they aren't just about creative genius, narrower product focus, or superior innovation. Those factors create the conditions for success but are rarely sufficient for sustaining it. Pursue strategies limited to those ideas and you're playing a game that's not too different from a lottery. Embrace product connections and you'll probably be around a lot longer.

Product connections are the second part of the Connections Triad. Instead of defending your existing product at all costs, look for value-creating opportunities beyond it. Instead of defining your business in terms of the "c every fire that comes your way, find the seeds of regrowth amid devastation.

In short, Expand to Preserve.

PART III

CONTEXT—FUNCTIONAL CONNECTIONS

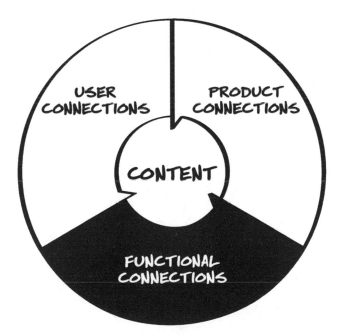

20

A DIGITAL CONTRAST

"DIGITAL-FIRST" AT SCHIBSTED

I've been traveling around the world telling these stories and showing them to others. And the reaction invariably is: "It must be something in the Norwegian air."
—Espen Egil Hansen, editor in chief of *VG*, Schibsted

Few traditional media organizations anywhere in the world have succeeded in the digital arena as well as Schibsted. But the paradox of Schibsted's success is that it came not from trying to leverage its roots in traditional media but from trying to get rid of them. When I met Espen Egil Hansen, one of Schibsted's seniormost editors, in 2013, he struck me as the embodiment of a traditional newsperson. Yet he noted, "Digital-first was central to our reinvention. It meant trying to forget about the paper, to start afresh. We wanted as few stories from the newspaper as possible, and instead wanted to make our own. That was the core idea."

Digital-first is a term often used to characterize reinvention efforts where digital strategies are constructed by intentionally distancing from or even discarding analog habits. A digital-first approach was the foundation of many news practices at *VG* while it led Schibsted's digital transformation. There was the three-layered approach to news that emphasized rapid publishing rather than careful editing. There was the picture-intensive presentation of stories, rather than text-heavy descriptions. There was real-time updating. There was the exceptionally long front page. Visit the website of nearly any traditional newspaper even today and you'll see the contrast Hansen referred to. Online news at most sites is still rarely a digital-first operation. Its format, cycle, design, and approach remain influenced, often heavily, by print parents.

Of course, digital-first at Schibsted never meant favoring the digital organization over print. It simply meant rethinking what news should—

and *could*—look like in the online domain. It also meant not indiscriminately transferring the approaches and conventions of print. Making this happen, however, required keeping a certain organizational distance from print. Torry Pedersen and Hansen were the only ones who "crossed the line" from print to digital at *VG;* everyone else was hired from outside. Hansen told me about other aspects of the novel culture that this spawned:

> We felt technology should have a seat at the table rather than be relegated to the backwaters. This led to many advantages: new tools and services for our users in real time, readership metrics we could track and respond to in real time, and sensitivity to certain features of the website—such as the time it takes to load a page—that we would have never thought about on our own. Even when digital was reintegrated with print a few years ago, our digital culture was preserved. Experimentation continues to this day.

The impressive digital successes at Schibsted and organizations like it might lead one to conclude that there's a recipe for success in the digital age: Act early. Separate and protect the digital business from the smothering tendencies of the print mother ship. Embrace a digital-first philosophy. Update content in real time. Offer interactive tools for user sourcing of content. Relentlessly experiment. And launch free. The advantages of these actions are well accepted by now, and they ought to be part of any strategic effort to digitally transform.

But before locking in this conclusion, let's consider another narrative.

"A SEVERE CONTEST BETWEEN INTELLIGENCE AND IGNORANCE"

Seven hundred miles south of Oslo, in central London, are the headquarters of *The Economist,* which resided until recently on St. James's Street. Like many of its neighbors—art and antique dealers, cigar retailers, and members-only private clubs—the appeal of *The Economist* for most of its first hundred years after its founding in 1843 was to an exclusive group that roamed the corridors of power: politicians, bureaucrats, bankers. By 1960 circulation had grown to a mere 3,700 subscribers. But global travel and trade propelled the magazine during the next forty years, and by 2000 its circulation had increased more than two-hundred-fold, to roughly 750,000 subscribers.

The Economist covered a far broader range of topics than most other magazines: macroeconomics, business, politics, and technology. It covered virtually every corner of the globe, but had far fewer journalists than other outlets employ. In 2013 it had slightly under ninety full-time journalists—roughly one-fourth the number at *Newsweek, Fortune,* and *Forbes.* In several other respects the choices of "The Paper" (as it was referred to internally) remained markedly different, even archaic. For example, it bucked the trend toward specialization over generalization; it was not uncommon even in 2015 for reporters to transfer between beats as distant as Asian politics and Silicon Valley.

As other magazines have looked to celebrity journalists, *The Economist* valued anonymity; sticking with a journalistic tradition from a bygone era, it has had no bylines. And as other magazines moved toward regionalizing their editions, *The Economist,* even in 2015, published only one edition worldwide.

Even more striking than any of this, for a long time *The Economist* displayed an almost casual indifference toward the Internet. Its reaction to online platforms was so slow that it did not even register the domain name theeconomist.com in time. (For more than a decade, that URL merely returned a photo of Alan Greenspan.) While most print organizations made digital content free, *The Economist* erected a paywall. And archive access was restricted to subscribers, who paid more than $100 a year.

Further, though its topic coverage necessarily grew in the digital era, the intellectual roots of the magazine's editors barely budged. Many still came from Oxford University and traced their roots to the debating union there. Online organization and content strategy was still closely integrated with print and, till very recently, determined by print editors. Digital separation was really never considered; nor were other elements of a digital-first approach. The online magazine's format, style, and content mimicked print features till very recently, largely eschewing blogs and offering content taken almost entirely from the print magazine. Digital product innovations were few and far between, and those few, such as its online "Debates" and "Tea with *The Economist,*" borrowed heavily from print formats and culture. The website was updated relatively infrequently and included almost none of the hyperlinks ubiquitous on most sites. Indeed, the editors made a conscious decision *not* to link to the outside world.

Media entrepreneur John Batelle noted in 2006 that "increasingly, sites which wall themselves off are becoming irrelevant. Not because the writing or analysis is necessarily flawed, but rather because their business model is. In today's ecosystem of news, the greatest sin is to cut oneself off from the conversation. Both the *Economist* and the *[Wall Street] Journal* have done that."

Yet in 2009—the worst year for the print industry in fifty years, with 369 magazines shutting down that year alone—*The Economist's* subscription revenue increased by 6 percent. That year, both its advertising revenue and operating profit increased by more than 25 percent. At the same time as the readerships of *Newsweek, Time,* and many other weeklies shrank rapidly, *The Economist's* appeal turned the other way. For the period 2000 to 2015, *The Economist's* print circulation more than doubled, and operating profit nearly tripled (to over £60 million), even as print advertising declined recently.

DECODING *THE ECONOMIST*

The stories of Schibsted and *The Economist* present a remarkable contrast. Their responses to the digital threat—the *same* digital threat—could not be more different. The table below summarizes these differences. It also raises a natural question: How are we to make sense of them?

TABLE 12. THE RIGHT DIGITAL STRATEGY?		
	Schibsted	***The Economist***
Speed of response	Fast and aggressive	Slow
Digital organization	Separate, then integrate	Integrated with print throughout
Hiring for digital	Mostly outsiders	Staffed with insiders
Content strategy	New content approach online	Largely replicate print approach
Updating frequency	Very frequent	Very infrequent
Revenue streams	Expand to new areas (for example, dating and weight loss)	Same as print
Reliance on print content for online	Low	High
Reliance on aggregation and user-generated content	Yes	No
Links	Many hyperlinks	No hyperlinks
Price	Free	Paid

Why did *The Economist* prosper, despite an Internet strategy that appeared slow, complacent, and as disinterested as scores of other magazines that failed? And why has it continued to grow and thrive, despite confronting the same fiercely competitive online threats that every other leading magazine faced?

It's tempting to think simply that *The Economist* presents higher-quality content—smarter, deeper, more incisive than other publications'. Many subscribers swear by its coverage and its ability to uncover insights that an unaided reader would not see.

In itself, though, the quality explanation is not convincing. Many publications offer quality coverage, and they often draw from journalistic pools that are larger, more diverse, and more experienced than *The Economist's*. Nonsubscribers and digital readers naturally find the explanation hard to swallow too. *The Atlantic's* Michael Hirschorn noted, sarcastically, that "the *Economist* prides itself on cleverly distilling the world into a reasonably compact survey. Another word for this is blogging." He concluded that the magazine "has never been quite as brilliant as its more devoted fans would have the rest of us believe."

One might expect *The Economist's* most loyal readers to dispute these observations. Not so. Even Andrew Rashbass, *The Economist's* former CEO, bluntly disavowed best-in-world claims while he was still at the publication's helm. He told me then, "If you take any single article from *The Economist,* you will find a comparable article somewhere on the Web. There is nothing we cover where we will be the only search result returned. As a product that provides quality analysis, it's hard. That proposition can still exist, but to try to do in real time is nearly impossible."

The clues to *The Economist's* success must lie elsewhere.

Let's start by recognizing what the magazine *doesn't* do. Never will you find a "breaking news story," a recent crisis, or an international incident first reported in *The Economist*. Nor will you find a story about the "real reason behind . . . ," one on the backroom drama of politics, or one based on months-long investigative reporting. Such reporting requires a far bigger newsroom and a different kind of journalistic activity—traveling around the globe, uncovering behind-the-scenes sources, and sleuthing for several months. It doesn't come from largely sitting in downtown London, where nearly two-thirds of *The Economist's* journalists are located.

What *The Economist* offers in its pages every week is not news but opinion—and a significant chunk of it. It's the magazine's interpretation of, and perspective on, global events, delivered at a regular cadence, Rashbass noted a few years ago. "It's our weekly package," Chris Stibbs, the current CEO, recently told me, using a phrase familiar to most everyone in the organization. "We offer perspective that our readers have no time for—they look to us for it. And we offer breadth—the entire world, every week."

Weekly opinion on international events is not *The Economist's* exclusive domain. A host of other publications, including *Time* and *Newsweek,* offered the same. The difference, Stibbs says, is less substance than style:

> There is a style to making balanced arguments. There is a style to basing them on facts. Most important, there is a homogeneous voice to our weekly package; it's not just an individual journalist's view, it's *The Economist's* view of the world. You could pick up an *Economist* article blindly and read it, and most of our readers would know straightaway it was ours. What you are getting is consistency.

Stibbs's observation will ring true to many. Read any two articles in *The Economist* and it feels like they were produced by the same writer. Read two issues published thirty years apart and even then it feels like you're reading the same person. Many media organizations center their efforts around quality. Few focus their entire editorial and organizational methods on such a rigorous mantra of consistency.

That there is value in quality journalism is hardly surprising to those who drive media content. That there can be so much value in *consistency of voice* is far less appreciated. *The Economist's* readers aren't just looking for smarts or individuality—they can get that from many sources. They're looking for someone to help them make sense of events, with a coherent and consistent point of view.

How does *The Economist* do it, and how has this approach been institutionalized? The magazine's relentless consistency is driven by an unusual set of norms.

At the core are *The Economist's* famous Monday morning meetings, where editors and correspondents debate the week's stories. The meetings mirror the famous Oxford Union debating society, to which many of its journalists trace their intellectual roots. They are conversations, probing and impassioned. The upshot is that the opinions *The Economist* brings to its readers aren't those of individual journalists but the collective opinions of everyone who works and writes for it. The magazine doesn't strive for balance; it strives for opinion based on evidence—a style deeply rooted in its simple and elegant 1843 mission statement: "*The Economist* is a publication of sometimes radical opinion with a reverence for facts." In contrast to the many outlets whose individual journalists may ruminate in isolation, Monday morning meetings at *The Economist* exemplify a different approach to journalism—team production.

The "weekly package" that emerges from the Monday debates not only makes sense of global trends but does so with a remarkably consistent perspective. Team production also makes it hard for any one writer to claim complete ownership of an article or opinion. That's one reason for the lack of bylines.

Anonymity has other benefits. It lets journalists move across different beats without being pigeonholed, and without readers even noticing the difference. It provides a level playing field for inexperienced and experienced journalists. And of course there's the earned media every time a reader refers to an article. Never is a reader able to refer to an individual writer, as in "Did you read what [*Atlantic* columnist] Fareed Zakaria said?" Instead readers ask, "Did you read what *The Economist* said?"

In other words, at the center of *The Economist*'s appeal is not a celebration of a large and diverse set of voices but an emphasis on a single voice. This comes not from a rigid style guide or blueprint but from collective production and debate. The important aspect is consistency more than superior quality. And the consistency is preserved across dozens of articles, across coverage of hundreds of countries, across decades of time. The result is "an editorial approach so institutionalized," Stibbs noted, "that if several of our most senior journalists left tomorrow, that approach would still be very embedded in what we do."

All this is an appealing explanation for why *The Economist* is uniquely successful. But that's not all. The magazine's mystique is reinforced by witty advertising campaigns (see Figure 24), which are legendary not only for their effectiveness but for how little they say about what the content actually is. One white-on-red advertisement simply urges readers to "leave no answer unquestioned," another—on an airport luggage trolley—to "rest your case." (My own personal favorite: "If you read rubbish in *The Economist*, it's because there must be something interesting to say about rubbish.")

What's most striking about these advertisements is how little they tell you about the product and what they try to persuade you about *yourself*. Sean Brierley, author of *The Advertising Handbook*, notes that "*The Economist*'s marketing campaign . . . has never emphasized the quality of the

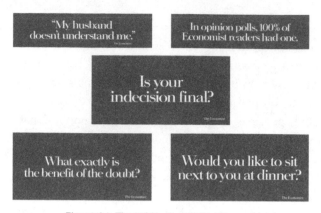

Figure 24: The White Out of Red Campaign

editorial product, but it has always concentrated on the self-image of the readers. It is a badge brand—one that executives like to be seen with, but are hardly ever seen reading."

That's the power of status marketing for *The Economist*. It offers value not just to those who read it, but also to those who buy it and don't read it.

The shrewd marketing is not limited to the white-on-red advertisements, either. The marketing strategy in the United States—the centerpiece of *The Economist*'s growth during the past decade—relied not on national TV ads but on city-level blitzes. Stibbs told me, "We were very careful about what cities we went after: not San Francisco or New York, but ones where we think there's the highest penetration of likely readers and the lowest penetration of actual readers." The result was not only effective—within a decade, U.S. circulation grew by more than 150 percent, to over 750,000 subscribers by 2010—but economical, costing far less than a blanket national campaign.

That's not to say *The Economist* eschews marketing spend. Its cleverness in marketing is reinforced by the large amounts devoted to it—more than virtually any other magazine. Its marketing budgets—20 percent of revenues—are enough to make others blush with envy. Stibbs said,

> Marketing is absolutely fundamental. People outside major cities like London, New York, and a few other places just don't think they should subscribe to *The Economist*. You have to sell the product. It's fundamental to what we do.

Stibbs was highlighting not what makes *The Economist* better in its marketing approach but what makes it *different*. First, it is interested primarily in full-paying subscribers. "We don't discount heavily like others do, just to get audience so that we can then drive advertising revenue. We try to find the person who's prepared to pay full price, and we will spend a considerable amount on 'subscriber acquisition costs'" (the marketing expense incurred in acquiring each new reader).

Second, its approach is driven by a careful assessment of who its *potential* global subscribers are—"roughly between 65 million and 130 million persons, based on various filters we apply," Stibbs noted. "We first identify our target audience and where they reside, and *then* hit them with a combination of traditional and social marketing efforts."

Third, the product isn't customized for different markets. "We believe that our appeal and therefore our message is very similar across markets—an *Economist* reader in New York has more in common with an *Economist* reader in Kuala Lumpur than with the person who lives two houses down on the road—even though how you actually reach readers varies."

The combined result of these factors is a more differentiated product and—more important a certain protection from what the Web brings. Center your magazine on individual writers, on breaking news, or on the diversity of voices you offer, and the Internet—as well as the hundreds of competitors it brings—is poised to destroy you. Center it around a collective voice, curation, and status, and it's far harder for others to undermine your advantage.

This explains *The Economist's* conscious indifference toward the Web when it first came along.

Stibbs talked about what this indifference was like early on. It wasn't that *The Economist* didn't have interesting content to offer on its website, he told me. Instead, it was that

> [o]ur dot-com has no curation. It doesn't have the weekly package. It's just like any other website, a collection of lots of stuff. So if you go into our dot-com as a reader, you've got to find your own way around it to find out what's interesting. When the Web came along, we weren't seduced into acting. Everyone was telling us to rush into the digital era. But we really never understood how the "lean-back" perspective that we offered worked with the Internet. You come to the website, you see an article, and then you go away. The biggest opportunity we have on our website is to get people to sample what we do and try to convert them to paid readers.

This was also the reason why *The Economist's* response to later digital platforms was so different: "When the tablet and smartphone appeared,"

Stibbs noted, "we aggressively pursued them, because we saw that here is where our lean-back experience could transfer well. A reader got the same experience we were offering in print: You go in, sit down like you would at Starbucks, and spend an hour or more. It's the weekly package and curation all over again."

These differences led to some counterintuitive decisions, too—around pricing and speed of response across the various digital platforms. On the Web, much *Economist* content could and still can be accessed free. Use a tablet, however, and *the same content* could be retrieved only by forking over a $150 annual subscription. A similar logic, Stibbs noted, lay behind the fact that "we were intentionally slow in our response to dot-com. But we were fast and aggressive in reacting to tablets."

Ask any organization about pricing and the distinction invariably made is between "digital" and "print." Ask about reacting to change and the response is that you've got to act fast. *The Economist* bucked both trends. Its pricing and its speed of response were strikingly different across various digital platforms, and these differences weren't a coincidence. They were driven by differences in the reader experience across these platforms, not by differences in content.

Look at the content in any single article of *The Economist,* and you're likely to find something similar elsewhere. But try reproducing the style, the consistency, and the status that the magazine offers and its position appears more robust. Indeed, understand these things and you'll understand a far more general message: Consumer experience matters more than content quality in the abstract.

The Economist reacted slowly to the Internet, in other words, not because it was unaware, lazy, or complacent but because it could afford to.

SCHIBSTED VERSUS *THE ECONOMIST:* WHAT TO MAKE OF IT

While the differences between the digital approaches of Schibsted and *The Economist* are striking, it's not surprising that two successful organizations would make different choices. What is surprising is how different their digital strategies are. Differ in one or two arenas and one can chalk it up to coincidence or noise. Differ in virtually every aspect and it demands a better explanation.

The differences between these organizations don't arise from geography. Several media outlets in the United Kingdom (where *The Economist* resides) look more similar to Schibsted in their responses. Several others in Scandinavia look more like *The Economist*. Nor are the differences explained by frequency of publication. Many weekly newsmagazines also reacted slowly, like *The Economist,* but they paid for it. And other daily newspapers tried to move aggressively, like Schibsted, but it hasn't worked.

To understand the reasons for these differences between the two organizations, it's useful to look more carefully at the choices made by each—not as individual decisions but as a series of *closely connected* ones.

Let's start with *The Economist*'s no-bylines policy, which, as I've discussed, arose as a natural by-product of the collective production philosophy. That in turn fashioned a culture of generalists, and made possible reporters' frequent movements across beats. The magazine's consistency of voice emerged not from a fiercely rigid style guide or superior training for new hires—it too is a by-product of team production. And the unchanging print format and design is not because such innovations aren't generally valued by consumers, but because in the context of what *The Economist*'s readers expect—consistency of voice and a refuge from product clutter—they aren't.

When viewed as whole systems of interrelated decisions, the differences between *The Economist* and Schibsted start to make a lot of sense. Understanding the connections between the mosaic of choices fashioned by *The Economist* over 150 years also explains why its digital approach was so different from Schibsted's. Consider the Schibsted tabloid *VG*, whose success was built on breaking news and entertaining stories. Along comes the Web, with hundreds of substitutes that offer the same. Compete on those elements and you have little option *but* to compete on faster and more entertaining stories. Real-time updating, pictures replacing text, bolder headlines, and more news resulted. But consider that *The Economist*'s strength and appeal come from curation and consistency. Bring on the Web and not much changes in the value you offer. If you tried to compete on faster and more entertaining stories, chances are you'd undermine the very appeal you had for your readers. They're looking for you, after all, not to link to others or to the growing information overload, but to get them away from it. Compete in this manner and you can afford to be slow—"intentionally slow," as Stibbs said—in your response to the Web.

The success of *The Economist* comes not from a series of accidental or haphazard choices, but from a network of closely connected ones. Figure 25 illustrates *The Economist*'s network of connected choices.

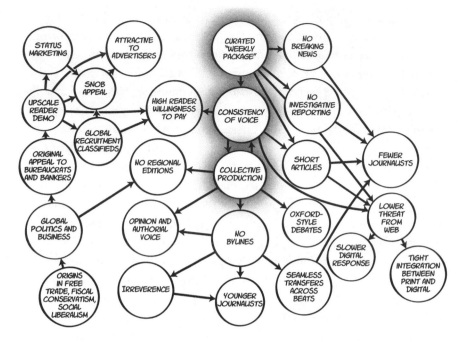

Figure 25: *The Economist:* Functional Connections

This web of connections across functional areas—what we might term "functional connections"—not only clarifies *The Economist's* success today but also makes it virtually impossible to emulate. Its high subscription price is very hard to match without the same status, perceived quality, and marketing philosophy. Eliminating bylines would most likely backfire unless you could also emulate team production and consistency of voice. Reducing the size of your newsroom without fundamentally altering your news approach—cutting out breaking news and investigative reporting—would diminish your product's quality.

Further, *The Economist's* intertwined choices evolved over time, making it even harder for others to run with the same things. Trying to copycat without recognizing the connections across functional choices and the complexity of the ecosystem is very likely to fail.

In 2008 *Newsweek* announced its intention to explicitly revise its positioning to more closely emulate *The Economist.* It would do away with breaking news coverage and rely on "intellectual scoops rather than informational ones." It would eschew newsstand discounting and unprofitable readers in favor of a smaller, more affluent circulation base. And it would abandon "celebrity news" in favor of opinion essays. Jon Meacham, the editor, explained:

> As the number of news outlets expands, it is said, attention spans shrink; only the fast and the pithy will survive. Some people in our business believe print should emulate the Internet, filling pages with short, web-like bites of information. We disagree. There is a simple idea behind the changes in the issue of *Newsweek* you are holding: we are betting that you want to read more, not less. Other media outlets believe you just want things quick and easy. We think you will make the time to read pieces that repay the effort.

Offering smart opinions as an alternative to an increasingly sound-bite-driven news world wasn't unreasonable. But doing so with star columnists, each working in isolation and commanding high sums, led to a collection of clever but idiosyncratic views, rather than a consistent voice. And it was costly. *Newsweek* couldn't replicate the highbrow appeal of *The Economist* overnight, so its effort to raise subscription prices backfired. As *Vanity Fair* had predicted when *Newsweek* announced its reinvention effort, "While raising subscription and newsstand prices might not be a bad idea, trying to imitate *The Economist* in other ways is a fool's errand."

In 2010 *Newsweek*'s owner, the Washington Post Company, sold the magazine for $1.

Newsweek's demise reflects the Content Trap—or more precisely, the third expression of it. It speaks to the tendency to focus on content rather than understanding context. It speaks to the tendency to look to others for answers—about what content to offer, in what form, at what price, and on what platforms—rather than shaping them yourself. It speaks to the tendency to pursue content initiatives singly rather than recognizing and exploiting connections among them, and in doing so to miss how context shapes nearly every content decision.

Functional connections are the third leg of the Connections Triad. And the message for content businesses harks back to what's come before. Just as you can't consider users in isolation or any product in isolation, you can't make any one decision about content in isolation.

Companies everywhere fall into this trap. In what follows I will explore the reasons they do, where we see this mindset on display, and the solution for it.

21

CONNECTIONS AND STRATEGY

The Economist's story is not unique. A successful organization's choices are often deeply intertwined. This idea of functional connections has long-standing roots in economics and management. But take this observation seriously and you'll see that its implications for business strategy—particularly in digital worlds—are profound.

Functional connections arise from the fact that the payoff from any single decision nearly always rests on other decisions. Raise subscription prices and the chance of success depends in part on how much you've spent on marketing. Offer one edition for the entire world and the response depends in large part on the content you offer everywhere. Eschew bylines and the risk of losing talent will be mitigated only if prestige or some other quality makes it appealing to work at your publication.

In each case, the benefits from any single choice are amplified by other decisions made. Or the costs of it are mitigated by others. Economists refer to these connections as "complementarities": Pursue one choice and you're better served by choosing a second, complementary one. This should be a familiar idea—we encountered it in our earlier discussion of product complements. And it's an idea that is foundational to our understanding of the Content Trap in this chapter.

The idea of complementarities was first made explicit by two Stanford economists, Paul Milgrom and John Roberts, more than twenty-five years ago. They were trying to understand one of the most vexing questions at the time: why Japanese firms were forging ahead of American ones, and what it would take to catch up.

Their starting point was a simple and then well-accepted observation, namely that "a unique set of institutional arrangements, organizational structures and managerial practices" propelled Japanese firms. But then they went further, invoking a lens of complementarity through which to view Japanese success:

We will argue that these features together constitute a system of complementary elements, each of which fits with the others and makes the others more effective than they would otherwise be. Further, this system has been particularly well adapted to the demographic, social, macroeconomic, legal, political and regulatory environment in which Japanese business has operated since World War II. *The result is a coherent whole that is much greater than the sum of the individual parts.* (emphasis added)

The result of this more holistic lens? The realization that "the individual features and their contribution to the success of the Japanese economy *cannot be properly understood by examining them one at a time, in isolation from the other complementary elements of the system or the environmental context* in which the system has been embedded."

It was a simple but powerful observation: Organizational choices are connected. Viewing them this way not only permitted an understanding of the Japanese phenomenon; it also underscored the importance of cross-functional alignment in *any* organization. Milgrom and Roberts went on to flesh out the idea of complementarities in their book *Economics, Organization and Management.* They discussed the concept's role in modern manufacturing strategies that were emerging to take advantage of "rapid, low-cost communications, highly flexible equipment, and computer-aided design." They wrote, "When complementarities are present, the[se] various aspects of a firm's strategy must be aligned properly for the firm's strategy to be optimal."

In other words, managers needed to identify and respect the functional connections that knit their organizations together.

Economics, Organization and Management was probably its authors' least technically sophisticated research, but it is their most widely cited. It had the broadest practical implications and had a significant ripple effect in business strategy over the next two decades.

Harvard professor Michael Porter fleshed out those implications in a 1996 *Harvard Business Review* article, "What Is Strategy?" It would become one of the most influential articles in the publication's history. Porter drew a distinction between operational effectiveness—an idea that had become widely popular in business and management during the prior decade—and the essence of business strategy. Operational effectiveness was about doing things better, activity by activity. Business strategy was about being different, and combining connected activities. Recognizing the difference was central to success.

The reason, Porter argued, had to do with competition. In a world where every organization pursued operational excellence, each might get better, but there would be little to differentiate any one from any other—creating no competitive advantage for anyone. As a result, pursuing operational excellence was futile. You had nothing to show for it at the end of the day.

This sobering conclusion about the pursuit of operational excellence is reminiscent of Lewis Carroll's *Through the Looking Glass,* a wonderful tale of imagination and fantasy. At one point in the book the Red Queen, whom Alice is chasing, explains the nature of Looking-Glass Land, where the faster each person runs, the more it appears that no one is moving: "Here, you see, it takes all the running you can do to keep in the same place."

The Looking-Glass Effect has application in evolutionary biology: Change is required just to keep up with competing organisms. It also finds application in business, encapsulating why initiatives thinking is treacherous. Strive for operational excellence and you might improve your business—but so will competitors who are doing the same. The result: no differentiation, and no advantage. You've run faster just to end up in the same place.

In contrast, striving to be different—the heart of sound strategy—holds greater promise, because of the connections between activities. "It is harder for a rival to match an array of interlocked activities," Porter noted, "than it is merely to imitate a particular sales-force approach, match a process technology, or replicate a set of product features. Positions built on systems of activities are far more sustainable than those built on individual activities."

Pursuing excellence was good for business. Being different was even better—it allowed you to capture the fruits of your efforts in a way that others couldn't match.

As Porter was presenting this argument—an argument that became self-evident once the idea of complementarities was understood—a graduate student of his, Jan Rivkin, was going about *proving* it. Rivkin observed that "when the decisions that embody a strategy are numerous and tightly linked to one another, a firm that discovers an effective combination of choices is protected against imitation in three ways." First, connected choices made it harder for others to rediscover the successful strategy—seeing the various choices that others made wasn't a guarantee that you could decode the connections among them. Second, it was undesirable to mimic a successful firm's decisions one by one—since by doing so, you'd miss the benefits from the connections across them. Third, mimicking a competitor's entire set of connected decisions was nearly impossible, since that could quickly get overwhelmingly complex. And even if a rival imitated most aspects of a firm and missed a mere handful, it might still fail.

While these authors were crafting their ideas, researchers in distant fields—Jay Forrester in systems dynamics, Stuart Kauffman in evolutionary biology—were making similar contributions. They approached the same problem in different ways: Some invoked formal mathematical models and simulations, others relied on logical consistency and inductive inference. But the central message in all their works was the same. And as it applied to business strategy, this message was as follows: Organizational choices are connected. Functional connections amplify the impact of any single decision. As a result, connections require you to look beyond isolated decisions and toward the logic of the whole. And they make it hard for competitors to match what you do.

In sum, connections are at the heart of business strategy and competitive advantage.

HOW CONNECTIONS AFFECT STRATEGY

Connections Generate Sustained Success: Why No One Could Stop Walmart—as Early as 1985

Perhaps the most famous example of sustained business excellence during the past half century is found in the retailer Walmart. Founded in 1961, Walmart was the largest retailer in the world by the early 1990s. By 2015 its annual revenue reached nearly $500 billion—more than the gross domestic product of Austria, and of another 150 countries. The intensity of its operations was no less impressive. For example, each year the company's drivers logged roughly 700 million miles, enough to circle the Earth nearly 30,000 times.

Dozens of books have been written about Walmart's success, including one by the company's founder, Sam Walton. A new article appears virtually every day. Walmart is perhaps the most studied company in the world. Yet what's most striking is that it has turned out to be one of the hardest to replicate.

It's tempting to attribute Walmart's spectacular success to the fact that it was one of the first to enter discount retailing and therefore grew large more quickly than everyone else. But that was not the case. In 1985, a full twenty-five years after Walmart's founding, it was still smaller than Kmart and only a fraction of the size of Sears. Yet no one could stop it.

The reason for Walmart's success rests not on the fact that the organization was smarter, faster, or better than the others. Its advantage came from a myriad of decisions that collectively were hard for others to mimic. Its advantage came from connections.

Here's one example. In 1990 roughly 2 percent of Walmart's cost advantage came from its savings on regional offices: It had none. Yet regional offices can perform useful functions—price setting, store control, coordination. Where were these functions handled at Walmart? Some, such as pricing, were pushed down to store managers. Others were pushed up to the corporate center.

That raises another question: If eliminating regional offices saved 2 percent, why didn't competing retailers do the same? Giving store managers pricing autonomy or shifting more responsibilities to the corporate center wouldn't seem particularly hard to replicate. But they were. Giving store managers pricing latitude didn't just mean empowering them; it meant making sure they had information on product demand. So, starting in the 1970s Walmart invested billions of dollars in sophisticated IT systems that could provide daily information on every single SKU—what was selling and what wasn't. Similarly, corporate managers could take on more control because of relatively seamless information transfers between the stores and the center.

The reason competing retailers couldn't mimic Walmart's "no regional offices" policy was not that they didn't know how to shut the offices down but that they wouldn't want to. It would have required substantial follow-on investments—in retraining managers, in reworking incentive structures, in information technology. Absent these investments, eliminating regional offices would only create havoc.

A similar logic extends to virtually every other activity in Walmart's operation—and why it was hard to pick them off, one at a time. Consider Walmart's famous "Everyday Low Prices" mantra and its accompanying "no sales" policy. Here, too, it might seem easy enough for another retailer to match Walmart by eliminating sales—except that for most retailers, sales and promotions played a tremendously useful role: They got rid of end-of-month inventory. Walmart didn't need to run sales because its sophisticated IT system kept inventories low to begin with.

And there's Walmart's early strategy of locating stores in rural areas rather than urban centers (its first store was in Rogers, Arkansas, with a population of just under six thousand at the time). This has received more attention than virtually any other part of the chain's approach, and it too seems as though it could easily be mimicked. But it turns out that locating in a small town isn't easy and in fact brings with it several nuisances of its own. Suppliers might refuse to ship to a remote location. The population density might be too low to support a store's fixed costs. Walmart's answer to these challenges had been to locate stores in regional clusters, which in turn allowed it to profitably build its own regional warehouses and distribution centers. Locating in small towns without a cluster strategy would not have been economically feasible.

We often believe that the key to business success is to make choices that are better or smarter than anyone else. The Walmart story turns this idea on its head. The reason that Walmart's success was so hard for others to mimic—the reason for its *sustained* success over five decades—wasn't that all these choices were "better" or "smarter" than its rivals', but that they were so well connected. For competing retailers, the prospects of matching Walmart were bleak: Copy any single choice and, because it's connected to so many others, you'll actually be worse off. Try to copy, say, ten of them at once and it will be exponentially harder to do so.

CONNECTIONS AND TRADE-OFFS: THE CURIOUS CHOICES OF EDWARD JONES

The idea of connected choices extends far beyond this behemoth retailer; it is seen in nearly every sector. It extends even to businesses like financial service brokerages, where you'd think differentiation would be hard. Managing other people's money would appear to be just a question of knowing where to invest smartly. But that's not so.

One of the fastest-growing brokerage companies in America over the past three decades is Edward Jones, a company that quietly grew to become the country's fourth-largest brokerage. On the face of it, the company's decisions about which markets and customers to serve have been strange.

Here's a small sample. Edward Jones chose to target customers not in large metropolitan areas but in small towns, many with incomes far lower than average. It chose to serve customers of all income brackets in *exactly the same way* rather than customize fees or service offerings to favor more wealthy individuals. It chose to staff its offices with just one financial advisor, while competitors had up to fifteen; as a result, its per-advisor overhead costs were the highest in the industry. As recently as 2010 it charged $100 per trade, even though customers could access similar services from firms like E-Trade and TD Ameritrade for less than one-tenth that price. It chose not to trade on its own account, in effect forgoing huge gains from investment banking activity—even though most competing financial institutions made their profits there. And even in 2016 it still offered mostly "plain vanilla" products—mutual funds and bonds—rather than more sophisticated offerings like derivatives, hedge funds, penny stocks, and swaps, all products that had increasingly become "table stakes" for competing in the brokerage business.

Through these choices, and by choosing to compete in the manner that it did, Edward Jones appeared to leave massive amounts of money on the table every day. Yet the company grew, quietly but steadily. It even grew during the Great Recession of 2007–08, when other brokerages shrank. And it was consistently regarded as one of the "best places to work" in America. Even more surprising, year after year it generated some of the highest returns on equity of any brokerage in the country.

What explains Edward Jones's puzzling array of choices and its even more puzzling success? As with Walmart, the answer has to do with connections.

Consider the company's stated objective for where it chose to play. These come directly from its three-line strategy statements, which have been carefully revised, every year for the past thirty, by the general partners. Here's a recent version (from 2009):

> We aim to grow to 17,000 financial advisors by 2012 (from 10k today) by offering trusted and convenient face-to-face financial advice to conservative individual investors who delegate their financial decision making through a national network of one-financial-advisor offices.

Read this simple statement carefully. Then read it again. It not only clarifies where Edward Jones chose to play—it also describes what opportunities it *wouldn't* pursue. It would pursue customers looking for trusted advice and long-term returns, *not* ones trying to beat the market daily. And customer trust, it was felt, meant having an advisor from the same community, locating their advisory offices in strip malls that created a "one of them" feeling with customers, rather than in a downtown office suite fifteen miles away. It meant simple products that customers could feel secure about, not complex securities with a flavor-of-the-month feel. It meant eschewing proprietary securities in favor of arm's-length relationships with third-party vendors. It meant having just one advisor in each office, so that relationships were personal rather than organizational. Ironically, it meant hefty fees that served as a powerful incentive *not* to trade frequently. And it meant not trading on its own account, reducing the conflicts that have plagued other financial services firms over the past decade.

Viewed one by one, Edward Jones's decisions appear shortsighted, strange, and counterintuitive. Viewed as a whole, a completely different picture emerges—of an organization making sharp trade-offs in its decisions, respecting these trade-offs, and choosing not to compete where others played but playing on its own terms instead.

The story of Edward Jones isn't of interest only to brokerages. It calls into question the notion of a "best practice," an idea that has infiltrated management and consulting thinking around strategy for years. Put in its simplest form, it's the idea that there exists an approach that's right for everyone. Find the firms who are doing well, the argument goes, then follow and mimic their efforts closely.

Acknowledge the notion of complementarities and you see why best practice thinking can backfire. Mimic one choice without making the follow-on decisions required for it to work and you'll be worse off than before. "If there were only one ideal position," Porter wrote in 1996, "there would be no need for strategy. Companies would face a simple imperative— win the race to discover and preempt it. The essence of strategic positioning is to choose activities that are different from rivals'."

Porter's forecast about best-practice thinking was depressing. But it drew attention to certain concepts in economics and strategy that are as evergreen as they come. First was the idea of economic trade-offs: Nearly every decision has not only a benefit associated with it, but a cost—and mitigating the cost requires other follow-on decisions. (There's no free lunch.) Second was the distinction between creating value and capturing it. Creating value for your customers by mimicking others who've found success is one thing. Capturing some of that value is quite another—it requires you to be different. And that's not where best-practice thinking will take you.

In 1996 John Bachmann, Edward Jones's managing director, wrote a remarkable memo titled "Trade-offs," describing the firm's entire approach:

> Trade-offs require clear choices, yet in a world of powerful forces, it is often easier to compromise than to make difficult choices. By making trade-offs, aspects of the organization become unique and each trade-off makes the organization slightly more difficult for a competitor to emulate. A series of wisely considered trade-offs makes emulation nearly impossible.

Bachmann then listed the trade-offs Edward Jones had chosen:

> The individual investor is our only customer.
> Our investment approach is to buy good securities and keep them for a very long time.
> We encourage face-to-face relationships.
> We do not offer every product.
> We do not manufacture our own products.
> We are averse to closed-end underwritings, B shares, and most preferred stocks.
> Offices are staffed by one financial advisor and one assistant.

And the list went on.

Bachmann was saying, We make trade-offs. We know what they are. And we respect them. Few other organizations have ever said this quite as simply or gained so much advantage from the idea. The reason for Edward Jones's advantage was not that it had somehow figured out a way to overcome the trade-offs embedded in its decisions, but that it deliberately made them.

22
FROM ATOMS TO BITS

1. CONNECTED CHOICES IN DIGITAL WORLDS

It's tempting to think the successes of Walmart, Edward Jones, and other businesses like them come from the complexity of features that characterize traditional businesses—supply chains, modern manufacturing, real estate, and face-to-face relationships. It's tempting to think that their webs of connected choices are peculiar to analog worlds. That's not the case. Success in digital worlds often comes from the same factors.

Reed Hastings founded Netflix in 1999 with a simple proposition: Order up to three DVDs at a time from your computer, get them shipped quickly, and hold on to them for as long as you like, with no late fees. Over the next ten years Netflix grew impressively. By 2008 it had $1.3 billion in revenue, nearly ten million subscribers, and $83 million in profits. Its success, many observers noted, came from a combination of factors: a simple and elegant customer interface, a powerful algorithm for recommending movies to subscribers, an elegant "queuing" tool that allowed customers to record their preferences for up to fifty movies in advance rather than each time they returned a DVD, and—most important—its decision to aggregate, obtaining content elsewhere rather than producing its own. At the time many experts argued that aggregation was the winning strategy—it made it faster for companies to scale and easier for them to offer variety.

For all these reasons, Netflix's online offering was much more compelling than those of physical video retailers like Blockbuster, the major incumbent at the time. But the real reason for Netflix's success—the reason no other *online* retailer could mimic it—lay elsewhere.

Designing a simple user interface, allowing customers to create a personalized video queue, and offering them useful recommendations weren't hard-to-replicate features—smart entrepreneurs could quickly serve them up. Nor did they translate into a higher price—Netflix's effective per-rental price was lower than Blockbuster's. What really set Netflix apart

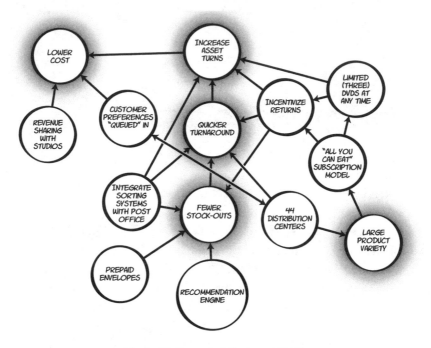

Figure 26: Connected Choices at Netflix

was its back-end, highly complex physical infrastructure for sorting, distributing, and delivering DVDs.

From 1997 to 2008 Netflix expanded from a single distribution center to forty-four across the country, a significant capital expenditure. It was this system that anchored a set of other choices around it. Netflix's queueing system, widely regarded as a tool to enhance user convenience, was instead really a powerful lever for demand forecasting: It told the company exactly what movies every customer in every part of the country wanted next, letting it tailor inventory in different warehouses to local preferences. The recommendation engine, also thought of as a means of increasing customer satisfaction, doubled as an inventory management tool: It let the company recommend not only movies a customer might like, but also those that were in stock! Netflix integrated its sorting machines with the U.S. Postal Service to make deliveries more efficient. It even hired a former postmaster general to guide its operations. And its distributed warehouse system allowed it to secure DVD titles at a relatively low cost per user, since it minimized inventory and maximized turns. The cumulative effect of these choices was impressive: By 2007 Netflix's inventory management costs were one-third those of Blockbuster.

Netflix's appeal to customers came from product variety, convenience, and service. But its massive *advantage* over anyone else—and its ability to turn an appealing offering into a profitable one—came from these interlinked choices.

Netflix's story is not unique. Let's look again at the retail giant Amazon. From 1996 to 2008 it grew from a fledgling start-up online bookseller to become the world's largest e-commerce player. Often lost in the story is the fact that Amazon never really was a digital e-commerce company. It was a powerhouse online retailer of *physical* content: print books, DVDs, and CDs. And its advantage, like Netflix's, came not from front-end operations but from the massive scale of its back-end operations, including fulfillment, delivery, and warehousing—operations as complex as any physical retailer's.

In 2008 Netflix shifted its emphasis to focus on the new trend in consumer video—digital streaming. Streaming seemed a more attractive business than DVD delivery. Netflix wouldn't need to acquire and store multiple copies of a movie; one copy could be watched simultaneously by a million users. Delivery was instantaneous and cheaper. Netflix wouldn't need to incur the costs of its warehousing and distribution system.

What could Netflix do to adapt to this new business reality?

In 1996, Nicholas Negroponte, then the head of the MIT Media Lab, wrote *Being Digital,* in which he coined the now-famous distinction between atoms and bits. Atoms are physical objects, and bits the information stored in computers. The two had very different business implications. The business of bits, Negroponte argued, had tremendous advantages over that of atoms. Bits were infinitely durable. They never went "out of print." They were easy to replicate, obviating the need for inventory and stock. They moved at the speed of light, providing instant global access. And they never get caught up in customs.

Netflix's business had shifted from "moving atoms" to "moving bits." It promised to deliver on Negroponte's promise of a better business: cheaper, faster, and safer. But that wasn't the case.

Negroponte's analysis was right on nearly all counts. But it missed one important point: Atoms are scarce, bits are not.

When it comes to the ease of creating a business, bits win any day of the week. When it comes to creating business advantage *relative to others,* however, bits are more challenging. The reason for this? The easier it is for you to peddle bits, the easier it is for your competitors to do so, too—thereby reducing your uniqueness. The insight that had been missed was that business advantage comes not from lower cost or higher customer value but from lower cost and higher value *relative to your competitors.*

Video streaming was a fabulous business for Netflix when it came to lowering the costs of aggregation and reproduction. It was a terrible business when it came to lowering its *relative* cost—anyone could become a content aggregator now. In contrast to DVD delivery, where Netflix had faced virtually no competition, streaming spawned hundreds of competitors, including Amazon, Vudu, Roku, Apple, and HBO. Delivering DVDs required distribution centers, complex IT systems, and efficient sorting. Streaming required only computer servers. It was a business of lower costs, less complexity, and fewer connections—and therefore more-fragile business advantage.

From July 2011 to September 2012 Netflix lost more than 85 percent of its market value. Several observers pointed to blunders in pricing: In July 2012 Netflix had unbundled its DVD and streaming services, leading to virulent subscriber reactions and subscriber losses, too. But even after the company reversed its pricing its stock price continued to slide.

Then, nearly a year later, Netflix initiated an entirely different approach: producing shows of its own. In January 2013 it aired *House of Cards,* a dark American political drama that drew critical acclaim, lured back subscribers, and reduced subscriber churn. One feature of Netflix's airing that drew attention, and viewers, was the release strategy: Rather than releasing one episode at a time, the company released the entire season—all thirteen episodes of it—at once, generating the phenomenon of "binge watching." Six months later Netflix followed with another series, *Orange Is the New Black,* a prison drama that used the same release strategy.

It's tempting to view these actions as serving to reduce Netflix's dependence on outside content. But their effects went much further. With a more stable subscriber base, Netflix saw its profits rise, which allowed it to invest more in original content—which in turn drove profits. And as its subscribers grew, so did its negotiating leverage in acquiring content from elsewhere: Its large subscriber base made it more attractive in licensing deals, and rivals found it harder to compete in acquiring expensive content. Each decision created its own virtuous circle of connections.

Within nine months Netflix's stock regained all the value it had lost in the prior two years.

Moving bits can create a whole lot more value than moving atoms. But because anyone can do it, it's also harder for a business to capture any of that value. Moving atoms is more costly and more complex. But greater complexity implies more connections and therefore more opportunities for differentiation.

Functional connections are often ignored in our fascination with digital businesses. Yet they are as relevant in environments of low-cost bits as they are in environments of atoms.

It's tempting to view Netflix's periods of success through the lens of its content strategy—make it yourself versus source it from others. Conventional wisdom holds that its success in DVDs came from aggregation, its success in streaming from original content production. The truth was neither. Aggregation was never the root of its advantage in a DVD world. Original production was not the reason for its advantage in streaming. In each case, differentiation and connections were responsible.

We believe that success or failure comes from the content you offer, or where you source it. We search for the magic bullet, the eureka moment, the next big thing. These biases are a reflection of the Content Trap. They miss the connections that actually underpin success. Although content and innovation can create success, they rarely allow a business to preserve it, as other firms copy, borrow, and learn. Connections preserve differentiation by making it harder for others to mimic.

This idea of functional connections builds on the earlier ideas about connections and offers new ways to create and capture value. Network effects and complements create value by virtue of connections between users and products. Network *ownership* and *exclusive* complements are ways to capture value, too. Get ahead in a networked market and it's likely you'll stay ahead—the decisions of your users tomorrow are connected to those of users today. Offer up exclusive complements and the benefits for your core product will be greater than for anyone else's. Functional connections create sustained differences not because of such user or product connections but because they link everything you do. Connected decisions preserve and amplify winning strategies.

2. COPYCATTING CONTENT INITIATIVES

a. Running into the *Times* Paywall

By the time *The New York Times* launched its paywall in March 2011, the industry was in dire straits. Dozens of papers were closing, and profits were plummeting; industry watchers predicted doomsday. The paywall was a landmark event for the industry. "Every newspaper is watching the experiment," noted NPR. If the paywall failed—if readers were unwilling to pay for content from the revered *Times*—the outlook for papers everywhere would be bleak. If it succeeded, it might signal a new era.

As early positive results filtered in, the cheers were heard in nearly every news building around the country. As the *Times* continued to experiment with new digital products, one thing was clear: It had created a robust revenue stream that was independent of the vagaries of advertising. In the ensuing months newspapers everywhere rushed to embrace digital paywalls and user charges. Over the next two years no fewer than 150 newspapers introduced online subscriptions, meters, or paywalls of their own.

Analyses of the *Times*'s experiment cropped up everywhere. Some saw it as dramatic evidence that users would now pay for news online. Others concluded that a metered model allowing readers some number of articles free worked better than a hard paywall. (Indeed, *The Times* of London had implemented a hard paywall a few years earlier, with disastrous results.) Still others noted that the experiment offered encouraging evidence that declines in the numbers of casual readers—declines triggered by paywalls—weren't large enough to compromise advertising revenues.

But there's a different and equally plausible conclusion from the *Times*'s success. The reason the paywall worked for the *Times* is that, well, it's the *Times*. Few other outlets have the prestige and brand appeal needed to persuade users to pay. Few offer coverage on a range of topics so wide and boast a pool of opinion columnists so broad that readers can't do without them. Fewer still command the scale of its subscriber base, central to generating a revenue base large enough to recover the fixed costs of a newsroom.

Consider the last point. The *Times*'s online reader base numbered more than sixty million. Even that was just enough to generate a digital subscriber base of roughly 1.3 million, or less than 2 percent of online readers. For small regional papers, with perhaps one-fifth the newsroom costs but just one-tenth the readership base, the math was simply not going to work.

Scale, brand, and differentiated content are just some reasons why the paywall worked at the *Times* but still failed elsewhere. Denise Warren, one of the *Times*'s early paywall evangelists, told me:

> I would like to think that what we did is generalizable, because I care desperately about the state of journalism and I know how challenging it is

on the advertising side. We've met with hundreds of news organizations who have tried to understand our secret sauce. I would say the single most important thing is to really understand what your readers uniquely value about your content. At the end of the day that's ultimately what pushed us over the edge.

So it's really important to truly understand what differentiates you, because that's the only key to your success. That's what people will pay for. If you don't have something that's differentiated, that's a real problem.

Arthur Sulzberger, the *Times*'s chairman, recently spoke to the need to avoid the trap of being too quick to copy a peer, noting that the challenges and opportunities that "*The New York Times* faces are very different than the challenges and opportunities that a metro daily, like, *The Washington Post, The Boston Globe,* the *LA Times,* has. Very different, yet, again, are the truly small, local, local papers, *The Topeka Capital-Journal.* Each one of those categories is going to have to find the answers. But, they're not going to be the same answers. There will be similarities. There will be significant differences."

For most newspapers, the rush to mimic the *Times* by charging readers online was sobering, to say the least. Many attempts completely failed. Hundreds of newspapers went out of business during the last few years. Among those that survived, few are generating enough revenue to offset the decline in ad dollars as readers flee paid sites. Nearly every one of these papers fell into the same trap: copying *what* others do rather than understanding *why* what they do works.

Mark Thompson, the CEO of the New York Times Company, recently remarked, "In modern media, you could make the case that the best way forward is to listen carefully to what the industry has to say and then do the exact opposite." Thompson was referring to the paywall, widely predicted to be a disaster. But his observation applies equally forcefully to those who subsequently launched their own paywalls, seduced by the success of the *Times*.

b. The Reality of Virtual Currencies

The benefits of recognizing and embracing differences rather than mimicking others don't apply just to decisions about *whether* to charge; they apply to decisions about *whom* to charge. Recall the contrast between

Facebook and Tencent, two of the largest social networks in the world. Each has more than a billion users, had 2015 revenues in excess of $15 billion, and has a market value upwards of $200 billion. Yet in 2013, nearly all of Facebook's revenues derived from advertising, whereas more than 80 percent of Tencent's came from user charges.

How could two companies with similar products, similar user bases, and similar operating financials have such different business models? It's natural to ask, Which model is "better"? But if you look at the business models in the context of connections, you'll realize that's the wrong question to ask.

One difference between the two companies, as I've described earlier, involves virtual currency. Tencent makes nearly all its money through virtual currency, Facebook nearly none. Why is that the case? And what does this difference imply for the prospects of each going forward?

In 2009 Facebook introduced Credits, a virtual currency that allowed users to pay for goods, services, and in-game apps on its platform. Eighteen months later it retreated; Credits wasn't working.

What went wrong? It couldn't be that virtual credits never work—witness the success of Tencent. A more plausible conclusion would be that Facebook simply messed up. It never really encouraged users to share credits with one another, which might have increased awareness and acceptance. It didn't educate users about what the currency could be used for beyond social games. And because it charged its partners a 30 percent tax, it never encouraged users to find other ways of using credits. "Startups would be wise to avoid this crippling trifecta of mistakes," one postmortem noted.

But there's a different explanation. Perhaps the difference in the success of virtual currencies had nothing to do with execution but reflected differences in context.

When Tencent introduced its virtual currency, in the early 2000s, payment systems were still poorly developed in China at the time; roughly 1 percent of the population had a credit card, and payment systems such as PayPal, already robust in the U.S. market, weren't present there. Advertising revenues were meager; in 2003 they amounted to only about $13 billion for all of China, as compared to more than $250 billion for the United States. Perhaps most important, Internet access was different: Roughly 30 percent of Chinese users accessed the Web through Internet cafés and third-party servers rather than their own PCs. For them, sharing personal information such as photos and videos was cumbersome. To address this hindrance, Tencent gave users their own Internet IDs (in lieu of email addresses, which very few users had) and their own avatars (in lieu of photos). As Tencent's IM exploded, so did user demand for personalization and differentiation, including better-dressed avatars and easy-to-remember or lucky numbers.

So virtual currency was valuable to a Tencent user for two reasons: it allowed her to purchase virtual products that distinguished herself from everyone else online, and it substituted for the lack of a formal payment mechanism. In these respects Facebook users had it easy: They could easily upload personal information and photos, making virtual differentiation immaterial, and formal payment systems were well established. Virtual currency never caught on with Facebook users because they didn't need it.

This explanation has very different strategic implications from the others.

The argument that contextual differences matter will be familiar to most companies. But these differences are often hard to discern. Ask most entrepreneurs why Chinese Internet companies rely on virtual currencies and you'll hear that the reason is "culture"—a knee-jerk argument that ignores the real contextual factors at play.

This argument surfaces elsewhere, too. Look at any Chinese or Indian website and you'll notice that it's far busier than any in the West. The pages are longer and more cluttered. Ask why and the customary answer is, again, "culture." But the real reason can be traced to slower Internet speeds in those markets a decade ago, which led businesses to load as much information as possible onto their pages so that users wouldn't have to refresh them. The habit stuck.

In other words, infrastructure, not culture, is better at explaining why Chinese users pay for virtual goods and put up with cluttered Web pages. Fail to understand this and it seems there's nothing to learn from Chinese experiences. But grasp it and a number of lessons appear.

The tendency when trying to extrapolate from news paywalls in the United States has been to see newspapers around the country as largely similar—but they're actually very different. The tendency when trying to extrapolate from virtual currencies around the world has been to zoom in on differences in culture—but the lessons are far more general.

We see these errors elsewhere. Vertical integration, the practice of marrying content and distribution, is thought to be the answer to every content producer's problem—until the next big merger fails, and then it isn't.

View vertical integration as a best practice that every firm ought to embrace and you'll be utterly confused as to why it sometimes fails and why some companies do fine without it. Recognize it as a practice that is sensible only under certain conditions—for example, when a content producer is trying to get coveted shelf space for launching new properties that aren't known—and you realize why it *shouldn't* be adopted by everyone.

In every case the error in decoding the success or failure of a content initiative lies in misidentifying or entirely missing the role of context—the set of *other* choices organizations make, or the features of the geographic markets in which they reside. The error lies in missing these connections.

CONTENT VERSUS CONTEXT: WHY GEOGRAPHY (STILL) MATTERS FOR DIGITAL BUSINESSES

The Structure of Commerce Around the World

When it comes to tailoring practices to local context, virtual currencies are an extreme case—they either work in certain geographies or they don't. More commonly, successful strategies succeed or fail because of local adaptation.

Adaptation is hard. Ask Walmart. For all its success in North America, it has struggled overseas. Walmart began its international journey in the early 1990s and over the next two decades expanded to nearly thirty countries. But in 2015 roughly 80 percent of its overseas profits were generated from just three markets—Canada, Mexico, and the United Kingdom (where it entered through acquisition). Why?

One possible answer is that it grew complacent. Another is that it was simply too American. Or perhaps it underestimated competition in new markets.

In fact Walmart's struggles go to the very heart of its previously successful strategy.

Build distribution centers and warehouses in far-flung locations in the United States and you get speedier, more efficient delivery. Try the same in markets without decent roads and you'll find it's a different story.

Integrate your IT systems with small vendors in the States and you can share information with them more quickly. Try it in markets where small vendors are distrustful of larger ones (for example, some small vendors in

Brazil viewed IT integration as a conduit for reporting information to tax authorities) and you'll find it *harder* to improve supply chain efficiency.

Build stores in suburban areas of America and it will pay off—real estate is cheap there, so people live in those areas. Build stores outside of cities in markets where urbanization is the norm and you'll generate little traffic.

Build large parking lots near stores in the United States and you've created a delightful convenience for shoppers. Do the same in markets where shoppers arrive by bus or cycle, as in Mexico and China, and you're forcing them to trudge across the lots with their shopping bags, at great inconvenience.

You can stand for "everyday low prices" in the U.S. market, where your wage bill is relatively low as well. In markets with strong unions (think Germany), it's a hard proposition.

These are more significant than mistakes in merchandising. Those kinds of missteps—like selling American footballs in soccer-crazy Brazil or ice-fishing huts in tropical Puerto Rico, as the firm initially did—are fairly easy to correct. The challenges that Walmart experienced in so many markets around the world arose for a different reason: Many of its decisions that had paid off handsomely in its home market flopped when they were decoupled from its home market *context*.

These are the connections between Walmart's choices—choices that make it so hard for competitors in the U.S. market—and home market *context*. Roads and infrastructure, tax compliance, suburbanization, and labor laws enabled Walmart's domestic success but were the very reasons the company found it hard to extend its advantage abroad. Decouple certain choices from the rest of the tightly connected activity system in which they were built—the connections that made it hard for others to imitate—as Walmart was forced to do when adapting to new markets, and your initial advantage is undermined.

This is the paradox of success arising from connections. While strategy professor Jan Rivkin was exploring how connected choices deter imitation in his Ph.D. dissertation, he also noted that "replication and imitation often go hand-in-hand. The factors that permit a system to defy imitation can forge equally strong barriers to replication." Intricately connected choices can be heartening for successful organizations trying to fend off imitators. But for the same reason, they pose a challenge to organizations trying to expand their success from one domain into other areas—in effect, for organizations trying to imitate themselves.

The same story played out for the successful British retailers Tesco and Marks & Spencer, two of the United Kingdom's most successful retailers, but which have had trouble going west. When Tesco launched its "Fresh & Easy" brand in California, it found that it didn't enjoy the (more European) benefits of the "passing trade"—shoppers walking off the street to buy food; most Americans drove to the supermarket. When Marks & Spencer tried to reproduce its supplier network in Canada to avoid high tariffs, it found that the new suppliers couldn't meet its quality standards, leading it to import goods from its traditional ones. Worse, "Canadian and European consumers were unfamiliar with the St. Michael's brand, and employee enthusiasm was difficult to re-create."

On the face of it, digital businesses shouldn't confront these problems. Aren't they run similarly everywhere, that being the virtue of digital? Online storefronts can be perfectly replicated, transactions costs should be similar across markets, communication costs are negligible, payment systems are rapidly converging, and servers are everywhere. The usual reasons why retailers struggle to expand overseas—differences in real estate costs, brand awareness, product access, and employee skills, among other things—are no longer differentiators.

But consider the structure of e-commerce around the world and the ability of Amazon to reproduce its domestic advantage abroad. Amazon's story in e-commerce has been eerily similar to Walmart's in physical commerce. The reasons why competing retailers found it hard to match Amazon in the U.S. market—the difficulties of reproducing its distribution centers, warehouses, and fulfillment operations—are precisely why it has been harder for Amazon to quickly scale abroad. By 2013 Amazon had nearly fifty fulfillment centers in the United States but just over forty in the rest of the world. Of those, more than thirty-five were located in a mere four geographics (the United Kingdom, Germany, China, and Japan), leaving the rest of the world open to an array of local e-commerce entrepreneurs.

Adapters—and How They Break Connections

The Rise of Flipkart

Flipkart is the leading e-commerce player in India. It's not that the knowledge required to start it eluded Amazon—the firm was started by two former Amazon employees. One of them, Binny Bansal, recently described to me the reasons for their success in India. It's a story of local context shaping strategy.

Its start wasn't much different. Like Amazon, Flipkart started by selling books online; customers paid by credit card. When the company moved into electronics, things took a different turn. Customers were unsure whether products would be delivered in good condition, would match their order, or would be delivered at all. "Book sales had been growing at 40 percent month over month, but we were stuck at 100 orders a day for electronics," Bansal noted. "Then we realized there was a trust problem with online retailers. So we told customers, You don't have to pay up front—pay on delivery." This was accompanied by a thirty-day replacement guarantee. "It was amazing—we went from $10 million in sales to $100 million within a year."

Cash-on-delivery spread throughout the industry. But there was a problem: Customers had to be present to take delivery. Since few wanted to do this at work, Flipkart built pickup centers to make it more convenient for customers on the ride home. Pickup centers had another trigger: If packages were left outside a customer's home, there was no knowing whether they would be there when the customer returned. That's typically not a problem in the United States, so it isn't surprising that Amazon didn't feel the need to build pickup centers in its first nineteen years of doing business there.

There were other differences between the markets, such as the choice of which product categories to enter. In the United States, media was a natural place for Amazon to start, but the retail market for CDs and DVDs was an order of magnitude smaller in India. In contrast, mobile phones were a natural category for Flipkart, because in India, inefficient mom-and-pop stores were the alternative to online sales—unlike in the U.S. market, where phones were sold through carriers, a system hard to penetrate. On top of that, U.S. carriers aggressively subsidized the cost of the device in order to sell voice and data plans, leaving device margins razor-thin for retailers. Fashion was another growth category for Flipkart. Unlike in the United States, "most fashion sales in India are through small retailers selling unbranded stuff," Bansal noted, making the category ripe for online growth. "And, the Indian market is more functional than aspirational."

Then there were the infrastructures themselves. Mobile phones saw an explosion in India within a very short period of time, making it imperative to build e-commerce around them. And the inefficient supply chain there meant that as Flipkart built out its own delivery infrastructure, thousands of physical retailers could benefit from using it—unlike in the United States, where most retailers had their own infrastructures.

Nearly every decision Flipkart made as it grew was tailored to local conditions—and by 2015 Flipkart commanded nearly 45 percent of the country's e-commerce market. The game was hardly over, of course. Amazon was present and gaining traction—but in order to do so it was having to adapt much of its global playbook to local market needs. Even as the e-commerce war was heating up, Bansal was blunt in his assessment: "There is little advantage to being global in e-commerce."

The Inspiration for Hotstar

Adapting content to local conditions can be done by incumbents, but it may require breaking the connections that made them successful and adopting an entirely different mindset. For years Star TV couldn't figure out how to crack the market for online video streaming in India—until it decided to pursue a different approach.

Star TV, a wholly owned subsidiary of global media giant News Corporation, is the country's leading television company. That's not usually a recipe for how to adapt strategy to local context. Like that of many other large media organizations, Star's longtime standard operating procedure was to learn what worked in Western markets and adopt similar practices locally. But when it came time to create digital platforms, that didn't work.

Uday Shankar, Star's CEO, recalls the initial effort: "We had a digital unit when I came to Star, in 2007. But we didn't really know digital, nor how to go about it." Ajit Mohan, a Wharton graduate who had worked for McKinsey and recently joined Star, elaborated: "We did what Western media firms were doing. We created a website. We offered sports content under the banner Star Sports. We created a paywall." The subscription price was reasonable: 50 rupees, or one dollar, for the entire cricket World Cup tournament. Yet Star attracted just 200,000 paying subscribers—0.02 percent of the population.

Seven years later things were much the same in Indian television. TV content was still ubiquitous, and TV viewership was still growing. Wireless capability wasn't there yet. And other than YouTube, there was no real competitor in video streaming. Yet Shankar and his team—Mohan, along with Chief Operating Officer Sanjay Gupta—decided to take another go at digital because, as Shankar noted, "time spent per consumer in viewing content had been steadily growing, but most of the incremental time was coming from the Internet. Not playing there was shortsighted, in my view."

I met Mohan and Shankar for lunch in the spring of 2014. It was sweltering in Mumbai. I was being drawn into an online education effort that Harvard Business School was launching. Shankar was thinking about how to initiate video streaming at Star. At Harvard, as I'll discuss in the following chapter, we'd decided to make our offering digital-first. Shankar wanted to make Star's video offering mobile-first, because cellphones were the platform of choice in the Indian market.

Eighteen months later Shankar told me how things had gone. First Star had focused again on sports, acquiring the digital rights to the 2015 Cricket World Cup in addition to its TV rights. Acquiring content rights was expensive, but that was the easy part. From that point virtually everything Star did was different from its previous try—this time it adapted to the local market, and to mobile.

Tailoring to mobile triggered a series of follow-on decisions. "We didn't create a website," noted Mohan, tapped by Shankar to lead the Hotstar effort. "It was entirely app based." Then there was the pricing decision: free. Payment gateways in India were still relatively immature and credit card transactions through mobile were rare. But more than that, or the fact of low incomes, the decision to price free was influenced by the structure of mobile data charges. "One of the things we'd learned was that users did not view free content on mobile as being free," Shankar said. "You pay for data as you go—there are very few fixed mobile plans, unlike in the U.S. So users think that charging for content smacks of profiteering."

It was a simple but profound insight: "Free" to the content provider wasn't the same as "free" to a local user, who paid variable data charges. Users viewed the price of content according to what they were charged for its complement.

Next was the challenge of optimizing the video feed for different bandwidth speeds and screens. India had enormously different bandwidths, from 64 kbps to broadband. But Shankar was determined not to compromise, in large part because of his experience in TV: "There, if you have power, you get the feed." He pushed his team to do the same with mobile.

Network quality was the biggest variability. To create a seamless user experience, the engineering team, working with external vendors, tried to figure out how to adjust the video feed to a user's bandwidth—automatically and in real time. "At low bandwidth," Shankar said, "you might not get video, but we ensured you'd receive an audio track; if you were stationary, you might still receive video. As you moved to areas with higher speeds, the video quality automatically readjusted itself to get sharper, without any interruption."

The engineering problem was hardly trivial. And "we had to design for different-sized screens. India has the largest number of screens of any market in the world, from the iPhone 5s to local feature phones. We designed for each."

Mobile-first also required new features that users expected as a matter of course: a pause button; scoring timelines in the cricket game that users could interact with; conversation around the programming that occurred on a dashboard. "For a mobile user, the content is not just the sports or the acting, story, and dialogue in a drama," Shankar noted. "All the other features make up the entire digital experience of how they see content." At the same time, Star didn't offer real-time content, long considered a must-have in sports. There was a five-minute delay, "to mute the noises from the TV team," Shankar wryly noted. "Users didn't appear to care."

Star tailored its brand campaign for mobile as Go Solo. "We wanted to contrast it with TV, which is a family affair," Shankar observed. "Mobile is an individual experience. It makes viewing private and gives you control as an individual."

Mobile-first didn't stop there. Star began hiring differently, too—young producers who were creating short-form content for YouTube rather than TV. "The talent, behaviors, reward, and engagement are all very different from a mainstream entertainment and sports organization," Shankar said. "Hiring from the outside is hard, but hiring from the media industry is suicidal."

The new hires, in turn, required a different culture:

> Our first conversation was about standards and procedures guidelines for content: what is permissible, what expressions we use, what words, what visuals. That's all necessary for TV. But the Internet is delightfully, or disgustingly, free of such restrictions. My legal team said that every bit of their content would violate our guidelines. Ultimately I had to give the new team my word: If you have a problem, call me.

Hotstar, as Star would call its mobile app, was scheduled to launch a few months before the World Cup. It actually launched just nine days before. The delays in creating the app were problematic, but the results were anything but. Mohan said, "We had targeted 2 million downloads in the first two months. We got 1 million in the first five days. In 40 days we reached 10 million." It was the fastest download of any app anywhere across the world. Three months after launch there were 35 million downloads.

Hotstar is not just a story of video streaming. It's a story of breaking apart the television model and adapting it for mobile, one feature at a time. There was technology: optimizing for different screens and designs. There was innovation in streaming and the capacity required to serve a large audience. There was the mobile-first advertising campaign. There was the pricing decision, influenced by mobile data charges. There were new hires. And there were new standards for content, ones that directly confronted familiar practices inside the parent.

That's what it takes to break the paradox of success.

Mobile-first for Star was a journey eerily similar to that of Schibsted when that company started down the road of its digital-first transition, three thousand miles away. Both were profound cultural changes. And both were triggered by a simple question: How can we tailor content to the local device of choice?

23

A STRATEGY PROCESS FOR ALL SEASONS

Winning strategies come from figuring out what's right for you rather than from looking to others. But an equally perilous conclusion is thinking that "anything goes." That's because although successful organizations end up with many different answers, the strategy *process* they follow to get there is invariably the same.

Why is it so hard in practice to get this right?

A few years ago I visited a regional newspaper in the United States. Its leadership team was in the midst of a "strategy reboot," trying to figure out what to do next. To jump-start the process, they did something reasonable. Their CEO asked every functional leader to come up with one or two initiatives he or she thought the paper should pursue. It's an exercise many organizations undertake at one time or another.

At the time of my visit, the leadership team was poring over the suggestions that had come back. Here's a partial list:

1. Transition to a free model.
2. Create new products and services for print.
3. Pursue stronger marketing in local areas.
4. Lower the price of the Sunday paper.
5. Bundle print and digital offerings.
6. Rationalize the newsroom.
7. Include more features in sports pages.

There were more.

The list of initiatives was plausible. But there's a problem with this list. Viewed individually, many of the ideas seem reasonable enough to pursue. View them together, however, and they give little sense of what the organization is trying to achieve. Where should the paper be going? How would it differ from the dozens of other papers trying similar things? Worse still, certain ideas were inconsistent with one another. Cutting prices would require lowering costs—but adding sports pages would increase costs. Rationalizing the newsroom would save costs—but more aggressive marketing would increase them. Taken together, these seemingly sensible initiatives appear incremental, undifferentiated, and misaligned.

A reasonable process had led the organization into the trap of pursuing content initiatives one by one rather than recognizing the connections between them. This points to an important insight about strategy process: To create and exploit connections, don't start by making functional decisions, hoping they'll add up to a coherent whole. Start with what you want to achieve and *then* consider the implications for individual functions.

One sees this even in the questions that managers and entrepreneurs often pose. "How should we price our mobile app?" "Should we favor advertising or subscriptions?" "Create open platforms or closed ones?" Frame the choices in this way and you'll fall into the same trap we encountered earlier when trying to make sense of Schibsted versus *The Economist*—of considering each choice in isolation, rather than in relation to the context within which it is made.

How to avoid the single-initiatives trap? The answer might seem straightforward. "Frame alternatives not as individual choices but as integrated ones," strategists often advise. This would force you to recognize connections. But where do the integrated alternatives come from in the first place? What questions must you ask to get there, and how do you create advantage? To this I turn next.

TWO QUESTIONS

The term *competitive advantage* is central to business strategy and goes back decades. The practice of strategy goes back even further—to battles waged centuries ago. It's become fashionable nowadays to probe the exploits of Alexander and Napoleon, the writings of Sun Tzu and Machiavelli, for insights about strategy. But regardless of where you look, there are two questions any strategist must answer: Where will you play, and how will you win?

These two questions are heard over and over again—in strategy, games, history, and politics. That's because they force you to think about more than competing. They force you to think about, respectively, context and execution. They force you to think about advantage, not mimicking. They force you to think about what you bring to the table that's different.

In the context of business, these questions force us to remember the basics of good management and what's at the center of it—your customers and the value you create for them. So when it comes to strategy *for business,* rather than for the battlefield or politics, here's an even sharper and simpler set of considerations to guide you:

Figure out which customers to go after and what they really want. Then deliver on it in a unique way.

It's that simple.

1. Understand Your Customer: Creating a Point of View

"Know your customer" is the oldest advice in business. But too often it has come to mean knowing what customers buy from you and why. If you're a retailer, it means knowing who shops in your store and for what. If you're an airline, it means knowing who flies in your planes and when. If you're a hotel or food chain, it means knowing who visits you most often and what they like. By learning these things, we think we can understand the customer. But they're not enough.

Recently a very different view of customers has arisen. Don't look only at customers you serve—look also at those you don't. Find underserved customers and go after them. Look at customers on the fringes and see what you can offer. Such advice can be useful, and it's one way to get rid of your organizational blind spots. But it too falls into the trap of telling you whom to serve without first figuring out whether you ought to be serving them at all.

To guide strategy, don't ask why your customers come to you—do exactly the opposite, first taking yourself, your product, and your organization entirely out of the picture when trying to understand customers. *That's* what will help you figure out where to play. "It's not about your organization at all," Andrew Rashbass once told me. "It's only about the outside world, and having a point of view about what's happening in that world."

Rashbass has had to confront this question many times during the past decade. He's led three successful media organizations during this period—first, *The Economist,* then Reuters, and most recently, Euromoney. They're three organizations that are about as different as they come. The first eschews breaking news, the second is all about it, and the third combines it with analysis and data for business customers. To find success in these very different organizations, Rashbass followed a simple rule: Form a worldview about how customer behavior is changing, but never start with your product while doing so. "If you're in media," he noted, "don't start by understanding what you offer to readers. Start with a view of how people are finding out about news, how they're using news, and how they're buying news."

Forming such a worldview is important everywhere. If you're a television executive, you need to have a view about where people are likely to watch video (at home or on the go?), what they are likely to watch it on (smartphones, computers, or television sets?), and what they're likely to watch (three-minute bytes or thirty-minute dramas?). You need to have a view on whether cord-cutting happens because television offerings have become stale for everyone, or because low-income viewers are migrating toward cheaper offerings elsewhere or none at all, or because young viewers have grown up on mobile. More important, you need a view on whether television sets will disappear or whether a multi-platform world will win. If you're a book publisher, you need to have a view on whether reading will increase or fall, on whether e-books will replace or supplement print. And so on.

These are not straightforward questions to answer. Five years ago most publishers thought their print business would collapse as e-book sales exploded. They were wrong. Recently, with digital sales stabilizing at about 20 percent of the market, some executives are saying that the rise of e-books is over. They may turn out to be wrong, too.

The reason isn't just that it's hard to know what will happen in the future. More often than not, the information is right before us—but we miss it. Sometimes we get the insight wrong because we lack empathy. We get the analysis wrong because we didn't look at the data. We get the conclusion wrong because we failed to understand the economics. But far more often we are wrong because we start with the product rather than with really understanding the customer. We insert ourselves into the process of forming our worldview when we shouldn't.

"Coming up with a worldview is a chaotic process," Rashbass says frankly. "But you go over and over it and you throw out hypotheses and you try to come up with others. The reason that traditional organizations often fail is that they hold on to what they currently have. And they do that because they haven't quantified the risk of the status quo. And they haven't quantified the risk of the status quo because they don't have a worldview."

2. Know What to Deliver Uniquely: Prioritization and Alignment

Once you've formed a worldview about customer behavior, you're ready to tackle the second part of the strategy process: figuring out what to offer customers in a way that matches *their* behavior with *your* unique capabilities. This question gets at the heart of differentiation and competitive advantage. It's the question that determines where you will focus your efforts as an organization, and what you will prioritize. It's the question that speaks to how you will win.

"Once you get a view of the world," Rashbass observed, "you say, all right, if that's the way the world is and I'm here as an organization, now what? Connecting your worldview to what you do as an organization is strategic insight.

"So if you're *The Guardian,* your worldview might be that polarization of news is increasing, with globalization and new distribution mechanisms and so on. And your strategic insight, your pivot, is that that there is a gap in the market for an authoritative authentic purveyor of left-leaning news. And *that* crystallizes what you need to do." So figure out what you want to do by matching customer wants with your objectives as an organization and your unique capabilities.

To make this work requires aligning everything you do in the organization around it. This is where functional connections come in. For a book publisher, for example, digital strategy isn't just about offering e-books. It's about reevaluating your sourcing strategy—how to find authors online. It's about revisiting your production strategy—what to do with those physical warehouses. It's about rethinking your marketing strategy—moving from trade to consumer marketing. It's about revising your pricing strategy— instead of considering books to be the unit of pricing, maybe it's chapters or bundles. It's about reassessing your marketing and data analytics capabilities, and how to build them.

This process is hardly earth-shattering. But look carefully and you'll see what it implies for strategy and where it's so different from initiatives thinking. It involves starting with context—a worldview of your customers—and *then* using that to figure out where to play and how to win. It means prioritizing across initiatives and then aligning across functions. It's strategy leading initiatives, not the other way around.

Where do organizations go wrong? Often they jump to answer the second question—how will you win—without answering the first—where will you play. That's like trying to find a solution without identifying the problem. Ironically, this error has little to do with what we usually consider to be the problem with successful incumbents—laziness or complacency. It's exactly the opposite, coming from a "bias for action." We give ourselves little time for analysis or reflecting; we prefer to just act.

Now let's apply this process to the world of digital content, and see what emerges.

STRATEGY IN ACTION: PRIORITIZATION AND LEARNING TO SAY NO

Imagine that you're crafting a digital strategy for a content business. Your first charge is to figure out what readers want. You give some thought to it, look around, perhaps even ask them. Here's a partial list of what you come up with:

Breaking news
Personalization
Blogging
Conversation
Curation
Aggregation
Consistency
Variety
Hyperlinks
Real-time updates
Entertaining stories
Important stories
Pictures
Multimedia
Rapid loading speed
Limited advertising

Free news
Easy search
Deep archives

Good luck trying to find a digital strategy that is not only feasible, but also profitable.

As a mantra, user centricity is intoxicating. As a practical matter, it can seem a never-ending muddle. With so many possibilities for what you can offer—in a digital world, seemingly more and more all the time—every choice you make requires forgoing others. The core challenge for content businesses isn't what to provide but what *not* to—where to say no.

In an analog world, you might have gotten by with content offerings that were "good enough" in many ways. Geographic boundaries, after all, protected businesses from competition. In a digital world, one must now confront a real choice about *where* to be world-class, because it's impossible to offer everything readers want. Saying no is even more imperative for digital businesses.

But how to prioritize and say no?

Let's go back and first see how Walmart does it. Walk into any Walmart store; chances are you'll find what you're looking for. And the price will probably be lower than anywhere else. Walmart shoppers can reel off a long list of reasons they like the stores: variety, availability, price, convenience. But store ambience is rarely on the list.

Indeed, Walmart is as well known for its no-frills layout, sterile ambience, and utilitarian design as it is for low prices. But why is it that the world's largest retailer, and one of the most profitable companies on the planet, doesn't invest in providing a more upscale, warmer shopping environment for its customers?

Similarly surprising behavior can be seen from leading companies in other industries. Southwest Airlines, the most profitable airline in the United States for most of the last two decades, is also consistently near the top in customer satisfaction surveys, except in one category: food. Apple, the most valuable company on the planet, also has customer ratings that are off the charts, except when it comes to two attributes that electronics buyers often care about—compatibility with other products, and low prices. To this day Apple products are more "closed" and more expensive than those of virtually every peer.

It's not that Walmart believes stores should be sterile, or that Southwest believes passengers shouldn't eat while flying, or that Apple believes people want all their products from one firm. The reason that these companies appear to stick it to their customers on these fronts is that doing so allows them to endear themselves on many others.

Spending more to upgrade Walmart's stores would compromise the retailer's cost structure and its ability to offer lowest-in-the-world prices— which is why people *really* go there. The time it takes to deliver food on board would increase Southwest's turnaround times and compromise its impressive on-time arrival and departure record—which is what its customers *really* value. Lowering prices or opening up systems would compromise Apple's high R&D spend and its ability to deliver user-friendly plug-and-play products—the reasons its most loyal customers *really* revere it.

Customers do value retail store ambience, airline food, and low prices for electronics—just not enough. And that's why Walmart, Southwest, and Apple *choose* not to provide these things. In order to be best-in-class at certain things, these companies choose to compromise on others. That's because, first, they understand what their customers want *most,* and second, they recognize the connections among the choices they need to make and the trade-offs embedded in those choices.

You can find a hundred things your customers want. But catering to every one of them is impossible. No organization has the resources to do so. Nor would connections across choices *allow* it. Connections create the need to choose and to prioritize: saying yes to one thing forces you to say no to something else.

Ironically, being user centered requires saying no to your customers, and often.

HOW TO SAY NO IN CONTENT BUSINESSES: BREAKING THE COST-QUALITY TRADE-OFF

Learning to say no doesn't come easy to content businesses. The worry is that by cutting costs somewhere, you compromise quality, making it harder to draw in readers, which in turn affects profitability, in turn making it even more important to cut costs. *How* do you say no in a content business, when your readers demand everything? How do you maintain quality while cutting costs? These are familiar refrains heard all around the world. Coming up with answers appears impossible. It's a classic trade-off, one that offers no simple way out.

Except that there is. Managers and entrepreneurs are making such trade-offs every day. The lessons from their experiences are instructive, and shed light on the process of strategy *they* are following.

1. Differentiating on Content—or, What *Not* to Cover

Recall *The Economist*'s high-quality and global coverage, all with ninety journalists. Its trade-off is not to give up what it does best but to compromise on everything else. It says no to many things—breaking news, investigative reporting, Web TV, frontier technology, interactivity. But saying no is what allows it to be a world-beater when it comes to what its readers *really* value from it, curation and consistency.

How does the magazine institutionalize saying no? I posed the question to CEO Chris Stibbs. His first response was reflexive: "Resisting the urge to say yes is part of our DNA." But Stibbs is also astute enough to recognize that "trying to turn this into a real answer, as opposed to some fluffy things about DNA, is the hard part." After some reflection, he identified three reasons.

First, there's the mission of *The Economist,* which dates from 1843 and involved the repeal of British common laws. "We were first published not to make money but to support a cause," Stibbs noted. "That mission has lived on, and there is a very strong identity in the organization about who we are and what we do." Second, there's the belief within the organization— the "real, continuing belief"—that what readers really want from the magazine is "our view of the world in a hundred articles this week. As soon as you fall into other ways of thinking—that it's about offering articles to anyone or about anything, or about pushing them around the world for free or very cheap—that isn't how we satisfy our mission." Third is the hard-nosed recognition that this approach will never appeal to everyone. Stibbs says:

> If your belief is that the total number of people in the world who might be interested in you numbers around 65 million—as we believe is the case for *The Economist*—then you simply cannot be Google or eBay or Yahoo!, whose potential audience is five billion. You just can't play a mass-market game. Our belief about our potential target audience puts us on a global leash.

Few organizations would ever acknowledge that the appeal of their product is limited. Fewer still dare to put a concrete number on just how limited this appeal is. But doing so can have a large payoff, as Stibbs described: "Based on these beliefs, if something comes along, our first question is: *Why* is that a threat? *Why* can someone do what we do better? We have a certain confidence that comes from thinking that *in what we do, we're as good as it gets*. And that confidence allows us to take a step back and say, All right, what would this do to us?"

The strategy of *The Economist* is deeply anchored around our two familiar ideas—knowing where to play, and how to win. It's a philosophy as deeply rooted in saying no. It's an approach, Stibbs argues, that can extend to many others:

> The thing I believe in very, very strongly is that whether you are running a business, managing people, or playing a sport, is always play to your strengths. If you have a team of three people, don't work on their weaknesses—build a team where the strength of the three gives you the complete solution. That's the one thing that *The Economist* absolutely does day in and day out. That's what gives you the strength to say no.

The Economist had been cultivating the habit of saying no for 150 years. So when digital came along, the magazine didn't need to change. Far more common is the experience of a paper like *Deseret News,* which, by contrast to *The Economist,* is having to learn to say no for the first time when thinking through digital priorities. That often requires dramatic change. Let's look at how that is playing out.

Story-Level Accounting, Organization-Level Prioritization

Clark Gilbert is not your typical media CEO. He used to be a business school professor—he trained under Clay Christensen. When he took over as CEO of *Deseret News,* based in Salt Lake City, Utah, it was an organization that had had modest regional success, and it was confronting the digital challenges every paper faced. Crafting digital strategy and knowing where to prioritize is one thing. To do that, you need to understand where you're doing well. But few people there knew what to do—for good reason:

"Because newspapers were natural monopolies, thanks to classifieds," Gilbert told me, "they had never really had to think about the cost of the core product. All we knew was the general cost of the newsroom. No one had ever looked at things on a cost-per-story basis, ever."

That's where the Web brought transparency, making unit economics clear at a story level. "Online, the market tells you what story was read every single day," Gilbert said. "So we started doing the math, which wasn't very complicated." They divided the total cost of an employee by the number of stories each person put out, to get a measure of productivity, or cost per story. They brought in data on traffic per story and created a two-by-two matrix: audience per story versus cost per story. "We found some very counterintuitive things: Some journalists who we didn't expect were superstars—very productive, and commanding large audiences. But there were some other people—even people our newsroom loved—who not only weren't very productive, but what they wrote wasn't that compelling to our audience."

Story-level accounting was relatively straightforward and offered clues about where the organization's reporting strengths were. But to figure out what to prioritize—deciding where to play, not just where they could win—they needed to look beyond traffic numbers. "You can't take a straight mathematical look at story-level numbers," said Gilbert. "Some stories might have strategic importance to the paper—we'd want to publish them regardless of traffic."

The more important realization, however, was that decisions about priorities needed to be made for the entire organization—not separately by every employee, as had become common practice: "What we realized was that rather than the paper making those decisions strategically, every employee was making that decision independently. If you're a freelance market, that's fine. But if you're the *Deseret News* or *The Washington Post,* you ought to be strategic about what's important."

The paper was discovering the tension between strategy and initiatives. And Gilbert was about to reverse the entire process. Leaders identified six areas of editorial emphasis: family, faith, values in the media, education, care for the poor, and financial responsibility. "Some of these stories, such as those about care for the poor, don't do as well in terms of traffic," Gilbert said. "But we believe at the highest levels of the organization that they are really important to us. We made that decision strategically. However, we didn't let someone six or seven layers down in the organization decide that environmental stories were really important. They might be for some people, but that's not our strength, so if that's what he wants to do, he should go somewhere else. It's just like a person who might be writing fantastic faith-based stories at another newspaper but is undervalued since those aren't an organizational priority there."

The priorities were set. Now the organization had to be aligned around them. For that, leaders turned to data, and measurement.

They started with story-level data, making it visible—"creating dashboards in the building that showed per-story traffic that you could sort by section and journalist." They set minimum targets, which differed by beat: Long-form enterprise journalists did two long-form pieces and three news roundups a week; those in the newsroom, in beat reporting mode, did two stories a day. The traffic and productivity data were combined with "quality scores that were peer reviewed and used ten metrics: things like 'does the story make the reader better-informed'; 'does it avoid polarization'; 'are all perspectives considered'; and so on." These were inherently subjective but could be easily measured. "Everyone has their own opinion, but every senior editor and leadership team evaluates quality every day. We have the entire company do it for a month twice a year. We built a quality rubric that takes ten minutes to score for a story. So we created something that not only reinforced our mission, and fit our brand promise; it was very easy to do."

Gilbert described the impact of the changes in the newsroom: "Journalists like recognition and praise, but they don't like feedback. We were building a culture of feedback. We praised great work, but we also gave feedback on how to improve things. Evaluation and measurement had never been part of the culture. It became part of ours."

The results of this process were clear, Gilbert said:

We reduced costs—we had to lay off 87 people. But we raised quality. And by creating a distinct brand promise, we're now better at everything we do. Prioritizing at the level of the organization was a major decision. And the reason was our realization that, for example, we were never going to be the watchdog on the federal government that *The Washington Post* is. Any dollar I spend on that is a wasted dollar, since I'm never going to be the first choice for that story in a digital world. So I will say to *The Washington Post,* you do political coverage better than anyone in the country. But I will also say that if a story relates to the American family, the *Deseret News* in Salt Lake City will beat you every single time, because we have focused our resources and our writers know that better than anyone. If every news organization had the discipline to do that, the quality of journalism in America would go up dramatically.

The strategy process at the *Deseret News* was instructive not only for what it did but also for what it didn't do. First was the question of *where* to say no. Most content businesses try to tackle the cost-versus-quality trade-off by cutting across the board—"proportionately scaling down." That approach is simple and easy to justify. But it's the opposite of where good strategy will take you. That will start you down a vicious circle, where quality downgrades result in fewer readers, greater financial urgency, and in turn further cost reductions. Prioritization, by contrast, meant a very different path, Gilbert noted—one that didn't imply across-the-board cuts. Rather, it was about making choices about where to cut and where *not* to.

Second was the question of which decisions were made where. At the start, costs were known at the level of the entire news organization, rather than for each story. But decisions about which news areas to prioritize— critical to preserving quality in the face of cost reductions—were being made by every journalist, rather than at the level of the entire organization. Gilbert's approach was to reverse this, combining story-level accounting with organization-level news prioritization, rather than the other way around. Story-level accounting clarified the economics, impacting productivity. Strategic prioritization overturned the initiatives mindset—the one-at-a-time decision making that had come to characterize the paper's approach to content. It allowed the organization to play to its strengths rather than in areas "where we could never compete."

Respect your mission. Recognize your strengths. Prioritize and then align. It's the simple, and familiar, process that *Deseret* had followed in charting out its own course.

By 2013 the *Deseret News* was in 200 syndication partnerships around the country. Website traffic experienced 40 percent year-on-year growth— especially impressive for a fifteen-year-old site. Story-level traffic had increased tenfold.

2. Differentiating on Experience: Three Stories About Television News

The Economist and *Deseret News* accounts offer a window into the process of prioritizing content—what to offer, or what not. But it's one thing to prioritize content. It's another to differentiate on all the other aspects of a user's experience—which are often ignored. Recognizing this distinction holds clues about differentiating *without changing your content*. Television offers some lessons here and illuminates some blind spots to avoid.

a. A Story About Reagan

During the 1984 presidential campaign, CBS News reporter Lesley Stahl put together a five-minute, forty-second story broadly critical of President Reagan's funding cuts for children with disabilities and his opposition to public health funding. Stahl recalls the episode and the reaction from White House Deputy Chief of Staff Dick Darman. Says Stahl, "I knew the piece would have an impact; it was practically a documentary in *Evening News* terms. I worried that my sources at the White House would be angry enough to freeze me out. . . . But that isn't what happened. . . . When it aired, Darman called from the White House."

> **DARMAN**: Way to go, kiddo. What a great piece. We loved it.
> **STAHL**: Didn't you hear what I said?
> **DARMAN**: Nobody heard what you said.
> **STAHL**: Did I hear you right? Come again?
> **DARMAN**: You guys in Television Land haven't figured it out, have you? When the pictures are powerful and emotional, they override if not completely drown out the sound. I mean it, Lesley. Nobody heard you.

The pictures accompanying Stahl's report were of Reagan visiting a children's hospital. Darman's implication: Nothing else mattered for the viewer.

Stahl had obsessed about getting the "content" right. Instead, the accompanying pictures carried the entire day.

b. An Experiment About Clinton

A few years ago my colleague Rafael Di Tella and I asked 250 MBA students in four classes to assess an interchange between a pair of journalists that went like this:

> **JOURNALIST 1**: Do you think Bill Clinton is an honest person?
> **JOURNALIST 2**: Yes, I think he is. I think at core he's an honest person. I think you can be an honest person and lie about any number of things.

The question we asked the students: Do you think the response by Journalist 2 is biased toward the right, biased toward the left, or neutral?

Their responses were as follows:

TABLE 13. SOURCE AWARENESS AND PERCEIVED BIAS		
Response by Journalist 2 is:	Biased toward the left	Biased toward the right
Classes 1 and 3	22%	48%
Classes 2 and 4	61%	13%

At first glance these differences seem strange: two of the classes viewed, by a margin of more than 2:1, the response to be right-biased. Two other classes viewed, by a margin of nearly 5:1, the response to be left-biased. The classes were demographically identical.

But we'd made one alteration in the scenario we posed to the different classes. For groups 1 and 3, the interchange was presented this way:

FOX NEWS JOURNALIST 1: Do you think Bill Clinton is an honest person?
FOX NEWS JOURNALIST 2: Yes, I think he is. I think at core he's an honest person. I think you can be an honest person and lie about any number of things.

For the others, it was:

CNN JOURNALIST 1: Do you think Bill Clinton is an honest person?
CNN JOURNALIST 2: Yes, I think he is. I think at core he's an honest person. I think you can be an honest person and lie about any number of things.

The differences had nothing to do with content—the thing content businesses everywhere obsess about. They were driven entirely by the identity of the reporting source.

The examples above illustrate the difference between content—or product—and how customers experience it. Yet we repeatedly miss this distinction.

Newsrooms fixate on how compelling their stories are, when the speed of loading their websites may be just as or more important to the reader experience. Google recognized this in 2010 and announced that website loading speed would affect how it ranked its search results; Facebook did too in 2015 when it used faster load speeds to differentiate its new offering, Instant Articles, and attract publishers. Taxis focus on the quality of the ride itself, but it's the ease of getting a cab *before the ride* or paying for it *afterward* that in large part set apart $50 billion upstart Uber. Focus on content or product and you may prioritize the wrong things. Understand user experience and you'll see real opportunities for differentiation.

c. Differentiating on Cable News

Television news was already a crowded market in 1995—there were four broadcast news networks and three general cable news networks, including a 24/7 channel. News viewership wasn't growing, and market share gains were tough to come by. The cost economics weren't favorable, either: Television is largely a fixed-cost business, where programming costs don't vary with the number of viewers. Nonetheless, Fox News decided to enter.

Within a decade it overtook CNN in ratings—not by producing better (and more expensive) news, and despite a lower cost structure. During its early years, Fox News had three bureaus, CNN had twenty-three; CNN had 2,300 employees, Fox, 100. How did the network do it?

By now the broad strokes of the story will be familiar. Differentiation was central to the Fox News strategy: targeting a certain segment of viewers (self-reporting to lean right on the political spectrum, on average) rather than serving everyone. It didn't stop there. It prioritized certain issues that resonated with this audience, rather than covering all equally; amplified its style tone, and energy, even taking a combative stance rather than the traditional measured approach to news; and eschewed viewer reach in exchange for loyalty (looking for "fans" is how it described its objective). These were the ways Fox looked to differentiate. And it worked remarkably well for it.

For the longest time news organizations have tried to differentiate by making their content "better." At CNN, this even got codified in a mantra: "News is the star." That approach was now running out of steam.

Fox News found a payoff not from making better content but from targeting a specific user. But even that has led it to focus on just one aspect of differentiation. There are other ways to differentiate. In a study of cable news programs a few years ago, we examined differentiation based not on the content that each offered, but on how viewers *perceived* them. The idea was simple: Infer how similar or dissimilar a pair of programs was, based on their share of common viewers. If two programs had a high viewer overlap, they were considered similar; if not, they weren't.

The results surprised us. One might expect two Fox News programs to be perceived as more similar than a Fox News and a CNN program. But that wasn't always the case. Roughly 30 percent of CNN's *Larry King Live* viewers regularly watched Fox's *O'Reilly Factor,* and vice versa—a greater overlap than between King and *any other* CNN program or between O'Reilly and most other Fox programs. (Large joint audiences were observed for other pairs of CNN and Fox programs, too, though some programs—*Hannity & Colmes* on Fox, *Anderson Cooper 360* on CNN— were less likely to draw viewers from the rival network.)

The more striking finding in all this was that there was another dimension of news differentiation that mattered to cable viewers, one that had nothing to do with right-versus-left ideology. It had to do with how "heavy or light" the tone of the news coverage was. Offer political news in a serious or hard-hitting, finger-pointing way and you'll draw in news junkies— but not many others. Combine the same content with humor or wit and you'll appeal to a broader audience, including folks who might never otherwise watch political news.

Cable news networks, busy trying to grab their particular share of political viewers, had left a large part of the market unserved. That's where Comedy Central entered, with Jon Stewart's *Daily Show,* which overtook the highest-rated program on Fox News within a few years. And its viewers were younger, better educated, more affluent, and better informed than national news viewers and newspaper readers.

The cable news networks had focused on differentiating in the market for serious news. But *not* taking yourself too seriously turned out to be an equally powerful strategy. The strategic insight came from asking what viewers are looking for, rather than merely focusing on how to differentiate from others already *in* the market.

A retired senior cable executive recently talked with me about the central challenge facing news organizations: "It's about how you make the interesting important and the important interesting." That's a question whose answer fundamentally resides in better understanding the viewer rather than just the content.

3. Differentiating on Business Model: How "Indies" Do It

The cost-quality trade-off affects other parts of the media, too. Movie executives have long grumbled about it. Reduce costs, they say, and you can't compete against other blockbusters for commercial success or attract the stars necessary to break through the clutter. From 1980 to 2010, even after accounting for inflation, the average cost of making a movie in Hollywood increased fourfold. Hollywood studio spending increased roughly 50 percent since 2000, with nearly all the growth coming from big-budget (over $100 million) films—a trend that many argued was unsustainable. The result was nail-biting opening-day releases for movie executives, an increased reliance on a swing-for-the-fences approach, and a trend toward safer, ostensibly less creative, bets such as sequels (or "franchises," as executives decorously term them).

But why are movie budgets skyrocketing? There are three commonly mentioned culprits. First, star actors draw in crowds but command big bucks. Second, large up-front marketing spends are perceived as required, because most movies gross half their receipts during the first weekend. Third, talented creative directors are hard to rein in on tight budgets and, the advice goes, shouldn't be reined in, either; otherwise "you'll get what you paid for." In other words, spend more and you'll attract quality. Spend less and you're doomed to commercial failure. It's a refrain that's as commonplace in Hollywood as fast cars and raucous parties.

And yet, there's a part of the movie industry that has proved otherwise—independents like Focus Features, Fox Searchlight, Lionsgate, and the Weinstein Company—and before them, Miramax.

Here's how the indies did it. First, they paid their stars less—up front. Profit participation, also called back-end deals in Hollywood, or more commonly referred to as equity sharing, was initiated by the indies and is now increasingly common. Some independent studios, for example, committed to never paying an actor or a producer more than $500,000, a director never more than $1 million. "It didn't matter who you were," recalls one indie executive. "Robin Williams might have been getting $20 million a movie, but he received no more than $500,000 from an indie. Of course, profit participation would often make up for it. A decade ago actors were getting paid on the front end *and* the back end. In essence, the studio had been working for the actors, not the other way around."

Second, indies saved on marketing by releasing movies overseas first—reversing prior norms whereby foreign distributors piggybacked on the attention from U.S. releases. "It allowed cheaper deals for domestic distribution after we'd established success overseas," one executive explained. "On top of that, we turned to phased releases—also called 'platform releases,' where a movie was rolled out across theaters nationwide gradually, and in response to viewer demand—rather than wide release, where you'd often risked spending up front for 2,000 theaters on opening weekend and might have nothing left."

Third, when it came to dealing with profligate directors, the indies' answer was simply "don't give in." Of course, that's easier said than done. But the trick was a negotiating ploy familiar in other industries: Don't negotiate yourself but have others negotiate for you. The approach is familiar to anyone who's bought a car from a dealership (recall that the salesperson always says "I'll check with my manager" before approving your deal?). Rather than employing dubious salespersons, the indie studios would use insurance companies and banks. Insurance companies would offer a bond to guarantee the film's completion—an assurance the bank needed to lend the money. In return, it would keep a watchful eye on the finances. One indie executive explained, "If the filmmaker's and our interests were aligned, we would invariably just approve the budget increase. If they weren't, we might say, 'Look, you can either deal with me in a collegial, collaborative way, or you can deal with the insurance company.' It was a mechanism for helping to manage filmmakers."

Equity participation, staged release, reverse piggybacking, and third-party negotiators. These were the levers used by the indies in an effort to break out of the cycle of profitless, big-budget movies. The result of all the levers? Better odds of both creative and commercial success. Fox Searchlight, for example, was launched in 1994 by News Corporation as the specialty film unit of 20th Century Fox. It began with period pieces and expanded its slate of offerings over time. Like Miramax before it, it had a remarkable record. From 1998 to 2006 Searchlight produced eighteen movies. All were profitable, and many were critically acclaimed as well. During that time Searchlight returned to its corporate parent $1 billion in profits on $3 billion of revenue—figures any media executive would pray for.

It's often thought that creativity requires financial freedom. Not so, argues a former indie executive: "Being constrained financially is not a bad thing," he says. "It allows you to take creative risks without the fear that undermines creativity. When there's a lot to fear about how much you could lose, you're willing to take fewer risks. Fear is the enemy of risk."

LESS IS MORE

1. Initiatives Versus Strategy—and a Firm That Has Mastered Both

Managers everywhere have come to believe that good business rests on good initiatives. This mindset is amplified in digital worlds and content businesses, where we've come to believe that there's one winning approach, one right answer, which we could find if we only looked hard enough at others like us. It's the mindset of the Content Trap.

The trap is to focus on individual decisions rather than the sum, to pursue best practices rather than strategy. The trap is missing the functional connections that link individual decisions together and tie them to context. So far we've looked at organizations that are trying to master the art of strategy. But perhaps the most illuminating example of sound strategy that I've encountered is a company that, ironically, has come to be known for exactly the opposite of what good strategy entails: It's a firm regarded as the exemplar of best-practice management in the United States.

Danaher is the best-performing Fortune 500 company you've never heard of. It's a $65 billion industrial conglomerate headquartered in Washington, D.C. Few U.S. companies have matched its performance during the past thirty years. From its founding, in 1985, to 2015, its share price growth compounded at a stunning 23 percent a year. Not even Warren Buffett's Berkshire Hathaway has returned that kind of money during this period. And Danaher achieved these gains while operating for a long time in businesses as mundane as machine tools, tests and measurement, and product identification.

Danaher started as a private equity shop. Within a couple of years its founders refashioned it as an operational firm modeled on Toyota. Japanese firms were outperforming their American counterparts by large margins at the time, achieving impressive productivity on shop floors. Process improvement was the rage, terms like *lean manufacturing* and *kaizen* the buzzwords. Danaher embraced it all, and then some.

Lean processes and continuous improvement became part of the company's famous toolkit, the Danaher Business System, which it refined and enlarged during the next three decades and applied relentlessly across the businesses it acquired, "Danaherizing" them by sending managers at all levels through DBS training. They learned new tools around product development, problem solving, personal development, pricing, and customer research. Training programs centered around action learning, not classroom theory. Performance measurement was hard-nosed and widespread—"everything is measurable" was the company-wide conviction—but it was combined with a "blameless culture." Stretch targets were set for every individual, and outcomes were color-coded red or green depending on whether targets were met. Performance reviews were penetrating, involving a rigorous ("5 whys") approach to understanding root causes. Numbers were scrutinized with the intent to learn and improve rather than evaluate or fire. The DBS process system became, as one analyst said, "the soul of Danaher. It guides their planning, deployment, and execution."

Virtually no other company anywhere is as relentless and unyielding in its rigorous application of a common set of processes throughout the entire organization. On the face of it, Danaher is a "best practice" machine, a company that just "does it better" than others. Many analysts and competitors view it in these terms. But Larry Culp, the firm's longest-serving CEO, who held the reins from 2001 to 2014, argues otherwise:

> It's so easy, given how prominent DBS is and the strong cultural undercurrent it has, for new hires to come in and just say, "I'll do this or that." And it may appear at first blush that they're being a good corporate citizen by doing so. But as much as we teach DBS as "this is how you would do X or Y," every other sentence is a reminder that everything we do has a time, a place, and a context. And understanding context for us is critical.
>
> So a good part of what we do today is train people in *when* to use the tools, to have a thoughtful conversation around *what* tool and what process is right in what context, and *where* is it likely to have impact. That continues to be a battle, because folks often think about solutions before they identify problems.
>
> You need to make sure you're asking the right question and understanding what problem you're trying to solve in every situation, rather than the reverse. That's what we think we do uniquely. Many companies try to copy us, but they're invariably just trying to fit the facts into the solution, and that's a recipe for disaster. You can't deploy the tools if you don't have the right questions up front.

For Danaher, those questions start with its strategy process. The familiar mantras of "where to play and how to win" have been etched in its strategy playbook. The company uses them first to guide the businesses it acquires and the merger criteria it follows—criteria as disciplined as its process rigor. It explicitly shies away from companies that operate in cyclical, volatile, or low-growth environments, or those not centered around tangible products. It is careful about entering new sectors, not because there aren't opportunities there but because "there are so many potential acquisitions in our core markets that we don't need to. There's a lot of room still left on the runway," Culp remarked. The result is that while it sees about 500 potential acquisitions each year, it turns down 98 percent—a ratio virtually unheard-of in corporate America today.

Saying no extends beyond mergers and acquisitions, and to prioritization of projects. Danaher starts by identifying three-to-five year "breakthrough" initiatives, a list that is very small. Culp said:

> There is a strong emphasis around the "critical few." We like to say, "Less is more." We really try to create a cultural bias towards the reality that you can't do everything. It's really hard. Our senior team comes in and says, Yes, we need to do all those things. But priority setting is about avoiding an agenda that's a mile wide. Instead, we are trying to create a digestible load for ourselves, and better focus. So we say, Let's be realistic—we're not going to do them all this year. We may not even do them all in the next three years. But let's also be clear about what we *really* need to do this year. That may mean cutting the list by half or two-thirds.

Three-year breakthroughs are broken down into one-year initiatives, which are then coupled with metrics to track every one of them. That's how alignment happens—cascading the metrics down from senior managers to each team member, all the way to the janitor on the shop floor. The "less is more" approach extends to talent development, too: "Fewer but better people, particularly at the leadership level, can be a better bet than a legion of B and C players," Culp told me. "A smaller team is likely to be more effective and more efficient, with fewer handoffs and less coordination. Over time we were able to go into certain companies and say, We think you can go from 20 to 15 people. But it's not just that we're going to whack five people. We're going to get you to a place where you have a flat-out better team."

The entire strategy process is referred to as policy deployment, or PD. It's a translation of the Japanese *Hoishin Kanri*. "That's where it was first developed," observed Culp. "At its core, it's the cascading of strategy." Most important to remember about PD is that every initiative, every decision, and every metric is linked to every other one. It's a process of recognizing, respecting, and leveraging functional connections.

Danaher doesn't succeed because it has a magic bullet or a well-guarded secret, or because it's stumbled on some creative geniuses. Everything it does is commonsense and open-book. Yet others have found it hard to match. Culp said,

> When I was young, I could never fathom why in the world Toyota was letting all the folks from GM and Ford into its factories, letting them do their fact quest. But we do the same today. We're unafraid to tell the world what we do in great detail. And I think the reason Toyota had, which we understand a bit, is that you can see all of it, but you may not see it in 3-D.
>
> It's the same when we do competitive intelligence. When we see our peers doing something interesting, our first reaction is never to say, "Let's do it." It's to ask, "*Why* are they doing it?"

Danaher's success comes from understanding context and seeing connections. Doing so requires discipline, relentlessness, and saying no. That's not the fashion in business today, as Culp acknowledged:

> Saying no might come across as anti-entrepreneurial or anti-innovation. It's tempting to let a thousand flowers bloom. But we'd rather come out of our strategic discussions and be really clear about the three to five big ones we want to pursue—and then reinforce that operationally throughout the entire organization.

2. Strategic Experimentation at Tencent

It might seem easy for managers at Danaher to say no when they have the luxury of hundreds of projects to choose from and the wind at their back. It's far harder to say no when one operates in a fast-changing environment, confronting technology disruptions nearly every day.

But let's revisit how things are playing out at China's Tencent, which operates in as unsettled a technology environment as any. The challenge of dealing with copycats is more urgent in that country than in the United States. And it's harder to get users to pay. The transition from desktop to mobile usage occurred earlier there than in the West. Chinese customers are brutally candid in their assessment of new technology products and services, and their loyalty to any one is negligible. The result is that innovation in China is an extreme form of innovation in any entrepreneurial setting: You throw spaghetti at the wall and see what sticks.

That's how nearly every Chinese Internet entrepreneur operated for the past fifteen years. That's also how Tencent functioned during that period. Yet, something strange happened in 2013, after Tencent launched We-Chat, the all-purposeful mobile app that is quickly expanding beyond domestic borders. The firm decided to offer less, not more.

Several months after the launch of WeChat, the president of Tencent's Online Media Group (OMG) approached its creator, Allen Zhang, with the idea of launching a news service on WeChat. The idea was attractive and approval was quick. When the news service launched a few months later, it had some unusual features. Instead of pushing stories in real time onto a user's device, it did so only twice a day, at 8 A.M. and 8 P.M. (except on rare occasions when there was significant breaking news). Instead of offering hundreds of stories, it offered four—just enough to fit on a single mobile screen. Instead of using algorithms to decide what stories to offer, editors decided, sometimes choosing stories that weren't expected to boost traffic. And instead of replacing low-traffic stories, Tencent made no revisions during the course of the day—this despite the fact that traffic data was instantaneously available throughout. The news feed initially allowed for no user conversation and no personalization. There was no real-time tracking of user time on the service—not because the company couldn't, it was doing that on its microblog Weibo—but because it chose not to, believing that with the limited number of stories on offer, it had little to gain.

On a product that was as contemporary, dynamic, and feature-full as any mobile app in the world, the news service was as simple and uncomplicated as, well, print.

The day I was in Beijing, the four news stories on WeChat were about a worker who donated sixty-nine houses to his laborers; the imminent change in China's single-child policy; a fire in Beijing; and a lawsuit related to a celebrity's son that had made its way to the Supreme Court. Those were the stories for the twelve daytime hours. That was it.

As news moved across different media during the past two decades, first from print to digital, and then from the desktop Web to the iPad and smartphone, it was supposed to bring more breaking news, more personalization, more on-demand information, more frequent updates, and more user-generated content. The WeChat news product offered none of that.

But it didn't seem to matter: About 40 percent of users came to WeChat for its news product, and 53 percent clicked on its stories every day. It was among the three or four most valued features of the application.

One OMG executive explained the logic behind its unusual decisions:

> As a media product on WeChat, we are different in how we attract users and what we can do. One of the most important design features was the idea that *less is more*. That's really what makes it a great product. Users don't want personalization—they want the important news that everyone's reading. They don't want clutter—they want simplicity. They don't want interference—they want curation. If I sent you a message that said, "Here's a great *New York Times* article for you," do you want to look at it right away? You don't! But we rarely thought about that earlier.

WeChat's simplicity and its remarkable success had ripple effects throughout the company. The executive said,

> WeChat has had a huge impact on the entire organization of Tencent, not just mobile QQ. First, it pushed us toward mobile in a big way and away from the desktop. Every division has now been charged with transitioning to mobile. Second and more fundamental is a new philosophy: Less is more.
>
> Every department is now forced to think about elite products it can develop—not just any product. We are doing fewer projects, not more. This may appear counterintuitive. But earlier we were doing everything that every other company did. It was a culture of rapid imitation and of leveraging our core product, QQ. We'd build something, put it on QQ, and think we'd be successful. In reality, of course, you need a good product, not just the channel benefit. The WeChat experience made Pony Ma [Tencent's CEO] look again at the entire organization. Every department is shifting from smaller projects and opportunities to big ones. And the right to initiate a project has been taken away from our GMs and VPs and given to a ten-person group.

The irony was that in its efforts to be more innovative, the company was cutting back.

> To make any product elite, the user experience has to be supergood. You have to care about every detail. We can't do that without intense focus. We are cutting other projects at a rate we never did. If we know it won't work out, we cut it immediately. We focus only on the important ones.

The organization has become more nimble. Tencent had grown into an organization where the feeling was of working together to build a company—everybody was close, no one wanted to hurt the feelings of others. Now the company is perceived as good for people who want to get work done. It's far better. Fewer projects, better products.

Close your eyes and you'll be excused for thinking you're talking to Larry Culp. Danaher and Tencent are about as different as any two organizations you can find. One's business is industrial manufacturing, the other's is mobile networks. One is traditional American, the other brand-new Chinese. One's philosophy centers on continuous improvement, the other's on creative possibilities. One is built on commonsense management, the other on uncommon entrepreneurs. Yet both converged on the same organizational and innovation philosophy: Less is more.

24
DARE TO NOT MIMIC

You're in charge of a digital transformation effort at a content business, and you're crafting your strategy for what to do. Here's what you decide: Go slow. Borrow organizational routines from your core. Reproduce your analog content online. Hire insiders.

If you were to ever design a digital strategy destined to fail, these would be its characteristics. Yet that's exactly what *The Economist* did for much of the past decade. And it's yielded more success than most other magazines. How to reconcile?

The secret lies in avoiding the temptation to look at content initiatives one by one and instead seeing them as a series of closely connected decisions. The secret lies in avoiding the view that the choices you make should be based on someone else's or in identifying best or worst practices that *everyone* should adopt or avoid.

These biases surface everywhere but are more pronounced in content businesses, where we've been trained to search for magic bullets. And they're most pronounced in digital worlds, where technologies change with such ferocity that managers and entrepreneurs are often at a loss to articulate or craft their digital response. It's natural that they would look at peers—others who are similarly struggling to stay afloat or just keep up—for any ideas that might work, any clues about what to do, and any hints about what strategies to embrace.

We hear these ideas all the time: Aggregate, don't produce. Build, don't buy. Erect paywalls. Create virtual currencies. Look at others making content similar to yours and with business models similar to yours. Copy what they're doing. Imitate and borrow. And whatever you do, do it quickly.

Follow these prescriptions and you're likely to end up on the wrong side of success.

Each of these prescriptions reflects the Content Trap. It's the trap where we look at others like us—others making similar content and also trying to navigate digital worlds—for answers to these struggles, rather than figuring out on our own what's right *for us*.

When everyone is trying something new, that's when understanding the role of context is more important than ever. When user behaviors are evolving at a rapid clip and technologies present new opportunities even more rapidly, that's when it's most important to think about where you'll say no. When costs are lowered and distribution is limitless so that everyone can participate, it becomes more, not less, important to think about how you're different.

Winning strategies come from recognizing the context you operate in, not the content you make. They come from recognizing the connections among choices, not from viewing choices in isolation. They come from setting priorities and saying no, rather than following the herd and grabbing every opportunity that comes your way.

They come from going back to the basics of strategy: Know your customers and what they want, and align your organization to deliver it in a unique way. That requires seeing, respecting, and making connections across your decisions.

Functional connections are the third wheel of the Connections Triad. They extend beyond connected users and connected products to the connections between choices themselves. *These* connections are what create competitive advantage and allow firms to differentiate themselves from so many others trying to do the same thing. They are where successful strategies reside.

Recognize this and it has profound implications. You'll understand why strategies of firms like Walmart and Danaher—elegantly simple and astonishingly open-book—have stood the test of time, nearly impossible for competitors to match. You'll understand why the most successful retailer in the world won't spend money improving the ambience of its stores and why the fastest-growing brokerage in America charges users more than $100 per trade.

Even digital winners are learning about these ideas firsthand. Amazon and Netflix enjoyed scarcity as online retailers in large part due to the physical infrastructure they'd built up, not any peculiar digital economics of the arenas where they fought. Now, as they move into retailing digital products, they are being forced to find new ways to differentiate themselves from hundreds of others who can do the same. Even the Internet giant Tencent, competing in an increasingly networked world with massive winner-take-all dynamics, has recently embraced the philosophy that less is more. Media organizations, even as they compete in a digital world where their product is increasingly commoditized, are learning to differentiate not just on content, but on customers and experiences.

Digital economies promise abundance. But competitive advantage ultimately comes from scarcity and differentiation. Marrying the two is the key to digital success.

So don't just follow the herd when figuring out your own digital path. Dare to *not* mimic.

PART IV

EVERYONE'S A MEDIA COMPANY

25
ADVERTISING—THE PROMISE AND DEBATES

Predictions about the impact of the Internet are as old as the Internet itself. But few predictions aroused as much excitement during the early 1990s as those concerned with its effect on advertising. "The future of advertising is the future of media," one observer wrote in *Wired* magazine. And the future seemed bright.

Advertising is hardly a recent phenomenon: The first ads we've discovered date to ancient Egypt, Greece, and Rome, when sales messages and lost-and-found notices could be found on papyrus. The basic approach remained unchanged for centuries: Put out an ad, and hope people respond.

There were challenges, however. As the nineteenth-century retailer John Wanamaker is said to have lamented, "Half the money I spend on advertising is wasted—I just don't know which half."

One reason it was hard to assess the effects of advertising, until recently, is that most ads were placed through mass media—TV, newspapers, radio—meaning that companies couldn't really target the recipients. Everyone who watched the medium got exposed to the ads placed there. Measuring advertising exposures was hard, too: Advertisers often had little clue about who saw or heard their ads. They had some broad demographic data about the audience but only limited information about individual exposure.

The Internet would change all that, it was believed. Advertisers could target precisely—so precisely that they could even choose which particular individuals to send their ads to. "In the one-to-one world the Net promises," wrote celebrated journalist and technology analyst Esther Dyson, "advertising will often be tailored and of higher quality. Those with more money to spend will get higher-quality advertising." In addition to precise targeting, measurement would improve, too. Companies would know precisely how many people were exposed to an ad and what they did in response. On top of all this, the Internet was interactive. Consumers could click through ads or ask for more—in undreamed-of ways.

Accompanying the optimism about Internet advertising were gloomy forecasts about TV advertising. In 2000, the first digital video recorders (DVRs) were introduced, with TiVo and Replay appearing at about the same time. All were simple boxes that viewers connected to their TVs, and all had features familiar from the days of VCRs: They could record programs and let viewers skip commercials while watching later on. But the new boxes made it preposterously easy to perform both functions, and they could do much more. Early studies were sobering: a whopping 88 percent of TV ads were unwatched by DVR owners. "If no one watches commercials, then there is no commercial television," *The New York Times* concluded.

As for targeted advertising, few companies anywhere elicited as much excitement about its promise as Facebook. Targeting requires knowledge of consumer preferences, of course, and Facebook had deep knowledge of its more than one billion users: It knew their age, gender, education, location, relationship status, work, media preferences, and friends. Better still, most of this information was being uploaded to Facebook by its own users, voluntarily. The potential for improving ad effectiveness seemed limitless.

So, three sets of predictions about the impact of new features on advertising markets were clear. Targeting, measurement, and interactivity would radically improve Internet ads. Fast-forwarding through commercials would be the bane of TV advertisers and broadcast networks. And one-to-one, real-time targeting based on demographics, social graphs, and behavioral information promised unlimited advertising potential. These predictions all originated with experts; all were backed by data and charts. And all were wrong.

THREE PUZZLES ABOUT ADVERTISING

Twenty years after the early predictions about online advertising, its promise is still relatively obscure. The dominant ad format for most Web publishers is not much different than in 1994, when banner ads of varying size surrounded the screen text. Targeting has become easier but has not delivered on its tremendous promise: Click-through rates (CTRs) for most ads are 0.1 percent, on average, meaning that roughly one person in a thousand actually clicks on the ad. Ways of measuring exposure have become more precise, but that hasn't helped advertisers tell what the returns on their ad investment (or their "ROI") are. Indeed, ad effectiveness remains as nebulous as ever, and marketing executives still can't figure out if their digital campaigns are worth it. (Even when they think they know, they are often wrong, as I will describe later.) Finally, "high quality" advertising has not translated into higher prices for most publishers. In fact, advertising prices—measured in "cost per 1,000 impressions," or CPMs— are falling every year.

When it comes to TV advertising and its foreshadowed demise, the picture is even more puzzling. DVRs were supposed to signal the end of broadcast advertising revenues. But from 2000 to 2015, even as DVR penetration grew to more than 40 percent of U.S. households, TV broadcast revenue held firm at about $40 billion a year; it still accounts for the second-largest share of the U.S. advertising pie. This wasn't due to some magical tricks conjured up by TV executives. A recent study by Duke University researchers showed that the high rates of ad skipping in DVR households had almost no impact on product sales, the metric of *ad effectiveness* that advertisers really care about. There was virtually no difference in product purchases between households that owned a DVR and ones that did not.

As for the promise of Facebook? That was challenged as well, although not because it's difficult to target ads to users. For several years click-through rates on Facebook had hovered around 0.3 percent—10 to 40 times lower than on Google, despite Facebook's superior user data. Now, one reason that Google's CTRs might be artificially high was "last click attribution": The fact that a consumer clicked on a Google search ad might simply reflect that she had gone to the search engine with the intent to purchase, rather than reflecting her response to the ad. But that wasn't the reason for the differences here. Facebook's CTRs were not only lower than Google's; for a while they were lower than the average for *all* sites on the Web.

Why do offline dollars translate into online pennies? How is it that apparently rampant ad skipping hasn't destroyed TV revenue? And why, for several years, were Facebook's click-through rates a fraction of Google's despite superior user information and a similarly large user base?

The answer is that the assumptions underlying all the early predictions were wrong. Get more eyeballs, the logic went, and you'll be able to expose more of them to your ads, generating more revenue. And to do this, use any means to get those ads in front of consumers since, left free to choose, most of them would turn away from ads. Implicit in this view, advertising is an irritant that consumers would love to do without.

Hold this view and you'd believe that advertising was finished when ad-skipping technologies came along. Until you realize that skipping ads was not the reason for the problems with advertising in the first place. After all, ad skipping was possible, even rampant, before DVRs: Viewers could simply ignore commercials if they chose to. Bathroom breaks, refrigerator visits, and side conversations were as problematic as any ad-skipping technology could ever be.

Similarly, hold this view and you'd think that Facebook—with its superior customer information and one billion users—was an advertiser's dream. But think about *why* people came to the site in the first place and you'd realize that Facebook had a real problem. For regular e-commerce sites, users went there with the intent to purchase. On Facebook they were there to catch up with friends. The last thing they wanted then was someone shoving a product promo in their face.

In other words, the promise of advertising was never about reach and eyeballs—simply placing more ads in front of a user, expecting they'd respond. Nor was it merely about more user data. It's about the same question as it's always been: ad effectiveness—figuring out *why* ads work at all, and *how* they do.

TWO VIEWS OF ADVERTISING: A DEEP DIVIDE

The tension between "eyeballs and effectiveness" is a microcosm of a larger debate in advertising going back at least fifty years. In his 1958 book, *The Affluent Society,* John Kenneth Galbraith painted a somber picture of how advertising worked, along with the implications for consumer welfare. "Advertising convinced people to need things they don't really need," he wrote. This was the "dependence effect."

Galbraith was offering a view that captured what many consumers, and even marketing executives, believed. But there's another, radically different, view of why marketing works. It's a story of advertising as an instrument not of unwelcome persuasion, but of desirable information.

Interested in buying a car? You might have no idea where to start were it not for ads containing information about size, gas efficiency, and price. Feel like seeing a movie? Rather than be stuck with a bad choice for hours, you can watch a three-minute sample—a trailer—and then decide.

Advertising works in these cases not by persuading you to buy things you don't want but by giving you information you need. In other words, ads could be good not only for companies but also for consumers. And it was good because it helped them make choices that were right for them.

So which is it—does advertising work through persuasion or by providing information? Answering that question is not only incredibly important; it's incredibly difficult, for two reasons, as we'll see.

THE ENDOGENEITY PROBLEM

The first challenge in uncovering the effect of advertising is that regardless of any theory about *how* advertising works, it's hard to figure out *whether* it works. People exposed to an ad are often the consumers *already* predisposed toward purchasing the product. After all, you won't see ads in a women's magazine, for example, unless you first choose to read that magazine. You're more likely to see trailers for a kids' movie if you're watching another kids' movie. You're more likely to see a beer commercial on TV if you're watching sports—in which case you're probably already drinking beer.

In other words, the fact that you bought a product may have nothing to do with your having been exposed to an ad for it. It may be that your preferences for products are what lead you to watch certain ads in the first place—and this arises because advertisers target consumers, seeking out media channels where they're more likely to find consumers who are right for them. This is what scholars of economics and marketing call the "reverse causation" challenge, or the "endogeneity problem." Its central question: Does advertising exposure *lead to* product purchase, or do consumer preferences *result in* both ad exposure and product purchase?

Overcoming this empirical hurdle is not merely an academic exercise. It goes to the heart of marketing and whether advertising dollars are money well spent. Google earns more than $40 billion a year from paid searches— easily the most important form of advertising on the Web and the fastest-growing part of the marketing pie. But why are Google ads so effective? One answer is that they give consumers precisely the information they need to make a purchase. Another possibility, however, is that paid keywords (for Patagonia, say) are just a substitute for a search result (Patagonia.com) that a user would have clicked on anyway. If that's the case, attributing a purchase decision to an ad overstates the ad's impact.

Berkeley professor Steve Tadelis became concerned about the endogeneity problem after joining eBay as its Distinguished Economist and senior director in 2011, and while overseeing a marketing project aimed at pinpointing where the firm might best spend its marketing dollars. Tadelis said, "The question of how you maximize your returns on advertising across different media channels—what's commonly referred to as the 'media mix' problem—is a pretty straightforward problem if you know the returns. My initial reaction was, 'Wow, that's a really hard problem,' because I was thinking about the endogeneity issues that make it hard to accurately measure the returns on advertising in any particular channel."

eBay had commissioned a consulting firm to do the analysis for the project. As Tadelis poked around internally for answers, his eBay colleagues encouraged him to talk to the firm to better understand its approach. He recalled the conversation with the consultants:

> The first part of the call was essentially a marketing spiel describing how great they were—founded twenty-five years ago, had tons of experience, and so on. Then they talked about their methods—"proprietary transformation functions" is what they called them—and how computationally burdensome it was to run their models. It took us ten or fifteen minutes to realize that there was nothing proprietary here; these were plain-vanilla regression models with nonlinear variables added in. You can run more flexible versions of their models on essentially an iPhone today.
>
> When we probed further, they talked about adding variables to the model—stock market behavior, time of the year, holidays, etc.—to measure the "incremental lift" of advertising, as they called it. It was clear that did nothing to address the problem of endogeneity. Finally, when pressed against the wall, they mentioned using Lagrange multipliers to solve the problem.

Lagrange multipliers are used to figure out the maximum or minimum value of a given function, subject to certain constraints. On the face of it, the consultants' answer wasn't crazy—after all, eBay was trying to figure out what spending mix would maximize the returns on its ad dollars, subject to its returns on advertising in different channels. But as Tadelis noted, "To know the answer, you need to know the function and the constraints. They had just pulled a fancy term out of their heads to intimidate us so that we would fold. Except that I teach this stuff. That's when I knew they were bullshitting me."

The firm presented its results to eBay a few weeks later. Its main finding was that the highest return on investment—1,200 percent—came from spending on the keyword *eBay.* Tadelis recalled, "I raised my hand and suggested that keyword bidding is probably negative one hundred percent ROI, since if you don't serve someone the ad, they're probably going to click on the organic search result that appears right below it. They started saying, 'You can't think about it this way, it's really long-term branding,' and so on. It was clear then that this was all just smoke and mirrors."

So Tadelis and a few eBay colleagues decided to probe the matter on their own.

Eventually they carried out a series of experiments that directly addressed the endogeneity problem by trying to separate the effects of paid and natural, or organic, searches. As they noted, the stakes were not trivial: "eBay manages over 100 million keywords and keyword combinations daily using algorithms that are updated daily and that automatically feed into Google's, Microsoft's, and Yahoo!'s search platforms." And the consequences of mismeasurement are particularly severe for paid search: "If you place an ad in *The New York Times* on a particular day and more people see the ad for whatever reason, you aren't going to pay more. And if people don't see the ad, you aren't going to pay less. That's not true of Internet advertising, and in particular of paid search—the more people click, the more you pay."

In one experiment, eBay halted all search engine marketing (SEM) queries for keywords involving the eBay brand (for example, "eBay shoes") on the Microsoft and Yahoo! search engines while continuing to pay for them on Google. In another, it ceased all bidding for nonbranded keywords (for example, "shoes") on Google in a sample of randomly chosen geographic areas for sixty days. The results of both experiments were sobering. In the first experiment, almost all the traffic forgone through paid clicks was compensated for by natural searches. That is, "shutting off paid search ads closed off one (costly) path to a company's website but diverted traffic to natural search, which is free to the advertiser" (in this case, eBay). In the second experiment, for nonbranded keywords, the results were similar: Search engine marketing had a small but negligible effect on sales. And most of the effect was from new registered users who were infrequent shoppers (buying one or two items on eBay the year before). Paid searches proved to have no effect on frequent shoppers—they would have gone to the site and bought the product anyway. Tadelis noted, "For people who bought on eBay more than three times in the previous year, or who frequented eBay in the past 90 days, advertising has literally close to a negative 100% return on investment: these people would have come anyway, and if you put the ad in front of them they'll click on it instead of coming in some other way. But that doesn't cause them to buy more." As for the overall returns on search advertising? The study concluded that because "frequent users whose purchasing behavior is not influenced by ads account for most of the advertising expenses," it resulted in "average returns that are negative."

In other words: Paid searches are essentially wasted money.

This was perhaps the cleanest study to date on the effects of online advertising—and it certainly was one of the most provocative. It was published in one of the most prestigious economics journals. Regarding the industry reaction, Tadelis said that "when the paper hit the media, Google was not a very happy camper." Google had released its own report, which showed a large incremental lift in clicks when using paid search. "Their result was right," Tadelis noted, "except that the real question is whether incremental clicks are incremental sales. We showed in the eBay data that by reducing paid search, we lose clicks—just as Google said—but we don't lose sales. The reason is that most clicks come from people who visit the site a lot anyway, so when you advertise more, you just get more clicks to the site—not more sales."

Did the results generalize beyond eBay? For large companies with well-known brands, the endogeneity logic ought to raise similar concerns about paid-search effectiveness, the authors noted. For lesser-known brands or new products—for which, in effect, there were few "frequent shoppers" like with eBay—paid search might very well pay off by increasing awareness or providing information about their existence (more on this later). But most reactions to the paper were generally of a different ilk, Tadelis recalled:

Several bloggers in the business of Internet marketing analytics argued that "of course, paid search didn't work for eBay—eBay's a stupid company, and it doesn't know how to spend its money." Was eBay stupid in that it was using the wrong keywords? Absolutely not—by then eBay had learned a lot about keyword bidding from prediction models developed by a very sophisticated group of Ph.D. computer scientists. But the models fell under the category of machine learning, where all you care about is correlation, not causation. Was eBay wasting a lot of money? Yes—just like any company that's not aware. And that's practically all companies using the industry's best practices, which are flawed because of the endogeneity problem.

eBay hadn't set out to understand how the endogeneity problem affected the returns on paid search. And Tadelis would never have thought about the question if he hadn't been at eBay. The study had come about entirely through these circumstances. But it cast a spotlight on one of the most important areas of Internet advertising, one that, strangely, no one had examined. Tadelis candidly reflected on the lack of prior inquiry:

> The field of marketing analytics and Internet advertising is a bit like seventeenth-century medicine. There are snake oil salesmen trying to sell their wares. They charm or intimidate you with jargon, their methods are a black box, and no one can evaluate whether or not their approach is solid. Reports from publishers appear credible and smart but are ultimately self-interested. And then there's the question of marketing budgets. What would happen if we figured out that half the budget, as Wanamaker said many years ago, doesn't need to be spent, and with the digital economy we know where it doesn't need to be spent? Ad agencies might lose half their budgets, and I don't think that's something anyone, even the client's chief marketing officer, wants. So there's a classic agency problem. Most marketing people aren't trying to cheat the company— they really believe this works. The client wants to believe it, too. But they don't trust the science because they don't have the training or skills, and they end up going largely on gut instincts.

And how did eBay respond? "It stopped bidding for the keyword *eBay*—if you type 'eBay' into Google, you will not get an eBay ad. For non-keyword bidding, the firm has revised its bidding strategy" based on the research of Tadelis and his coauthors.

PERSUASION VERSUS INFORMATION

If overcoming the endogeneity problem isn't enough of a challenge—if one could in fact establish that advertising works—a second hurdle looms:

sorting out *how* advertising works. The reason is that finding that ad exposures result in product purchases is consistent with either story—persuasion or information. Persuasive advertising seduces consumers to buy a product even if they may not want it. Informative advertising leads some consumers—those for whom the product is "right"—to make a purchase. Regardless of the story, the result is the same in both cases: Advertising exposure results in product purchase.

Sorting out these competing explanations for *how* advertising works—through persuasion or information—has large consequences, as we'll see. But they are hard to sort out. One way to determine which story is correct would be to look for consumers who *should not* like a product—and then assess the impact of ads they were exposed to. But that's easier said than done. A priori evaluations of consumer preferences are hard. Identifying occasions when consumers were "mistakenly" exposed to ads is even harder. After all, companies try to target consumers they think will purchase their products.

My former colleague Ron Shachar and I tried to overcome this empirical challenge vis-à-vis promos for television programs, a context we chose for two reasons. First, as we described earlier in Part II, viewers have clear, and clearly different, preferences over TV programs, ones that are predictable. Older viewers like shows with older characters, younger viewers like shows with younger actors. Viewers like shows whose characters match their own gender, income, or education. (We are a narcissistic people: We like to watch shows about ourselves.) Second, because TV ads cannot be precisely targeted—everyone who's watching a show is exposed to a promo placed there, whether or not the promoted program was a good match or not with their preferences—there are numerous instances of "mistaken" exposures—exposures to ads for programs that weren't a good match for the viewer.

The results were striking. Look at the large effect of promos overall and it's easy to reason that they work by persuading any viewer to watch a program, whether or not that program is "right." But look at the effect of promos across different viewers and the "information" story dominates: Viewers predicted to be a poor match with a program were even less likely to tune into it if they saw the promo than if they hadn't seen it. In other words, the study suggests, advertising works primarily through matching and information, not (just) by persuasion.

The persuasion versus information stories reflect two competing philosophies of advertising. One is a "product-centered" mindset, whereby advertising persuades, irritates, interrupts, and ultimately brainwashes users. The other is a "user-centered" approach, whereby advertising acknowledges and even embraces consumers' control over their choices, giving them information when they need it. Product-centered advertising is designed to convince you to purchase a product even when you might not want it. Consumer-centered advertising makes it easier for you to find a product that you want. It's a distinction between battling, bombarding, and convincing the consumer to watch versus partnering, informing, and getting the consumer to share. As I'll describe in the following pages, the two views have vastly different implications for how we advertise, how we perceive digital technologies and their impact on marketing, and what we're likely to see going forward.

USER-CENTERED MARKETING AND WHAT IT IMPLIES

The idea of user centricity has been tossed around in marketing for decades. Yet marketing is as product-centered as any activity today. Consider advertising metrics: terms like *reach, eyeballs, sales,* and *product purchase* are de rigueur. Those are the metrics that matter, taking no account of whether consumers are pleased with the product they purchased or how they were led to make the purchase. A similar disconnect applies to incentives for marketing and sales. "Create a campaign that is memorable" is the mandate of the chief marketing officer, regardless of whether that campaign helps the consumer. "Harness effort that results in sales" is the directive for the head of sales, whether or not his team tricks consumers into buying. Similar mandates are given to ad agencies, ad networks, and anyone else involved in marketing. It's all about the results, not how we obtain them. *User centricity* may have been coined by marketers, but beneath the euphemism, it involves pounding and ultimately overwhelming the consumer.

The challenge of what metrics to focus on is relevant not only to marketers; it's also a challenge for those who determine what does and doesn't count as advertising. Consider this: The Interactive Advertising Bureau sets the rules for advertising on the Internet, in large part to create standards that can guide payments from advertisers to media firms. Several years ago the IAB ruled that even though 50 percent to 70 percent of users reported very negative associations to brands using pop-ups, "as some advertisers employ these ad types, we must sustain the viability of this ad type." More recently it ruled that as little as three seconds of exposure to a digital video ad was enough to merit compensation from an advertiser. Ever wonder why YouTube gives you the option of skipping ads after just three seconds? That's long enough to charge the advertiser. "The system is broken," a senior marketing executive told me. "Advertising networks want to continue with it, so they get paid. Clients could stop it but don't. Advertising agencies have every incentive not to stop it."

If ever a philosophy centered on fooling not just the consumer but the advertiser as well, this is it. Consumers who interact with online ads face increasing risks, too. Cisco's 2013 annual security report noted that "clicking on an ad was 182 times more likely to install a virus on a user's computer than surfing the Internet for porn."

It's not just incentives or metrics where these competing philosophies collide. These contrasting views of advertising—product-centered versus user-centered—apply everywhere.

Consider ad measurement, for starters. For the longest time, Nielsen (easily the most important) and other metrics firms collected data by medium (TV, radio, Internet), not by consumer. That's fine if you want to know which sorts of consumers watch TV or listen to the radio or go to certain websites, and therefore what a campaign for each different medium should look like. But try to understand how to best reach *a particular consumer* or optimize your integration of campaigns across different media and you are at a loss. Only in 2014 did Nielsen change its approach to tracking ad exposure, by measuring exposure for each individual across different media, rather than measuring it for different individuals on a given medium.

Or consider trends in advertising rates and the accompanying analysis. Online CPMs are low and sinking. By 2015 they were a fraction of print CPMs. The popular explanation is that there's too much supply: "Every website is a publisher now," we hear, and every ad network is commoditizing reach by allowing firms to target precisely the individuals they want. Unlimited ad inventory is a challenge for media firms, no doubt. But there's another explanation for low CPMs, one that gets less attention: Perhaps the ads simply aren't effective, so consumers don't care enough to click through. Indeed, if online advertising worked marvelously, then with its low prices, the return on investment would be enormous (ROI, after all, is just effectiveness divided by price). This, of course, is not the case, nor what most marketers believe. (If they did, ad budgets would be shifted instantaneously, and in massive amounts, to the digital arena—and that hasn't happened either: In 2014, consumer packaged goods companies, among the largest advertisers in the economy, spent less than 10 percent of their entire budget on digital ads.) CMOs are still waiting to be convinced. And the reason is that the "pricing problem" may have as much to do with low ad effectiveness as with high ad inventory.

The same tension applies to the newest trend in marketing, "big data." With words like *retargeting, real-time bidding,* and *efficiency* thrown around every day, you might think that having more information on users, and more ways of analyzing it, will solve marketing's problems. But lost in all this is what one might call the Facebook Problem. Early on, as the company sought to shape its advertising strategy, the mantra was data: graphs, demographics, targeting. It failed to yield the desired results. Eventually, Facebook veered away from individual targeting and toward social advertising, where ads were integrated into social relationships rather than merely being pushed onto recipients. (Simple examples were recommendations from friends, Facebook likes, shared stories, or price discounts made available through friends. Prominent examples included the "ice bucket challenge," where friends were tagged to either douse ice water on themselves or donate toward research on amyotrophic lateral sclerosis [ALS]; or, Budweiser's "Buds for Buds" campaign, which allowed Facebook users to buy a friend a beer by sending them a receipt redeemable at their local bars.) The differences were noticeable: Click-throughs increased dramatically. As Facebook learned along the way, more data alone wasn't enough to convert a lousy ad into a good one, or persuasion into information. By itself, it won't help us understand why advertising works. It won't solve the endogeneity problem. And it's no substitute for understanding users, and user behavior, more deeply.

Digital advertising is still "a black box," one analyst noted recently. "We have a long way to go."

NATIVE ADVERTISING—AND WHAT IT'S REALLY ABOUT

On January 14, 2013, a story on the Church of Scientology appeared on the website of *The Atlantic,* the nationally renowned magazine devoted to cultural and political news. In itself, this wasn't surprising. What was surprising was its content—curiously and unabashedly complimentary of

Scientology's controversial leader, David Miscavige. On the top left corner of the article was a banner indicating that the article was "sponsored content," a euphemism for a paid advertisement. That wasn't nearly enough to quell scathing criticism, which came within hours. "The Theft of Credibility," screamed *Wired*. "The Lessons of the *Atlantic's* Scientology Blunder" was the headline of a *Guardian* piece making the point that "trust is more easily squandered than earned." *The Atlantic* published an apology within a day, with the simple opening, "We screwed up."

"Native advertising" means embedding an ad message in other content. The idea itself isn't new. It's been around for a long time. Magazines refer to it as "advertorials." In television, it's called "product placement" or "branded entertainment"—recently exemplified by huge Coke cups on *American Idol* and by the Donald Trump–anchored *Celebrity Apprentice,* where challenges included creating a new ice cream flavor for Walgreen's store brand or producing a ninety-second video for LG's home entertainment system.

It's one thing for entertainment programs to augment ad revenues this way. It's another thing when news outlets start doing the same. That trend has turned up the heat in the debate over native advertising.

On the face of it, there are two simple, opposing perspectives. One regards native advertising as a creative approach to news organizations' increasing revenue challenges, ones that have become more pressing as digital advertising prices fall and digital displays or banners are increasingly ignored. The other considers it a willful fooling of the customer, one that dangerously undermines the integrity of journalism by compromising the long-held separation of church from state, or editorial from advertising content.

It's tempting to view the debate over native advertising in this way—between those who are determined to preserve journalism versus those who are determined to exploit it. But what makes the debate more vexing is that this is not the only way people are lining up on both sides of the aisle. The debate is bringing together strange bedfellows. And the reason is that, ultimately, the debate over native advertising is not really about church versus state, but about a product-centered versus a user-centered mindset toward advertising and which one will prevail.

To see this, it's useful to understand how the recent trend toward native advertising started. *The Huffington Post* played a more prominent role in its rise than any other organization. But it was inspired not by an innate preference for the approach or by the revenue shortfalls that later drove other publishers, but by its content management system (CMS).

CMSs are computer applications used by media organizations to upload, display, organize, store, and manipulate content on their websites—seemingly mundane sets of tasks that would hardly differentiate one news organization from another. But at *The Huffington Post,* it did.

"In most traditional content organizations, when you published an article your job was done," Janet Balis, former publisher of *Huff Po,* said in a recent conversation. "At *Huff Po* that was just the beginning." The CMS analyzed who read every article, who shared it, and how often. This data was relayed back to the editors' desks, where dashboards displayed this data side by side with the content.

Paul Berry, appointed chief technology officer of *Huff Po* in 2007, was key to the creation of its CMS. He told me, "We were really the first organization to allow editors to track reader metrics in real time. We were really proud that through these stats and dashboards, we were able to allow the editorial staff to manage their activities." *Huff Po*'s CMS turned out to be formidable at driving traffic around search and social. "It was the most extraordinary architecture to connect content to conversation," summarized Balis.

Huff Po's CMS was designed to track how well a piece of content performed. What no one initially realized was its value in tracking the performance of advertising. This quickly became clear, as Berry described: "We'd see the CMO of a large organization, do a demo, and show how our content was created, together with the audience tools. Then we'd look to sell them sponsored blog posts, banners, and curtains. They invariably would ask, How can we get your content management platform? That's what we really want." Advertisers had seen *Huff Po*'s growth in content and traffic, and now wanted the same tools.

This insight led to the creation of an entirely new role within *Huff Po:* social marketing managers. They were trained on the same tools as the editorial team; they knew how to optimize traffic and sharing, and how to use the dashboard. The only difference was that they reported back to advertisers to tell them how their ads were doing. Jonah Peretti, one of the founders of *The Huffington Post,* would later recreate this approach at BuzzFeed. Berry himself went on to found RebelMouse, a platform that could be accessed by any publisher looking to track reader metrics and content sharing in real time.

Janet Balis noted the significance of this moment in *Huff Po,* when advertising began to mimic the look and feel of content. "The recognition that the CMS could be used as an advertising technology was important. If the goal of advertising was click-throughs and conversions and engagement, that's what our content teams were focused on, too. Use the same tools and the same experts, and similar metrics, and you start to see the same look and feel and design. You start to see the lines getting blurred."

Though acutely aware of the seeds of dangers in this trend, Balis also underlined the benefits—including those for readers.

> There are various positive things that come from doing what the best content creators on the planet have been doing. Why shouldn't advertisers emulate the quality of the recipes that come out of Martha Stewart's test kitchen when placing their messages there? Why shouldn't they emulate the viewpoint of *The Economist* when inserting their messages there? Doing so just means you're the best at your craft. And understanding that has value to consumers.

Her argument was simple but important. Traditionally an ad was tailored to a product and then the same ad was placed in hundreds of different media channels. Native advertising, in effect, allowed an ad to be tailored not only to each product but to each media channel as well. The payoff from aligning the ad message with the brand context was improved advertising effectiveness.

But what about the effect of ads on consumer perceptions of editorial quality? That, one might expect, also depends on brand context. Experiments support this idea. Recall the experiment on "names" described earlier, where we compared the effectiveness of the same editorial content on different websites. We ran the same experiment again, this time randomly exposing participants to a different set of advertising messages inserted in each source. Among the participants who read an article on *The Economist*'s site, a third saw no ads, a third saw beautifully crafted ads (from American Express, Jaguar, and the like), and a third saw cheap pop-up ads. A similar randomized treatment was conducted with participants who read an article on *The Huffington Post* and one on the unbranded website.

The result? Among those who saw ads on the unbranded site, exposure to *any* form of advertising increased perception of editorial quality. Readers might infer that if someone were willing to pay for ad space there, the site couldn't be too lousy. Among those reading *The Economist*, the results were very different: Quality ads got the same response in terms of perceived editorial quality as no ads. But insert low-quality ads and perceived editorial quality fell. As for *The Huffington Post*? There was no difference in perceived editorial quality between seeing ads of any type and seeing none at all.

The key point is that the effect of ads on editorial quality is strikingly different for sites with different brand legacies. It's an intuitive idea: It matters who you are. But it explains why the incentive to experiment with advertising in all its forms—native or otherwise—has been, and should be, different from publisher to publisher. Offer trust and quality and you're playing with fire if you experiment too far. Lack these attributes and ads *of any kind* might lend credibility.

A recent study by two Stanford professors, Navdeep Sahni and Harikesh Nair, explicitly examined how native advertising works, and whether it does so by deceiving consumers. The setting was a mobile app for restaurant searches; both the format (native or not) and frequency of ads were randomized in the experiment. To separate the effect of a consumer's *propensity to purchase* from an ad's *propensity to confuse,* the researchers examined the specific manner in which consumers responded to native ads. While such ads were very effective—on average, they increased calls to a restaurant by 67%—it wasn't because they tricked consumers into purchase: Consumers continued to search *after* viewing the native ad and, if they did eventually select the advertised restaurant, they did it through regular search or organic clicks, suggesting low support for the *naïve consumer* view. It's not that consumers are never fooled, of course. But the "default presumption that consumers are easily tricked," the authors cautioned, is probably not the case either.

The bottom line: Done the right way, advertising doesn't help only advertisers; it can also help publishers and readers.

Raju Narisetti recently amplified this point when we talked. Narisetti knows a thing or two about church and state: He's been a newsroom insider who has traversed *The Economic Times* and *Mint* in India and *The Wall Street Journal* and *The Washington Post* in the United States. Narisetti is adamant that the church-state separation of editorial from advertising is a relic of the past, something out of touch with today's reality. At first, you'd think he's sold out. Until you hear he's saying something different. His argument isn't driven by a desire to make advertising work. It's driven by a desire to make content work.

Newsrooms used to believe that great content was their unique selling proposition. Increasingly, great content is a given—table stakes. If you put any content out, within thirty seconds ten other people have something similar to say. I believe that for newsrooms to be successful, they will have to pivot from focusing only on content to focusing on reader experiences. That's a profound change, because all those experiences—good or bad—come through the intersection of content and technology.

That's a more challenging thing than anything we've done so far, because these two sets of people—technologists and journalists—inhabit very different universes. They are usually on separate floors or even in separate buildings. Their language and vocabulary are different. Most developers think the art is the code and everything else is stuff; most journalists think the art is words and everything else is stuff. The only way to overcome this is by changing the language of newsrooms from creating great content to creating great experiences. To create a structure around experience creation means that in addition to editors and writers, you have to have developers in the mix, product people in the mix, user interface people in the mix, and data analytics people in the mix. That's where the idea of church versus state is causing us huge problems—because everything outside the newsroom is considered "business."

And this is without even getting into the question of advertising people in the newsroom or native advertising. That would just be a natural evolution of what we need to do.

Narisetti's idea isn't to merge church and state. It's to create the sensibilities of each in the other.

I would create a company-wide advertising innovation process team with decision-making authority from the newsroom product, technology, analytics, and advertising; but working primarily on creating innovation rather than fielding it. Not one newsroom in the U.S. has a cross-silo Ad Innovation Team. That's because of church and state. The unintended consequence is that we've abdicated the relationship of readers to advertisers.

As a result, most advertising innovation today is just intrusion masquerading as innovation. Pre-roll is a great example of that, where for fifteen seconds you can't do anything but watch an ad—that's like saying, We know you want to get to the content, but let's stop you first and drive you nuts. This type of innovation is pretty much on auto play. We need to change that, to create ads that are part of the experience.

That's what makes the debate about native advertising interesting—and maddening. Balis and Narisetti dream of creating better customer experiences by having advertisers develop newsroom sensibilities, and having newsrooms more integrated with the rest of the organization. Others worry about a slippery slope, where the loser is journalism and the integrity of news. Who's right? It depends on your mindset as you execute this idea. One mindset envisions integrating content with other parts of the business—design, technology, user interface, advertising—to create a better experience for the customer, yet remains unabashedly committed to transparency and disclosure. Get it right and readers should *want* to see ads, read sponsored content, and link to related stories—with completely open eyes. The other embraces native advertising as another way to make a buck and fool the customer, with disclosure in name only. The result will be more of the kind of cynicism and outrage that *The Atlantic* unfortunately experienced.

The debate over native advertising, in other words, isn't only about swindlers versus guardians of journalism. It's also a debate between those trying to preserve content and those trying to improve experiences—between those with a product-centered mindset and those with a user-centered one.

26
REIMAGINING ADVERTISING

WINDS OF CHANGE: HOW USER-CENTRICITY MIGHT YET SHAKE UP THE ADVERTISING INDUSTRY

1. Users as Partners

When I met John Winsor, we were both leading digital ventures in larger organizations: he at the advertising conglomerate Havas, I at Harvard Business School. As we shared experiences about trying to "innovate from within," I was struck by one thing. He was swimming upstream.

Winsor was, then and until recently, the chief innovation officer of Havas. But he's hardly your typical advertising executive.

He hails from Boulder, Colorado, and embodies its famed outdoor culture. He's run triathlons, competed in professional inline skating events, and set a world speed record running up Mount Kilimanjaro. He's spent much of his time recently surfing in Mexico, even as he headed Victors & Spoils, one of the fastest-growing advertising agencies in the United States. And he's trying to shake up the advertising world with his approach to user-centered marketing.

It began in 1989. Winsor told me,

If you live in Boulder, all your friends are professional athletes. My wife was one—she competed in the world triathlon championships. So were so many of our other friends. You'd sit around with a bunch of professional athletic women and they'd say, "There are all these men's athlete magazines, why isn't there a women's?" That's how it all started.

Women's Sports + Fitness (WSF) was one of the only magazines in the 1980s entirely devoted to female athletes. Started as *womenSports* by tennis legend Billie Jean King ten years earlier, it had been bought by *Redbook*. But, Winsor recalls, "It quickly ran into financial trouble. It just wasn't in the right place at the right time. It's almost as bad to start a business that's too new as to start a business whose idea is too late."

Part of the magazine's problems might have stemmed from being too innovative too early. The other part was rooted in its advertising-driven model. Winsor said,

> The game of the day was maximizing ad dollars per subscriber. And the fastest way to charge your advertisers more was to grow your subscriber base—genuinely or artificially. The magazine ostensibly had 450,000 subscribers when I bought it. But most of them were fake. So the first thing I did was try to give away the bad circulation. I became the laughingstock of the advertising industry for trying to do so. People were like, "Winsor just bought a bankrupt magazine and he's going to cut the circulation. Can you believe it?" I would go to conferences and they would basically say, "What an idiot."

The idiotic strategy paid off.

> I cut circulation dramatically, to 150,000. But I told the advertisers we were focusing on our core subscribers, that these were the ones you want, and that you can get these subscribers for only half of what you were paying last week. No advertiser dropped out. So I cut circulation by two-thirds, but advertising revenues only in half. I quickly went from being very unprofitable to being really profitable.

Focusing on core subscribers was the first step. The next step was leveraging those subscribers, smartly. Doing that, however, required an understanding of who their customer base really comprised. "This was somewhat serendipitous," Winsor noted. "Our data showed that our readers said, on average, that they told twelve other people what to buy, how to do exercise, and so on. This was key in our rebranding."

Two of *WSF*'s major competitors at the time were the magazines *Self* and *Shape*.

> Our previous owners had said, "We are like *Self* and *Shape*." We said, "No, we are not. *Self* and *Shape* are the people who come to the yoga class. We are the yoga instructors."

This "high-end" repositioning proved attractive to advertisers, too. Then *WSF* ventured beyond its core customer base.

We then created a high school sports magazine. To sell it, we targeted coaches. We sent a booklet called *How to Coach Better* to every coach of every women's sports team in America, accompanied by forty-five copies of the magazine. And we said, "Thank you so much for leading the way and building these future leaders. We are going to help you with this magazine, and would you please hand out the magazines to the athletes."

Soon *WSF* had moved beyond creating magazines to creating research reports as well: "We had barely convinced advertisers that women did sports. They weren't interested in high school girls' sports. So we created a product called the Reporter." The reports were merely daily logs of what women athletes did—"ethnographic descriptions," Winsor said. But the information proved invaluable to companies and advertisers trying to build businesses targeted at women athletes. *WSF* spent $5,000 to create each report. It sold them for $25,000 apiece.

That's when I realized how distorted the advertising funnel was. We had the early adopters. We had the product ideas. We had the research insights. Yet we were capturing only a small fraction of the product and marketing value created in the business. So much of it went to the ad agencies. That's when I asked, what happens if we take these early adopters and put them *on top* of the funnel?

In 1998, Winsor sold *Women's Sports + Fitness* to Condé Nast and started Radar Communications, a strategy and research agency styled on the philosophy of "co-creation" in marketing: users as partners in the product generation and communication process. He'd been deeply influenced by Boulder, and by firms like Nike. "Nike did this brilliantly. They'd fly my wife and her pro athlete friends to Portland for a few days. They'd just sit around trading stories, doing sports, hacking with their designers. This was user-generated product, and then the products marketed themselves."

Next came a book outlining Winsor's philosophy. But "my publisher titled it *Beyond the Brand*. They wouldn't let me call it *Co-Creation*. That will never happen, they said. User-centered marketing will never happen."

Pro women athletes had been the first user-marketer-designer partnership for Winsor. And it had come naturally there: "Boulder is all about athletic hacking. Climbers would break things to make it easier to climb. Inline skaters would hack equipment. Nordic skiers would tweak materials. If you have the best hack, chances are it will help you win the race."

But Radar quickly moved beyond athletics to launch several more partnerships: Levi's signature brand ("we found fifteen mothers and their twelve-year-old daughters, paired them with a designer, and the job was to build a new line of products for the Signature Line"). Toyota. Intel. Hewlett-Packard.

Winsor's dramatic early successes, now spanning two companies and more than fifteen years, had all come from a simple marketing philosophy: Think of users as partners.

Women's Sports + Fitness and Radar were embracing a different approach to marketing. They weren't telling their readers to buy things they couldn't care about. Quite the opposite: They'd invite readers in to help them understand who to sell to, how to market, and even what to make. Users were partners in selling and they were partners in idea generation.

In 2007 Winsor sold Radar to another ad agency, Crispin Porter + Bogusky. But he wasn't done.

2. Crowdsourcing the Creative

After selling Radar, Winsor joined Crispin Porter + Bogusky (CPB), overseeing strategy and product innovation. CPB was a self-styled creative firm currently being led by Alex Bogusky—"a creative genius, a freak, an awesome idea machine," according to Winsor. And it was going from success to creative success. It created campaigns for Burger King, BMW's Mini, Nike, the antismoking campaign Truth.com, and Microsoft's audacious "I'm a PC" refrain. It grew from 200 to 1,200 employees within two years. It thumbed its nose at Madison Avenue, choosing to locate headquarters in Boulder instead. And it famously refused to pitch for business; clients approached it, rather than the other way round. For its creative work, CPB was anointed "Agency of the Year" by the trade press a stunning thirteen times. In 2010, *Advertising Age* named it "Agency of the Decade."

In 2009, Bogusky and Winsor wrote a book, *Baked In,* describing the basic CPB philosophy to product design and marketing. The central thesis: These should be integrated activities. "Rather than creating a product first and then thinking of marketing, businesses and products should market themselves." The philosophy was in part an offshoot of Winsor's earlier experience with *WSF* and Radar. Now, they'd test it even further.

By 2010 CPB had more business than it could handle. "Along came a smaller client, Brammo motorcycles, to design a logo. We had too much work, but this was a passion project. We decided to do it."

To do so, the agency pushed their limits even further.

> We'd just seen a friend, Ben Malbon, who decided to crowdsource a new logo for BBH Labs. They used the open platform crowdSPRING, on which the buyer would continually provide scoring feedback to submissions that were visible to all, a platform feature designed to allow buyers to shape crowd work in a preferred direction. The industry reaction was predictable: "We are making money, don't blow a hole in this." Alex and I looked at each other and said, "Oh, this is kind of cool." So we decided to use crowdSPRING for the Brammo work.

CPB put out a simple brief for Brammo's work on crowdSPRING. They also offered a prize—$10,000 for the winning submission. "It was ten times more than anything that had been offered on the crowdSPRING platform. And this was the first crowdsourcing work ever offered by the ad industry on behalf of a client."

The contest attracted thousands of designers in the first week alone. It persuaded Bogusky and Winsor to write a business plan for a new agency, one based entirely on crowdsourcing principles.

> Our parent company's reaction was: "Are you kidding me? This destroys our entire economic value." So I went out, got a VC to back me, got a few friends from Boulder, and we started Victors & Spoils.

Winsor's world was changing fast. What had started out twenty-five years earlier as an invitation to users to participate in marketing had grown into an "open" philosophy around marketing: Invite users, invite designers, invite anyone who can contribute to marketing ideas and strategy. Invite them in rather than work against them. Winsor described the tension:

> In the traditional marketing world, it's us versus them. Company versus customer. It's as if the interests aren't aligned. But think about the greatest brands and marketers: Apple, Nike, Patagonia. They have a different approach. If you go to the Nike campus and look around, you are like, "Oh, that's a customer. That's an athlete. That's a designer." They are all there. It's what I refer to as an *eco-tone*. It's a place where two ecosystems come together, a transition zone. For instance, if you have a wetland and

a forest, in the eco-tone the attributes of both coexist and thrive. It's like a petri dish that fuels both kinds of things. The best marketers have large eco-tones. It's not us versus them.

FROM CO-CREATION TO CONNECTIONS

a. User Connections I: From Viewing to Sharing

Partnering and co-creation are examples of user-centered marketing. Connections take you even further.

Winsor recalls an incident from college that shaped his thinking:

Mine is a fifth-generation publishing family. During my college summers I worked for my father, who was a newspaper publisher at the *Canton Daily Ledger* in Illinois. One summer I worked there on the city desk, and we had an article about some old ladies in a nursing home in Canton who went to Peoria, the big town. And how Betty Sue got a cheeseburger and Julie got some fries and a shake. I said, "Come on, dad. This sucks for a collegiate guy. Who cares about what some old lady in Canton had to eat?" My father gave me a dressing down. He said, "You don't understand the world. The way you sell newspapers is you make it about your readers, by your readers, and for your readers. That's the way you create interest in what you write, because when Julie reads the newspaper at her nursing home she is going to tell all her friends. And everyone else will buy a newspaper. It's a community activity."

This was a huge influence in everything I did beyond that.

Getting consumers to like your advertisement is one thing. Getting them to like your product is better. And better still is when they tell others to like it. That's when advertising moves beyond a message from a firm to its customers and becomes messages from customers to one another. That's an example of ad sharing, or what we now refer to as "viral advertising." It's one expression of user connections.

Viral advertising, word of mouth, and *social advertising* are some of the hottest terms today. Understanding what drives ad sharing, however, is elusive. Why do certain TV ads go viral? What increases peer-to-peer sharing of news articles? Why are certain messages retweeted more than others? Marketers have been studying these things for years. And certain findings have emerged: Make your ads humorous and they're viewed more—but not shocking, or they'll be shared less, reported a study exploring what made certain TV ads viral. Arouse awe or anger and a story will be shared more; arouse sadness and it won't be shared—reported another study on the sharing of *New York Times* articles. Surprising or useful information increases sharing. Some firms have tried to build a business around "engineering virality." Mekanism, an ad agency launched in 2000 that gained some renown, had some success for several years. Much of it came from "paid influencers"—people with large followings who were compensated for spreading the word—rather than from actually cracking the code of what made content viral.

BuzzFeed is perhaps the most successful effort at building a business around virality. In 2006 Jonah Peretti, a graduate of the Massachusetts Institute of Technology and a former editor at *The Huffington Post,* set out to "make things social." At first he could do so only after the fact: BuzzFeed would pick up stories that were already being shared, then place them on its own site. Over time, it moved toward trying to predict rather than merely piggyback on virality. Every piece of its content was tracked in terms of its "virality lift." Sharability across Twitter, Facebook, and Pinterest was separated so that the company could understand the drivers of each. Continuous tracking and algorithmically driven replacement of stories on the site let editors monitor what pieces of content were being shared. And lessons were shared across editorial teams.

Perhaps the most intriguing part of BuzzFeed's approach was also its most outwardly scientific. In 2007, Peretti and network sociologist Duncan Watts (famous for his research on "small-world" connectivity in social networks, and now serving as an advisor to BuzzFeed) published a paper in *Harvard Business Review* describing their approach to making things viral. It involved a simple equation. $R = b \times z$, the authors noted, describes the spread of infectious diseases, where R is the reproduction rate, or the expected number of new infections generated by each existing one (b is the probability that a disease transmission actually occurs between one person and any other, and z is the average number of persons whom any one person might "infect"). Conventional wisdom was that if R was greater than 1, each person would spread the disease to more than one other person, resulting in an epidemic. If R was less than 1, the rate of spread would drop, resulting in "failure."

"There is an important flaw in the epidemic analogy, however," Watts and Peretti noted. The reason was that the rate of spread depended not only on the reproduction rate but also on the number of people who were infected to begin with. Infectious diseases start with one person, so a high R is necessary to spread. But advertising campaigns could start by "seeding" a large number of people, so even a low reproduction rate could generate virality. (Procter & Gamble's campaign to promote their laundry detergent Tide Coldwater, Peretti and Watts noted as an example, "registered a low reproduction rate of 0.041 but was initiated with such a large seed—900,000—that it still reached some 40,000 more individuals than it would have without the forwarding capability.") In effect, Peretti and Watts were making the idea of sharing scientific, proposing to combine traditional media campaigns—through TV, email lists, or direct ad buys on the Internet—to generate a large number of potential transmitters. The big insight was that one needed neither influencers nor high reproduction rates to make things viral.

Peretti and Watts were honest about their approach to cracking the code of virality: "Our notion of big-seed marketing lacks the mystique of truly viral marketing, [but] it is straightforward to implement and can reliably improve advertising yields at low cost."

By 2014, BuzzFeed was one of the fastest-growing websites in the world, attracting more than 150 million unique visitors each month— twice as many as *The New York Times*. This was the power of sharing—the power of user connections.

Yet there is a long way to go.

Despite its rapid and impressive growth and perhaps the most scientific approach to predicting virality—employing randomized testing, continuous monitoring, and large initial "seeds"—BuzzFeed's model of virality had at best a few robust variables: humor, animals, lists, and pictures, for example. "Stories of cats turned out to be eminently sharable," noted one report on the firm. Predicting what made things go viral remained hard. Less than 20 percent of the variance—the difference in virality across different pieces of content—could be explained by BuzzFeed's models.

Even native advertising content was subject to a form of A/B testing, with multiple stories simultaneously created for the same campaign. "Winners would be favored with more space and better placement, the losers starved." In effect, BuzzFeed's devotion to rapid A/B testing was also an acknowledgment of sorts: "We don't know what works."

Connections, when identified, are powerful. Recognizing and engineering connections can be elusive. But even some progress pays, as Watts noted: "You can make money with that. If [BuzzFeed is] predicting 20 percent of the variance and the competition is predicting 10 percent of the variance, they're kicking ass."

b. User Connections II: From Individuals to Communities

In November 2011, Patagonia ran a full-page ad in *The New York Times* with the tagline "Don't Buy This Jacket." It wasn't a picture of a competitor's jacket. It was one of their own.

Why would a company tell its customers not to purchase more? On its website, Patagonia explained:

> It's time for us as a company to address the issue of consumerism and do it head on. . . . [In order to] lighten our environmental footprint, everyone needs to consume less. Businesses need to make fewer things but of higher quality. Customers need to think twice before they buy.

A disingenuous campaign designed to sell more? The company addressed that question, too:

> But we're in business to make and sell products. Everyone's paycheck relies on that. Moreover, we are a growing business, opening new stores and mailing more catalogs. What do we tell customers who accuse us of hypocrisy?
> It's part of our mission to inspire and implement solutions to the environmental crisis. It would be hypocritical for us to work for environmental change without encouraging customers to think before they buy.

It's not hypocrisy for us to address the need to reduce consumption. On the other hand, it's folly to assume that a healthy economy can be based on buying and selling more and more things people don't need—and it's time for people who believe that's folly to say so.

Nevertheless, Patagonia is a growing business—and we want to be in business a good long time. The test of our sincerity (or our hypocrisy) will be if everything we sell is useful, multifunctional where possible, long lasting, beautiful but not in thrall to fashion. We're not yet entirely there. Not every product meets all these criteria.

The following year, Patagonia created a film, *Worn Wear,* encouraging consumers to repair their old clothes rather than buy new ones. It even published a series of free repair guides.

Patagonia was founded in 1973 by Yosemite rock climber Yvon Chouinard with a commitment to environmental activism. Its mission was "Build the best product, cause no unnecessary harm, use business to inspire and implement solutions to the environmental crisis." Some of the ways in which it grew appeared strange—until one recognized the consistency with the firm's roots and mission. The company sold through catalogs, not brick-and-mortar stores. And its catalogs were published only twice a year. Customers who wanted to order dialed a toll number. But people seeking information about climbing locations could use a toll-free line. The firm engaged in no surveys, focus groups, or customer research. Its employees were "die-hard" customers who "built for themselves." The company encouraged them to take time off to surf. And it prided itself on making clothes that lasted longer than anyone else's.

If you view the ad and the film as stand-alone marketing campaigns, they can very well seem odd and manipulative. But in light of the company's entire history, they're entirely consistent and legible.

Patagonia's strength—the real reason for its deep customer loyalty, "cultlike following" (as competitors often put it), and impressive growth—lay not in its ability to produce good products or market them well. It came from its "community"—the group of users, employees, climbers, and environmentalists it had built up over the years. It came from connecting them all.

Patagonia's growth in the two years after the "Don't Buy This Jacket" ad exceeded 40 percent. The *Worn Wear* film quadrupled traffic on the brand's channel within five months. It also attracted media attention the firm never had to pay for—"earned media," as experts refer to it.

c. User Connections III: From Purchasing to Giving

Black Friday is becoming a day few Americans look forward to. Long lines, odd hours, unpleasant shoppers, and stock-outs. And it's only the first day of the holiday shopping experience. Retailers have started taking a black eye for it too. In 2014, as—increasingly—in prior years, shoppers complained of brusque retail employees and discourteous service. Prevailing consumer sentiment about Black Friday was that retailers wanted to cash in, rather than help out. "Jingle Bells" was becoming gloomy bells.

Until JCPenney decided to take a different tack.

On December 3, Penney surprised a few shoppers with "acts of giving." They were approached by strangers—other shoppers who'd been spontaneously co-opted by the store to participate on its behalf. The recipients were presented with a simple offer of a gift: Receive anything in the store, with any price tag, for free that day. The reactions were stunned surprise, appreciation, and emotion—and not just from the recipients, but also from the givers. It was all recorded on camera and played as a commercial with the tagline "Is Giving Better Than Receiving?"

A cynical reaction to the campaign would see it as just another retailer trying to drum up sales, this time under the guise of gift-giving. But there was a twist: The gift had to be to a complete stranger—a powerful idea that's alien to most of us nowadays. That turned the commercial on its head. That's what got it shared.

Victors & Spoils had conceived the campaign. Winsor described its genesis to me the day before it launched:

> We felt there was a tension around holiday shopping. Anybody in America these days can't help feel a bit disgusted by the overconsumerism in Black Friday. So this idea of convincing a brand like JCPenney to take on this tension is a pretty cool thing. It's all about just asking a simple question: Isn't it more important to give than to receive?
>
> The crazy thing is that JCPenney has enough guts to not put their logo on it. The film has only a hashtag: "#JustGotJingled." You can obviously discover when you go to #JustGotJingled that it's JCPenney. And there are hints that it's a JCPenney store. But the entire premise was that if everyone is going one way—saying we've got better deals, take 75 percent off another TV, look at all the great stuff in our store—you go the other. JCPenney is asking: Isn't giving the true spirit of Christmas?
>
> We expect it'll change the conversation. And the best thing about it is that it's true to the DNA of the firm. When you go way back in the history

of the company, Mr. Penney, back in the day, liked to talk about *their* Golden Rule: Give unto others before you receive.

People cry in the video. When people watch the video, they will cry. It's powerful because it strikes at the heart what we should be thinking of. My sense is everybody is going to say, damn, I want to be a part of that community.

The commercial worked. Within a week, the "Just Got Jingled" video had been viewed or shared more than three million times on Twitter alone, making it one of that site's most-watched commercials. It worked for two reasons. It was stirring—it made people feel good about themselves. And it did so by connecting them to others.

The story offers a simple but powerful lesson in what makes for social connections—and why it's often so hard for companies to take advantage of them. A former colleague, Mikolaj Piskorski, is an expert in social strategy. He's studied nearly every online social network, along with ones that aren't still around. His takeaway for companies trying to leverage social connections: Stop trying to sell your product. Think social first, product later. The possibilities become not only more and more powerful, but also more authentic.

Connections are about precisely that: making people connect. They aren't about selling. Get the first part right, though, and the second usually follows.

d. Product Connections

User connections can turn good campaigns into great ones. Connecting media can help, too.

Ask any advertiser or agency about its latest campaign and chances are it was largely restricted to one medium. Did you see that TV ad, or did you see the Facebook campaign—is how *we* remember campaigns. Even when media do connect, it's usually by happenstance—a TV ad goes viral, say. Far more infrequent are campaigns that use all media synchronously, or truly integrate them. And for good reason, you might think: Print ads don't lend themselves to TV, nor do Twitter or Facebook campaigns that rely on those medias' interactive, real-time nature.

Think again.

In 2010, hip-hop megastar Jay-Z was about to publish his first book, *Decoded*. Like most Jay-Z projects, this was different. It wasn't a straightforward biography, but a "lyrical memoir" in which the artist described the hidden meanings of many of his most provocative songs. To promote it, Jay-Z wanted something different, too, and he got it from Droga5, a start-up creative agency that had grabbed attention with campaigns for Puma, Kraft, and Prudential and won Agency of the Year.

When conceptualizing the book launch, Droga5 did something unusual even by its own standards. It devised a campaign to be integrated across every media outlet—TV, billboards, Facebook, Twitter—and a range of nonmedia locations too, from swimming pools to restaurant menus, sub-way stations, and bus shelters. It worked like a scavenger hunt. Every page in the book would be distributed as a single placement in some location around the world—one page a day, with the sites carefully and cleverly chosen to correspond to something on that page. For example, the page describing Jay-Z's restaurant would be printed on a restaurant menu or placemats. Participants were given clues daily through social media about which pages in the book were being "revealed," and they could search for them using Microsoft's Bing search engine. Microsoft, itself trying to grab market share from Google at the time, partnered with Jay-Z and Droga5 to create an integrated online game in which participants could figure out where each page fit into the book, gradually assembling a digital version of the entire work. Whoever assembled the entire book would win two life-time passes to Jay-Z concerts.

It worked: The campaign generated nearly one billion media impres-sions and returned twice the $2 million investment (it also contributed to Bing's highest market share increase in a year). The book launched at number three on the *New York Times* bestseller list.

The *Decoded* campaign wasn't about replaying the same ad in different outlets. Each outlet was chosen for its relevance to content. And it wouldn't have worked with fewer outlets; each medium would have been useless without the rest. It was a genuinely integrated campaign. One plus one plus one equaled thirty.

It's not that more advertisers wouldn't want to do this sort of thing. It's that they're not organized to pull it off. Agencies are typically structured as media "verticals"—there's a TV arm, a radio arm, a social media arm, and so on. Their clients are, too, with the heads of digital media, TV, and so on all reporting to the CMO. So launching a marketing campaign is likely to consist of ten different media campaigns, each laying claim to a share of the marketing spend. And even if a company could create an integrated program, figuring out its effectiveness would be problematic. Nielsen and other ad measurement companies aren't organized to track ad effectiveness across media; they collect data by one ad medium after another.

But that's changing, slowly, as organizations seek to manage and exploit product connections. Increasingly, ad agencies are looking to overcome their silos. Firms are reorganizing to take advantage of such opportunities. And in 2014 Nielsen moved toward a more integrated data collection and reporting structure. They are each recognizing, and trying to exploit, the power of media connections.

Let's look at another example of what an array of different media channels can offer at once.

Unilever's Dove soap is one of the most recognized consumer brands, with products sold in more than ninety countries. In 2014, Dove's global digital team was looking for thought leadership at their global digital summit. It invited several companies to present, led by Victors & Spoils, Facebook, Google, and Pinterest. Winsor described the event:

> Each of us presented our point of view and saw what the others were doing. That's probably not normal—but our platforms are not really competitive with each other.
>
> Facebook got up and showed a few very impressive things: ads tailored to local markets by changing the ethnicity of the person in the video. They had the data to show the impact in each market—there was unbelievable upswing. Where it got really interesting was when they talked about their Facebook studio—essentially an internal ad agency. And they said, "We didn't have anything else going on, so we just created this thirty-second spot for Dove." They played the entire thing during the pitch—which any other agency would charge one to two million dollars for. What happened next was extraordinary: They said, "If you want to use this ad, great—just take it. If you don't, no big deal. It's just a gift, our gift to you." We just looked at each other and went, "It's over, right?" At that point I thought our traditional ad world was finished.

In creating internal agency-like capabilities, Facebook is not alone. In 2014, BuzzFeed, Tumblr, and other upstarts did the same—BuzzFeed created a ninety-person team entirely devoted to creating ad copy for clients. These companies were essentially giving away their work. Why? It's not because they think their ads are any less valuable than others', or because they are pricing low in an effort to win market share. It's because they want clients to spend more advertising dollars on their sites. Anything that makes it easier for clients to do so helps.

In the old days, media channels—TV networks, newspapers, radio—sold media space to ad agencies. Now, new-media publishers—Internet upstarts and giants—were giving away ads to clients in order to then sell space to them. They were becoming agencies. Winsor said:

> It's this incredible dynamic of consolidation and democratization at the same time. On the one hand, anybody can be a creator today—anybody can produce a YouTube video. On the other hand, there's this impressive consolidation where Google, Facebook, and others are saying "The best way for us to get dollars on YouTube (or other sites) is to create YouTube studios." Today, Google is creating state-of-the-art studios around the world—in L.A., London, Singapore, New York. To me, it's the endgame for why agencies won't exist.

The future for agencies may be unfamiliar. But the principle at work here surely isn't—it's the power of complements again. To sell a product, give away the complement for free. And for ad agencies, there's a familiar lesson: When your core business becomes someone else's complement, it's time to wake up.

It turns out that this game is not new. As Winsor recounted from his early days, newspapers and magazines used to do it all the time:

> It's the same process as when I worked for my dad's newspaper, the *Canton Daily Ledger*. There was a Ludlum's grocery store down the street. They'd run ads in our paper. But there was no agency to create the ads. I would run down to Ludlum's every day and ask, "What's the price of beef today?" They would tell me the prices of meat. And I'd create the "advertisement." If we didn't do that for free, we wouldn't get their media spend.
>
> When I started Rocky Mountain Sports, it was the same thing. We'd ask a local running shop, "Would you like to run an ad?" They'd say, "Yes, but we don't have any creative." We'd say, "No problem. We'll create the ad for you." Or, since we were a women's sports and fitness magazine, if they didn't have any woman in their ad, we'd reshoot it with a woman, for free—in return for their media spend.

e. Differentiation

Two thousand thirteen was not a pretty year for JCPenney. CEO Ron Johnson was fired in April, after just seventeen months on the job. He was coming off a quarterly performance in 2012 described as the "worst in the history of major retail." Johnson had tried to model Penney's retail approach on Apple's, whose strategy he'd engineered several years before. Promotions were cut, store layouts were redone, the logo was redesigned. Thousands of managers were fired.

None of it helped. Price-sensitive consumers left for better deals elsewhere. When promotions were reintroduced, those customers didn't return. Morale was low. The rebranding efforts had been confusing. Logo awareness dropped from 84 percent to 56 percent.

In early 2014, the company needed a marketing makeover. But it couldn't afford one.

Conventional wisdom was that TV was where you built your brand, and social media was how you leveraged it. JCPenney decided to try the reverse.

Within minutes of kickoff of the 2014 Super Bowl, the first tweet came:

> @jcpenney: Who kkmew theis was ghiong tob e a baweball ghamle. #lowsscorinh 5_0

The reaction on Twitter was fast and sardonic. Had someone hacked the account? Was an intern on the job drunk? Half an hour later, a second tweet surfaced:

> @jcpenney: Toughdown Seadawks!! Is sSeattle going toa runaway wit h this???

The Twittersphere went crazy. The post received more than 21,000 retweets. It wasn't just viewers retweeting; other brands did, too, from Doritos to Kia Motors to Snickers, and even rival Macy's. The opportunity to mock a bungling rival was golden.

A half hour later, the next tweet appeared:

> @jcpenney: Oops . . . Sorry for the typos. We were #TweetingWithMittens. Wasn't it supposed to be colder? Enjoy the game! #GoTeamUSA

JCPenney was the official sponsor of the U.S. Winter Olympic team—and its mittens. The Olympics was still a few weeks away, but the campaign, planned throughout, drew extraordinary attention. Although it didn't save the brand from its structural and operational troubles, it was the most successful non-TV campaign of the Super Bowl. And the firm had spent no advertising dollars on it.

What prevents traditional agencies from doing the same? There are two big reasons.

First, habits can be hard to break. There are "ways of doing business"— TV metrics (reach, exposure), creative approaches (100-person teams, months-long campaigns), pricing models (15 percent commissions on ad expenditures), and measures of success (water cooler conversation, Cannes awards). "Creative" is thought of as art. Agencies view themselves as arbiters of culture. Changing any of this means breaking habits, and risking both viable business models and prestige.

Second, certain incentives have led agencies to favor the status quo. Traditionally, agencies were paid on commissions—15 percent of the amount clients spent on a campaign. If a campaign cost the client $100 million, the agency made $15 million; if it was $500 million, the agency take increased to $75 million—although the cost of producing the two campaigns might be roughly the same. In an effort to change this incentive structure, compensation moved to a cost-plus model many years ago—compensation would be based on how many agency employees were actually needed to produce a campaign. But that didn't help, either. When this move occurred, so did the urge for agencies to inflate costs.

Such is the power of habits, structures, and incentives. Few agencies have been able to break away from these forces. Some are trying. Fewer still are able to succeed. But that's where competitive advantage resides.

ADVERTISING AND THE CONTENT TRAP

Advertising today is consumed by three questions. First, from the advertisers' perspective, how to reach more eyeballs at the lowest cost. Second, from the publishers' perspective, how to preserve ad revenue in a world of falling ad prices. Third, what new metrics to use in a world of digital advertising, social media, and hypertargeting.

These questions, and the mindset behind them, add up to the Content Trap.

View customers as eyeballs to send messages to, view advertising as a business to be preserved at all costs, view digital advertising as the next big thing, and you've been ensnared just as the music, newspaper, and book industries were.

The promise of advertising lies not in bombarding consumers with messages they don't want, but in inviting them to be a part of something they do. It's not about eyeballs; it's about sharing, networks, and communities. That comes from understanding user connections.

The promise of advertising lies not in figuring out the most creative campaign for any one medium—whether TV or social, new or old—but about integrating campaigns across media. It's not about preserving the value of advertising as a business and trying to prop up prices at all cost; it's about understanding how the economics of that business change when it becomes someone else's complement. That comes from recognizing product connections.

The promise of advertising lies not in trying to mimic the leaders in social media or TV advertising; it lies in understanding your needs, your context, and your strengths. Create a network effect around your product and you won't need to advertise—users will be your advertisers. Create an ad that users love and you won't need to target; users will do it for you. Create a community that is specific to your culture and you won't have to seek customers out; they'll find you. Every company faces different possibilities—which can be harnessed by understanding functional connections.

It's one thing to draw in viewers through an effective campaign. User connections multiply the effect. It's one thing to create powerful campaigns for social media *or* TV *or* radio. Integrated campaigns multiply the impact of each—where $1 + 1 = 3$. It's one thing to keep track of the best marketing approaches, be they in social media, ad campaigns, or business models, and mimic them. It's another to be ahead of the curve, to go one way when everyone's going the other—and to shape culture rather than follow it.

These are user, product, and functional connections at work. They offer a guide to the trends we see in marketing today, and where to look for new ones.

It's easy to be seduced into thinking new technologies will alter marketing. They won't. It's easy to believe that understanding the latest metrics and terms in online advertising—CPMs and CPAs; CPCs and CTRs; exchanges versus networks, filtering and retargeting; native, embedded, display, banner, interstitial, and search ads—will help you understand how to proceed online. It won't. Even marketing executives find it hard to keep up with these terms or agree on common definitions and metrics.

The real tension in advertising and marketing is not between traditional and digital, as most are led to think. It's the tension between product-centered and user-centered thinking. Banner ads, pop-ups, and native advertising are not fundamentally new strategies; they're new expressions of an approach and mindset that have always been around. Bombard users; fool them; irritate them; trick them—as long as you can sell your product. A product-centered mindset is a zero-sum game. Unsurprisingly, it's the consumer who often loses.

"If you aren't thinking about connecting with your audience, building trust when selling your products or services . . . you need to reexamine your motivations," wrote David Ogilvy, the "Father of Advertising," decades ago. "Information about the product is more important than persuading the consumer with adjectives." These were cautions at a time when the marketing world was intoxicated by the seemingly limitless possibilities of mass media. Today's new technologies seem to bring limitless possibilities, too. But the real potential for marketing doesn't lie in the technologies themselves but in the ability to embrace them with a mindset that's both old and frankly new, one built around user centricity and user connections.

User centricity has been promulgated by marketers and marketing experts for decades. The irony is that the normal marketing mindset remains generally indifferent to the idea. Get the sale, then deal with the experience later. The real power of great campaigns—authenticity, user centricity, and consumer trust—won't go away anytime soon. If anything, it's finding greater expression in digital media. That's also where advertising has the promise to change dramatically.

Whether it does depends on which mindset wins. *Co-creation, communities,* and *sharing,* are not new terms (granted, *eco-tone* is). But they represent a philosophical shift, one based around understanding the importance of authentic connections between brands and users and between users themselves—not forced, manipulated, or engineered ones.

Look through a product-centered lens and you'll confront many puzzles—why offline dollars turn into online pennies, why DVRs haven't destroyed TV advertising, why Facebook's click-through rates were so low for so long, and why CPMs continue to be. Take a user-centered lens and these aren't puzzles anymore.

27

EDUCATION AT A CROSSROADS

"A revolution has begun" in higher education, *The Economist* noted recently. "The result will be the reinvention of the university." In this last part of the book, I examine the changing world of higher education, how it's being affected by digital technologies, and certain strategies that are emerging to cope with, and embrace, the transformations that lie ahead.

On the face of it, education appears to be a very different product from media, entertainment, and other content businesses. But in fact, there are important commonalities.

Music, movies, radio, television programs, books, news, and advertisements are all examples of information goods—things that can be reduced to bits and bytes and transmitted digitally. So too is education—a product whose delivery remained unchanged for nearly three centuries. Until now.

The same digital technologies and phenomena that impacted these other businesses are now creating cataclysms in education, too: broadband delivery, multisided platforms, apps, search, new devices, and software innovations. And in this world, just as in other content businesses, doomsday scenarios are plentiful, digital possibilities are simultaneously frightening and exhilarating, and new models, new organizations, and new investors are emerging everywhere.

Throughout this book, I've tried to show how digital forces are profoundly affecting practically every aspect of our culture. In what follows, as I turn to education, there's one difference: My analysis won't be that of a dispassionate observer—this is my world. In recent years colleges and universities throughout America have been rethinking their online role. I was fortunate enough to be involved in those efforts at Harvard Business School.

My main argument is that the central lessons from the digital transformation of content businesses like media and entertainment have much to add to the conversations around strategy taking place in institutions of higher education today. Higher education is already being transformed, and the shape this transformation takes in the future depends on the choices we make now.

But first, let's take a step back.

THE CHANGING LANDSCAPE

Universities seem to be in trouble. New technologies are shaking up their world. And the full transformational potential of those technologies can't even be predicted yet.

One Ivy League professor laid out a "compelling vision for the future of higher-level instruction" in which there'd be no textbooks or campuses. It would start with a simple idea: Professors could, in their classrooms, deliver a lecture while, simultaneously, hundreds of thousands of people "are receiving an education without even leaving the limits of their own neighborhoods." "The nation has become the new campus," another observer noted. A journalist went further: "Will the classroom be abolished and the child of the future be stuffed with facts as he sits at home or even as he walks about the streets?" Universities, meanwhile, are rushing to offer courses using new technologies and platforms. Investors are pouring money into new educational ventures. Experts are warning about impending disruption.

These descriptions capture the quandaries facing higher education today. Except that they were written one hundred years ago. They were describing the state of higher education when radio first emerged.

The debates today are eerily similar to ones in the 1920s and 1930s. New technologies—radio then, the online revolution now—promised to revolutionize education. Universities' costs rose then, as now, along with tuition. And in both eras critics warned of impending disruption.

What's different this time?

A (Very) Brief History of Technology and Education: 1920–2010

The idea of "learning at a distance" predates even radio. The first distance-learning course was offered in Boston in 1724, via regular mail. Correspondence courses were popularized in the 1840s by Sir Isaac Pitman, who offered instruction in his shorthand system. Radio courses followed nearly a century later.

Between 1920 and 1938 more than two hundred city school systems and numerous universities applied for federal radio broadcasting licenses. Radio was a new and exciting technology that would allow professors to transmit information to students hundreds of miles away. Indeed, it could offer "a college education for everyone who wants it." New York University established a radio broadcast station in 1922. Columbia, Tufts, Wisconsin, and Harvard followed suit.

Several university courses were offered for credit. But, as an article in *The Chronicle of Higher Education* described,

> Gradually problems emerged, and doubts spread that on-air courses would ever fully replace traditional colleges. First was the issue of attrition. Like most modern-day courses taught at a distance, completion rates were disappointing. Of those enrolled in one course, only half took exams. There were reports that listeners' interest in erudition often competed with the temptations of entertainment. Listeners might tune into a lecture occasionally, but not with the regularity or dedication ardent advocates predicted.

These observations were prescient. And again, almost the same words could be used to describe what's happening today.

By 1940, the hype around radio education had dramatically diminished. The number of radio courses in the United States offered for credit had fallen to exactly one.

Television soon appeared, offering its own promises for education. The hype quickly faded there as well, as TV struggled to attract audiences to educational content. There were exceptions: the revolutionary children's program *Sesame Street* in the United States, and the TV-based Open University in the United Kingdom, founded in the 1970s with a radical open admissions approach. But by and large, like radio, television didn't have the impact on traditional modes of teaching or on educational institutions that so many predicted.

The computer and Internet revolutions followed. The first computer-based adult learning center was established on the East Coast (in New Hampshire) in 1982. The first virtual university was formed by a consortium of colleges on the West Coast (in California), fifteen years later. Enrollments soared: By 2009, more than 5.5 million people in the United States had taken at least one online course. Still, traditional universities remained more or less the same.

A colleague of mine recently described the modern university as a "force for inertia." It was a tongue-in-cheek observation, but it's rather true. Since 1636, when Harvard opened its doors, its brick-and-mortar model has remained roughly the same. By the late 1800s (and largely shaped by then university president Charles William Eliot), its model was of a "hybrid university," looking to combine world-class research with a multi-year preprofessional education anchored in the liberal arts. Admissions were highly selective, and the curricular offering was broad.

The hybrid model "all made sense—in theory," noted Kevin Carey recently in *The End of College*. But it was a bundle of contradictions. Most salient was the concern, first expressed more than a century ago by Harvard philosopher William James in an essay titled "The Ph.D. Octopus," that excellence in research had little to do with excellence in teaching. James's concern would grow over time.

Some institutions chose a different route. Liberal arts colleges focused entirely on undergraduate education and on the liberal arts, humanities, and sciences. They doubled down on teaching. They admitted smaller cohorts. And they emphasized the student experience over faculty "star power."

State universities had their own strengths (larger student pools, lower tuition, greater access) and challenges. And then there were community colleges—in the United States, by 2014, more than 1,100 of them serve some seven million students, or more than 40 percent of all undergraduates. More than one-third of those students are the first generation in their families to attend college. Community colleges admitted students even more generously, targeted adult learners more than teenagers, eschewed high-cost residential experiences, and focused on practical skills. Given their sheer number, they were at the center of many education reform initiatives.

Over a long period of time colleges and universities learned to differentiate themselves from one another, and this has generally served them well. For instance, it has allowed schools to compete for students even if those schools are in close proximity. As of 2014 the Boston area contained more than one hundred colleges and universities, almost all of which have been around for at least three decades.

But challenges have emerged over time: rising tuition, increasing costs, a growing reliance on endowments to cover these costs, a diminished emphasis on teaching, and a perceived gap between the liberal arts and the skills required for the workplace. This last issue is sometimes described as the tension between the intellectual and the practical, the esoteric and the vocational, "how to think" and "what you need to know."

Most concerning was that students appeared to be paying more to learn less. National student debt recently surpassed $1 trillion. Graduation rates were falling: By 2015 hundreds of colleges were graduating less than a third of their entering students. Literacy levels were alarming: In a recent study by the Organisation for Economic Co-operation and Development, more than a third of college graduates failed to demonstrate basic numeracy and problem-solving skills, and sociologists Richard Arum and Josipa Roksa noted in their book *Academically Adrift* that a third of college students made no gains in critical thinking, analytical reasoning, and communication skills during their four years in school.

Higher education appeared not just ripe for change, but destined for it.

Seeds of Disruption

Sal Khan grew up in New Orleans, the son of South Asian immigrants. He was an accomplished student, talented enough to get accepted to MIT and earn three degrees there (in mathematics, electrical engineering, and computer science). At twenty-seven he graduated from Harvard Business School and went to work for a Silicon Valley hedge fund. It was a normal start to what would soon become an abnormal career.

In late 2004 Khan's thirteen-year-old cousin, Nadia, called him from New Orleans. She was having trouble with fifth-grade algebra. Khan gave her some guidance over the phone. It was helpful—so helpful that he was soon tutoring many more relatives and friends by phone. That wasn't manageable, so he created simple videos that they could all view, using off-the-shelf technology—Yahoo!'s Doodle notepad—and uploading them to YouTube. What happened next was extraordinary.

First, there were the reactions from his relatives, including Nadia, who seemed to prefer Khan's YouTube videos to his individualized phone discourses. Khan later reflected on why: "The worst time to learn something is when someone is standing over your shoulder going, 'Do you get it?'" Soon he was receiving appreciative comments on YouTube—not just from relatives, but from viewers around the world. He got letters as well. One was from a woman whose two disabled children had used the videos. "She said that her entire family prays for my family every night," Khan recounted. "To put that into context, at the time I was working for a hedge fund."

Khan was discovering, in effect, that education is an information good, just like any media or entertainment product. Education is "non-rivalrous"—any piece of knowledge can be consumed simultaneously by millions of users. Education is also "non-excludable"—access is increasingly hard to restrict, given mechanisms for free, instantaneous worldwide distribution (and other times, piracy).

So in 2009, just a few years after he had joined the world of high finance, Khan quit his day job to start Khan Academy, a nonprofit dedicated to "a free world-class education for anyone, anywhere." Its resources were "almost comically meager," he later said. The academy "owned a PC, $20 worth of screen capture software, and an $80 pen tablet. The faculty, engineering team, support staff, and administration consisted of exactly one person: me."

By early 2016 Khan Academy had roughly 10,000 videos on its site, on topics ranging from calculus to finance, biology, and government, and was attracting more than six million learners a month—"more than ten times the number of people who have gone to Harvard since its inception in 1636," Khan said. Its videos had been viewed more than 750 million times, by learners from varied age groups. And it was all free.

Microsoft's Bill Gates invested in Khan's enterprise after seeing his own kids learn math from Khan online. Google invested, too. In 2012 Khan was recognized as one of *Time* magazine's 100 Most Influential People, and the U.S. Department of Education funded a $3 million trial to assess the effectiveness of the academy's teaching materials.

Something *was* different this time.

The Majors Get In

Khan Academy was only the tip of the iceberg. Though it represented a fascinating breakthrough in the world of online K–12 education, its short-form videos were still not generally perceived as a major disruptive threat to higher education. That came with the tsunami launched by Stanford professor Sebastian Thrun in 2011.

Thrun had been a computer science professor, at Carnegie Mellon and then Stanford, for more than a decade. He specialized in artificial intelligence (AI) and in far-out projects that Google later called "moon shots." Like many Stanford computer scientists, he was closely involved with Valley start-ups—in his case, Google. Thrun had advised Google since 2007, led its program to develop a driverless car, and started Google X, the lab that developed Google Glass.

In 2010 Thrun was about to teach the AI course he offered every fall. But this time he also recorded his lectures and put them online. That would certainly benefit any of his Stanford students who missed a lecture or two. But his real motivation was to make his teaching available to anyone who was interested but would never set foot on Stanford's campus.

Thrun was shocked by what ensued. Within a few weeks about 50,000 online learners from around the world had registered for the course. By the end of the semester, there were more than 150,000. "It was this catalytic moment," Thrun recalled. "I was educating more AI students than there were AI students in the rest of the world combined."

The results were even more startling: Of the course's top 400 performers, none were Stanford students—all were online learners. (The best-performing Stanford student came in at 411.) Thrun had an epiphany: "I can't teach at Stanford again. I feel like there's a red pill and a blue pill. You can take the blue pill and go back to your classroom and lecture. But I've taken the red pill. I've seen Wonderland."

In June 2011 Thrun left Stanford to found Udacity, a for-profit enterprise backed largely by venture capitalists who saw immense promise in educational technology, or, "edtech." Udacity first reached out to university professors, and later companies, to create courses on its platform. Other players soon joined the fray. Stanford computer science professors Andrew Keller and Daphne Ng had also offered their courses online, enrolled more than 100,000 registrants, and subsequently left to form an online education enterprise—in their case, Coursera. These faculty-led spinouts, with their unnerving implications for the business model of universities, did not go unnoticed. East Coast institutions soon jumped in. In May 2012 Harvard president Drew Faust and MIT president Susan Hockfield announced the formation of a nonprofit, edX—an unprecedented online learning partnership between two major universities sometimes viewed as rivals.

edX's governance was different from Stanford's offspring's. It was a joint venture, with Harvard and MIT each committing $30 million. And it would solicit universities, not individual star faculty directly, for content partnerships. Despite these differences, its platform was similar to the others in form and function: A typical online course, referred to now as an MOOC (short for "massive open online course"), would consist of streamed video lectures coupled with "office hours" by the faculty or their teaching staff where students could ask questions, and a series of tests. edX also made its courses free.

The higher education landscape, relatively serene for three hundred years, was being dramatically shaken up. For the first time since the dawn of the Internet, elite universities were actively participating in the space and opening up their courses to anyone, anywhere in the world.

By September 2012 about 20 million learners had registered for courses on various platforms. There were more than 1,500 courses to choose from. More than 150 universities and other institutions, including the best in the country, offered some type of content. They were reaching a far broader audience than they ever had, and at a far lower cost to the learner.

The New York Times declared 2012 "the year of the MOOC." *Times* columnist Tom Friedman asserted that the "MOOC revolution is here . . . and it is for real." University presidents, deans, and administrators were staring down a path familiar to managers in music, newspapers, and book publishing. Major universities were taking an ambitious plunge into the online world—not always entirely of their own volition, but out of a felt necessity—because of forces like Sal Khan, Sebastian Thrun, and the scores of venture capitalists and media organizations entering the space.

This was the situation in the summer of 2012, when some of us at Harvard Business School (HBS) sat down to figure out our own digital future.

CRAFTING DIGITAL STRATEGY

"What should we do?" It's a question that nearly every school and university has been asking recently.

As we tried to answer this question ourselves, we were listening to the broader debates around online learning that were taking place. The implications for residential education weren't necessarily pretty. With waves of new learners enrolling in free online courses offered by some of the best professors in the world, university enrollments would almost certainly be affected. They already had been—applications to most business schools, for example, had been diving for a decade, fueled by the Internet's siren call to students to pursue their entrepreneurial dreams straight out of college, employers' increasing emphasis on their own on-the-job training programs, and questions about the value of an MBA. Meanwhile, managers and entrepreneurs were finding it increasingly hard to take extended periods of time away from their jobs to attend long executive programs. Free online courses would only accelerate these trends.

Online education offered opportunities, too. The possibility of reaching millions of talented learners around the world was consistent with the missions of many universities, including Harvard. The need for lifelong learning—upgrading or replacing employees' "human capital"—was as important as ever. Tom Friedman had written of a "flat world" in which people everywhere could access the same educational resources using technology. Barriers were falling.

And they were falling fast. There were serious worries about not moving quickly enough. As existing platforms partnered with more and more universities and professors, they would become increasingly attractive to learners. The potential for strong network effects—for winner-take-all platform dynamics, as eBay, Facebook, and Amazon enjoyed—was likelier every day.

The basic strategy for online education seemed clear: Do it fast. Do it cheap. This was the approach that Amazon, Facebook, and Google had embraced. Most of the experts warning of imminent disruption were advocating it now. Yet we decided it was not the right course of action for HBS.

Over the next few months, we carved out an online learning strategy that departed from the established MOOC model in virtually every respect. We decided to pass on the increasingly standard "camera in the classroom" in favor of a more expensive "digital-first" approach. We decided to build our own technology platform to host our courses, rather than rely on existing ones like edX or Coursera. We decided to charge for our courses. We eschewed broad reach in favor of engaging smaller groups of learners. And we decided that the online experience we created would involve virtually no live interaction with the faculty.

Each of these decisions was debatable in its own right. Together they appeared downright reckless. The last feature—no live interaction with faculty—was perhaps the most counterintuitive, particularly in light of our effort to engage learners. The prevailing wisdom held that the only way to improve the online learning experience, or to charge for online courses in an increasingly free marketplace, was to offer *more* live interaction with faculty and content experts—"value-added services," as they were loquaciously referred to. Our approach was a far cry even from the residential teaching approach at HBS—the case method approach—whereby professors and students engaged in vibrant exchanges of ideas.

The rest of this section probes our reasoning behind these choices, and the lessons we learned along the way. My hope is that these lessons go beyond what happened here at Harvard Business School, and will be useful for others tasked with crafting strategy in the face of digital change—and for those seeking to understand it.

28
CREATING HBX

OUR UNIVERSITY CONTEXT

In the spring of 2012, soon after the edX partnership was announced, Harvard University's provost, Alan Garber, began reaching out to the eleven different schools within Harvard and to faculty members.

Along with MIT provost L. Rafael Reif, Garber had been instrumental in forging the edX partnership. The vision for Harvard centered on three objectives. First, online offerings could dramatically increase the university's reach and impact. For centuries Harvard had restricted access to the select few chosen to come on campus. Now we could—and should—offer access to anyone who wanted it.

The second objective involved possibilities for new research, an activity that underpins the elite status of institutions like Harvard. Large amounts of data were becoming available through online user clickstreams. Parsing them could yield significant insights about learning and pedagogy.

The third objective was to use online learning to improve residential learning and teaching. But how? By the end of 2011, it was becoming clear that YouTube videos and online courses didn't just have the potential to benefit online learners. They had the potential to impact the residential learner, too. After all, if an online learner could watch a professor's classroom videos on his or her own time, so could that professor's on-campus students. And that in turn would impact classroom teaching. Lectures that ate up an hour or more of classroom time could be relegated online, freeing up valuable time for intimate, value-added in-class conversations between students and faculty.

In 2000, three economics professors coined the term *inverted classroom* to describe technology's potential to reverse the traditional teaching process. By 2012, the idea of inverted, or "flipped," classrooms had become part of the online vernacular and was being embraced by a growing number of schools and universities. Garber reasoned that on-campus students could not only leverage online materials, but also benefit from follow-on small-group conversations with their professors in the classroom. *That* was the real benefit of online education for residential students at Harvard.

Garber's first two objectives struck a deep chord with many of us at HBS. We had a harder time with the third. I didn't immediately know why at first; it hit me later: We'd been flipping the classroom for a hundred years at HBS.

OUR STARTING POINT: LEARNING BY DISCOVERY

HBS is known around the world for its research on business practices and management. It's even better known for its teaching approach—the case method. Rather than learn management from textbooks or theory, students grapple with the real-world problems that managers encounter and the decisions they must make—all captured in ten- to fifteen-page "case studies" written by faculty members.

The case method isn't the most efficient approach to teaching and learning. Quite the opposite: It can be frustrating for both student and teacher. Students might yearn for "the answer" but instead are encouraged to engage in reflection and conversation with their peers. Faculty might yearn to give "the answer," especially when student discussions veer onto a wrong path, but are committed to let students try to discover it on their own. Despite all this, the experience is often deeply engaging for students (Sal Khan recently referred to the HBS classroom as more engaging than "any traditional classroom I've ever been a part of"). Why? Students are almost always alert and prepared, in part because they need to be—the instructor might ask them at any time to speak (the dreaded "cold call"). Excellence was rewarded not only for mastery on exams but for daily contributions in class. Daily attendance almost always exceeds 95 percent—not just because absenteeism compromises students' grades, but because students (dare one say it?) enjoy the learning process. Students learn not only from the instructor but just as frequently from one another. They are challenged to think, often on their feet. They learn by discovery and through mistakes. The case method is a modern-day Socratic approach.

These are the fundamental differences between the case method approach and a traditional lecture-based one—between what many observers had come to characterize as "active learning" versus "passive learning." One might be excused for thinking that the difference in approaches boiled down to content or format—in one setting there was "the lecture," in the other, "the case." That couldn't be further from the truth. The difference in approach extended far beyond the content or format, to the learning process itself. At its heart, the case method was teaching centered on students and *how* they learned, not just what they learned. It was the flipped classroom.

While many institutions were aspiring to migrate toward a model of active learning, this was already our starting point. So when we looked at online education and the benefits it might offer students, the first question we asked ourselves was: *What is the problem we are trying to solve?*

WHY CHANGE?

Organizational change is invariably precipitated by fear. There is the fear of sticking to the status quo and becoming stale. There is the fear of being disrupted by new competitors or new technologies. And there is the fear that doing nothing might leave one ill-prepared to grab new opportunities as others march forward. These were among the reasons many universities were jumping into the online game.

At HBS in 2012, there was little dissatisfaction with the status quo: The case method approach was working well. Our existing programs were in fine shape, and our students were reporting high levels of satisfaction. There was little fear of impending disruption to the institution.

This last point was salient, coming as it did in the face of concerns voiced by one of our own colleagues, Clay Christensen. Christensen is perhaps the most famous theorist and scholar of disruption—and a vigorous proponent of the need for organizations to get out in front of it. He'd been bravely trying to rally our faculty for more than a decade, warning as early as 2001 of the dangers of the complacency that had beleaguered so many other sectors. He'd spoken articulately of the havoc online education would eventually wreak on our well-functioning operating model.

But, again, the effectiveness of our case-method-based active learning approach made us question whether online learning could possibly improve the classroom experience. It also gave faculty confidence—perhaps false confidence—that what we offered on campus was unlikely to be disrupted any time soon.

These conditions—a strong core product, satisfaction with the status quo, no burning platform, and a lower-quality substitute—are often described as precisely the conditions that eventually lead incumbents into the abyss. But our conversations didn't stop there. Our dean, Nitin Nohria, had, until recently, been skeptical about online education ("Not in my lifetime," he'd replied to a question about when Harvard Business School would offer online courses). Now, he and many other faculty were still keen to do *something* online. Why? We saw it as a tremendous opportunity to learn about what was possible with digital technologies. Perhaps those learnings could better inform a decision about whether we wanted to invest in online education for the long haul. There was an aspiration, best articulated by our dean: HBS had made its mark in residential business education for more than a century; now could we carve out a leadership position in multi-platform education? And there was a concrete decision to make: whether or not to offer MOOC-style courses on edX. In hindsight, the bold move forward by our university parent to cocreate edX had activated internal conversations at HBS on how *we* wanted to approach this space. Absent that, we might not have moved as quickly as we did, or at all.

So the question became, what could we do in online education that would not only benefit learners, but would be right for the institution, and leverage our strengths? It was this question that ultimately turned us away from the "camera in the classroom." MOOC-style streamed video lectures had benefits for millions of online learners. But there was no reason why we'd be any better than anyone else at delivering them. Moreover, they didn't fit with our classroom pedagogy. To succeed online, we'd need to build on something we did well—to leverage our institutional DNA. That something was the case method approach. So as we began conversations about HBX—the name we would apply to the initiative, borrowing from the increasingly ubiquitous X suffixes in online education—we did so with a belief in the strength of our existing approach to teaching, rather than a mindset geared toward overcoming its shortcomings. And we did so with a desire to differentiate, to build our online offerings around our strengths, rather than follow what was for us, in any case, a path we couldn't follow without changing our pedagogical DNA.

WHO'S THE LEARNER?

Very quickly, we ruled one option out. We decided we would not offer our MBA courses fully online. The MBA program is the crown jewel of HBS, the reason that hundreds of students paid a lot of money to enroll. It was in no danger from online education—or at least that's how we felt then.

This was not an obvious decision. Many other major universities were jump-starting their online offerings with some of their best residential courses—Justice, at Harvard, by Michael Sandel; Circuits, at MIT, by Anant Agarwal; Artificial Intelligence, at Stanford, by Sebastian Thrun. Why, one might think, would these institutions risk undercutting their most desirable residential offerings by making them freely and universally available? One reason was a desire for greater reach. Another was a belief that online courses were unlikely to cannibalize demand for residential programs—and that even if they did, that it was the right move. "Cannibalize yourself" has become a familiar refrain in business; indeed, many of us at HBS had been preaching it to companies for years. It's a sensible prescription when the threat of disruption is real. But again, few of us believed this was the case for us. At some point we might be forced into offering our MBA courses online. But we weren't going to start there.

So we began instead by asking: Who should we offer online courses to? To answer this question, we began by considering those learners closest to home—our own MBA students. In doing so, we identified a problem with our MBA program that had nothing to do with the program once classes were in session. It was a problem that occurred *before* the sessions started.

Roughly 15 to 30 percent of Harvard MBA students matriculate with little or no background in the basic language of business: accounting, economics, data analysis. (Some might think they have the requisite knowledge, but often realize later that they don't.) But knowledge of these areas—knowing how to read accounting statements, leverage economic principles in decision making, and analyze data—was essential to preparedness for our program, starting on day one.

For years we had tried to meet this challenge by offering two-week residential courses—primers—mostly before the start of regular MBA coursework. Some, like Foundations, offered exposure to a broad range of topics (problem solving, business history, economics). Others, like Analytics, focused on quantitative skills, finance, and accounting, accompanied by some online tutorials. But by the end of 2011, certain gaps in student preparedness were visible. Foundations had long been done away with; Analytics, despite its effectiveness, reached only roughly 15–20% of the students, and the program had been recently compressed further from two weeks to one. By now, several faculty members viewed our ability to fully prepare our students for the rigors of the MBA program as being somewhat compromised.

Now this presented a near-perfect opportunity to rework with an online version.

In December 2014, four of us—Youngme Moon (who as the chair of the MBA program had, along with our dean, initiated conversations about HBX), Janice Hammond and V. G. Narayanan (who together led Analytics), and I—gathered in a basement conference room on the HBS campus to explore whether our pre-MBA courses should make up HBS's first online offerings. It didn't take much debate—we were all in. We would create three online courses—Accounting, Business Analytics, and Economics— covering the fundamental concepts needed before embarking on an MBA program. They were the "basic language of business." This was the genesis of our first online program.

Our foray into online education had started with two seemingly un-eventful decisions: We would not touch our existing product, and we would start with a new offering for our existing students *before they walked onto campus.* It was akin to a company's offering a new digital product to its existing customers before they entered the physical store. Crafting digital strategy by focusing on your existing customers is often regarded as a recipe for failure. It can lead to organizational myopia, where a focus on existing customers' needs leads you to overlook what most other custom-ers want. But the distinction between products and customers is often misunderstood in these debates. Reinventing existing products can be hard because architectures are inflexible; creating new products to serve unmet needs of your existing customers is not. And often it's *those custom-ers'* unmet needs that are not just ignored, but present the most valuable opportunities to differentiate on. So, rather than looking far—to "non-customers," to those at the fringes of the market, to those far away from our own organization—we started by looking close to home.

This decision—to focus on the needs of our own MBA students—had two further implications. We soon realized that the potential demand for the materials we were creating might extend beyond our MBA student body. Other business schools might want to draw on the same preparatory online materials for their own MBA students. Employers might find it useful to offer these courses to their incoming hires. And undergraduates—not just those planning on getting an MBA—might find these materials valuable as they prepared for their own entry into the workforce.

This last point was particularly salient in light of the broader debates swirling around undergraduate education. The liberal arts had long been the cornerstone of higher education in the United States, but in recent years many had come to regard them as a luxury. The debate was often framed as "learn for a job" versus "learn for life," or "acquire marketable skills" versus "acquire a way of thinking." The debates were becoming increasingly heated. And no one was ceding any ground.

Although our first online program was conceived to prepare our own students—many of them formerly liberal arts undergraduates—for our MBA program, perhaps, if extended to a summer program for undergraduates anywhere, it could afford other students a chance to acquire an understanding of the basic "language of business" while still pursuing their passions for art history or literature, philosophy or chemistry. They'd acquire the critical thinking and communication skills that were valuable in the longer run, but be better prepared for their first day at work as well. This logic eventually gave rise to the name we'd ascribe to our online program—HBX CORe, or Credential of Readiness.

This was the first set of unforeseen implications that came from deciding to focus on the needs of our own MBAs. The second was that, like it or not, the quality bar would necessarily need to be high. Whatever we did online for our incoming students, we would need to create a "wow" experience, something comparable to what they'd encounter in our residential classrooms after they arrived on campus. CORe, after all, would be their first learning experience through HBS. It wouldn't do for the experience to be anything less than what they'd get on campus.

This last aspiration appeared to be no easy one, perhaps even a fool's errand.

A DIGITAL-FIRST APPROACH

We quickly realized it would be impossible to simply mimic our residential experience online. If we tried, we'd probably fail. So we decided we had to go "digital-first." Whatever we created would need to offer something that *only* online platforms could bring to the learning experience.

This realization moved us even further away from the "flipped class-room" approach. As attractive as the flipped classroom was, irrespective of how HBS taught, it contained a basic challenge: It was "classroom-first." Moving online that part of classroom instruction that involved little inter-action was appealing for the *in-class* learner—but it also had dispiriting implications for the *online* learner. He or she, after all, would now become subject to the same lecture approach that classrooms were trying to get rid of. Even in the case of HBS, where in-class learning involved active dis-cussion, merely recording these conversations for online learners wouldn't be stimulating or inspiring, we felt.

Let's embrace the digital medium for what it can offer, we argued. Let's imagine new possibilities there, ones that would moreover elevate online learners to prime-time status.

"Digital-first" came from a belief that if we tried to merely copy what we did in the classroom, it wouldn't work. Instead, digital-first meant that we'd distill the case study approach down to the basic tenets that made it so powerful, and then reimagine how each of those tenets might be ex-pressed online. We'd be borrowing the principles, not the particulars. Ev-erything else, we would try to forget. "Forget and borrow" would become a familiar mnemonic in the subsequent evolution of HBX. It was inspired directly by the experience of media firms like Schibsted and others.

What were the core principles? We identified three: real-world problem solving, active learning, and peer learning. Real-world problems defined case method learning. As with traditional cases, we'd motivate the learn-ing of each concept with stories of managers confronting real dilemmas that brought the concepts to life. Active learning required students not just to read or hear material, but to immerse and engage, reflect and dis-cuss. Case learning was a "lean-forward" approach; we'd want to create the same experience online. Peer learning was central, too—students would learn from each other.

We spiritedly brainstormed ways that we might bring these principles to life online. We knew there were some things we couldn't do as well, online, as a classroom could. But the question was whether we do other things *better*. Ideas began flowing. Short, dynamic videos of managers nar-rating case stories could be more engaging than traditional textual narra-tives, for example. Interactive exercises or graphs could be a better way to learn a concept than just seeing a drawing on the blackboard or a written formula. Students could ask questions at any time, unlike in the class-room, where airtime was scarce. Each could be required to reflect on their learnings before moving on. Those reflections could be shared instantaneously and widely. Students could slow down or speed up a video according to their needs. Several professors could be showcased in the same course or even in a single lesson, rather than having students exposed to a single voice only.

We came to realize that the digital medium itself wasn't an obstacle to creating a great online experience. Only our imagination was.

As we brainstormed ideas like these, we reached another sobering conclusion. There was no existing online learning platform that would let us create the experience we wanted. We'd need to build one ourselves, and fast.

We had no idea how to do this. It was no coincidence that all the major online education platforms had been built by computer science professors. We asked some colleagues from our information technology group to help us think through the possibilities. They did so enthusiastically, listening to our (we hoped) bursts of inspiration and sometimes (we suspected) outrageous ideas, letting us know what was feasible and what wasn't. As ideas were exchanged, something even more important was occurring: A continuous feedback loop between our content and technology teams was forming. This would be a pivotal point for us, and would create a culture that would anchor HBX in the months to come. If a faculty member had an idea, it could be implemented on the platform at very short notice.

29

FROM STRATEGY TO LAUNCH

QUESTIONS THAT MATTER

Our conversations were at times messy and chaotic—as conversations about product development or strategy often are. But beneath it all were two questions that formed a clear thread connecting everything we discussed. They were the two basic questions every strategist must ask: Where should we play? And how can we win there?

These aren't complicated questions. But it takes real effort to answer them. In our case it would have been easy to be seduced by the rhetoric surrounding online education. "Democratize education." "Flatten the world." "Embrace new technologies." These statements had undeniable merit, and they were motivating us too. But, while these statements might point generally to where the world of online education might end up, they weren't particularly useful in guiding any individual decision. The fundamental questions of strategy still mattered. Who's the learner? Where to differentiate? How to create a digital-first experience?

As universities or online platforms craft their online strategy and targets, a few axioms emerge time after time. "Have the broadest impact" is one. "Achieve maximum reach" is another. The means cited to reach these targets is also often the same: Offer great courses with star faculty, and learners will follow.

These aren't unreasonable approaches—until you realize that they offer little help in understanding who the learners are or what they actually care about. It's like offering a product in search of a customer, rather than the other way around. It would be taking a classic product-centered approach, rather than a user-centered one.

Starting with the simple question—"Who's the learner"—shifted us away from a bias toward content and faculty. And it mattered. Knowing our MBA learners, deeply, made it easier to know the range of materials they'd need in CORe to be equipped for our MBA program. It allowed us to know exactly where they struggled, and what concepts were essential to cover. And it set for us a clear quality bar.

Another consequence of not knowing your learner has to do with the metrics so often cited: reach and access. Having 100,000 students register for your online course had come to be accepted as a marker of success. But completion rates were low, typically in the single digits. Naturally, these figures had come to fuel skepticism about the online education trend. *The New York Times*'s 2012 "Year of the MOOC" gave way the following year to NPR's "The Online Revolution Drifts Off Course."

Focusing on the individual learner meant that we focused—ruthlessly—on a single metric: engagement, not reach. If we could crack the code of engagement, we felt, reach would follow.

PRIORITIZATION VERSUS EXPERIMENTATION

By early March 2013, the CORe offering was on its way to being crystallized. At the same time, hordes of other opportunities began surfacing, ones that might naturally fall under the umbrella of "digital education" and HBX. Should we create a portal to connect aspiring entrepreneurs with advisers and investors? Should we create digital platforms to enhance our research efforts at HBS? Should we seek to maximize the number of our educational offerings or start narrow? Should we offer "how-to" tools for managers? Should we try to use digital technology to enhance our existing on-campus programs?

Strategists and entrepreneurs are often viewed as operating in different worlds. The world of strategy, it is argued, applies to big, mature organizations whose ways of competing and competitors are well known, and where competing priorities are a reality. The world of entrepreneurs is seen as messy, innovative, and unknown. There, the priority ought to be to grab every opportunity that comes along, since it's impossible to know which might resolve in your favor.

This distinction is a red herring. Mature organizations also need to innovate. Young organizations also need to prioritize. During the early days of HBX, while we were trying to innovate, we were also being forced to prioritize.

Over the next few months, we got used to saying no. We decided to experiment with one more type of offering, short online courses for senior executives (Clay Christensen agreed to create the first one on, ironically, Disruptive Strategy—his research area). We couldn't take on more projects because we didn't have the resources—time or money—to devote. We didn't need to have a thousand flowers bloom. We hoped only that what we created might improve online education in some way. It was a seemingly odd juxtaposition of the worlds of strategy and entrepreneurship. And it turned out to be best captured in an informal directive from our dean: "Be as creative and as entrepreneurial as possible. But failure is not an option."

As our conversations about portfolio strategy were getting clearer, another clarifying event would soon take place. The irony wasn't that it surprised me, but that given what I'd been writing about, it shouldn't have.

A CLARIFYING EVENT: USER CONNECTIONS AND SOCIAL LEARNING

By May 2013 we were rolling. We were building the platform, hiring videographers, making calls on pricing, and architecting the content for each course.

For that last activity, in addition to hiring course research assistants and engaging some of our doctoral students, we enlisted three outstanding second-year MBA students to offer their input. If we were going to create a compelling and engaging online offering for entering MBA students, who better to inform the content creation process than our own students?

We met regularly to brainstorm. Three months in, I realized the MBA students had been saying something we hadn't been hearing. We'd been discussing the principles that made in-classroom case discussions work for months now. But our students were describing ways in which learning occurred *outside* the classroom as well—things that we ought to think about re-creating online. They talked about pre-class study groups, post-class emails, corridor conversations, lunchroom debates, and dorm room arguments. Those seemingly accidental peer-to-peer interactions were as much a part of case method education as anything else, they said.

Social learning had been one of our anchoring principles. We knew that the case approach relied heavily on students listening to and learning from one another. But we had paid little attention to the full scope of what that really meant. Instead we'd focused our efforts primarily around course architectures, platform design, and teaching quality—in other words, on delivering great content.

We were falling, remarkably, into the Content Trap.

It was a eureka moment. "We've spent 97% of our time on content creation and active learning, 3% on social learning," I wrote in a note to myself that month. "We need to dramatically reverse this emphasis: 97% social, 3% content." As it turned out, Moon was independently arriving at the same conclusion.

Over the next month, we focused on everything we could do to enhance the social learning features of our platform. Our faculty team had a series of meetings with our technology team. We threw out dozens of ideas. Nothing would be rejected offhand. Open the platform with a global map showing where students were at any moment, we envisioned. They'd know one another's identity: Anonymity and pseudonymity were out, profile pictures were in. Have students provide lots of information about themselves. Update interactive polls in real time to reflect everyone's answers. This seemingly small innovation could create a learning moment—the surprise that occurs right after you've answered a question, when you realize that many others answered it differently. Replace text-based answers with assignments that required students to upload photos that showed their understanding of concepts—and then make the images searchable. Prompt spontaneous virtual debates. Create study groups on the fly so that learners who'd reached the same point in the course could discuss a concept between themselves. Even try an online "cold call."

Cold calls are the most famous teaching technique in a case method classroom. An instructor might ask a question of any student at random, at any point during the class. The question could be simple or hard, conceptual or analytical. The instructor might move on quickly or probe the student for several more minutes. Cold calls are central to the Socratic approach. They are dreaded by students and often remembered for years afterward.

What makes the cold call so effective, we asked? It encourages preparation, of course—students have to be alert throughout class. It lets students learn from one another, and even from their mistakes—after all, rarely is a student's first instinct entirely right. And it can be terrifying because it's social: You have ninety students staring at you, in what often seems interminable silence, while you prepare to speak. It is, ultimately, the social pressure that makes cold calls so powerful. "We're far more afraid of embarrassing ourselves in front of our classmates than in front of the professor," numerous students had told us over the years. Now, as we thought about social learning online, we wondered how to capture that power for HBX.

And just like that, we created the HBX cold call. The design was simple: A pop-up would randomly appear as a student progressed through material online. It would present a question that had to be answered within a minute—a clock was ticking on the side—in thirty words or less. And the answer would be visible to everyone in the cohort, along with the student's profile picture to boot. This would be one of many features on the HBX platform to combine active and social learning.

The social features we designed were intended not just so that students could engage one another; we wanted them to help one another, too. But how? Discussion boards were common in online education, but rarely effective. Fewer than 10 percent of students participated in them. One reason why most stayed away was that they could be tedious to navigate. They were normally set up as "sidebars" to online course pages, and learners could post questions on any topic, at any time—but that made searching hard. Another reason was that students often had had no incentive to answer other students' questions—the most popular online courses often had armies of teaching assistants ready to jump in and answer questions themselves. And, on top of all this, students needn't register under their real names.

To address these challenges, we started with a simple design: Course materials were broken down into discrete lesson pages, and discussion boards were "local" to every page on the platform. Questions on a page could be triggered only by that page's content. It was a small feature, but it encouraged peer interaction by making search easier.

Then, we added explicit incentives. "Gamification" had increasingly populated the online world. The idea there was to reward participants for particular behaviors. Sometimes incentives worked well; other times they seemed gimmicky. But online education had one advantage over gaming and media companies: Participants received grades. So we decided to tie grades to participation. Answer other learners' questions and your course grade will improve. We'd graded students in our residential courses this way for years.

During the previous decade, social networks had exploded, and so had the study of them. One question receiving attention had to do with why some social networks succeeded in encouraging certain behaviors, while others did not. For example, how did LinkedIn encourage participants to post work-related information, whereas Facebook postings were more personal? Why were users on Friendster interested in dating rather than building friendships, as its founders had intended?

One emerging and powerful insight was that success rested on attracting the "right" users, giving them the "right" incentives to participate, and providing the "right" tools to engage in certain behaviors—it wasn't about platform quality or social features per se. We'd been teaching those principles to others, and now we put them to work ourselves. For every social feature we ideated, we encouraged our team to ask: How can we ensure that we elicit the right behaviors, attract the right users, and give them the right incentives? Our rules should be simple enough to understand but not so transparent as to be easily gamed.

The conversations about social learning resulted in a shift in emphasis around our platform design—from making it merely interactive to making it social, too. Our design principles for HBX were crystallizing. In May 2014 we sketched a four-layered design around which we would center our pedagogical approach (see Figure 27). The layers corresponded to four forms of learning: passive, active, adaptive, and social. The central question guiding us was how to boost engagement through each form.

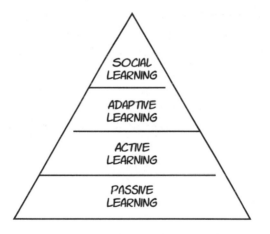

Figure 27: Four Layers of Learning

Passive learning was the simplest layer. Users could watch and listen without much effort. But it needn't be boring. Keeping videos short, enhancing the quality of animations, and grounding theoretical concepts in real-world examples were all ways to heighten interest.

Active learning was the second layer: Get users to do something. The principle of "trying and failing" underpins the case method in our classrooms; online, we would follow the same strategy, the key being getting students to try. Polls, reflections, cold calls, and interactive features were all examples of active learning. We would stick to a "three-to-five-minute rule"—learners couldn't go by for more than three to five minutes without doing something active in that time. This would differentiate even our video clips from typical MOOCs.

Next was adaptive learning: customizing learning to the needs of every individual. Online learning is by its very nature adaptive—learners can move through material at their own pace. But numerous other possibilities for customization existed. Get a question wrong, for example, and you could be given more until you got the answer right. Elementary and middle school kids were already learning math on platforms like IXL, which embodied this principle impressively. The problem was that the technologies needed for more sophisticated forms of adaptive learning weren't there yet. So we decided to focus on that later, and concentrate on optimizing other things for now.

Social learning was layer number four. This, as much as anything else, could differentiate our platform, we felt. We needed it to work well for another reason—namely, we weren't intending to have any live interaction between learners and faculty members once the course started.

When we first shared this idea with our team members, several were taken aback. It wouldn't work, some argued: The root of our success in case method teaching was the closeness of student-faculty interactions and the role of the faculty in guiding conversations. But if we pursued that classroom approach online, we would never be able to scale. Online learning would then require faculty to divert attention away from their residential responsibilities, which was impractical. We needed a learning model that worked well *without* faculty members present.

CAN QUALITY ONLINE EDUCATION SCALE?

The question of how organizations scale is crucial to most businesses. Thinking about it may require testing your assumptions about what's really important about what you're offering. The traditional circus industry is a case in point. Marvelous as the experience for circus-goers was, the industry had not succeeded in scaling for a hundred years. On any given day the circus performed in a single city; only when it was done there did it move on to another location. This was because trained animals and their handlers (particularly lions and lion trainers), often the centerpiece of the circus experience, were extremely hard to come by. By the late 1990s, a relatively new industry player, Cirque du Soleil, had not only carved out its own unique position, but also scaled up impressively, simultaneously offering shows in multiple locations around the world. How did it do so? Not by finding more lions and lion trainers, but by getting rid of them. That had meant questioning an old assumption—that lions were necessary for a great circus experience.

By now, most online learning platforms were gravitating toward one of two alternatives. The first was designed to scale—lecture formats in MOOCs, for example, were easily broadcast to hundreds of thousands of learners. Where they were challenged was increasing individual learner engagement. The second, and opposite, route focused on "active learning"—creating a rich, personalized experience for every learner, typically with faculty participating in live, small-group discussions with ten to twenty students. The result was often a superb experience for each learner—but the model was hard to scale. Either one needed more faculty, or existing residential faculty had to do more work.

As we designed HBX, this was a major issue. We sought *both* engagement and scale. The only way to achieve that was to avoid any live interaction with a faculty member. During one of our early conversations, we captured this idea on a simple chart.

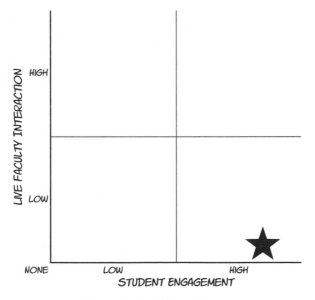

Figure 28: Scale Versus Engagement

Should we try this? Yes, we felt.

But how to achieve it? Few faculty members anywhere believe that one can have high learner engagement without live interaction with faculty members or teaching assistants. In fact, as online platforms sought ways to charge for a premium online learning experience, the dominant view was that faculty members should offer online office hours, live chats, and other kinds of interaction. We looked to reverse this approach.

To do so, we carefully thought through each part of the faculty role in the classroom, and how we might automate it. In class, faculty members guide the discussion when it veers off-topic. To achieve that online, we would allow for discussions at various points; then, anticipating how those would generally evolve on the basis of our classroom experience, we would inject prerecorded faculty videos at the appropriate moments to keep them on track. In class, faculty help generalize beyond the particulars of the case at hand. Online, we would insert questions that forced students to consider how concepts applied in different settings. In class, faculty members encourage students to reflect. Online, we'd insert "shared reflections" at key moments too. In class, faculty members ensure that students paid attention. Online, we would use the cold call. In class, faculty members answer questions. Online, that would have to rest on peer learning. This last feature meant that making social learning work wasn't just a luxury for us now; it was necessary if we were to scale. And it would test our faith in peer learning.

As we developed the courses, we were now not just producing the materials, but trying to think through every learning moment for students as they might proceed through them—then inserting the right teaching elements at the right moments to allow students to "learn through discovery." We were comfortable with this pedagogical approach in our classrooms. It was far harder to pull off online. Every learning moment had to be anticipated. Course learnings had to be robust enough to withstand variations and digressions in the discussions, yet flexible enough and rich enough to allow conversation.

In effect, we were designing a *process*—a process that might be thought of as guiding learners through a series of mysteries and puzzles, each time unlocking a new question for them to tackle on their own, interspersed with short videos of real-life managers or faculty, and followed by reflections, polls, or interactive exercises. By hard-coding these elements into the course flow we were determined to make ourselves as faculty redundant once the learning process began.

If we were successful in doing so, we felt we could reverse, for us, the economics of creating online courses. Traditional online offerings were relatively straightforward to create: Use a camera to record faculty lectures, stream them online, then add assessments. But while the up-front cost and effort might be fairly low, enhancing the student experience *after* the course started required ongoing faculty time and high ongoing effort. We intended to do the opposite: Our approach would demand a high up-front time commitment from our faculty but virtually no ongoing effort.

Could we succeed? We had no idea.

STRATEGY-SETTING AND FUNCTIONAL CONNECTIONS

By the end of the year, we had formulated an approach that differed from the "MOOC model" in many respects: selective versus open, proprietary platforms versus common ones, gated access versus flexible schedules, real identities versus virtual ones, paid versus free, and so on. To an outside observer, it could be tempting to ascribe these differences to different objectives: for example, that the paid model was a result of prioritizing monetization over access; or that the "platform build" decision resulted from an organizational preference for control. Our decision to eschew live faculty interaction might be viewed as an indication that we weren't taking online learning seriously, and our decision to restrict the release of new materials might have been viewed as puzzlingly at odds with the flexibility of online learning itself.

In fact the range of our differences from the MOOC approach didn't arise out of a desire to be different. They arose almost entirely from our different starting point: case-based learning. The philosophy of student-centered learning spawned every subsequent choice. Our differences from MOOCs arose because of connections.

Figure 29 illustrates these connections. "Learning by discovery" sparked ideas about interactive features and assessments—and the recognition that existing platforms weren't flexible enough to accommodate them. That led to a decision to build our own platform—in turn generating higher costs. Covering those costs would require a fee-based model. But fees created expectations for support, in turn further increasing costs. To then preserve broad access, we offered financial aid. And to verify aid need, we relied on college partnerships.

Peer learning had a domino effect on other choices, too. Students would need a *shared* learning experience—otherwise conversations would be fragmented. Shared experiences required a restrictive approach to content release, so that students would work through the courses more or less in tandem. They also required a linear flow through material, rather than allowing students to jump around or mix content from different modules. And they meant that high continuation rates were essential—if large numbers of learners dropped out, peer conversations would be disjointed.

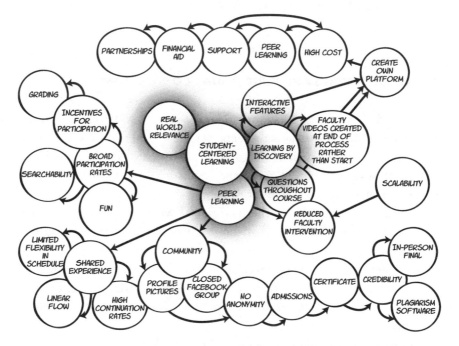

Figure 29: HBX: Elements of Strategy

Peer learning also required appropriate incentives—grades. It required that discussion forums be easily searchable. It required familiarity among participants. This led to our restricting the size of any single community of learners—larger waves would be divided into smaller cohorts. It was why we required participants to disclose their real identities and supply personal profile information, rather than be anonymous. It was why we created a closed Facebook group—to amplify social relationships. It was why we selected learners rather than letting anyone enroll. It was why we restrained content teams from intervening too often.

In other words, the differences between our model and the typical MOOC approach arose not as a series of coincidences, or from an innate desire to depart from that model in every way. They arose because the decisions we were making around price, platform, support, grading, community, admissions, and partnerships were deeply connected to one another. These are the functional connections that underlie strategy. In effect, it was a reprise of Schibsted versus *The Economist,* Walmart versus Target, and Edward Jones versus, say, Merrill Lynch.

View the differences in approach through this lens and you'll see prescriptive implications for other online learning strategies and the "right" approach. It could be tempting to argue that launching online courses free, quick, and open—the MOOC approach—is the "right" model for online education. That would be incorrect. It could be equally tempting to conclude that building proprietary platforms, targeting existing learners, having little faculty interaction—our approach—is the right one to pursue. That, too, would be incorrect. Our approach was triggered both by *our* own needs and our strengths, even as it was inspired by the practices we were seeing elsewhere, including in the MOOC world.

This is the heart of differentiation and strategy. These are the sorts of differences that have played out in many industries, analog and digital, in recent years.

CHANGE—AND A WORD OF CAUTION

Confronted with technological change, organizations often fail. By now, we know many of the reasons why. An organization might be rigid and inflexible, tied into existing ways of doing things. Managers may not want to change—they might be unwilling to take on multi-year transformation efforts or to trade sure near-term bonuses for risky longer-term payoffs. They may not even see a threat coming, being too focused on existing customers and products.

Sometimes, perversely, organizations fail because they are successful: Winning strategies contain the seeds of their own destruction. Effective strategy, after all, requires tailoring everything you do around serving a certain set of customers. But, as we've seen, that requires coordination across all parts of your organization—functional connections. And although these connections bestow success, they are also hard to unravel and change easily.

These reasons for organizational failure have been understood for a while. As we proceeded with our efforts, we were acutely aware of them. But, over the past decade, one idea had risen above all others in popular discourse: Clay Christensen's theory of disruptive innovation, generally regarded as one of the most influential ideas in management during the last decade.

Christensen himself had predicted the disruption of K–12 education ten years earlier in his book *Disrupting Class*. By now, analysts, entrepreneurs, and investors were warning about the impending disruption to higher education as well. So was the media: "Online Education: The Disruption to Come," noted *The Economist*; "Higher Education Is Now Ground Zero for Disruption," announced *Forbes*. What did it mean for us? More important, what did it mean for other institutions trying to carve out their own path? Disruption prescriptions—launch fast and free, to learners you've never served—were being followed by many institutions. They'd become a rallying cry, even a crutch, that many administrators were turning to for guidance on what to do. But there were reasons to exercise caution.

It's useful to first understand what the theory of disruptive innovation actually says.

Originally articulated in the mid-1990s by Christensen and his adviser, longtime HBS professor Joe Bower, the theory has been refined by others and applied to numerous technologies and industries. At its heart, though, are three simple and perhaps frightening observations.

First, incumbents get disrupted by new technologies not because they are unaware of them or unable to embrace them but because they rationally choose to ignore them. Why? New technologies often express themselves initially in products that are inferior in quality to existing ones. So firms focus on the needs of their current customers and rationally reject newer but lower-quality alternatives.

Beware of this, Christensen says: The behavior of customers on the periphery is often a harbinger of what's coming in your core business. This goes to his second observation: Things can change, sometimes quickly. Competitors who appear unthreatening today will migrate up a "quality spectrum" and become threatening tomorrow. In this sense, the theory warns against a static, once-and-for-all view of customer needs or competitor behaviors, and against ignoring those products or companies with ostensibly worse product quality today.

This leads to the third and related observation and prescription: Don't be too protective of your core. Eat your lunch today, or others will. The only chance of success, Christensen argues, lies in creating a separate organization that disrupts or destroys your core. It's the only way to be free from both the shackles and the seductive riches of your existing one.

Christensen documented these concepts in the context of steel mills, showing how high-cost incumbents like US Steel ignored low-cost "mini mills"—and eventually saw much of their business destroyed. Low-end rebars, he noted, were ignored and willfully ceded by high-cost incumbents like US Steel to lower-cost entrants. The decision to do so seemed fully rational at the time. Fast-forward thirty years, however, and these very same entrants were making steel of comparable quality, at lower cost, destroying the business of erstwhile successful incumbents in the process. The quality migration over time was documented clearly by Christensen, and the pattern used to describe similar dynamics elsewhere.

As examples from other industries accumulated, the theory of disruption gained credence as an explanation for what was wrong with incumbent organizations and why they fail. It became a metaphor for what Silicon Valley represented. And it was applied to a broader and broader set of industries.

And this is where its Achilles' heel also surfaced. Disruptive theory began to be seen as applying everywhere and to everything. Only, it didn't.

Part of the reason was that the vernacular of disruption became increasingly divorced from the original theory. Popular use of the term had butchered the original idea, and far outdistanced Christensen's definition, much to his own chagrin. Over time *disruption* came to mean different things to different people, embraced—and often misused—by managers, investors, and entrepreneurs to marshal arguments that served their needs. But the theory itself had built-in limits.

To start, there was the question of empirical universality. Disruptive innovation is at its heart a story of certain *industry-level* trends—not a story of every industry or of every firm within disrupted ones. Christensen had recognized this a few years back. Hotels, he'd noted, were not being disrupted by new technology, because there was no common "technological core" spanning different hotels. The more general point was that disruption is hardly a law of nature, as so many observers had come to believe. It is merely a possibility.

In addition, "disruptive dynamics" in practice needn't always start with low-quality alternatives. They could come from the high end, too. Apple's was the most expensive smartphone in the market when it came out, in 2006—and the most "disruptive" innovation in the phone industry for thirty years.

More salient for content businesses, the real threat came from elsewhere. Most frightening to book publishers wasn't the rise of self-publishing. Nor were Hollywood studios terrified by YouTube videos, bestselling musicians by YouTube covers, or *The New York Times* by bloggers. In each case, the far more relevant threat came from a different source: aggregators, platforms, and networks. In other words, the threat wasn't from low- or high-quality content alternatives; it was from businesses that exploited user connections.

The relative importance of "network dynamics" over "quality dynamics" was increasingly relevant in education as well. Initially higher education institutions were probably not worried about Lynda.com—a company that had been offering moderate-quality short video tutorials for software and business professionals for a decade—and perhaps rightly so. But in 2015, when that firm was acquired by LinkedIn—a business rooted in network connections—they instantly were.

Disruption theory warned incumbents about being too focused on their current customers. But increasingly, organizations were falling into a different trap: focusing excessively on current products. Recording studios had missed the opportunity in concerts by focusing on CDs. Newspapers had missed the opportunity in classifieds by focusing on news. Cable companies were increasingly threatened by Netflix not because they were too focused on customers; rather, they had focused obsessively around their product—content and pipes. In each case, the needs of *current* customers were unmet. Customer-centricity wasn't deadly; product-centricity was.

And, even if disruption was evident, the solution offered to incumbents didn't always follow. "Separate your innovative organization as much as you can from your core." "Launch quickly, at the low end." "Learn and improve over time." These prescriptions had a certain appeal; indeed, some organizations would have done well to follow them more closely. But these prescriptions too assumed an uneasy air of universality over time, and they collided with a core principle of good strategy: the value of being different.

Disruption theory led to a mindset that framed new technologies as substitutes for existing ones, rather than recognizing their potential as complements. It might explain the failures of organizations like *Newsweek* but not the simultaneous success of ones like *The Economist*. It extolled the advantages of separating start-up efforts from the core but not of reintegration efforts like those that had worked at Schibsted. It emphasized forgetting, not the virtues of forgetting *and* borrowing. Ultimately, it created a narrative centered on negative connections, rather than emboldening a focus on positive ones.

We were both informed and challenged by disruption theory in trying to figure out the right course for HBS, even if ultimately we did not follow many of its prescriptions. Trying to compete in online education by following the same approach as apparent "disruptors" at the other end would have made little sense. It wouldn't play to our strengths or leverage our existing capabilities. It might undermine some of our core assets, even the school's brand. Most important, it was not the only way forward. All of us involved in creating HBX became convinced that being "different" would be a virtue rather than a liability as we charted our course. We were confident, but far from certain. Things were evolving far too rapidly, and the behavior of online learners was far too unfamiliar, to warrant that.

LAUNCH AND RESULTS

Website Launch

We opened the HBX website on March 21, 2014. The site and everything about it—its tone, style, and content—were designed to convey three messages. First was our aspiration for online learning. We were embracing digital technology in a big way for the first time, and were trying to make online learning as engaging and powerful as the HBS classroom experience. Second, in order to do so, we were going to build directly on our strengths—the case method pedagogy. The primary screen shot on our website was not of an online learner but, seemingly counterintuitively, was of a traditional HBS classroom. We were signaling that we were approaching online with a distinctive teaching perspective in mind. Third, our approach would not be for everyone. We were looking for serious learners, not tourists; for active learners, not passive observers; for those committed to helping others, not just to learning on their own.

And there was the price. We would charge $1,500 for the first CORe program, lasting roughly ten weeks. But we'd provide financial aid to those who needed it. Our intention was clear: We would not restrict access on the basis of financial ability, only on the basis of motivation and commitment.

The price of CORe was a matter of internal debate. Like any such decision, it would be discussed by outsiders, too. HBS was not being ambitious enough about online learning, some might say, in prioritizing selectivity over scale. Others might worry about the opposite: By charging roughly one-thirtieth the cost of an MBA degree, we were making the brand too accessible and risked cheapening it.

If we attracted both views, some might say, then we were probably doing something right. But both views were, to our mind, incorrect. We didn't lack ambition or aspirations for reach and scale. But we had a degree of uncertainty, too—we would open up to more learners only *after* we knew the initial program worked. As for cheapening the brand, on an hour-by-hour basis the costs were roughly identical.

Charging for our online programs was intended to generate revenue and increase our odds of making the enterprise sustainable. Most other online platforms were struggling with sustainability. But our reason for charging was rooted in another belief, too. Offer a course for free and anyone will sign up—including those without motivation, ability, or commitment. That would be fine, we felt, for a solitary learning experience. But peer learning was central to our approach. To rely on social learning, you need to attract the right learners. Unmotivated learners might otherwise undermine the experience of those who were motivated. We couldn't afford to have 90 percent of learners withdraw—the typical dropout rate for MOOCs. Non-completers would have a negative externality on those who stayed in. Price could serve as a signal of motivation: Anyone who dared to pay $1,500 for an online program they'd never heard of should be committed to it.

Choosing paid versus free, in other words, wasn't only about generating revenue. It was about being consistent with the learning principles on which we were building HBX.

In early April, we presented HBX to our faculty colleagues. Until then, we'd operated in relative obscurity—separating the HBX project from the day-to-day rhythms of other campus programs and operations, with the exception of the faculty (who'd continued their regular campus assignments) and key staff hires (our executive director and a few staff members were "borrowed" from our MBA program, though many were hired afresh from the outside). The HBX team was located less than one-quarter of a mile from the main campus—close enough to tie in with the parent as necessary, yet far enough to confer a license to be different. Both the faculty dean and head of HBS staff had been involved in conversations throughout. Now, two months before program launch, we shared HBX in full detail with the rest of the faculty. The reaction was very encouraging. The dominant sentiment was that if we were going to do anything online, this was the way we ought to proceed. Now we could only hope it worked.

Will Anyone Enroll?

On April 11 we opened our website for applications to the CORe program, engaging in what I good-humoredly referred to as "silent marketing." HBS is not used to marketing its MBA program. When we open our website to MBA applications every fall, hundreds of applications stream in during the first few days alone. But who knew about HBX and CORe? Who would be willing to pay $1,500 for an online program no one had ever experienced?

A day later, the first application came in. There was a cautious cheer within the HBX team—until we realized the applicant was ineligible: He was from a college in California.

We had imposed a Massachusetts-only restriction. Why, when in principle online businesses are designed to break geographic boundaries? It reflected caution—we needed to learn on a small scale before rolling out everywhere. Local students could be more easily engaged for follow-on feedback and surveys, and having learners in the same time zone would make it easier for our technology and support team.

The first applicant from the Bay State came on the third day. Other applications trickled in. We informed our own undergraduates about the program, and alumni, too, in case their children or grandchildren were interested. We distributed flyers to other local colleges. By the time we were ready to start the program, we'd admitted just over 600 students.

Program Launch

At noon on June 11, with excitement and nervousness, we launched CORe to our first set of learners, whom we later affectionately dubbed the "pioneer" cohort. Within minutes, participants began uploading their profile pictures and personal information—over the next nine hours more than 300 participants did so. More astonishing still, there were more than 13,000 profile views on the first day alone—an average of more than forty views per participant. It was striking to see the online learners simply wanting to "check one another" out—and the first vindication of our belief in social connections and community.

The HBX team was glued to a big screen that day, tracking participants' activities. Some learners logged in, spent a few minutes registering, and logged out. Others dove right into the course content. The typical learner spent about thirty minutes on their first foray into the platform.

That evening we noticed something remarkable. One participant, Layla Siraj, completed the first module of all three courses by 9 P.M. We had designed this work to be spread across a week and a half and to take roughly fifteen hours. She had done it in one nine-hour stretch on the very first day.

Siraj was a rising junior at Harvard College, majoring in organismic and evolutionary biology. Her astonishing speed forced us to ask ourselves: Did we pace the program right? Is it too easy? Was Siraj simply too smart? Around the same time, I received an email from Siraj, unexpectedly. "I'm so excited to be starting HBX CORe," she wrote. "I am absolutely loving the program—it is so hard to tear myself away from the modules. Thank you for creating such an amazing experience."

Perhaps HBX would work after all.

The first day brought many emotions for our entire HBX team. There was satisfaction—we'd created the first online program at HBS. There was relief, and burnout—we'd met a tough deadline, after spending months of sleepless nights and with little time for our families. And there was a great deal of pride.

Over the next few weeks messages from other students appeared. One user posted on Facebook, "This is the most collaborative learning experience I have had in my entire life." We tracked the conversations between students and saw them gain momentum. As questions began popping up, our content teams monitored the boards, ready to intervene—but only if answers didn't appear, or if the wrong ones did.

For the first three weeks, the number of times our content teams intervened on the peer help forums was exactly zero. Nearly every question a student asked was answered correctly and precisely by some peer. Social learning was working better than we could have imagined. It was also slightly unnerving: Given the right incentives, platform, content, and curation, students could do without us.

We were seeing the power of user connections, in real time.

Learnings and Surprises

When the first program ended, in September, we tracked outcomes. The completion rate of the first cohort was 86 percent. Engagement scores were comparable to the ratings in our residential programs: more than 90 percent of participants rated the program a 4 or 5 out of 5. Student feedback was remarkable: "One of the greatest learning experiences I have had in my entire life," and, "This is the best proxy for any classroom experience that I have seen so far." One student wrote: "It felt personal." We had never met this student.

This was our first conclusion: Online learning can be highly engaging for some of the most demanding learners from elite institutions—even in a fully automated experience, without any live faculty interaction. We had created the conditions for scaling HBX.

Students found the program demanding and rigorous, a view that would be shared by subsequent cohorts. Yet the pioneer cohort performed impressively—perhaps not surprising for students drawn from some of the best colleges and universities in Massachusetts, including Harvard, MIT, Amherst, Williams, Wellesley, Northeastern, and Tufts. Six months later we opened CORe to learners around the world, admitting more than 900. The diversity of the second cohort was extraordinary. A few weeks after the program started, one learner noted on a LinkedIn post:

> Remember when I said my expectation was to meet American undergrads? Well, there are definitely some of them in our cohort. But there are many other people, and their path to HBX is something you would usually find in the beginning of a Tom Hanks movie. We have a Navy captain, a bomb defuser, a Portuguese oncologist, a German engineer, a Canadian psychologist, an Argentinean brand manager, a South-African Master's student, and a rehab center financial manager from Texas. We have a couple of guys working in Wall Street. An Australian school director. Four Brazilian lawyers. A bunch of MBA students, a couple of economists, and many, many others. The diversity of this group is, without a doubt, its most valuable asset, and the different perspectives each student brings to the table in every discussion we have is what makes HBX truly unique.

We had expected the vast majority of CORe learners to be undergraduates or recent graduates, those just entering the workforce. Here again we were surprised. The age distribution spread wide: Half the CORe learners were older than our entering MBA students, who averaged twenty-seven years of age. Why did they join? Several had been slotted into various functional roles through their careers—sales, IT, software development, design, creative, and so on—and had never been exposed to these learnings. As they'd describe to us later, they could now participate in meaningful "business conversations"—conversations around product development, pricing, business performance, and the like—in their workplace for the first time. Others were service professionals (lawyers, physicians, educators) who'd never trained in business and were looking to acquire the basics. Some were entrepreneurs, some were looking to enhance their career prospects. Others were managers who were familiar with many of these materials; but, they told us afterward, they'd not learned them this way.

We'd seen CORe as an opportunity for young adults entering the workforce: *Prepare* was the keyword we'd had in mind when we designed the program. *Empower* was what CORe learners were now telling us was the reason they'd found it most valuable.

Their global representation was impressive: On average, 45 percent of learners in each cohort would come from outside the United States, from more than ninety countries. More noteworthy about this global cohort was *their* performance. The CORe faculty (Hammond, Narayanan, and I) had thought we might never see another cohort quite like the pioneers. When we completed the program grades for the first global cohort, they had performed even better. Our assumptions about the location of talent around the world were being shaken. The possibilities were greater than we'd dared to think.

Social learning had been one of the anchoring principles of HBX. The participation rate in the discussion forums was roughly 75 percent. Peer discussions were effective, accurate, and engaging. More than that, they created an esprit de corps in ways we hadn't predicted. Students pushed one another to complete modules before deadlines. They commiserated, they calmed one another, they joked. These were the seeds of a community that would continue to grow with each cohort. For many learners, being a part of a diverse, talented, and engaged community would come to define their learning experience through CORe as much as the quality of the content, pedagogy, and platform did. Virtual interactions gave rise to physical meet-ups around the world—Tokyo, London, San Francisco, and other places. Students reached out to peers to collaborate on business ideas or engage in socially motivated work. The idea that online learning might fashion real-world relationships in this manner was astounding.

Most debates around online education focus on how learning outcomes are shaped by "supply-side" characteristics—content, pedagogical approaches, faculty quality, teaching assistants, and platforms. But I and my colleagues learned that "demand-side" characteristics matter just as much. CORe wasn't just for millennials; it was for older learners, too. They weren't waiting for their employers to pay; many were doing so on their own. They were taking control of their learning. Learners were talented, motivated, and diverse—characteristics necessary for effective peer learning. We had tried to create the norms and conditions for effective online conversations, but the learners were the ones bringing it all to life.

Then, of course, there were the core objectives we'd started with. One of these had been getting students with little or no background in business to achieve basic mastery in the "language of business" within eleven weeks. We encountered a few surprises here, too. We'd expected students with backgrounds in economics, statistics, or accounting to do better than other students in those courses—and they did. But the similarities were more notable. By the end of the program, the difference between four-year college economics majors and non-majors was roughly 3 percentage points out of 100. We saw similar results in accounting and statistics, the other fields of study.

In early 2015, with CORe established in the marketplace, we opened it up to our own MBA students, too—the group we'd had in mind at the start. Roughly 300 matriculating Harvard MBAs signed up for CORe in 2015—about one-third of our MBA class. We had come full circle. HBX and online education was now directly impacting our residential programs at Harvard Business School.

Meanwhile, investments for the future, and experiments, continued. Our second HBX platform—HBX Live—launched in August 2015. It was a virtual classroom (inspired by Youngme Moon) where, in effect, sixty physical seats were replaced by sixty TV screens, so that learners could participate in a live class discussion from anywhere in the world. Where we'd tried to "forget" our case method classroom in creating the online platform, HBX Live was designed to explicitly "borrow"—the only difference being that we collapsed geography. While traditional forms of digital interaction had perfected the use of live TV studios to anchor one-to-many forms of interaction, HBX Live would create a many-to-many experience. By the time it launched, we had run nearly seventy pilot sessions with faculty members and different groups of learners. Subsequently, we ran virtual reunions for our alumni, a live research seminar with faculty from nineteen universities, a pilot series titled "The Global Philosopher" with BBC Radio and Harvard colleague Michael Sandel, and we were starting to design entirely virtual executive programs. Our efforts to create engaging learning experiences on the online platform continued, too: With the launch of CORe and Disruptive Strategy behind us, more faculty colleagues began to create courses there, we were envisioning shorter-form content, and we'd started to design a mobile platform.

Where will this all lead? We aren't sure yet. But by creating two digital platforms through which we could now deliver learning experiences comparable to our residential classrooms, we were ready to envision a different future—combining residential and online learning experiences to create a true multi-platform education.

EDUCATION: WHAT LIES AHEAD

Online education efforts are proceeding in earnest. Yet we are still closer to the starting point than the finish line. As I reflect on the many efforts currently ongoing, it's clear that what we've learned about digital transformation, whether in media or elsewhere, over two decades, are not only relevant to a field like education; they are relevant in ways that even I did not fully understand or appreciate when I first joined our digital efforts.

By now three questions are central.

First, how does one offer the best content online, and the broadest selection of it, to reach the maximum number of learners? All the major platforms launched during the past few years—Coursera, Udacity, edX—have carved out strategies around this idea.

Second, will online education eventually be better than, or even displace, the traditional classroom? Pick up any article or listen to any debate about online education and this is the lens through which its promise and problems are seen. "Will MOOCs Kill Universities?" headlined *The Economist* recently; *Time, Fortune, The New Republic,* and scores of others have taken similar tacks. An equal number of commentators asked, "Is online learning a fad?"

Third, how can one get universities to move faster in their online efforts? With new platforms and ventures launched every few weeks, and new investors and business models introduced just as fast, the cost of not moving quickly is often said to be irrelevance.

These three ideas are now so commonplace that they've taken on an air of inevitability. Yet I would argue that they are all misplaced. And they reflect a line of thinking similar to what we've seen in other settings—the many industries described in the rest of this book. They exemplify the Content Trap.

The first question reflects a bias toward content rather than learning, toward a faculty-centered model rather than a student-centered one. The bias comes from missing the role of users and the power of user connections.

The second question falls into the trap of seeing traditional and digital forms of education as substitutes rather than complements. It falls into the trap of distressing about the future of the traditional classroom rather than seeing how technology might augment it. It misses opportunities and product connections.

The third idea provokes organizations to follow the herd rather than figure out what's right for themselves. For universities, more than ever, thinking about the future of education calls for creativity, imagination, and courage. It's about strategy and being different rather than me-too. It's about context and functional connections.

Flip these questions around—much as classrooms are being flipped— and you might see opportunities you've never thought of. You might see ways to deepen relationships among students online, rather than believing that ties will inevitably be weakened. You might see the power of "digital-first" approaches in creating new and distinctive modes of teaching, rather than assuming that online education is destined to be inferior and commoditized. You might see ways to carve out unique strengths for your organization, rather than entering a race where you're likely to fall short.

You might see connections.

Recognizing and respecting these connections was ultimately at the center of our efforts at HBX. Positive connections are what spur new ideas in many other parts of digital education. They will be central to the future and the promise of online learning.

When classroom teaching is at its best, the reason isn't that it's in-person, but that it focuses on student learning. Conversely, most of the time that classroom teaching is passive, uninspiring, or unengaging, the reason isn't that the content is inadequate, but that the student experience is being neglected.

The surprising part about digital education is not that it's so different from classroom education in these respects, but how profoundly similar it has looked so far. The first wave of online courses was built around sixty-minute lecture videos from faculty. They aspired to reach millions of learners rather than understand the individual motivation of any one learner. They centered on content rather than experience.

These courses were transformative in moving online education forward, but they weren't necessarily a transformative experience for the learner. They were in many cases the same old classroom experience simply delivered through a new medium. It will take more than that to transform learning.

Where online education does work, it shifts the center of attention from faculty to student, from enrollment to engagement, from content to experience. The material in Sal Khan's academy isn't considered breathtaking in its delivery, platform, or content. But it's effective because it offers something profoundly valuable to students when they need it most: brief, no-frills explanations of useful concepts. Southern New Hampshire University has one of the fastest-growing online programs not because it has figured out how to teach masterful courses with dynamic new content but because it is masterful in keeping students engaged amid everything else going on in their lives by supporting them through a nattily branded army of "Sherpas." 2U offers effective online programs through university partnerships not because by doing so it can create the best courses but because it focuses on what else students need—brand credibility, degrees, and, above all, attention. And the Minerva Project, a two-year-old enterprise offering a four-year online liberal arts degree, is drawing high-quality students from across the world not because it's cheap or free, but because it focuses entirely on small-group discussions and critical thinking rather than lectures.

Viewed this way, the challenges traditional classrooms face actually have nothing to do with digital technologies. They're a result of focusing primarily on content rather than learning. That's something we don't need digital technologies to fix.

But to focus on learners, you need to understand learners—their motivations, abilities, incentives, and problems. It's surprising how easy it can be to ignore these things, and how little attention is often paid to them. Create the content, offer the best courses, make them accessible, and the rest will take care of itself: That's exactly the Content Trap.

What I and my colleagues realized after looking further into the minds of learners is that effective learning is not just about content; it's about purpose. It's about students taking ownership of what they need to learn. It's about students having the will to ask questions and the courage to try to answer them. It's about students taking responsibility for setting the right tone in the learning environment, for teaching others, and for learning from others, too.

That's where learning and delivery, content and classroom, student and faculty, come together. To allow students to do all this, you need to give them tools. You need to give them not just the right content but the right platform. You need to give them materials not just to learn but to engage and inspire. You need to give them ways to interact with one another. You need to create the right tone and encourage the right norms. Above all, you need to trust that they'll enhance all these things on their own. You need to leave it to them to do more than you ever envisioned they could.

That's the responsibility of students *and* educators. It always has been. And it has little to do with classroom versus online.

AFTERWORD

When I began writing this book, I knew that many things around us would change by the time I had finished it. They did, and in predictably unpredictable ways.

Who would have thought, even a few months ago, that an app whose content vanishes almost as soon as users create it would be worth billions? Or that you could learn from unknown drivers three miles ahead of you that a cop is waiting on the side of the road? Or that investment bankers would moonlight as drivers? These kinds of things are not even rare; they are commonplace, happening every day.

It's clichéd but true: Our world is changing faster than ever. In this book I've tried to provide a snapshot of a world in which even as *things* change, certain ideas don't.

Here's the concept at its core: The process of creating content has not changed much in some domains (like writing a book or performing in a concert), while it has changed radically in others (see above). But in every case, *managing* content couldn't be more different than it was even a few years ago. The reason is connections.

We can connect with others today in ways not possible before—that's obvious. So is our craving for experiences that connect products more closely and in new ways. But connections aren't always obvious, and taking advantage of them requires recognizing them in the first place.

Succeeding now also requires more courage than before—the courage to be different. Follow others and chances are you'll be too late, too similar, or too misaligned. Are Facebook, BuzzFeed, or Tencent the only routes to follow? No. Is the *New York Times* paywall the only approach to success in news? Surely not. Is HBX a model with universal applicability? Hardly. We can learn a lot from these stories. But the most successful organizations don't mimic successful others; they do what's right for *them*.

The potential for success today is enormous. In a connected world, it's not merely large or well-funded organizations that succeed—and you don't need to be an entrepreneur or a CEO to do so, either. Virtually any idea, from any source, has the potential for huge impact. Every person, from seasoned veterans to middle managers to new hires, has the ability to light a spark that spreads. Like Yellowstone in 1988, digital forests are dry, and the trigger can come from anywhere.

Media is far from dead. As this book goes to press, e-book growth has flattened. Concerts are still thriving. Paid news subscriptions to *The New York Times* have increased. Television cord-cutting has slowed. Cable bundles haven't unraveled. Movie box office receipts have grown.

But many media businesses remain challenged. It's not because their content is getting worse. It's because of fixed cost structures. It's because of competing networks and platforms. It's because of the fragility of being someone else's complement. The challenges come from connections.

Strategies themselves can connect. As we speak, Schibsted is trying *New York Times*–type paywalls; the *Times* is embracing Schibsted's digital-first approach. Content businesses like *The Washington Post* are pivoting toward platform thinking, even as platforms including Tencent, Amazon, and Netflix are investing in their key complement—content. TV Everywhere—a model that adapts *Times*-style bundling to television—appears primed to grow.

And connected change isn't confined to what we read, watch, or listen to. A fitness group consisting only of people who get together to work out for free has spread, almost like a grassroots movement, to seventeen cities. A mobile app that allows free exchanges of money between users saw $7.5 billion in transfers in 2015, as friends use it to split restaurant bills and roommates share rent.

Political campaigns, too, are experiencing the force of connections. Jon Miller was part of the team that helped seed the social media campaign of Barack Obama in 2008. Miller was an experienced businessman but a political neophyte; his noteworthy experience had been in leading digital ventures at USA Networks and AOL. "When we started," he told me, "we knew we had no chance of competing for big donations, super PACs, and traditional media. We knew we had to be different. So we looked to social media. We had little idea of its eventual power. After we won Iowa, all of us on the team looked at one another and thought—maybe we can win this thing." Eight years later the trend toward "connected campaigns" would continue on both sides of the political spectrum. One presidential candidate, Bernie Sanders, raised more money per month and in total through $27 donations from people connected through social media than rivals who took in the $2,700 maximum per-person donation. Donald Trump didn't wait for news outlets to cover him—*he* called *them,* and tweeted at a prodigious rate. Sanders's donations exceeded $200 million; Trump's earned-media coverage exceeded $4 billion. Both candidates relied exclusively on connected media as the trigger.

This book has described changes in the worlds of information goods. Similar changes are occurring in "hard" goods, too. Thermostats, refrigerators, lightbulbs, door locks, and cars are becoming "smart"—the term used to describe products that contain sensors and software to relay information, all belonging to the "Internet of Things" (or, IoT). Hard goods are beginning to resemble information goods. Manufacturing is becoming media.

But if traditional content businesses teach us anything, it's that the smart products that win will be the ones that figure out connections.

Some already are. Smart homes allow refrigerators to turn off lights and lock doors. Smart farms tie irrigation systems to weather information and crop prices. Smart cars connect hardware performance to service calls. Experts call these trends "product systems," or "systems of systems."

The benefits of connectivity go beyond products. More accrue when information is shared directly among users—as in the case of traffic (Waze), video cameras (GoPro), fitness bands (FitBit), and weather (Weathermob). Some possibilities are even more audacious—for example, the idea of using excess solar energy from one house to help power others close by. Connected users and products, not just smarter products—that's where the biggest benefits of the emerging IoT lie.

The forces we've seen for more than two decades in content businesses are playing out in these new arenas, too. Companies with hundred-year histories of making "product"—engines, thermostats, lightbulbs, refrigerators—are seeing new players such as Amazon, Apple, and Google enter their domains by introducing products that don't require traditional manufacturing competencies. They are entering to connect.

The same questions about strategy that content businesses have been forced to confront are in play even among traditional manufacturing companies. Car companies are used to investing in engines and transmissions, looking to grab differentiation there. But some of them, including BMW, have begun licensing their technologies to others. Their reasoning? That superiority in hardware will be short-lived, even superfluous, as the shift toward electric cars (inspired by Tesla), self-driving cars (inspired by

Google), and ride sharing (inspired by Uber) shifts the locus of differentiation toward sensors, controls, and software. It's a familiar story: As competition moves from products to connected portfolios, it pays to know whose complement you are—or, to put it another way, which business you are really in. Define your business as engines and power trains, and you might just hear the whispers of the recording studios in your ear. It's CDs and concerts, all over again.

We tend to describe these kinds of changes in terms of technology. We'd do better to describe them in terms of ideas. Yes, technology is the trigger, but ideas are the cause—ideas ultimately rooted in how we connect.

My own world, the world of education, continues to change, too. As I walk on the Harvard Business School campus nowadays, I not only marvel at the beauty and spring colors as students graduate to head off into the world. I also think about those who are now impacted by our programs without ever setting foot on campus.

As I was completing this book, the worlds of HBS and HBX met.

Earlier this year we noticed that peer learning—one of the anchor "connecting" principles of HBX—had gone far beyond what we'd envisioned. Online interactions had given rise to physical meet-ups between learners, to social projects, to spontaneous conversations that jump-started business ventures. In March we decided to nurture these relationships by inviting HBX learners to campus for the first time to engage in a day of community building and interaction.

Nearly five hundred learners came on May 7—from Australia, Kenya, India, Qatar, Ecuador, Colombia, Denmark, and elsewhere. Participants expressed gratitude for what they'd learned. Many described how the program had touched their lives. A pastor spoke of wanting to leverage a similar approach to connect churchgoers more meaningfully. A student with learning disabilities noted that he'd struggled all his life with traditional modes of instruction, and that the short bursts of content and peer conversations online had renewed his desire to learn. A young woman talked about how the knowledge she'd gained gave her the confidence to make decisions for her family and its fledgling business. The stories were moving and inspiring. They originated in peer learning and community. They originated in connections.

Create to connect. Expand to preserve. Dare to not mimic. These are simple ideas. Yet so often we fall into the trap of doing exactly the opposite.

These are the ideas I first set out to write about, not knowing they would shape my own world before I was done. These are the ideas I hope you might take with you in whatever you do, using them to find success wherever you are.

ACKNOWLEDGMENTS

I am immensely grateful to the many people who contributed to this book.

My interests in strategy, media, and digital change were inspired by certain serendipitous research projects that I embarked on many years ago, and they later grew during programs on media strategies that I cocreated at Harvard Business School (HBS) with my colleague Felix Oberholzer-Gee. I have spent so much time teaching and discussing many of the ideas in this book with Felix that he might easily have coauthored parts of it.

Along the way, several other people were directly or indirectly influential in shaping the ideas in this book: Barry Nalebuff, who sparked my early interest in strategy and continued to motivate and challenge me over the years; Ron Shachar and Alexander Galetovic with whom I spent endless hours on various projects despite living on different continents; and Rafael Di Tella, Tarun Khanna, Rajiv Lal, Nitin Nohria, and Jan Rivkin, who were my early thought allies at HBS.

I have been fortunate to have worked with an outstanding group of scholars, first at Yale and then at HBS, and have benefited not just from their work but often from the many conversations in the proverbial hallway. Thank you to Adam Brandenburger, Dmitri Byzalov, Ramon Casadesus-Masanell, David Collis, Tom Eisenmann, Anita Elberse, David Garvin, Pankaj Ghemawat, Ranjay Gulati, Rebecca Henderson, Elon Kohlberg, Vineet Kumar, Cynthia Montgomery, Das Narayandas, Ariel Pakes, Krishna Palepu, Misiek Piskorski, Michael Porter, Julio Rotemberg, Thales Teixeira, Dennis Yao, and David Yoffie; and particular thanks to my other collaborators involved in creating the Digital Initiative at HBS: Sunil Gupta, Marco Iansiti, Karim Lakhani, and Colin Maclay.

The HBX Initiative has been a transformational personal experience that has brought me close to other colleagues from whom I continue to learn: Jan Hammond, V. G. Narayanan, Youngme Moon, and Clay Christensen; the present and former executive directors, Patrick Mullane and Jana Kierstead; and an exceptional team that has inspired me in so many ways. Throughout, I have benefited from Nitin Nohria's leadership, Angela Crispi and Jean Cunningham's wise counsel, and my university colleagues "across the river" for being engaging partners on this journey.

The HBS case method teaching approach allows the faculty to learn as much from students as they do from us. I have been a privileged beneficiary of this environment. I cannot count the ideas, stories, and projects of my students—MBAs and executives alike—that I have learned from over the years. As a business scholar, I have encountered many remarkable business leaders and executives through research, case writing, and consulting. In particular, conversations with Koos Bekker, Caitlyn Chen, Larry Culp, Craig Moffett, Mark McCormack, Sverre Munck, David Perpich, Andrew Rashbass, Peter Rice, and Uday Shankar helped refine some of the ideas in this book.

I am extremely grateful to all those who were willing to be interviewed about, and to reflect on, their experiences: Kjell Aamot, Janet Balis, Binny Bansal, Paul Berry, Caitlyn Chen, Ben Colayco, Scott Cook, Larry Culp, Anil Dash, Markus Dohle, Pieter du Toit, Clark Gilbert, Espen Egil Hansen, Karim Lakhani, Anne Messitte, Benjamin Mako Hill, Phil Kent, Madeline McIntosh, Jon Miller, Craig Moffett, Ajit Mohan, Sverre Munck, Barry Nalebuff, Raju Narisetti, Martin Nisenholtz, Felix Oberholzer-Gee, Torry Pedersen, David Perpich, Andrew Rashbass, Jan Rivkin, Rolv-Erik Ryssdal, Terje Seljeseth, Uday Shankar, Carl Shapiro, Paul Smurl, Robert Steen, Peter Stern, Chris Stibbs, Ole Jacob Sunde, Steve Tadelis, Denise Warren, Carl-Nicolai Wessmann, John Winsor, Ali Yurukoglu, and Dylan Zhang.

This book would not have been possible without the research assistance of Suresh Balu, Carolyn Brown, Benjamin Chowdhury, Tom Dan, Jeffrey Engler, Daven Johnson, Mackenzie Lowry, Jonny Moran, and Aleksander Rosinski. Beyond their painstaking efforts, their greatest contribution was that their enthusiasm for the project matched my own.

I worked with an incredible team at Random House, guided by Susan Kamil. Peter Olson convinced me years ago that writing a book still had merit. Markus Dohle was unflagging in his encouragement to pursue this project. Gina Centrello is the quintessential "author's publisher." She introduced me to my editor, Will Murphy, whose combination of editorial brilliance, good humor, and encouragement is plainly rare. Will read and reread every draft meticulously and made the process surprisingly enjoyable.

I also greatly benefited from Amy Meeker, whose ability to suggest edits that tightened and clarified the text while remaining true to the content is a singular gift; Campbell Schnebly-Swanson, who offered valuable suggestions at key moments; Christopher Linnane and Daeun Jeong, whose artwork brought visual form to several of the ideas; Sheila Linehan, who looks out for me and makes my work easier every day; Mika Kasuga, who was patient, professional, and skilled in coordinating all parts of the project; and my agent, Don Fehr, who provided necessary counsel early on and at important phases throughout.

Many colleagues and friends read parts of the book and offered useful comments: Travis Connors, Sunil Gupta, Jan Hammond, Purnima Kochikar, Rajiv Lal, Dan McGinn, Barry Nalebuff, V. G. Narayanan, Nitin Nohria, Ishan Raina, Danny Samit, Venkat Srinivasan, and Michael Tushman. I can't thank them enough for their time and their willingness to work with my deadlines.

Finally, my deepest gratitude is to my family: my late mother, who would have wanted to read this book more than anyone else; my father, whose proud enthusiasm was demonstrated by repeated violations of the cardinal rule never to ask "When will it be done?"; my parents-in-law, who supported the project with anticipation and bias; Amit, for being the best brother one could have; Nitin and Monica, for always keeping me grounded; and most of all my wife, Anju, whose remarkable love and support I am blessed with every day, and our daughter, Rhea, who has changed my world.

SELECTED BIBLIOGRAPHY

Ackerberg, Daniel. "Empirically Distinguishing Informative and Prestige Effects of Advertising." *RAND Journal of Economics* (2001). 32, no.2, 316–33.

Alcacer, Juan, Abhishek Agrawal, and Harshit Vaish. "Walmart Around the World." HBS No. 9-714-431. Boston: Harvard Business School Publishing, rev. December 6, 2013.

Anand, Bharat. "Strategies of Related Diversification." HBS No. 705-481. Boston: Harvard Business Publishing, Revised April 11, 2005.

Anand, Bharat, and Kate Attea. "International Management Group (IMG)." HBS No. 702-409. Boston: Harvard Business Publishing, rev. September 16, 2002.

———. "News Corporation" HBS No. 702-425. Boston: Harvard Business Publishing, rev. June 27, 2003.

Anand, Bharat, David Collis, and Sophie Hood. "Danaher Corporation." HBS No. 708-445. Boston: Harvard Business Publishing, rev. November 30, 2015.

Anand, Bharat, and Alexander Galetovic. "Strategies That Work When Property Rights Don't." In *Intellectual Property and Entrepreneurship*, vol. 15, *Advances in the Study of Entrepreneurship, Innovation, and Economic Growth*, edited by Gary Libecap, 261–304. Greenwich, CT: JAI Press, 2004.

———. "How Market Smarts Can Protect Property Rights." *Harvard Business Review* 82, no. 12 (December 2004).

Anand, Bharat, and Sophie Hood. "Schibsted." HBS No. 707-474. Boston: Harvard Business Publishing, April 16, 2007.

Anand, Bharat, and Samhita Jayanti. "Strategies of Unrelated Diversification." HBS No. 705-480. Boston: Harvard Business Publishing, rev. April 11, 2005.

Anand, Bharat, and Tarun Khanna. "Must Zee TV." HBS No. 700-122. Boston: Harvard Business Publishing, rev. February 10, 2003.

Anand, Bharat, and Peter Olson. "The Random House Response to the Kindle." HBS No. N1-710-444. Boston: Harvard Business Publishing, rev. February 7, 2011.

Anand, Bharat, and Ron Shachar. "Advertising the Matchmaker." *RAND Journal of Economics* 42, no. 2 (Summer 2011): 205–45.

———. "Brands as Beacons: A New Source of Loyalty to Multiproduct Firms." *Journal of Marketing Research* 41, no. 2 (May 2004): 135–50.

Anderson, Chris. *The Long Tail: Why the Future of Business Is Selling Less of More*. New York: Hyperion Books, 2008.

Anton, James, and Dennis Yao. "Expropriation and Inventions: Appropriable Rents in the Absence of Property Rights." *American Economic Review* 84, no. 1 (March 1994): 190–209.

Armstrong, Mark. "Competition in Two-Sided Markets." *RAND Journal of Economics* 37, no. 3 (Autumn 2006): 668–91.

Arum, Richard, and Josipa Roksa. *Academically Adrift: Limited Learning on College Campuses*. Chicago: University of Chicago Press, 2011.

Bagwell, Kyle. *The Economics of Advertising*. Cheltenham, UK: Edward Elgar. 2001

Barker, Rocky. *Scorched Earth: How the Fires of Yellowstone Changed America*. Washington, DC: Island Press, 2005.

Barnett, William. *The Red Queen Among Organizations: How Competitiveness Evolves*. Princeton: Princeton University Press. 2002.

Berger, Jonah. *Contagious: Why Things Catch On*. New York: Simon & Schuster, 2013.

Berry, Steven T., et al. "Structural Models of Complementary Choices." *Marketing Letters* 25, no. 3 (September 2014): 245–56.

Bogusky, Alex, and John Winsor. *Baked In: Creating Products and Businesses That Market Themselves*. Chicago: B2 Books/Agate, 2009.

Boudreau, Kevin J., and Karim R. Lakhani. "The Confederacy of Heterogeneous Software Organizations and Heterogeneous Developers: Field Experimental Evidence on Sorting and Worker Effort." In Josh Lerner and Scott Stern, eds., *The Rate and Direction of Inventive Activity Revisited*, Chicago: University of Chicago Press, 2012. 483–502.

Brandenburger, Adam, and Barry Nalebuff. *Co-opetition*. New York: Currency Doubleday, 1997.

Bronnenberg, Bart J., Jean-Pierre Dubé, and Carl F. Mela. "Do Digital Video Recorders Influence Sales?" *Journal of Marketing Research* 47, no. 6 (December 2010): 998–1010.

Brown, Peter, Henry Roediger III, and Mark McDaniel. *Make It Stick: The Science of Successful Learning*. Cambridge, MA: Belknap Press of Harvard University Press, 2014.

Byzalov, Dmitri. "Unbundling Cable Television: An Empirical Investigation." Working paper, July 2010.

Carey, Kevin. *The End of College: Creating the Future of Learning and the University of Everywhere*. New York: Riverhead Books, 2015.

Caves, Richard E. *Creative Industries: Contracts Between Art and Commerce*. Cambridge; Harvard University Press. 2002.

Celly, Nikhil, and W. H. Lo. "Tencent: Expanding from China to the World." University of Hong Kong case no. HK1009, June 21, 2013. Boston: Harvard Business Publishing.

Chipty, Tasneem. "Vertical Integration, Market Foreclosure, and Consumer Welfare in the Cable Television Industry." *American Economic Review* 91, no. 3 (June 2001): 428–53.

Chopra, Sunil, and Murali Veeraiyan. "Movie Rental Business: Blockbuster, Netflix, and Redbox." HBS No. KEL616. Kellogg School of Management, rev. March 2, 2016.

Christensen, Clayton M. *Disrupting Class: How Disruptive Innovation Will Change the Way the World Learns*. Expanded ed. New York: McGraw-Hill, 2011.

———. *The Innovator's Dilemma: When New Technologies Cause Great Firms to Fail*. Boston: Harvard Business Publishing, 1997, 2000.

Christensen, Clayton M., Michael E. Raynor, and Rory McDonald. "What Is Disruptive Innovation?" *Harvard Business Review*, December 2015.

Chung, Kevin Y. C., Timothy P. Derdenger, and Kannan Srinivasan. "Economic Value of Celebrity Endorsements: Tiger Woods' Impact on Sales of Nike Golf Balls." *Marketing Science* 32, no. 2 (March 1, 2013): 271–93.

Cohen, Wesley, Richard Nelson, and John Walsh. "Protecting Their Intellectual Assets: Appropriability Conditions and Why U.S. Manufacturing Firms Patent (Or Not)." National Bureau of Economic Research, Working Paper No. 7552, 2000.

Collis, David, and Michael Rukstad. "Can You Say What Your Strategy Is?" *Harvard Business Review*, April 2008.

Collis, David, and Troy Smith. "Edward Jones in 2006: Confronting Success." HBS No. 707-497. Boston: Harvard Business Publishing, rev. March 21, 2012.

Cramer, Judd, and Alan Krueger. "Disruptive Change in the Taxi Business: The Case of Uber." National Bureau of Economic Research, Working Paper No. 22083, March 2016.

Crawford, Gregory, Robin Lee, Michael Whinston, and Ali Yurukoglu. "The Welfare Effects of Vertical Integration in Multichannel Television Markets." National Bureau of Economic Research, Working Paper No. w21832, December 2015.

Crawford, Gregory S., and Ali Yurukoglu. "The Welfare Effects of Bundling in Multichannel Television Markets." *American Economic Review* 102, no 2 (April 2012): 643–85.

Datar, Srikant, David Garvin, and Patrick Cullen. *Rethinking the MBA: Business Education at a Crossroads*. Boston: Harvard Business Review Press, 2010.

Deighton, John, et al. "The Future of Interactive Marketing." *Harvard Business Review*, November/December 1996.

Elberse, Anita. *Blockbusters: Hit-Making, Risk-Taking, and the Big Business of Entertainment*. New York: Henry Holt, 2013.

Elberse, Anita, and Kwame Owusu-Kesse. "Droga5: Launching Jay-Z's Decoded." HBS No. 513-032. Boston: Harvard Business Publishing, July 25, 2012.

Esteves-Sorenson, Constança, and Fabrizio Perretti. "Micro-Costs: Inertia in Television Viewing." *Economic Journal* 122, no. 563 (September 2012): 867.

Evans, David. "The Online Advertising Industry: Economics, Evolution, and Privacy," *Journal of Economic Perspectives*, 23, no. 3 (2009): 37–60.

Farhoomandr, Ali, and Elsha Yiu. "Tencent's Business Model." University of Hong Kong case no. HK 1003, July 5, 2013. Boston: Harvard Business Publishing.

Forrester, Jay. "Systems Dynamics and the Lessons of 35 Years." In Kenyon De Greene, ed., *A Systems-Based Approach to Policy Making*. New York: Springer, 1993.

Franke, Mary Ann. *Yellowstone in the Afterglow: Lessons from the Fires*. Mammoth Hot Springs, WY: National Park Service, 2000.

Galbraith, John Kenneth. *The Affluent Society*. 3rd ed. Boston: Houghton Mifflin, 1976.

Gans, Joshua. *The Disruption Dilemma*. Cambridge, MA: MIT Press, 2016.

Gentzkow, Matthew. "Valuing New Goods in a Model with Complementarities: Online Newspapers." *American Economic Review* 97, no. 3 (June 2007): 713–44.

Ghemawat, Pankaj. "Distance Still Matters: The Hard Reality of Global Expansion." *Harvard Business Review* 79, no. 8 (2001): 137–47.

———. "Fox Broadcasting Company." HBS No. 387-096. Boston: Harvard Business Publishing, rev. April 2, 1993.

———. "Leadership Online (A): Barnes & Noble versus Amazon.com." HBS No. 798-063. Boston: Harvard Business Publishing, rev. March 16, 2004.

Ghemawat, Pankaj, and Stephen Bradley. "Wal-Mart Stores in 2003." HBS No. 704-430. Boston: Harvard Business Publishing, rev. January 30, 2004.

Govindarajan, Vijay, and Chris Trimble. *Ten Rules for Strategic Innovators: From Idea to Execution*. Boston: Harvard Business Review Press. 2005.

Grossman, Gene, and Carl Shapiro. "Informative Advertising with Differentiated Products." *The Review of Economic Studies*, 51, no. 1 (1984): 63–81.

Guinan, Eva C., Kevin J. Boudreau, and Karim R. Lakhani. "Experiments in Open Innovation at Harvard Medical School." *MIT Sloan Management Review* 54, no. 3 (Spring 2013): 45–52.

Hagiu, Andrei. "Strategic Decisions for Multisided Platforms." *MIT Sloan Management Review*, Winter 2014.

Hagiu, Andrei, and Simon Rothman. "Network Effects Aren't Enough." *Harvard Business Review*, April 2016.

Hendricks, Ken, and Alan Sorensen. "Information and the Skewness of Music Sales." *Journal of Political Economy* 117, no. 2 (April 2009): 324.

Henry, Jeff. *The Year Yellowstone Burned: A Twenty-Five-Year Perspective.* Lanham, MD: Taylor Trade Publishing, 2015.

Hill, Benjamin Mako. "Almost Wikipedia: What Eight Early Online Collaborative Encyclopedia Projects Reveal About the Mechanisms of Collective Action." In *Essays on Volunteer Mobilization in Peer Production.* Ph.D. diss., Massachusetts Institute of Technology, 2013.

Interactive Advertising Bureau. IAB Internet Advertising Revenue Report: 2013 Full Year Results. 2014.

———. IAB Internet Advertising Revenue Report: 2012 Full Year Results. 2013.

Isaacson, Walter. *Steve Jobs.* New York: Simon & Schuster, 2011.

Katz, Michael, and Carl Shapiro. "Network Externalities, Competition, and Compatibility." *American Economic Review,* June 1985.

———. "Systems Competition and Network Effects." *Journal of Economic Perspectives,* Spring 1994.

———. "Technology Adoption in the Presence of Network Externalities." *Journal of Political Economy,* August 1986.

Kauffman, Stuart. *The Origins of Order: Self-Organization and Selection in Evolution.* Oxford: Oxford University Press, 1993.

Keating, Gina. *Netflixed: The Epic Battle for America's Eyeballs.* New York: Portfolio/Penguin, 2012.

Khan, Salman. *The One World Schoolhouse: Education Reimagined.* New York: Twelve, 2013.

Khanna, Tarun, and David Yoffie. "Microsoft–1995 (Abridged)." HBS No. 799-003. Boston: Harvard Business Publishing.

King, Andrew, and Baljir Baatarogtokh. "How Useful Is the Theory of Disruptive Innovation?" *MIT Sloan Management Review,* Fall 2015.

Knittel, Christopher, and Victor Stango. "Celebrity Endorsements, Firm Value, and Reputation Risk: Evidence from the Tiger Woods Scandal." *Management Science* 60, no. 1 (January 2014).

Knopper, Steve. *Appetite for Self-Destruction: The Spectacular Crash of the Record Industry in the Digital Age.* New York: Free Press, 2009.

Krueger, Alan. "The Economics of Real Superstars: The Market for Rock Concerts in the Material World." *Journal of Labor Economics* 23, no. 1 (April 2004): 1–30.

———. "Land of Hope and Dreams: Rock and Roll, Economics, and Rebuilding the Middle Class." Lecture delivered at Rock and Roll Hall of Fame and Museum, June 12, 2013.

Krueger, Alan, and Marie Connolly. "Rockonomics: The Economics of Popular Music." In *Handbook of the Economics of Art and Culture 1,* 667–719. Amsterdam and Boston: Elsevier North-Holland, 2006.

Kumar, Vineet, Bharat Anand, Sunil Gupta, and Felix Oberholzer-Gee. "The *New York Times* Paywall." HBS No. 512-077. Boston: Harvard Business Publishing, rev. January 31, 2013.

Kwak, Mary, and David B. Yoffie. "Apple Computer—1999." HBS No. 799-108. Boston: Harvard Business Publishing, March 1999.

Lafley, A. G., and Roger Martin. *Playing to Win: How Strategy Really Works.* Boston: Harvard Business Review Press, 2013.

Lage, Maureen J., Glenn J. Platt, and Michael Treglia. "Inverting the Classroom: A Gateway to Creating an Inclusive Learning Environment." *Journal of Economic Education* 31, no. 1 (Winter 2000): 30–43.

Lal, Rajiv. "Harrah's Entertainment, Inc." HBS No. 502-011. Boston: Harvard Business Publishing, rev. June 14, 2004.

Lambrecht, Anja, and Catherine Tucker. "When Does Retargeting Work? Information Specificity in Online Advertising." *Journal of Marketing Research* 50, no. 5 (2013): 561–76.

Lang, Larry H. P., and Rene M. Stulz. "Tobin's Q, Corporate Diversification, and Firm Performance." *Journal of Political Economy* 102, no. 6 (December 1994): 1248.

Lashinsky, Adam. *Inside Apple: How America's Most Admired—and Secretive—Company Really Works.* New York: Business Plus, 2012.

Leschly, Stig, et al. "Amazon.com—2002." HBS No. 9-803-098. Boston: Harvard Business Publishing, rev. February 13, 2003.

Levin, R. C., Alvin Klevorick, Richard Nelson, and Sidney Winter. "Appropriating the Returns from Industrial R&D." *Brookings Papers on Economic Activity* (1987): 783–820.

Liebowitz, Stan. "How Reliable Is the Oberholzer-Gee and Strumpf Paper on File-Sharing?" University of Texas at Dallas. Working paper. 2007.

Martin, Gregory, and Ali Yurukoglu. "Bias in Cable News: Persuasion and Polarization." Working paper, May 27, 2016.

McCormack, Mark. *What They Don't Teach You at Harvard Business School: Notes from a Street-Smart Executive.* London: Bantam Press, 1986.

———. *What They Still Don't Teach You at Harvard Business School.* London: Bantam Press, 1990.

McGrath, Rita. "The Problem with Groupon's Business Model." *Harvard Business Review,* July 13, 2011.

Meyer, Philip. *The Vanishing Newspaper: Saving Journalism in the Information Age.* Columbia: University of Missouri Press, 2004.

Milgrom, Paul, and John Roberts. "Complementarities and Systems: Understanding Japanese Economic Organization." *Estudios Económicos* 9, no. 1 (Winter/Spring 1994): 3–42.

———. *Economics, Organization and Management.* Englewood Cliffs, NJ: Prentice-Hall, 1992.

Milkman, Katherine L., Liz Rees-Jones, and Jonah Berger. "The Secret to Online Success: What Makes Content Go Viral." *Scientific American,* April 14, 2015.

Moak, Jacob. "Regulation of the Pay Television Market." *Kentucky Law Journal* 103, no. 2 (January 2015): 291–309.

Moffett, Craig, et al. "The Dumb Pipe Paradox." Bernstein Research, 2006.

———. "U.S. Telecommunications, Cable & Satellite: The Dumb Pipe Paradox, Revisited." Bernstein Research, June 11, 2009.

Mortimer, Julie Holland, Chris Nosko, and Alan Sorensen. "Supply Responses to Digital Distribution: Recorded Music and Live Performances." *Information Economics and Policy* 24, no. 1 (March 2012): 3–14.

Moshkin, Nickolay, and Ron Shachar. "The Asymmetric Information Model of State Dependence." *Marketing Science* 21, no. 4 (2002): 1–20.

Mulligan, Mark. *Awakening: The Music Industry in the Digital Age.* CreateSpace Independent Publishing Platform, May 3, 2015.

Nalebuff, Barry. "Bundling as an Entry Barrier." *Quarterly Journal of Economics* 119, no. 1 (2004): 159–88.

Narayandas, Das, Sunil Gupta, and Rachna Tahilyani. "Flipkart: Transitioning to a Marketplace Model." HBS No. 516-017. Boston: Harvard Business Publishing, rev. March 14, 2016.

National Park Service. "Interagencies Final Report on Fire Management, 1989." nps.gov. October 25, 2000.

―――. "The Yellowstone Fires of 1988." nps.gov. 2008.

Negroponte, Nicholas. *Being Digital.* New York: Knopf, 1995.

Nevo, Aviv, John Turner, and Jonathan Williams. "Usage-Based Pricing and the Demand for Residential Broadband." *Econometrica* (forthcoming).

Oberholzer-Gee, Felix. "BuzzFeed—The Promise of Native Advertising." HBS No. 714-512. Boston: Harvard Business Publishing, rev. August 15, 2014.

Oberholzer-Gee, Felix, Bharat N. Anand, et al. "The Economist." HBS No. 710-441. Boston: Harvard Business Publishing, rev. July 14, 2010.

Oberholzer-Gee, Felix, and Koleman Strumpf. "The Effect of File Sharing on Record Sales." *Journal of Political Economy* 115, no. 1 (February 2007).

―――. "File Sharing and Copyright." In Josh Lerner and Scott Stern, eds., *Innovation Policy and the Economy.* Chicago: National Bureau of Economic Research, 2010.

O'Reilly, Charles, and Michael Tushman, "The Ambidextrous Organization," *Harvard Business Review* 82, no. 4 (2004): 74–81.

Palepu, Krishna, Bharat Anand, and Rachna Tahilyani. "Tata Nano—The People's Car." HBS No. 710-420. Boston: Harvard Business Publishing, rev. March 28, 2011.

Park, Sangin. "Quantitative Analysis of Network Externalities in Competing Technologies: The VCR Case." *Review of Economics and Statistics* 86, no. 4 (November 2004): 937–45.

Piskorski, Mikolaj Jan. *A Social Strategy: How We Profit from Social Media.* Princeton, NJ: Princeton University Press, 2014.

Piskorski, Mikolaj Jan, et al. "Facebook." HBS No. 808-128. Boston: Harvard Business Publishing, rev. March 20, 2014.

Porter, Michael. "The Five Competitive Forces That Shape Strategy." *Harvard Business Review,* January 2008.

―――. "What Is Strategy?" *Harvard Business Review,* November 1, 1996.

Porter, Michael E., and Gregory C. Bond. "Edward Jones." HBS No. 700-009. Boston: Harvard Business Publishing, rev. June 15, 2000.

Prahalad, C. K., and Gary Hamel. "The Core Competence of the Corporation." *Harvard Business Review,* May/June 1990.

Rayport, Jeffrey, and Louie Dickson. "Amazon.com (A)." HBS No. 897-128. Boston: Harvard Business Publishing, rev. April 9, 1998.

Reinhardt, Forest, et al. "Patagonia." HBS No. 711-020. Boston: Harvard Business Publishing, rev. October 19, 2010.

Reinhart, Karen. *Yellowstone's Rebirth by Fire: Rising from the Ashes of the 1988 Wildfires.* Helena, MT: Farcountry Press, 2008.

Rivkin, Jan. "Imitation of Complex Strategies." *Management Science* 46, no. 6 (June 2000): 824–44.

―――. "Key Concepts in a Module on Strategic Failure." HBS No. 706-471. Boston: Harvard Business Publishing, rev. March 21, 2006.

―――. "An Options-led Approach to Making Strategic Choices." HBS No. 702-433. Boston: Harvard Business Publishing, December 2001.

―――. "Reproducing Knowledge: Replication Without Information at Moderate Complexity." *Organization Science* 12, no. 3 (May–June 2001).

Rob, Rafael, and Joel Waldfogel. "Piracy on the High C's: Music Downloading, Sales Displacement, and Social Welfare in a Sample of College Students." *Journal of Law and Economics,* 49, no. 1 (2006): 29–62.

Rochet, Jean-Charles, and Jean Tirole. "Platform Competition in Two-Sided Markets." *Journal of the European Economic Association* 1, no. 4 (June 2003): 990–1029.

———. "Two-Sided Markets: A Progress Report." *RAND Journal of Economics* 37, no. 3 (Autumn 2006): 645–67.

Rogers, Jim. *The Death and Life of the Music Industry in the Digital Age.* London: Bloomsbury Academic, May 9, 2013.

Rohlfs, Jeffrey. "A Theory of Interdependent Demand for a Communications Service." *Bell Journal of Economics,* no. 1 (Spring 1974): 16–37.

Rosen, Sherwin. "The Economics of Superstars." *American Economic Review* 71, no. 5 (December 1981): 845.

Sahni, Navdeep, and Harikesh Nair. "Native Advertising, Sponsorship Disclosure, and Consumer Deception: Evidence from Mobile Search-Ad Experiments." Working paper.

Salganik, Matthew J., Peter Sheridan Dodds, and Duncan J. Watts. "Experimental Study of Inequality and Unpredictability in an Artificial Cultural Market." *Science,* February 10, 2006.

Seamans, Robert, and Feng Zhu. "Responses to Entry in Multi-Sided Markets: The Impact of Craigslist on Local Newspapers." *Management Science* 60, no. 2 (February 2014): 476–93.

Shachar, Ron, and Bharat Anand. "The Effectiveness and Targeting of Television Advertising." *Journal of Economics & Management Strategy* 7, no. 3 (Fall 1998): 363–96.

Shapiro, Carl. "Antitrust in Network Industries." United States Department of Justice, March 7, 1996.

Shapiro, Carl, and Hal Varian. *Information Rules; A Strategic Guide to the Network Economy.* Boston: Harvard Business Review Press, 1998.

Shih, Willy, Steve Kaufman, and David Spinola. "Netflix." HBS No. 607-138. Boston: Harvard Business Publishing, rev. April 27, 2009.

Shih, Willy, Howard Yu, and Fang Liu. "WeChat: A Global Platform?" HBS No. 9-615-049. Boston: Harvard Business Publishing, June 17, 2015.

Simpson, Ross. *The Fires of '88: Yellowstone Park and Montana in Flames.* Helena, MT: Farcountry Press, 1989.

Spence, Michael. "Job Market Signaling." *Quarterly Journal of Economics* 87, no. 3 (August 1973): 355–74.

Stone, Brad. *The Everything Store: Jeff Bezos and the Age of Amazon.* Boston: Little, Brown, 2013.

Tadelis, Steven, Chris Nosko, and Thomas Blake. "Consumer Heterogeneity and Paid Search Effectiveness: A Large-Scale Field Experiment." *Econometrica* 83, no. 1 (January 2015): 155–74.

Teixeira, Thales. "A Consumer-Centric Model of Viral Advertising Calibrated on Face-Tracking Data." Harvard Business School Working Paper, March 2014.

———. "The New Science of Viral Ads." *Harvard Business Review,* March 2012.

Tushman, Michael, and C. O'Reilly. *Winning Through Innovation: A Practical Guide to Leading Organizational Change and Renewal.* Boston, MA: Harvard Business School Press, 1997.

Varian, Hal. "Newspaper Economics: Online and Offline." Google Public Policy Blog, March 2010.

Villalonga, Belén. "Diversification Discount or Premium? New Evidence from the Business Information Tracking Series." *Journal of Finance* 59 (2004): 479–506.

———. "Does Diversification Cause the 'Diversification Discount'?" *Financial Management* 33, no. 2 (2004): 5–27.

Waldfogel, Joel. "File Sharing and Sales Displacement in the iTunes Era," *Information Economics and Policy,* 22, no. 4 (2010): 306–14.

Walton, Sam, and John Huey. *Sam Walton, Made in America: My Story.* New York: Doubleday, 1992.

Watts, Duncan J., and Jonah Peretti. "Viral Marketing for the Real World." *Harvard Business Review,* May 2007.

Williams, James Allen, and Janet L. Yellen. "Commodity Bundling and the Burden of Monopoly." *Quarterly Journal of Economics* 90, no. 3 (August 1976): 475–98.

Winsor, John. *Beyond the Brand: Why Engaging the Right Customers Is Essential to Winning in Business.* Chicago: Dearborn Trade, 2004.

Wolff, Michael. *Television Is the New Television: The Unexpected Triumph of Old Media in the Digital Age.* London: Portfolio, 2015.

Yoffie, David, and Eric Baldwin. "Apple Inc. in 2015." HBS No. 715-456. Boston: Harvard Business Publishing, October 28, 2015.

Yoffie, David, and Renee Kim. "Wal-Mart Update, 2011." HBS No. 711-546. Boston: Harvard Business Publishing, rev. March 1, 2013.

Zakaria, Fareed. *In Defense of a Liberal Education.* New York: Norton, 2015.

Zhu, Feng, and Aaron Smith. "Baidu, Alibaba, and Tencent: The Three Kingdoms of the Chinese Internet." HBS No. 615-039. Boston: Harvard Business Publishing, January 13, 2015.

NOTES

Introduction

xv **The Yellowstone Fires of 1988** The account of the 1988 Yellowstone fires in this section draws primarily from the following sources: Rocky Barker, *Scorched Earth: How the Fires of Yellowstone Changed America* (Washington, DC: Island Press, 2005); Jeff Henry, *The Year Yellowstone Burned: A Twenty-Five-Year Perspective* (Lanham, MD: Taylor Trade, 2015); Mary Ann Franke, *Yellowstone in the Afterglow: Lessons from the Fires* (Mammoth Hot Springs, WY: National Park Service, 2000); Karen Wildung Reinhart, *Yellowstone's Rebirth by Fire: Rising from the Ashes of the 1988 Wildfires* (Helena, MT: Farcountry Press, 2008); Ross Simpson, *The Fires of '88: Yellowstone Park and Montana in Flames* (Helena, MT: Farcountry Press, 1989); "The Yellowstone Fires of 1988," National Park Service, U.S. Department of the Interior, 2008); Timothy Egan, "Ethic of Protecting Land Fueled Yellowstone Fires," *New York Times,* September 22, 1988; Mike Stark, "A Hellish Day: Yellowstone's Fires Devoured 165,000 Acres on 'Black Saturday,'" *Billings Gazette,* August 16, 2003; "Ex-Firefighter Relives Yellowstone's 'Black Saturday,'" NPR, last modified September 7, 2008, http://www.npr.org/templates/story/story.php?storyId=94324025; Michael Winerip, "Lessons From the Yellowstone Fires of 1988," *New York Times,* September 2, 2013.

xv **a still-burning cigarette** Barker, *Scorched Earth*; Associated Press, "Four Charged with Starting North Fork Fire," *Spokesman-Review* (Spokane, WA), January 31, 1989.

xv **Black Saturday** Franke, *Yellowstone in the Afterglow;* "Ex-Firefighter Relives Yellowstone's 'Black Saturday,'" NPR, last modified September 7, 2008.

xv **"snapped like toothpicks"** Quote from *Fire,* Yellowstone National Park: Park Vision, accessed June 6, 2016, http://www.shannontech.com/ParkVision/Yellowstone/Yellowstone17.html.

xv **20 percent of the entire area of Yellowstone** "The Yellowstone Fires of 1988."

xvi **"Barbee-que"** Barker, *Scorched Earth,* p. 7.

xvi **"Burn, Baby, Burn"** J. Carrier, "Burn, Baby, Burn," *Denver Post,* August 28, 1988, 13A.

xvi **"for too long"** NBC *Nightly News* transcript, September 7, 1988, as reported in Barker, *Scorched Earth,* p. 213.

xvi **"Targhee would not accept"** Barker, *Scorched Earth,* p. 199.

xvi **let it burn** Ibid., p. 190.

xvi **bulldozers to etch** Ibid., p. 199–200.

xvii **"Jingle Bells"** William C. Everhart, *Take Down Flag and Feed Horses* (Champaign, IL: University of Illinois Press, 1998), p. 195.

xvii **1.3 million acres** Gabe Fuentes, "Agoura Fire Plan Goes Up in Yellowstone's Smoke," *Los Angeles Times,* September 22, 1988; Barker, *Scorched Earth,* p. 220; Reinhart, *Yellowstone's Rebirth by Fire,* p. 6.

xvii **More than 2 million tons of particulate** Barker, *Scorched Earth,* p. 220.

xvii **"The fires will slow down"** Ibid., p. 205. Winerip, "Lessons from the Yellowstone Fires."

xvii **the devastating impact** Rinehart, *Yellowstone's Rebirth by Fire,* p. 88–98; Barker, *Scorched Earth.*

xviii **in the Arab Spring** "The Arab Spring: A Year of Revolution," *NPR,* December 17, 2011, accessed June 6, 2016, http://www.npr.org/2011/12/17/143897126/the-arab -spring-a-year-of-revolution; later, it was reported by *The Guardian* that "the slap" did not actually happen: Elizabeth Day, "Fedia Hamdi's Slap Which Sparked a Revolution 'Didn't Happen,'" *Guardian,* April 23, 2011; "The Slap That Sparked a Revolution," *Guardian,* May 14, 2011.

xviii **on a hunger strike** D. K. Singh, "Making Peace with Political Class: The Story Behind the Consensus Over Lokpal Bill," *Indian Express,* December 18, 2013; Ishaan Tharoor, "10. Anna Hazare's Hunger Fasts Rock India," *Time,* December 7, 2011; Chandrahas Choudhury, "Indians Divide Over Policing a Watchdog: World View," *Bloomberg View,* June 21, 2011; Sandeep Phukan and Sunil Prabhu, "Lokpal Bill Passed in Lok Sabha, but No Constitutional Status," *NDTV,* last modified December 28, 2011.

xviii **forty-dollar late fee** Willy Shih et al., "Netflix," HBS No. 607-138 (Boston: Harvard Business School Publishing, rev. April 27, 2009); the forty-dollar late fee has been disputed by other accounts as the story behind Netflix's creation, see Gina Keating's book for a detailed account: Gina Keating, *Netflixed: The Epic Battle for America's Eyeballs* (New York: Portfolio/Penguin, 2012).

xviii **Blockbuster chose** Greg Satell, "A Look Back at Why Blockbuster Really Failed and Why It Didn't Have To," *Forbes,* September 5, 2014; Luis Alfonso Dau and David T. A. Wesley, "Netflix Inc.: Streaming Away from DVDs," Northeastern University College of Business Administration no. W12850, April 5, 2012, via Harvard Business Publishing.

xix **in the cards for years** Bharat N. Anand et al., "eReading: Amazon's Kindle," HBS No. 709-486 (Boston: Harvard Business Publishing, February 27, 2009).

xix **declined by roughly 50 percent** David Goldman, "Music's Lost Decade: Sales Cut in Half," *CNN Money,* February 3, 2010; Tyler Durden, "How iTunes Destroyed the Music Business in 1 Simple Chart," ZeroHedge.com, May 24, 2015.

xix **even more sharply** Varian, "Google: Newspaper Economics," Federal Trade Commission, rev. March 13, 2010; Michael Barthel, "Newspapers: Fact Sheet," Pew Research Center, April 29, 2015; Vineet Kumar, Bharat N. Anand, et al., "The *New York Times* Paywall," HBS No. 512-077 (Boston: Harvard Business Publishing, rev. January 31, 2013).

xix **dropped like flies** Josh Sanburn, "5 Reasons Borders Went Out of Business (and What Will Take Its Place)," *Time,* July 19, 2011; Derek Thompson, "Books, Borders and Beyond: How Digital Tech Is Changing Retail," *Atlantic,* July 20, 2011; Ben Sisario, "Record Stores Fight to Be Long-Playing," *New York Times,* April 18, 2008.

xix **paying for television** Keach Hagey, "Cord-Cutting Is Accelerating," *Wall Street Journal,* December 10, 2015.

xix **Movie theaters closed** Dorothy Pomerantz, "How Subscriptions Could Save Small Movie Theaters," *Forbes,* October 22, 2014.

xx **is a far more common cause** "The Yellowstone Fires of 1988."

xx **in the 112-year recorded history** National Park Service, *Yellowstone in the Afterglow*; Egan, "Ethic of Protecting Land Fueled Yellowstone Fires."

xx **with uncharacteristic speed** Ibid.

xx **the result of policy that was decades in the making** Barker, *Scorched Earth,* p. 7–8.

xx **Harris led troops** Ibid., p. 4.

xx **they created separate areas** Ibid., p. 65.

xxi **Aldo Leopold** Barker describes the results of Leopold's efforts to restore eroded prairies through a series of experiments: "The fire opened native seeds, unleashing them to grow and thrive. Saplings and other brush that had tenaciously intruded into the area were killed. The invader weeds were brought under control as the almost three hundred species of prairie plants, which had evolved through centuries of frequent fires, took over again." Barker, *Scorched Earth,* p. 141.

xxi **the need for reducing animal populations** Ibid., p. 165.

xxi **"of the various methods"** Leopold, A.S., S.A. Cain, C.M. Cottam, I.N. Gabrielson, and T.L. Kimball, "Wildlife Management in the National Parks: The Leopold Report," National Park Service, March 4, 1963.

xxi **had taken firm hold** The new Park service fire policy, released in 1970, stated: "The presence or absence of natural fire within a given habitat is recognized as one of the ecological factors contributing to the perpetuation of plants and animals native to that habitat. Fires in vegetation resulting from natural causes are recognized as natural phenomena and may be allowed to run their course when such burning will contribute to the accomplishment of approved vegetation and/or wildlife management objectives" (Barker, *Scorched Earth,* p. 168).

xxi **From 1972 to 1987** Egan, "Ethic of Protecting Land Fueled Yellowstone Fires"; Rinehart, *Yellowstone's Rebirth by Fire,* p. 17.

xxi **Barbee let it burn** Barker, *Scorched Earth,* p. 190.

xxii **"sending an explosion of seeds"** Rinehart, *Yellowstone's Rebirth by Fire,* p. 90.

xxii **"15-foot-high lodgepoles"** Barker, *Scorched Earth,* p. 248; "Interagencies Final Report on Fire Management, 1989," nps.gov, October 25, 2000; Lary M. Dilsaver, ed., *America's National Park System: The Critical Documents* (Lanham, MD: Rowman & Littlefield, 1994).

xxii **"from the ash"** The natural fire policy would come under scrutiny in the years following the fires. But after a Fire Management Policy Review Team, appointed by the secretary of agriculture, concluded its detailed review years later, it noted that the objectives of prescribed natural fires were indeed sound. Only now, the policies would have to be refined to ensure that the fires burn under "pre-determined conditions" (*Report on Fire Management Policy: Departments of Agriculture and Interior,* December 14, 1988; and see Barker, *Scorched Earth,* p. 220–21). One of these conditions was that natural and prescribed fires would no longer be allowed in drought years.

xxii **"reborn, rebuilt, and rejuvenated"** Rinehart, *Yellowstone's Rebirth by Fire,* p. 8.

xxiv **more than 900 channels** "Industry Data," NCTA, accessed April 15, 2016, https://www.ncta.com/industry-data.

xxiv **are uploaded to YouTube** Anthony Wing Kosner, "YouTube Turns Seven Today, Now Uploads 72 Hours of Video Per Minute," *Forbes,* May 21, 2012; Susan Gunelius, "The Data Explosion in 2014 Minute by Minute," ACI Information Group, Featured Post, July 12, 2014. Much of this content is characterized as "long tail" content: see Chris Anderson, *The Long Tail: Why the Future of Business Is Selling Less of More* (New York: Hyperion Books, 2008).

xxiv **five exabytes . . . of data** San Diego Supercomputer Center, accessed July 9, 2016, http://www.sdsc.edu/news_and_events/press_kit.html.

xxvi **Figure 1** Constructed by author. Thanks to Dee Jeong for assistance with artwork.

xxvii **the digital transition** Bharat N. Anand and Sophie Hood, "Schibsted," HBS No. 707-474 (Boston: Harvard Business Publishing, April 16, 2007).

xxvii **2013 paywall experiment** Vineet Kumar, Bharat N. Anand, Sunil Gupta, and Felix Oberholzer-Gee, "The *New York Times* Paywall," HBS No. 512-077 (Boston: Harvard Business Publishing, rev. January 31, 2013).

xxxii **"we don't know"** Richard Caves terms this the "nobody knows" axiom of creative industries; see Richard E. Caves, *Creative Industries: Contracts Between Art and Commerce* (Cambridge: Harvard University Press, 2002).

xxxii **you "could have had the entire United States Army"** Associated Press, "Yellowstone Fires Grow," *Livingston Enterprise*, August 23, 1988.

Part I

3 **Schibsted's board was convening** Information about Schibsted here and in the rest of this book draws primarily from the following sources: Bharat Anand and Sophie Hood, "Schibsted," HBS No. 707-474 (Boston: Harvard Business School Publishing, April 16, 2007); Schibsted annual reports; various public sources of information as listed; and interviews with various company executives. I am grateful to the following executives at Schibsted for interviews over several years (November 2006, March 2007, April 2013, October 2013, January 2014, and email correspondence): Kjell Aamot, Frode Eilertsen, Christian Printzell Halvorsen, Espen Egil Hansen, Jan Helin, Eduardo Jacucci, Birger Magnus, Sverre Munck, Torry Pedersen, Rolv-Erik Ryssdal, Terje Seljeseth, Robert Steen, board chairman Ole Jacob Sunde, and Carl-Nicolai Wessmann.

3 **"Everything was going wrong"** Interview with Kjell Aamot, November 2006.

4 **"Who Killed the Newspaper?"** "Who Killed the Newspaper?," *Economist*, August 24, 2006.

4 **"Mourning Old Media's Decline"** David Carr, "Mourning Old Media's Decline," *New York Times*, October 28, 2008.

4 **to make money on its online operations** Carol Matlack, "Norway's Schibsted: No. 3 in Online Classifieds," *Bloomberg Businessweek*, last modified October 14, 2010.

4 **for 35 percent of operating profits** "More Media, Less News," *Economist*, April 24, 2006.

4 **into a profitable business** Anand and Hood, "Schibsted."

4 **nearly 60 percent that of the entire group** *Schibsted Media Group: Annual Report 2011*.

4 **Chinese Virtual Giants** Information about Tencent in this section and the rest of this book draws primarily from the following sources: Tencent annual reports; *Inside Tencent* (Beijing: Plus Eight Star, 2009); Ali Farhoomand and Elsha Yiu, "Tencent's Business Model," University of Hong Kong case number HK 1003 (through Harvard Business Publishing); Feng Zhu and Aaron Smith, "Baidu, Alibaba, and Tencent: The Three Kingdoms of the Chinese Internet," HBS No. 615-039 (Boston: Harvard Business Publishing, January 13, 2015); Willy Shih, Howard Yu, and Fang Liu, "WeChat: A Global Platform?," HBS No. 615-049 (Boston: Harvard Business Publishing, June 17, 2015); various analyst reports on Tencent Holdings Ltd. by Marketline (London, May 2013), Jefferies (London, February 2013 and March 2013), J.P. Morgan (New York, April 2013); and various public source information where listed below. I am grateful to various Tencent executives for interviews in November 2012 and November 2013, and particularly to Caitlyn Chen (editor in chief of Tencent's Online Media Group) for arranging them. Disclosure: In 2013, I was invited to give a paid keynote address (*Reinventing Media: Lessons from the News Industry*) at Tencent's Online Media Group's 10th anniversary celebration.

4 **Pony Ma and Zhang Zidong** Arianna Huffington, "Pony Ma," *Time*, April 23, 2014; "Tencent's Ma Becomes China's Second-Richest Man on WeChat Mania," *Bloomberg*

Business; Dorinda Elliott, "Tencent the Secretive, Chinese Tech Giant That Can Rival Facebook and Amazon," *Fast Company*, April 17, 2014.

4 **for local telecom operators and paging centers** Farhoomandr and Yiu, "Tencent's Business Model."

4 **to copy from the West** Huffington, "Pony Ma"; "Tencent's Ma Becomes China's," *Bloomberg Business*; Elliott, "Tencent the Secretive"; "An Internet with Chinese Characteristics," *Economist*, July 30, 2011.

4 **AOL's ICQ** Elliott, "Tencent the Secretive"; "AOL Acquires Instant Message Firm," *CNET*, June 8, 1998; "ICQ Celebrates 100 Million Registered Users," TimeWarner, May 9, 2001; Nikhil Celly and W. H. Lo, "Tencent: Expanding from China to the World," University of Hong Kong case no. HK1009, June 21, 2013.

4 **such as chat rooms and a mobile service** Elliott, "Tencent the Secretive"; Zhu and Smith, "Baidu, Alibaba, and Tencent: The Three Kingdoms of the Chinese Internet"; Celly and Lo, "Tencent"; "Internet Value-Added Service," Tencent, 2016.

5 **to slow it down** Bruce Einhorn, "Tencent: March of the Penguins," *Bloomberg Business*, April 4, 2011.

5 **into a single offering—for free** "Walkie Talkie," WeChat, 2015; Ryan Bushey, "300 Million People Use WeChat to Text with Strangers, but Most Americans Probably Haven't Heard of It," *Business Insider*, December 16, 2013; Willy Shih et al., "WeChat: A Global Platform?"

5 **as much as LinkedIn's and Twitter's combined** Annual reports of Tencent, LinkedIn, and Twitter.

7 **Hal Varian** Hal Varian, "Newspaper Economics: Online and Offline," Google Public Policy Blog, March 2010; "Newspaper Economics: Online and Offline," presentation to Federal Trade Commission, March 9, 2010.

8 **beginning in the 1980s** "Demographic Trends in the 20th Century: Census 2000 Special Reports," United States Census Bureau, last modified November 2002.

8 **aggregate newspaper readership** Hal Varian, "Newspaper Economics."

9 **fell by 20 percent** Newspaper Association of America.

9 **fully 74 percent** Ibid.

9 **Figure 4** Data from Newspaper Association of America, various years; Pew Research Center (stateofthemedia.org), various years; U.S. Census Bureau; Statista. Thanks to Carolyn Brown for assistance in collecting the data.

10 **of just 0.5 percent a year** Data from *New York Times* quarterly and annual reports.

12 **"A Theory of Interdependent Demand"** Jeffrey Rohlfs, "A Theory of Interdependent Demand for a Communications Service," *Bell Journal of Economics*, no. 1 (Spring 1974): 16–37.

12 **Richard Schmalensee** Richard Schmalensee, "Jeffrey Rohlfs' 1974 Model of Facebook: An Introduction with A Theory of Interdependent Demand for a Communications Service by Jeffrey Rohlfs," *Competition Policy International* 7, no. 1 (Spring 2011).

13 **Apple went head-to-head** David Yoffie and Eric Baldwin, "Apple Inc. in 2015," HBS No. 715-456 (Boston: Harvard Business Publishing, October 28, 2015); Erik Sandberg-Diment, "Personal Computers; Hardware Review: Apple Weighs In with Macintosh," *New York Times*, January 24, 1984; Michael Rogers, "Will Apple's Macintosh Beat IBM?," *Newsweek*, January 30, 1984.

13 **one of the most-watched** Jacquelyn Smith, "Experts and Viewers Agree: Apple's '1984' is the Best Super Bowl Ad of All Time," *Forbes*, January 30, 2012.

15 **"Personal computers were just beginning"** I am grateful to Carl Shapiro for an interview in November 2014.

15 **antitrust policies for networked markets** Carl Shapiro, "Antitrust in Network Industries," United States Department of Justice, March 7, 1996; for more on the early

literature on network effects, see also Michael Katz and Carl Shapiro, "Network Exter-nalities, Competition, and Compatibility," *American Economic Review*, June 1985; Mi-chael Katz and Carl Shapiro, "Technology Adoption in the Presence of Network Externalities," *Journal of Political Economy*, August 1986; Joseph Farrell and Carl Sha-piro, "Dynamic Competition with Switching Costs," *RAND Journal of Economics*, Spring 1988; Michael Katz and Carl Shapiro, "Product Introduction with Network Ex-ternalities," *Journal of Industrial Economics*, March 1992; and Michael Katz and Carl Shapiro, "Systems Competition and Network Effects," *Journal of Economic Perspec-tives*, Spring 1994. For an early and comprehensive treatment of strategy in networked markets, see Carl Shapiro and Hal Varian, *Information Rules: A Strategic Guide to the Network Economy* (Boston: Harvard Business Review Press, 1998).

16 **"We look for opportunities with network externalities"** Tarun Khanna and David Yoffie, "Microsoft–1995 (Abridged)," HBS No. 799-003 (Boston, MA: Harvard Busi-ness Publishing), July 1998.

16 **VHS won out over Betamax** Stanley M. Besen and Joseph Farrell, "Choosing How to Compete: Strategies and Tactics in Standardization," *Journal of Economic Perspec-tives* 8, no. 2 (Spring 1994): 117–31; Sangin Park, "Quantitative Analysis of Network Externalities in Competing Technologies: The VCR Case," *Review of Economics and Statistics* 86, no. 4 (November 2004): 937–45; Hiroshi Ohashi, "The Role of Network Effects in the US VCR Market, 1978–1986," *Journal of Economics & Management Strategy* 12, no. 4 (Winter 2003): 447–94.

16 **someone was to download it** Matthew J. Salganik, Peter Sheridan Dodds, and Dun-can J. Watts, "Experimental Study of Inequality and Unpredictability in an Artificial Cultural Market," *Science*, February 10, 2006.

17 **He told me about the events** I am grateful to Scott Cook for an interview in May 2014 (all quotes attributed to him are from this interview).

17 **Yahoo! Auctions ultimately closed** "Yahoo Plans to Close U.S. Auction Site," *New York Times*, May 9, 2007.

19 **"in this sandbox but me"** Hayley Tsukayama, "Google Plus Review: Fun, Interest-ing, and Totally Empty," *Washington Post*, June 30, 2011.

21 **Facebook introduced Facebook Platform** Mikolaj Jan Piskorski et al., "Facebook," HBS No. 808-128 (Boston: Harvard Business Publishing, rev. March 20, 2014); Mi-chael Arrington, "Facebook Responds to MySpace with Facebook Connect," *Tech-Crunch*, May 9, 2008.

21 **Marketplace** Stig Leschly et al., "Amazon.com—2002," HBS No. 803-098 (Boston: Harvard Business Publishing, November 21, 2002).

21 **the App Store** John Markoff and Laura M. Holson, "Apple's Latest Opens a Develop-ers' Playground," *New York Times*, July 10, 2008.

21 **to more than a billion** Barbara Ortutay, "Facebook Tops 1 Billion Users," *Associated Press*, October 4, 2012; Julie Sloane, "Facebook Got Its $15 Billion Valuation—Now What?," *Wired*, October 26, 2007. Arrington, "Facebook Responds"; Brad Stone, "Face-book Aims to Extend Its Reach Across the Web," *New York Times*, November 30, 2008; Charlene Li, "Facebook Connect—Another Step to Open Social Networks," *Harvard Business Review*, May 17, 2008.

21 **iPhone users** "iPhone App Store Downloads Top 10 Million in First Weekend," Apple.com, July 14, 2008.

21 **when it restricted its service** Judd Cramer and Alan Krueger, "Disruptive Change in the Taxi Business: The Case of Uber," National Bureau of Economic Research, Working Paper No. 22083, March 2016.

21 **"product versus platform"** See also Jean-Charles Rochet and Jean Tirole, "Platform Competition in Two-Sided Markets," *Journal of the European Economic Association* 1, No. 4 (June 2003), 990–1039; Mark Armstrong, "Competition in Two-Sided Markets,"

RAND Journal of Economics, 37, no. 3 (Autumn 2006), 668–91; Jean-Charles Rochet and Jean Tirole, "Two-Sided Markets: A Progress Report," *RAND Journal of Economics*, 37, no. 3 (Autumn 2006), 645–67.

21 **in 1996** Nick Statt, "Rare Pokemon Card Attracts Record-Breaking $50k Offers on eBay," *CNET*, September 5, 2013.

22 **indirect network effects** Andrei Hagiu, "Strategic Decisions for Multisided Platforms," *MIT Sloan Management Review*, Winter 2014; Andrei Hagiu and Simon Rothman, "Network Effects Aren't Enough," *Harvard Business Review*, April 2016; and Rita McGrath, "The Problem with Groupon's Business Model," *Harvard Business Review*, July 13, 2011.

24 **Schibsted** Information about Schibsted in this section and the rest of the book draws primarily on the sources listed earlier.

24 **"Let me digress"** This and all other quotes from Sverre Munck are from interviews conducted in November 2006, April 2013, and October 2013, and email correspondence.

24 **as early on as 1995** Anand and Hood, "Schibsted."

25 **Terje Seljeseth** This and all other quotes from Terje Seljeseth are from interviews conducted in November 2006 and October 2013.

25 **Robert Steen** All quotes from Robert Steen are from an interview conducted in November 2006.

25 **with Yahoo! a few years later** Miguel Helft and Steve Lohr, "176 Newspapers to Form a Partnership with Yahoo," *New York Times*, November 20, 2006; Anand and Hood, "Schibsted."

26 **"people who understood the business"** Interview with Terje Seljeseth, November 2006.

27 **"The ad department"** Ibid.

27 **"forget certain behaviors"** The idea of "forget, learn, and borrow" has been described in V. G. Govindarajan and Chris Trimble, *Ten Rules for Strategic Innovators: From Idea to Execution* (Boston: Harvard Business Review Publishing, 2005), and is reminiscent of the "ambidextrous organization" described by Michael Tushman and Charles O'Reilly in *Winning Through Innovation: A Practical Guide to Leading Organizational Change and Renewal* (Boston: Harvard Business Publishing, 1997), and in Charles O'Reilly and Michael Tushman, "The Ambidextrous Organization," *Harvard Business Review* 82, no. 4 (2004): 74–81.

27 **the dot-com crash** Anand and Hood, "Schibsted."

27 **"Within a year"** Interview with Robert Steen, November 2006.

27 **115 percent market share** Schibsted annual report.

28 **"We thought Blocket"** This and all other quotes from Rolv-Erik Ryssdal are from an interview in October 2013.

29 **"Today the valuation"** Ibid; and email correspondence with Sverre Munck, July 9, 2016.

29 **"Our Finn model"** The Finn model was also successful in Austria, where a joint venture with the local media company Styria Medien Group was established in the mid-2000s based on the FINN technology and its B2C go-to-market strategy. According to Sverre Munck, Austria is the "exception that proves the rule: scaling globally at a rapid pace could not be done with this technology and go-to-market strategy" (email correspondence dated July 1, 2016).

30 **"postponing management"** Interview with Terje Seljeseth, October 2013.

30 **to merge their classifieds** Naspers' current CEO, Bob Van Dijk, worked for Schibsted in 2007–08.

31 **"We are still not sure"** Interview with Carl Shapiro, November 2014.

31 **"We started with a very small team"** All quotes in this section, unless otherwise stated, are from interviews with Espen Egil Hansen conducted in October 2013.

32 ***The Innovator's Dilemma*** Clayton M. Christensen, *The Innovator's Dilemma: When New Technologies Cause Great Firms to Fail* (Boston: Harvard Business School Publishing, 1997).

34 **"there were sections"** Interview with Torry Pedersen in March 2007; see also Anand and Hood, "Schibsted," for a description of differences between the online format and print format.

34 **ESPN** Paul Melvin, "ESPN Launching New ESPN.com on Site's 20th Anniversary," *ESPN MediaZone*, March 31, 2015.

36 **including *The New York Times*** Anand and Hood, "Schibsted."

38 **The *New York Times* Paywall** I am grateful to the following *New York Times* executives for various interviews conducted in April 2013, October 2013, April 2014, and March 2016: Martin Nisenholtz, David Perpich, Paul Smurl, and Denise Warren. The information about *The New York Times* in this section and the rest of this book draws primarily from these interviews and the following sources: Vineet Kumar, Bharat Anand, Sunil Gupta, and Felix Oberholzer-Gee, "The *New York Times* Paywall," HBS No. 512-077 (Boston: Harvard Business Publishing, rev. January 31, 2013); company quarterly and annual reports; and various public information sources cited where relevant.

38 **The decision to tailor** Charging different prices to different consumers is often referred to as "price discrimination" by economists. One of the challenges in designing price discriminatory strategies is ensuring that consumers prefer the pricing bundle designed for them rather than that designed for another consumer group—this is referred to as the "incentive compatibility constraint" in pricing problems. Ensuring incentive compatibility requires a careful understanding of how preferences, and purchase decisions, of different consumers interact.

38 **"largely on gut"** Interview with Denise Warren, November 2013.

39 **"This effort was organized differently"** This and all other quotes from Martin Nisenholtz are from an interview in April 2013.

39 **"We were coming out"** This and all other quotes from Denise Warren are from an interview in, November 2013.

39 **would not pay for such content** Kumar, et al., "The *New York Times* Paywall."

40 **Many observers were critical** Jason Rosenfeld, "*The New York Times'* Baffling On-line Strategy," *Silicon Exit,* July 5, 2015.

41 **"The lion's share"** Interviews with Martin Nisenholtz (April 2013) and Denise Warren (October 2013).

42 **Richard Fairbank and Nigel Morris** The description of Capital One's strategy draws primarily from Bharat Anand et al., "Capital One Financial Corp.," HBS No. 700-124 (Boston: Harvard Business School Publishing, April 24, 2000).

42 **financial services firms in America** "Capital One Earns Place on Fortune 500," *Capital One,* April 14, 2013.

43 **"Some of the workarounds"** This and all other quotes from David Perpich are from an interview in April 2014.

44 **"Would people pay for digital"** This and all other quotes from Paul Smurl are from an interview in April 2014.

46 **"Commodity Bundling"** William James Allen and Janet L. Yellen, "Commodity Bundling and the Burden of Monopoly," *Quarterly Journal of Economics* 90, no. 3 (August 1976): 475–98. Also see Adam Brandenburger and Barry Nalebuff, *Co-opetition* (New York: Currency Doubleday, 1997), p. 250–51, for a more informal treatment of price discriminatory bundling. While price discrimination expands the pie, bundling has also been analyzed as an entry barrier; see Barry Nalebuff, "Bundling as an Entry Barrier," *Quarterly Journal of Economics* 119, no. 1 (2004): 159–88.

50 **four billion videos** Edmund Ingham, "4B vs. 7B: Can Facebook Overtake YouTube as No. 1 for Video Views and Advertisers," *Forbes*, April 28, 2015.

50 **"cord cutters"** Keach Hagey, "Cord-Cutting Is Accelerating," *Wall Street Journal*, December 10, 2015; "Americans Cutting the Cable TV Cord at Increasing Pace," *eMarketer*, December 10, 2015,.

50 **"but then became unstoppable"** Vikas Bajaj, "Ready to Cut the Cord?," *New York Times*, April 6, 2013.

51 **the five largest** In May 2016 Charter merged with Time Warner Cable, creating the country's second-largest cable provider.

51 **"Music got transformed"** I am grateful to Ali Yurukoglu for an interview conducted in January 2014 (this and all other quotes attributed to him are from this interview).

52 **Sling TV** "Sling TV to Launch Live, Over-the-Top Service for $20 Per Month; Watch on TVs, Tablets, Computers, Smartphones, Game Consoles," Dish.com, January 5, 2015; Emily Steel, "Dish Network Unveils Sling TV, a Streaming Service to Rival Cable (and It Has ESPN)," *New York Times*, January 5, 2015.

52 **CBS announced its** Sarah Perez, "CBS Announces Its Own Live TV and Streaming Service, CBS All Access," *TechCrunch*, October 16, 2014; Emily Steel, "Cord-Cutters Rejoice: CBS Joins Web Stream," *New York Times*, October 16, 2014.

52 **HBO made a similar announcement** Steel, "Cord-Cutters Rejoice."

52 **"the most critically acclaimed network"** Derek Thompson, "First HBO, Then CBS: The Cable Bundle Is Slowly Coming Apart," *Atlantic*, October 16, 2014.

52 **"the cable bundle isn't going anywhere"** Victor Luckerson, "The Cable-TV Bundle is Finally Starting to Unravel," *Time*, October 16, 2014.

55 **each recognized something neat** The relevant papers are Gregory S. Crawford and Ali Yurukoglu, "The Welfare Effects of Bundling in Multichannel Television Markets," *American Economic Review* 102, no. 2 (April 2012): 643–85; Dmitri Byzalov, "Unbundling Cable Television: An Empirical Investigation," working paper, July 2010. See also Jacob Moak, "Regulation of the Pay Television Market," *Kentucky Law Journal* 103, no. 2 (January 2015): 291–309.

56 **One business publication** Jim Edwards, "TV Is Dying, and Here Are the Stats That Prove It," *Business Insider*, November 24, 2013.

57 **"The Dumb Pipe Paradox"** See Craig Moffett et al., "The Dumb Pipe Paradox," Bernstein Research, 2006; and Craig Moffett et al., "U.S. Telecommunications, Cable & Satellite: The Dumb Pipe Paradox, Revisited," Bernstein Research, June 11, 2009.

58 **"dramatically counter-intuitive"** I am grateful to Craig Moffett for interviews conducted in March 2015 and June 2015 (all quotes attributed to Moffett are from these interviews).

58 **some smaller cable companies** Victor Luckerson, "This Small Cable Operator May Help Unravel the Pay TV Industry," *Time*, October 1, 2014; Mari Silbey, "Is Dumb Pipe the Smart Move?," Light Reading, October 2, 2014, accessed June 7, 2016, http://www.lightreading.com/video/video-services/is-dumb-pipe-the-smart-move/d/d-id/711207.

59 **Starz upped its charge** Julianne Pepitone, "Starz Videos Disappear from Netflix," *CNN Money*, February 29, 2012.

59 **35 percent of all** Todd Spangler, "Netflix Streaming Eats Up 35% of Downstream Internet Traffic: Study," *Variety*, November 20, 2014; Adam Epstein, "Netflix Now Accounts for 35% of Bandwidth Usage in the US and Canada," *Quartz*, November 20, 2014.

59 **at no additional cost** Michael Learmonth, "TV Everywhere—As Long As You Pay for It," *Advertising Age*, March 2, 2009; Andrew Hampp, "8 Things You Should Know About TV Everywhere," *Business Insider*, October 28, 2009.

59 **from $300 to $58** Emily Steel, "Netflix, Growing, Envisions Expansion Abroad," *New York Times*, July 21, 2014; Yahoo! Finance stock quotes.

59 **Netflix recovered impressively** Julia Greenberg, "Netflix Is So Hot Because It Gives Us What We Want: TV," *Wired*, July 2, 2015.

60 **Time Warner Cable launched** Moffett, interview; see also Tom Lowry, "Time Warner Cable Expands Internet Usage Pricing," *Bloomberg,* March 31, 2009; Martin H. Bosworth, "Time Warner Cable Backs Down on Bandwidth Caps," *Consumer Affairs,* April 16, 2009.

60 **$45 billion megamerger** Emily Steel et al., "Comcast Is Said to End $45 Billion Bid for Time Warner Cable," *New York Times,* April 23, 2015.

60 **"accelerated industry regulation by a decade"** Moffett, interviews.

60 **introduced usage-based pricing** Moffett, interviews. One of the few academic studies on usage-based pricing is by Aviv Nevo, John Turner, and Jonathan Williams, "Usage-Based Pricing and the Demand for Residential Broadband," *Econometrica* (forthcoming); they use data on broadband usage under current pricing plans to estimate what would happen if various forms of usage-based pricing were implemented. See also "Moving Towards Usage-Based Pricing," report by Cisco Internet Business Solutions Group, March 2013; Bruce Upbin, "The Netflix Effect: Results from a Revealing Study in Canada," *Forbes,* January 7, 2011; Gillian Shaw, "Netflix and Usage-Based Billing: Does It Make a Difference to Your Internet Bill?," *Vancouver Sun,* January 27, 2011; Alex Sherman, "Netflix Viewing Seen Swelling U.S. Cable Bills Next Year: Tech," *Bloomberg Business,* November 30, 2011; David Lieberman, "Netflix Prepares to Respond as Broadband Providers Push Usage-Based Pricing," *Deadline,* September 25, 2013, accessed June 2016, http://deadline.com/2013/09/netflix-prepares-to-respond-as-broadband-providers-push-usage-based-pricing-596302.

62 **"the guy who keeps astronauts alive in space"** I am grateful to Karim Lakhani for an interview in December 2013.

63 **NASA ran a two-week contest** Kevin J. Boudreau and Karim R. Lakhani, "The Confederacy of Heterogeneous Software Organizations and Heterogeneous Developers: Field Experimental Evidence on Sorting and Worker Effort," in Josh Lerner and Scott Stern, eds., *The Rate and Direction of Inventive Activity Revisited* (Chicago: University of Chicago Press, 2012), pp. 483–502.

63 **Bara Reyna** From e-mail correspondence with Lakhani, June 2016.

63 **For the contest** Eva C. Guinan, Kevin J. Boudreau, and Karim R. Lakhani, "Experiments in Open Innovation at Harvard Medical School," *MIT Sloan Management Review* 54, no. 3 (Spring 2013): 45–52.

64 **"If you view community"** I am grateful to Anil Dash for an interview in December 2013. All quotes in this section from Dash are from this interview.

65 **Mako Hill noticed something interesting** Benjamin Mako Hill, "Almost Wikipedia: What Eight Early Online Collaborative Encyclopedia Projects Reveal About the Mechanisms of Collective Action," in *Essays on Volunteer Mobilization in Peer Production* (Ph.D. diss. Massachusetts Institute of Technology, 2013). I am grateful to Benjamin Mako Hill for an interview in January 2014. All quotes in this section from Mako Hill are from this interview.

67 **The norms on Wikipedia** I am grateful to Alan Wu for a very informative description of Wikipedia norms; interview conducted in April 2016.

68 **is in the title itself** Anil Dash, "If Your Website's Full of Assholes, It's Your Fault," anildash.com: A Blog About Making Culture, July 20, 2011, accessed June 9, 2016, http://anildash.com/2011/07/if-your-websites-full-of-assholes-its-your-fault.html.

71 **Amazon's Kindle** I am grateful to Penguin Random House executives Markus Dohle and Madeline McIntosh for interviews conducted in October 2013. Information in this section draws on Bharat Anand and Peter Olson, "The Random House Response to the Kindle," HBS No. 709-486 (Boston: Harvard Business Publishing, February 27, 2009); Peter Olson and Bharat Anand, "The Kindle: Igniting the Book Business," *Book Business* 12, no. 4 (June 2009): 26–28. Disclosure: I taught a paid executive education program for senior executives at Penguin Random House in 2013 and 2015.

72 **"Reinventing the Book"** Steven Levy, "Amazon: Reinventing the Book," *Newsweek*, November 17, 2007.

72 **"If it's allowed to take hold"** Ken Auletta, "Publish or Perish: Can the iPad Topple the Kindle, and Save the Book Business?," *New Yorker*, April 26, 2010.

74 **the top ten CEOs of the past decade** "The Entrepreneurs of the Decade: 2000 to 2009," *Inc.*, December 2009.

74 **is the day big problems and questions arose** Luis Alfonso Dau and David T. A. Wesley, "Netflix Inc.: Streaming Away from DVDs," Northeastern University College of Business Administration no. W12850, via Harvard Business Publishing.

75 **The Vanishing Newspaper** Philip Meyer, *The Vanishing Newspaper: Saving Journalism in the Information Age* (Columbia: University of Missouri Press, 2004).

75 **6 percent in the year following 9/11** "The Impact of September 11, 2001, on Aviation," International Air Transport Association, 2010 report.

75 **more than 21 percent—higher than almost any other company** Yahoo! Finance.

75 **Some of the company's choices are well-known** Information about Walmart in this section is drawn primarily from Pankaj Ghemawat and Stephen Bradley, "Wal-Mart Stores in 2003," HBS No. 704-430 (Boston: Harvard Business Publishing, rev. January 30, 2004); David Yoffie and Renee Kim, "Wal-Mart Update, 2011," HBS No. 711-546 (Boston: Harvard Business Publishing, rev. March 1, 2013); Juan Alcacer, Abhishek Agrawal, and Harshit Vaish, "Walmart Around the World," HBS No. 714-431 (Boston: Harvard Business Publishing, rev. December 6, 2013). Disclosure: I was invited as a paid speaker at a Walmart executive leadership program in 2016.

76 **Take Amazon** Information about Amazon draws primarily from Stig Leschly et al., "Amazon.com—2002," HBS No. 803-098 (Boston: Harvard Business Publishing, rev. February 13, 2003); Pankaj Ghemawat, "Leadership Online (A): Barnes & Noble versus Amazon.com," HBS No. 798-063 (Boston: Harvard Business Publishing, rev. March 16, 2004); Jeffrey Rayport and Louie Dickson, "Amazon.com (A)," HBS No. 897-128 (Boston: Harvard Business Publishing, rev. April 9, 1998); John R. Wells et al., "Amazon.com, 2016," HBS No. 716-402 (Boston: Harvard Business Publishing, rev. May 10, 2016); Brad Stone, *The Everything Store: Jeff Bezos and the Age of Amazon* (Boston: Little, Brown, 2013); and company annual reports.

78 **Book publishers have been experiencing** Information for this section primarily drawn from interviews with Markus Dohle and Madeline McIntosh (previously cited); Bharat Anand et al., "Random House," HBS No. 704-438 (Boston: Harvard Business Publishing, rev. April 2007); Anand and Olson, "The Random House Response to the Kindle."

79 **a new TV talk show, *Satyamev Jayte*** I am grateful to Uday Shankar for interviews conducted in November 2013 and December 2013 (all quotes in this section are from these interviews).

82 **Planned Journalism** This section primarily draws from "Fast and Slow," Svenska Dagbladet report, August 28, 2012; Schibsted annual reports; and interviews with various Schibsted executives (previously cited).

84 **Tencent is the most interesting** Information about Tencent in this section draws primarily from the various public sources listed earlier, and interviews with company executives in November 2013.

84 **Facebook versus Tencent** Facebook and Tencent annual reports, respectively; and Yahoo! Finance.

86 **the value of signals** Michael Spence, "Job Market Signaling," *Quarterly Journal of Economics* 87, no. 3 (August 1973): 355–74.

87 **signal its quality through advertising** Paul Milgrom and John Roberts, "Price and Advertising Signals of Product Quality," *Journal of Political Economy* 94, no. 4 (1986): 796–821.

87 **on the Hong Kong stock exchange** Nikhil Celly and W. H. Lo, "Tencent: Expanding from China to the World," University of Hong Kong case no. HK1009, June 21, 2013, Harvard Business Publishing.

88 **"Virtual goods weren't big"** I am grateful to Ben Colayco for an interview conducted in January 2011.

89 **"You're paying us with fake money?"** *"Diary of a Wimpy Kid 2: Rodrick Rules* Movie Clip 'Mom Bucks' Official (HD),'" video file, YouTube, posted by Clevver Movies, March 17, 2011.

90 **When it first introduced** Rajiv Lal, "Harrah's Entertainment, Inc.", HBS No. 502-011 (Boston: Harvard Business Publishing, rev. June 14, 2004).

90 **nonredeemable tokens** Alexis C. Madrigal, "Chuck E. Cheese's, Silicon Valley Startup: The Origins of the Best Pizza Chain Ever," *Atlantic,* July 17, 2013; David Wolman, *The End of Money* (Cambridge, MA: Da Capo Press, 2012).

91 **China's Central Bank** David Barboza, "In China, New Limits on Virtual Currency," *New York Times,* June 30, 2009; Geoffrey Fowler and Juying Qin, "QQ: China's New Coin of the Realm?," *Wall Street Journal,* March 30, 2007; David Barboza, "Internet Boom in China Is Built on Virtual Fun," *New York Times,* February 5, 2007.

93 **WeChat was the creation** Information in this section drawn primarily from public sources listed earlier; and interviews with various Tencent executives in November 2013.

95 **article in *TechCrunch*** Frank Yu, "Why WeChat Is a Chinese Mobile Game Changer for Tencent," *TechCrunch,* July 16, 2012, accessed June 2016, http://technode.com/2012/07/16/why-wechat-is-a-chinese-mobile-game-changer-for-tencent.

Part II

101 **"Most Powerful Persons in Sports"** Bharat Anand and Kate Attea, "International Management Group (IMG)," HBS Case No. 702-409 (Boston: Harvard Business Publishing, rev. September 16, 2002).

101 **He'd practically invented the industry** Information about Mark McCormack and IMG in this section and the rest of the book is primarily drawn from Anand and Attea, "International Management Group"; Mark McCormack, *What They Don't Teach You at Harvard Business School: Notes from a Street-Smart Executive* (London: Bantam Press, 1986); Mark McCormack, *What They Still Don't Teach You at Harvard Business School* (London: Bantam Press, 1990); conversations with Mark McCormack in March and April 2002; and various public sources of information listed where relevant.

101 **"I had no chance"** All quotes in this section are from Anand and Attea, "International Management Group."

103 **"war" between Hollywood and Silicon Valley** Laura Sydell, "A California Civil War Over Internet Piracy," NPR.org, last modified February 23, 2012, accessed April 25, 2016, http://www.npr.org/2012/02/23/147294229/california-industries-spar-over-internet-piracy.

104 **in a single week in 2002** Felix Oberholzer-Gee and Koleman Strumpf, "The Effect of File Sharing on Record Sales," *Journal of Political Economy* 115, no. 1 (February 2007): 1–42.

104 **averaging 3 to 5 percent per year in the late 1990s** This and other data on CD sales are obtained from RIAA data, various years.

104 **"Who Killed the Music Industry?"** See for example, Stephen Deusner, "Who Killed the Music Industry?" *Salon,* December 3, 2012, accessed June 7, 2016, http://www.salon.com/2012/12/03/who_killed_the_music_industry/; Kabir Sehgal, "Who

Killed the Music Industry?," CNBC.com, August 11, 2015, accessed June 7, 2016, http://www.cnbc.com/2015/08/11/who-killed-the-music-industry-commentary.html. For more detailed explorations of the changes in the music industry, see Steve Knopper, *Appetite for Self-Destruction: The Spectacular Crash of the Record Industry in the Digital Age* (New York: Free Press, 2009); Jim Rogers, *The Death and Life of the Music Industry in the Digital Age* (London: Bloomsbury Academic, 2013); Mark Mulligan, *Awakening: The Music Industry in the Digital Age* (CreateSpace Independent Publishing Platform, 2015); Bharat Anand and Estelle Cantillon, "The Music Industry and the Internet," HBS No. 703-513 (Boston: Harvard Business Publishing, rev. January 4, 2004).

104 **the price of live concert tickets** Alan B. Krueger and Marie Connolly, "Rockonomics: The Economics of Popular Music," *Handbook of the Economics of Art and Culture 1* (2006).

105 **Figure 9** Figure is adapted from Krueger's "Land of Hope and Dreams: Rock and Roll, Economics, and Rebuilding the Middle Class," lecture delivered at Rock and Roll Hall of Fame and Museum, June 12, 2013. Data for 2003 to 2014 on top 100 North American tours is from Pollstar *Year End Business Analysis Reports*. Data for 1981 to 2003 is from Krueger. Average ticket price for all North American concerts is assumed to grow at the same rate as the top 100 North American concerts. Thanks to Ben Chowdhury for assistance in data collection.

105 **The average price of a ticket** Data from Krueger and Connolly.

105 **didn't much care** There are exceptions, of course; see, for example, Taylor Swift, "For Taylor Swift, the Future of Music Is a Love Story," *Wall Street Journal*, July 7, 2014.

105 **"It doesn't affect me"** The quotes attributed to the various artists in this paragraph of the text are from: Jeff Stone, "Neil Young Says Internet Piracy Is the 'New Radio,' Campaigns for a New Musical Format," IBTimes.com, February 9, 2013, accessed March 24, 2016, http://www.ibtimes.com/neil-young-says-internet-piracy-new-radio -campaigns-new-musical-format-1073582; "Artists Speak Out on Music Piracy," UpVenue, accessed March 24, 2016, https://www.upvenue.com/article/1590-musician -stances-on-music-piracy.html; James Martin, "Radiohead's Ed O'Brien Interview Part 2," Midem Blog, 2010, accessed March 24, 2016, http://blog.midem.com/2010/01 /exc/; Mike Masnick, "Lady Gaga Says No Problem If People Download Her Music; The Money Is in Touring," TechDirt, May 24, 2010, accessed March 24, 2016, https:// www.techdirt.com/articles/20100524/0032549541.shtml, *Daily Mail* Reporter, "Shakira Hits Back at Lily Allen in Illegal Downloading Row as She Claims File-Sharing 'Brings Me Closer to Fans,'" *Daily Mail,* October 20, 2009.

105 **an artist took home** Jan Rivkin and Gerritt Meier, "BMG Entertainment," HBS No. 701-003 (Boston: Harvard Business Publishing, rev. September 22, 2005); Neil Strauss, "Pennies That Add Up to $16.98: Why CD's Cost So Much," *New York Times*, July 5, 1995.

105 **more than 70 percent** Krueger and Connolly, "Rockonomics"; Felix Oberholzer-Gee and Koleman Strumpf, "File Sharing and Copyright," in *Innovation Policy and the Economy*, edited by Josh Lerner and Scott Stern (Chicago: National Bureau of Economic Research, 2010); *Billboard* Staff, "*Billboard* Money-Makers List: Music's Top Earners of 2014," *Billboard*, May 1, 2015.

105 **upwards of $100 million** *Billboard* Staff, "*Billboard* Money-Makers List."

106 **"many of the forces that are buffeting the U.S. economy"** Krueger, "Land of Hope and Dreams."

106 **Using data on more than 200,000 concerts** This section describes the analysis in Alan Krueger, "The Economics of Real Superstars: The Market for Rock Concerts in the Material World," *Journal of Labor Economics* 23, no. 1, p. 1–30. See also Krueger and Connolly, "Rockonomics," and Julie Holland Mortimer, Chris Nosko, and Alan

Sorensen, "Supply Responses to Digital Distribution: Recorded Music and Live Performances," *Information Economics and Policy*, 24, no. 1 (March 2012): 3–14.

107 **although top bands** In a separate analysis, Mortimer et al. (2012) show that concert revenues grew faster for smaller bands than top artists during the period 1995–2004.

107 **and popularized recently by** See the book by Adam Brandenburger and Barry Nalebuff, *Co-opetition* (New York: Currency Doubleday, 1997).

108 **Two products are complements** An analogous definition applies to the cost side; Two products are complements if the cost of producing both is lower than the cost of producing each alone. Demand-side complementarities can arise in different ways: They can be technological complements (hardware and software), behavioral complements (for example, habit that causes consumers to purchase two products offered in succession), or informational complements (common brands). I will explore these different forms of complements in the rest of Part II. In Berry et al., we offer a more detailed, and related, categorization of the range of ways in which products can be complementary. For example, they can be "quantity complements" (left and right shoes), "cross-category complements" (hardware and software), or "dynamic complements" (television programs appearing at different times), among other reasons. See Steven Berry, Ahmed Khwaja, Vineet Kumar, Andres Musalem, Kenneth Wilbur, Greg Allenby, Bharat Anand, Pradeep Chintagunta, Michael Haneman, Przemyslaw Jeziorski, and Angelo Mele, "Structural Models of Complementary Choices," *Marketing Letters* 25, no. 3 (September 2014): 245–56.

108 **"we're the beneficiaries, in all honesty"** "Larry Vallon on How Music Piracy has Changed the Concert Business," YouTube video file, uploaded by ArtistsHouseMusic, last accessed March 30, 2016, https://www.youtube.com/watch?v=xk-_zKFCdT4.

108 **Music complements** See the discussion in Bharat Anand and Alexander Galetovic, "Strategies That Work When Property Rights Don't," in Gary Libecap, ed., *Intellectual Property and Entrepreneurship*, vol. 15 (Greenwich, CT: JAI Press, 2004); and Oberholzer-Gee and Strumpf, "File Sharing and Copyright."

109 **Figure 10** Figure is adapted from Oberholzer-Gee and Strumpf, "File Sharing and Copyright." Data for digital and physical sales is from RIAA *Year End Shipment Statistics*; iPod sales data is from Apple Annual Reports; concert sales data is from Pollstar *Year End Business Analysis Reports*. After 2009, iPod functionality was integrated into the iPhone; while there are various estimates of the iPhone's effect on iPod sales, we take a conservative estimate here and assume that iPod functionality accounts for 5 percent of the value embedded in an iPhone. Further, we take a conservative estimate of North American iPod and iPhone sales as accounting for an average of 50 percent of worldwide sales across the years. Thanks to Ben Chowdhury for assistance in data collection.

110 **Apple and Complements** The analysis in this and the next section has benefited greatly from numerous conversations with Felix Oberholzer-Gee, and David Yoffie, over the years.

110 **An Inconvenient Truth** The information about Apple in this section and the rest of this book draws in large part on David Yoffie and Mary Kwak, "Apple Computer—1999," HBS No. 799-108 (Boston: Harvard Business Publishing, rev. May 24, 1999); David Yoffie and Michael Slind, "Apple Computer: 2006," HBS No. 706-496 (Boston: Harvard Business Publishing, rev. May 30, 2007); David Yoffie and Penelope Rossano, "Apple Inc. in 2012," HBS No. 712-490 (Boston: Harvard Business Publishing, rev. August 14, 2012); David Yoffie and Eric Baldwin, "Apple Inc. in 2015," HBS No. 715-456 (Boston: Harvard Business Publishing, rev. October 28, 2015); Walter Isaacson, *Steve Jobs* (New York: Simon & Schuster, 2011); Adam Lashinsky, *Inside Apple: How America's Most Admired—and Secretive—Company Really Works* (New York: Business

Plus, 2012); company annual reports; and public sources of information that are listed where relevant.

110 **and a market share of 3 percent** Dennis Sellers, "Mac OS Global Market Share Shows Promise," *Macworld,* January 9, 2002, accessed March 30, 2016, http://www .macworld.com/article/1002940/marketshare.html.

110 **"insanely great"** This is how Steve Jobs famously referred to the Macintosh at its launch event in 1984, and subsequently to many new products; see also Jessie Hartland, *Steve Jobs: Insanely Great* (New York: Schwartz & Wade, 2015); *Billboard* Staff, "Steve Jobs: A Collection of His Classic Quotes," *Billboard,* last modified October 5, 2011.

112 **the iPod wasn't the first** Daryl Deino, "Five Portable Mp3 Players That Arrived Before the iPod," Examiner.com, May 25, 2013, accessed June 7, 2016, http://www .examiner.com/list/five-portable-mp3-players-that-arrived-before-the-ipod.

112 **Between 2002 and 2013 more than ten billion songs** "iTunes Store Tops 10 Billion Songs Sold," Apple press information, Apple.com, February 25, 2010, accessed June 7, 2016, https://www.apple.com/pr/library/2010/02/25iTunes-Store-Tops-10-Billion -Songs-Sold.html.

112 **Apple made almost nothing** Yoffie and Rossano, "Apple Inc. in 2012"; Yoffie and Baldwin, "Apple Inc. in 2015." In 2016, Apple's profits from iTunes were estimated to be growing slightly, but were still very small in relation to the rest of its business.

113 **was only about $130** Slash Lane, "iPod Classic: The Last Hurrah for HDD-Based iPods?," *AppleInsider,* October 11, 2007, accessed June 7, 2016, http://appleinsider .com/articles/07/10/11/ipod_classic_the_last_hurrah_for_hdd_based_ipods; *MacNN* staff, "iPod Classic May Be a 'Stopgap' Device," *MacNN,* October 11, 2007, accessed June 7, 2016, http://www.macnn.com/articles/07/10/11/ipod.classic.teardown/.

113 **"Thoughts on Music" . . . "DRM Free" . . . "create a truly interoperable music marketplace"** Memorandum by Steve Jobs, "Thoughts on Music," originally published on Apple's website, February 6, 2007, accessed March 30, 2016, http://web .archive.org/web/20080517114107/; http://www.apple.com/hotnews/thoughtsonmusic.

114 **the numbers hadn't increased much** "Apple's iTunes Store Passes 35 Billion Songs Sold Milestone," *MacDailyNews,* May 29, 2014, accessed March 30, 2016; http://mac -dailynews.com/2014/05/29/apples-itunes-store-passes-35-billion-songs-sold-milestone -itunes-radio-now-has-40-million-listeners/.

114 **"If anything can play on anything"** John Markoff, "Jobs Calls for End to Music Copy Protection," *New York Times.*

115 **A tire manufacturer** I owe this example to Felix Oberholzer-Gee.

116 **"This isn't a device, it's a service"** Jeff Bezos quoted in Steven Levy, "Amazon: Reinventing the Book," *Newsweek.*

116 **In 2009 Tata Motors** Information about Tata Nano here and elsewhere in the book is drawn primarily from Krishna Palepu, Bharat Anand, et al., "Tata Nano—The People's Car," HBS No. 710-420 (Boston: Harvard Business Publishing, rev. March 28, 2011), and public sources where listed.

116 **Safety concerns** Information in this paragraph also draws from Vikas Bajaj, "Tata's Nano, the Car That Few Want To Buy," *New York Times,* December 9, 2010; Pankaj Doval, "Cheapest Car Tag Hit Tata Nano: Creator," *Times of India,* August 21, 2014; Vipin Nair, "Tata Doubles Nano Warranty, Adds Maintenance Plan as Sales Fall," Bloomberg.com, December 9, 2010.

117 **revenue was more than** Apple quarterly and annual reports.

117 **It had all of nine applications** Yoni Heisler, "The History and Evolution of iOS, from the Original iPhone to iOS9," BGR.com, February 12, 2016, accessed June 6, 2016, http://bgr.com/2016/02/12/ios-history-iphone-features-evolution/.

118 **were accounting for more than 55 percent** Katy Huberty et al., *The Mobile Internet Report*, Morgan Stanley research report, December 2009.

118 **During the first three days** "iPhone App Store Downloads Top 10 Million in First Weekend," Apple Press info, July 14, 2008.

118 **and Android's was more than 75 percent** Brad Reed, "It Could Be Worse: IDC Pegs BlackBerry's Market Share at 0.6%," BGR.com, February 12, 2014, accessed June 6, 2016, http://bgr.com/2014/02/12/blackberry-market-share-q4-2013.

120 **even bizarre, accessories** John Fuller, "10 Bizarre iPod Accessories," HowStuff Works.com, accessed March 30, 2016, http://electronics.howstuffworks.com/bizarre -ipod-accessory.htm.

120 **the typical smartphone user** Felix Richter, "The Average Smartphone User Has Installed 26 Apps," Statista, September 5, 2013.

121 **"Companies are sufficiently focused"** I am grateful to Barry Nalebuff for interviews conducted in February 2014 and May 2016.

122 **View these frictions** See the related discussion of interdivisional conflicts in Anand and Galetovic, "Strategies That Work When Property Rights Don't."

122 **"Rip, Mix, Burn"** "Apple Unveils New iMacs with CD-RW Drives & iTunes Software: Rip, Mix, Burn Your Own Custom Music CD's," Apple Press info, February 22, 2001, accessed March 30, 2016, https://www.apple.com/pr/library/2001/02/22Apple -Unveils-New-iMacs-With-CD-RW-Drives-iTunes-Software.html.

123 **In early 2014 we analyzed** Research conducted by Bharat Anand, Brajesh Kumar, Venkat Srinivasan, and researchers at Rage Frameworks.

124 **and more recently Facebook** Facebook's Instant Articles (created in 2015, and in order to upload articles at faster speeds) relies in large part on articles from traditional major publishers.

124 **under a single umbrella** See, for example, efforts by Slovakian newspapers to create a combined paywall under Piano Media (William Baker, "A National Paywall that Works: Lessons from Slovakia," Columbia Journalism Review, February 4, 2012, and Catalina Albeanu, "It Takes Commitment: Lessons from Piano Media's paywalls," Journalism.co.uk, 21 April 2015, accessed July 11, 2016, https://www.journalism.co .uk/news/it-takes-commitment-lessons-from-piano-media-s-national-paywalls/s2 /a564829.) In 2015, Piano Media and another paywall technology firm, TinyPass, merged into a single firm, Piano.

124 **and would retain 70 percent** Thomas Catan, Jeffrey A. Trachtenberg, and Chad Bray, "U.S. Alleges E-Book Scheme," *Wall Street Journal*, April 11, 2012.

124 **Subsequent antitrust investigations** *U.S. v. Apple, Inc.,* et al. (July 10, 2013).

126 **quantifying the impact of piracy** Stephen Siwek, "The True Cost of Sound Recording Piracy to the U.S. Economy," report by the Institute for Policy Innovation, August 21, 2007.

126 **Stop Online Piracy Act** "H.R. 3261—Stop Online Piracy Act," Congress.gov, last modified December 16, 2011.

126, 127 **Figures 13, 14** All sales data is from RIAA *Year End Shipment Statistics.* Figure 14 shows CD unit sales normalized to a peak of 100. Thanks to Jonny Moran and Ben Chowdhury for assistance in data collection.

128 **In a 2005 study** Oberholzer-Gee and Strumpf, "The Effect of File Sharing."

129 **"It's one of those instances"** I am grateful to Felix Oberholzer-Gee for an interview conducted in August 2013.

129 **wasn't that the paper had nailed** The paper, and others that followed it on the same topic, has been heavily scrutinized. One critique of the analysis is a "fallacy of composition": an observed relationship between file sharing and CD sales at the album level need not imply that the aggregate relationship is the same; see Stan Liebowitz, "How Reliable is the Oberholzer-Gee and Strumpf Paper on File-Sharing?" University of

Texas at Dallas, Working Paper (2007); ideal data would also measure downloads and sales by person, rather than by album. Other studies on the same topic employ survey approaches; see, for example, Rafael Rob and Joel Waldfogel, "Piracy on the High C's: Music Downloading, Sales Displacement, and Social Welfare in a Sample of College Students," *Journal of Law and Economics* 49, no. 1 (2006): 29–62; and Joel Waldfogel, "File Sharing and Sales Displacement in the iTunes Era," *Information Economics and Policy* (2010), 22, no. 4, 306–14.

129 **The declines could come from** Joe Flint and Shalini Ramachandran, "Cord-Cutting Weighs on Pay TV," *Wall Street Journal*, August 6, 2015; see also Craig Moffett et al., "The Poverty Problem," Bernstein Research, 2011, for an analysis of the estimated impact of the 2008–09 recession on lowest-quintile incomes and the demand for pay TV.

130 **In 2014 Netflix's net promoter score** Rhys Wesley, "Net Promoter News: 2014 US Net Promoter Benchmarks at a Glance," CustomerGauge, March 13, 2014, accessed March 25, 2016, https://customergauge.com/news/2014-net-promoter-benchmarks/.

131 **thanks in part to a Supreme Court ruling** Stan J. Liebowitz, "The Elusive Symbiosis: The Impact of Radio on the Record Industry," *Review of Economic Research on Copyright Issues* 1, no. 1 (2004): 93–118.

131 **In *Universal v. Sony*** "1984: U.S. Supreme Court Decides *Universal v. Sony*, as VCR Usage Takes Off," History.com, 2016, accessed March 25, 2016, http://www.history.com/this-day-in-history/u-s-supreme-court-decides-universal-v-sony-as-vcr-usage-takes-off.

131 **One of the most careful** Bart J. Bronnenberg, Jean-Pierre Dubé, and Carl F. Mela, "Do Digital Video Recorders Influence Sales?," *Journal of Marketing Research* 47, no. 6 (December 2010): 998–1010.

131 **In 2012, a broadcast network** "NBC Universal's Prime-Time Olympic Viewership Soars Despite Time Delay," Instant.ly, accessed March 25, 2016, https://www.instant.ly/images/marketing/case-studies/Instantly_NBCOlympics_CaseStudy.pdf.

133 **in a celebrated 1983 survey** The survey results were analyzed and published in R. C. Levin et al., "Appropriating the Returns from Industrial R&D," *Brookings Papers on Economic Activity*, 1987, 783–820.

133 **the study was repeated** W. Cohen et al., "Protecting their Intellectual Assets: Appropriability Conditions and Why U.S. Manufacturing Firms Patent (Or Not)," National Bureau of Economic Research, 2000, Working Paper No. 7552.

133 **Michele Boldrin and David Levine** Michele Boldrin and David K. Levine, *Against Intellectual Monopoly* (Cambridge: Cambridge University Press, 2010); see also Michele Boldrin and David K. Levine, "The Case Against Patents," *Journal of Economic Perspectives* 27, no. 1 (Winter 2013): 3–22.

133 **writing in this area** See also James Anton and Dennis Yao, "Expropriation and Inventions: Appropriable Rents in the Absence of Property Rights," *American Economic Review* 84, no. 1 (March 1994): 190–209; James Anton and Dennis Yao, "Start-ups, Spin-offs, and Internal Projects," *Journal of Law, Economics & Organization* 11, no. 2 (October 1995): 362–78; Anand and Galetovic, "Strategies That Work When Property Rights Don't"; Bharat Anand and Alexander Galetovic, "How Market Smarts Can Protect Property Rights," *Harvard Business Review*, December 2004.

134 **You can stretch the list** The necktie example is now renowned among strategy colleagues at Harvard Business School, even though I am not aware who deserves credit for the original example. It is also mentioned in Michael Porter, "The Five Competitive Forces That Shape Strategy," *Harvard Business Review*, January 2008.

135 **the problem of "perception"** Jan Rivkin, "Key Concepts in a Module on Strategic Failure," HBS No. 706-471 (Boston: Harvard Business Publishing, rev. March 21, 2006), 1–15.

135 **of print and digital complementarities** Matthew Gentzkow, "Valuing New Goods in a Model with Complementarities: Online Newspapers," *American Economic Review*

97, no. 3 (June 2007): 713–44. Berry et al., "Structural Models of Complementary Choices," examines both the challenges that arise in estimating complementarities, and the range of ways in which this problem has been tackled in the economics, marketing, and strategy literatures.

138 **Fantasy sports** The information about fantasy sports is drawn from Nando Di Fino, "A New Kind of Pocket Protection," *Wall Street Journal*, September 1, 2009; Ben McGrath, "Dream Teams," *New Yorker*, April 13, 2015; Adam Satariano, "How Fake Sports Are Turning Man Cave Dwellers into Millionaires," *Bloomberg Businessweek*, January 15, 2015; Chris Chafin, "Living the Dream," *Fast Company*, April 29, 2015; Leigh Steinberg, "Fantasy Football Madness," *Forbes*, August 28, 2012; Nico Newman, "History of Fantasy Sports," Fantasy-Sport.net, November 4, 2015, accessed March 25, 2016, https://fantasy-sport.net/history-of-fantasy-sports/; Miranda Green, "NFL's Shadow Economy of Gambling and Fantasy Football Is a Multibillion Dollar Business," *Daily Beast*, October 6, 2012, accessed June 7, 2016, http://www.thedailybeast.com/articles/2012/10/06/nfl-s-shadow-economy-of-gambling-and-fantasy-football-is-a-multibillion-dollar-business.html; Nicholas David Bowman et al., *Fantasy Sports and the Changing Sports Media Industry: Media, Players, and Society* (Lanham, MD: Lexington Books, 2016); Jay Correia, *Daily Fantasy Sports* (Pennsauken, NJ: BookBaby, 2016). I am very grateful to Varun Anand as well for many informative conversations about fantasy sports.

141 **the Indian television market** Information about the Indian television wars in this section is drawn primarily from Bharat Anand and Tarun Khanna, "Must Zee TV," HBS No. 700-102 (Boston: Harvard Business Publishing, rev. February 2003); Bharat Anand, "Competing over the Airwaves," *Smart Manager* Q102 (January–March 2002): 22–36. I am grateful to Zee TV executives for interviews in 1999, and to Uday Shankar for interviews in November 2013, December 2013, and March 2015.

141 **"Competition is heating up"** Interview with Zee TV executive, October 1999.

143 **This pattern of "sticking around"** See, for example, Roland Rust and Mark Alpert, "An Audience Flow Model of Television Viewing Choice," *Marketing Science* 3 (Spring 1984): 113–27; Ron Shachar and John Emerson, "Cast Demographics, Unobserved Segments, and Heterogeneous Switching Costs in a TV Viewing Choice Model," *Journal of Marketing Research* 37 (May 2000): 173–86; Nickolay Moshkin and Ron Shachar, "The Asymmetric Information Model of State Dependence," *Marketing Science* 21, no. 4 (2002): 1–20; Bharat Anand and Ron Shachar, "Advertising, The Matchmaker," *RAND Journal of Economics* 42, no. 2 (Summer 2011): 205–45.

143 **at least four types of connections at work here** Ron Shachar and Bharat Anand, "The Effectiveness and Targeting of Television Advertising," *Journal of Economics & Management Strategy* 7, no. 3 (Fall 1998): 363–96; Bharat Anand and Ron Shachar, "Brands as Beacons: A New Source of Loyalty to Multiproduct Firms," *Journal of Marketing Research* 41, no. 2 (May 2004): 135–50.

144 **sought to understand the magnitude** Shachar and Anand, "The Effectiveness and Targeting of Television Advertising."

145 **"KBC worked as a program"** This and other quotes in this section are from interviews with Uday Shankar in November 2013 and December 2013.

147 **Figures 17, 18** NFL contract values are from Kevin G. Quinn, *The Economics of the National Football League: The State of the Art* (New York: Springer, 2012). Regular season viewership data is from Nielsen Media Research. Thanks to Ben Chowdhury for assistance in data collection.

148 **NBC is thought to have paid** Information about the 1990s TV deals in this section is drawn from Bharat Anand and Catherine M. Conneely, "Fox Bids for the NFL–1993," HBS No. 704-443 (Boston: Harvard Business Publishing, December 11, 2003); Bharat Anand and Catherine M. Conneely, "Fox and the NFL–1998," HBS No. 704-

444 (Boston: Harvard Business Publishing, December 2003); Bill Carter, "The Media Business: Outbid on Pro Football, NBC Retains 'E.R.' in Record Pact," *New York Times,* January 15, 1998; "'ER' Doctors Rescue NBC," *CNN Money,* January 14, 1998.

148 **more than three times that of any other channel** Frank Bi, "ESPN Leads All Cable Networks in Affiliate Fees," *Forbes,* January 8, 2015.

148 **"economics of superstars"** Sherwin Rosen, "The Economics of Superstars," *American Economic Review* 71, no. 5 (December 1981): 845–58.

149 **"forced cable operators"** Bharat Anand and Kate Attea, "News Corporation," HBS No. 9-702-425 (Boston: Harvard Business Publishing, rev. June 27, 2003).

150 **"We are not going to lose money"** Adam Bryant, "Beyond the Bottom Line: The New Math of TV Sports," *New York Times,* January 18, 1998.

151 **benefited from the same sort** Information about the Howard Stern and Sirius XM deals is from Howard Kurtz and Frank Ahrens, "Sirius Lands a Big Dog: Howard Stern," *Washington Post,* October 7, 2004; Felix Gillette, "Can SiriusXM Survive Without Howard Stern?," *Bloomberg Business,* March 11, 2015; Peter Lauria, "Howard Stern's New Deal: $2K a Minute," *Daily Beast,* last modified December 2009, accessed March 25, 2016, http://www.thedailybeast.com/articles/2010/12/09/howard-sterns-sirius-deal -the-400-million-contract.html; Georg Szalai, "Sirius XM Radio Ended 2010 with More Subscribers than Netflix," *Hollywood Reporter,* February 15, 2011.

153 **The difference in TV ratings** Jonathan Mahler, "The Tiger Bubble," *New York Times Magazine,* March 24, 2010; see also "Tiger's Impact on Golf Ratings," ESPN.com, February 19, 2010, accessed June 7, 2016, http://espn.go.com/blog/sportscenter/post /_/id/32264/tigers-impact-on-golf-ratings; and Roger Pielke, Jr., "Measuring the Tiger Effect," *Sporting Intelligence,* August 6, 2014.

154 **"There's nobody in the game"** Interview with Phil Mickelson on *Charlie Rose Show,* July 25, 2011, accessed June 7, 2016, https://charlierose.com/videos/13705.

154 **"I certainly don't live like a king"** Mahler, "The Tiger Bubble."

154 **"In 1996, only nine players"** Donna Barbie, ed., *The Tiger Woods Phenomenon* (Jefferson, NC: McFarland, 2012).

154 **A 2013 study** Kevin Y. C. Chung, Timothy P. Derdenger, and Kannan Srinivasan, "Economic Value of Celebrity Endorsements: Tiger Woods' Impact on Sales of Nike Golf Balls," *Marketing Science* 32, no. 2 (March 1, 2013): 271–93.

154 **he normally played in dropped 47 percent** "Tiger's Return Expected to Make PGA Ratings Roar," Nielsen, February 25, 2009, accessed March 25, 2016, http:// www.nielsen.com/us/en/insights/news/2009/tigers-return-expected-to-make-pga-ratings -roar.html.

154 **In 2009 networks charged 30 percent less** Michael McCarthy, "Financial Impact for Golf Felt All Around with Tiger Woods Gone," *USA Today,* January 28, 2010.

154 **or roughly $10 billion** Christopher Knittel and Victor Stango, "Celebrity Endorsements, Firm Value and Reputation Risk: Evidence from the Tiger Woods Scandal," *Management Science* 60, no. 1 (January 2014).

155 **In an intriguing study** Ken Hendricks and Alan Sorensen, "Information and the Skewness of Music Sales," *Journal of Political Economy* 117, no. 2 (April 2009): 324–69.

156 **Figure 20** Figure reproduced from Hendricks and Sorenson, "Information and the Skewness of Music Sales."

156 **The Cuckoo's Calling** Liz Bury, "Cuckoo's Calling by JK Rowling: Did You Know?," *Guardian,* July 15, 2013; "JK Rowling Revealed as Author of *The Cuckoo's Calling,*" BBC News, July 14, 2013, accessed March 25, 2016, http://www.bbc.com/news /entertainment-arts-23304181; James B. Stewart, "Long Odds for Authors Newly Published," *New York Times,* August 30, 2013; Ewan Spence, "The Real Winner of The Cuckoo's Calling Was Amazon, not J.K. Rowling," *Forbes,* July 15, 2013.

157 **in 2011, all ten were** "1981 Domestic Grosses," Box Office Mojo, March 29, 2016, accessed March 30, 2016, http://www.boxofficemojo.com/yearly/chart/?yr=1981&p=.htm.

157 **Roughly 20 percent** Stephen Follows, "Hollywood Sequels by the Numbers," June 15, 2015, last accessed March 30, 2016, https://stephenfollows.com/hollywood-sequels-by-the-numbers.

157 **recently ran an experiment** Bharat Anand and Aleksander Rosinski, "The Impact of Brands and Advertising on Perceptions of Editorial Quality," working paper.

158 **Figures 21a–c** Figures are from the experimental treatments in Anand and Rosinski study.

159 **an artist named Alex Goot** "GootMusic YouTube Channel Stats," VidStatsX, last modified March 25, 2016.

160 **"fundamentally changed our entire approach"** I am grateful to Pieter du Toit for an interview in October 2015 (all quotes in this section are from this interview).

161 **Figure 22** Data obtained from Pieter du Toit, *Beeld*.

161 **"The skeptics said that digital"** I am grateful to Anne Messitte for an interview in October 2013 (all quotes in this section are from this interview).

162 **vertical combinations between TV studios** For a history of the broadcast network industry, see Pankaj Ghemawat, "Fox Broadcasting Company," HBS No. 9-387-096 (Boston: Harvard Business Publishing, rev. April 2, 1993).

163 **A recent study of vertical integration** Gregory Crawford et al., "The Welfare Effects of Vertical Integration in Multichannel Television Markets," National Bureau of Economic Research, Working Paper No. w21832, December 2015. They examine not just the benefits that come from avoiding the double markup but also the foreclosure effects that come from limiting content access to rival distributors, and find that "program access rules" allow markets to reap the benefits of integration without its associated cost. See also Tasneem Chipty, "Vertical Integration, Market Foreclosure, and Consumer Welfare in the Cable Television Industry," *American Economic Review* 91, no. 3 (June 2001): 428–53.

165 **on a portfolio approach** Another, anticompetitive reason for the same observed behavior (also referred to as "tying") is that companies with market power bundle channels to make it harder for others to enter; see Barry Nalebuff, "Bundling as an Entry Barrier," *Quarterly Journal of Economics*, 119, no. 1, 159–87.

165 **Fox News in 1996** See Anand and Attea, "News Corp."; "The State of the News Media 2012," Pew Research Center's Project for Excellence in Journalism, 2012, accessed June 7, 2016, http://www.pewresearch.org/2012/03/19/state-of-the-news-media-2012/.

165 **$10 for every subscriber** Jesse Holcomb, Amy Mitchell, and Tom Rosenstiel, "Cable: CNN Ends Its Ratings Slide, Fox Falls Again," *The State of the News Media 2012*, Pew Center's Research Project for Excellence in Journalism, last accessed July 13, 2016, http://www.stateofthemedia.org/2012/cable-cnn-ends-its-ratings-slide-fox-falls-again/.

166 **When Tencent decided to launch** I am grateful to Caitlyn Chen for interviews conducted in October and November 2013.

166 **Schibsted discovered another way** I am grateful to Sverre Munck for interviews in April and October 2013 and to Carl-Nicolai Wessmann for an interview in January 2014 (all quotes in this section are from these interviews).

169 **they've exploited connections *after the fact*** The distinction between "ex-ante" versus "ex-post" synergistic opportunities, and its corporate implications, is also examined in Bharat Anand, "Corporate Strategies for Media and Entertainment Businesses," HBS No. 705-479 (Boston: Harvard Business Publishing, rev. April 13, 2005).

170 **"the stories change"** I am grateful to Uday Shankar for interviews conducted in November 2013 and December 2013.

171 **When we looked at the data** Anand and Shachar, "Brands as Beacons: A New Source of Loyalty to Multiproduct Firms."

172 **A 2003 study** Walter McDowell and Steven Dick, "Has Lead-in Lost Its Punch? An Analysis of Prime-Time Inheritance Effects Comparing 1992 with 2002," *International Journal on Media Management* 5, no. 4 (2003): 285–93. In a subsequent paper, Constança Esteves-Sorenson and Fabrizio Perretti obtained similar results using (even more accurate) data from Italian television: Constança Esteves-Sorenson and Fabrizio Perretti, "Micro-Costs: Inertia in Television Viewing," *Economic Journal* 122, no. 563 (September 2012): 867–902.

173 **"Curated packages appeared to have value"** I am grateful to Andrew Rashbass for this interview in November 2013 (all quotes in this section are from this interview).

173 **created a ratings bonanza** Paul J. Gough, "NBC Has Best Saturday Since 1990," *Hollywood Reporter,* August 17, 2008, accessed March 27, 2016, http://www.hollywood reporter.com/news/nbc-has-best-saturday-1990-117622; "Michael Phelps: Saturday Night Fever on NBC," *Variety,* August 17, 2008; Bill Carter, "NBC Banks on Olympics as Springboard for New Shows," *New York Times,* August 12, 2012; "The Final Numbers Are In: Olympics a Huge Success for NBC," *Sports Media Journal,* August 13, 2012.

175 **IMG's story** Information about IMG throughout this section draws primarily from the sources listed earlier.

176 **compared the market values** Larry H. P. Lang and Rene M. Stulz, "Tobin's Q, Corporate Diversification, and Firm Performance," *Journal of Political Economy* 102, no. 6 (December 1994): 1248–80.

178 **"you can literally pick an advertiser's needs"** Lawrie Mifflin, "Making a Media Giant: The Overview; Viacom to Buy CBS, Forming 2D Largest Media Company," *New York Times,* September 8, 1999.

178 **"I honestly believe"** Randall Stross, "Why Bricks and Clicks Don't Always Mix," *New York Times,* September 18, 2010.

179 **"When Barnes & Noble started"** Ibid.

180 **"S-curve of talent"** I am grateful to Peter Olson for an interview in September 2013.

180 ***Showdown at Sherwood*** Richard Sandomir, "Golf; Duval-Woods Rushing to Daylight," *New York Times,* July 21, 1999.

181 **was guaranteed NZ $3.7 million** "Ticket Sales Poor for New Zealand Open," *Golf Today;* "New Zealand Open Facing Big Loss," *Golf Today,* January 2002.

182 **"They were the only ones"** "Online Extra: Peyton Manning's IMG Dream Team," *Bloomberg Business,* July 12, 2004.

184 **offered a new twist** C. K. Prahalad and Gary Hamel, "The Core Competence of the Corporation," *Harvard Business Review,* May/June 1990.

185 **a lively debate ensued** Jose Manuel Campa and Simi Kedia, "Explaining the Diversification Discount," *Journal of Finance* 57, no. 4 (August 2002): 1731–62; Belén Villalonga, "Does Diversification Cause the 'Diversification Discount'?," *Financial Management* 33, no. 2 (2004): 5–27; Belén Villalonga, "Diversification Discount or Premium? New Evidence from the Business Information Tracking Series," *Journal of Finance* 59 (2004): 479–506; Bharat Anand and Samhita Jayanti, "Strategies of Unrelated Diversification," HBS No. 705-480 (Boston: Harvard Business Publishing, April 2005).

185 **the share of diversified firms** Bharat Anand and Dmitri Byzalov, "Systematic Heterogeneity versus Average Effects in the Returns to Diversification," working paper, 2011.

Part III

191 ***"I've been traveling around the world"*** I am grateful to Espen Egil Hansen for an interview in October 2013 (quotes in this section are from this interview).

192 **"A Severe Contest Between Intelligence and Ignorance"** The information about *The Economist* in this section and the rest of the book is drawn primarily from the following sources: Felix Oberholzer-Gee, Bharat Anand, and Lizzie Gomez, *"The Economist,"* HBS No. 710-441 (Boston: Harvard Business Publishing, rev. July 14, 2010); company annual reports, various years; Andreas Kluth, "Answering Questions about *The Economist,"* andreaskluth.org, June 12, 2008, accessed June 6, 2016, https://andreaskluth .org/2008/12/06/answering-questions-about-the-economist; Andreas Kluth, "A Generalist among Generalists—I Move On," andreaskluth.org, March 19, 2009, accessed June 6, 2016, https://andreaskluth.org/2009/03/19/a-generalist-among-generalists-i-move-on/; Michael Hirschorn, "The Newsweekly's Last Stand: Why *The Economist* is thriving while *Time* and *Newsweek* fade," *Atlantic,* July–August 2009; and public sources of information that are listed where relevant. I am grateful to Andrew Rashbass and John Micklethwait for interviews in May 2009, November 2009, and February 2010 (as part of our HBS case on *The Economist*), and to Chris Stibbs for interviews in October 2013 and December 2013, and subsequent email correspondence.

193 **slightly under ninety full-time journalists** Email correspondence with Chris Stibbs, December 2013.

193 **who paid more than $100 a year** By 2016, the subscription price was roughly $150 per year.

193 **Digital product innovations** In 2014, *The Economist* introduced a daily briefing for the first time via its "Economist Espresso" paid smartphone app, designed to "bring you up to speed in just a couple of minutes at the start of the day" (Economist.com, November 6, 2014). The content continued to be faithful to its roots: short, witty, and with no links.

193 **"increasingly, sites which wall themselves"** John Battelle, "From Pull to Point: How to Save *The Economist* and the *Journal* from Irrelevance," battellemedia.com, October 11, 2004.

194 **subscription revenue increased by 6 percent** Oberholzer-Gee, Anand, et al., *"The Economist."*

194 **advertising revenue and operating profit** *The Economist,* annual reports.

194 **For the period 2000 to 2015** Ibid.

195 **"the *Economist* prides itself"** Hirschorn, "The Newsweekly's Last Stand."

195 **"If you take any single article"** Interviews with Andrew Rashbass, 2009 and 2011.

196 **"It's our weekly package"** Quotes from Chris Stibbs, here and in the rest of the book, are from interviews in October 2013 and December 2013.

197 **an emphasis on a single voice** "Why Are *The Economist's* Writers Anonymous?," *Economist,* September 4, 2013.

197 **"The *Economist's* marketing campaign"** Oberholzer-Gee, Anand, et al., *"The Economist."* See also Samuel Chan, *"The Economist:* Advertising or Ego Satisfaction?" October 9, 2012, http://www.officialsamuel.com/blog/the-economist-advertising/.

202 **"intellectual scoops rather than informational ones"** David Carr, *"Newsweek's* Journalism of Fourth and Long," *New York Times,* May 23, 2009.

203 **"As the number of news outlets"** Jon Meacham, "Jon Meacham: The Editor's Desk," *Newsweek,* October 13, 2007.

203 **"While raising subscription"** Matt Pressman, "Why *Time* and *Newsweek* Will Never Be *The Economist,"* *Vanity Fair,* April 20, 2009.

203 **sold the magazine for $1** Dealbook, *"Newsweek's* Price Tag: $1," *New York Times,* October 7, 2010.

204 **was first made explicit** Paul Milgrom and John Roberts, "Complementarities and Systems: Understanding Japanese Economic Organization," *Estudios Económicos* 9, no. 1 (Winter/Spring 1994): 3–42.

205 **"We will argue that these features"** Ibid.

205 *Economics, Organization, and Management* Paul R. Milgrom and John Roberts, *Economics, Organization, and Management* (Englewood Cliffs, NJ: Prentice-Hall, 1992).

205 **"What Is Strategy"** Michael E. Porter, "What Is Strategy?," *Harvard Business Review*, November 1, 1996.

206 **Lewis Carroll's *Through the Looking Glass*** Lewis Carroll, *Through the Looking Glass, and What Alice Found There* (New York: Macmillan, 1898). See also William Barnett, *The Red Queen Among Organizations: How Competitiveness Evolves* (Princeton: Princeton University Press, 2008).

206 **"when the decisions that embody"** Jan Rivkin, "Imitation of Complex Strategies," *Management Science* 46, no. 6 (June 2000): 824–44.

207 **researchers in distant fields** I am grateful to Jan Rivkin for an interview in February 2014. See Jay Forrester, "Systems Dynamics and the Lessons of 35 Years," in Kenyon De Greene, ed., *A Systems-Based Approach to Policy Making* (New York: Springer, 1993); Stuart Kauffman, *The Origins of Order: Self-Organization and Selection in Evolution* (Oxford: Oxford University Press, 1993); S. Kauffman and S. A. Johnsen, "Co-Evolution to the Edge of Chaos: Coupled Fitness Landscapes, Poised States, and Co-Evolutionary Avalanches," *Journal of Theoretical Biology* 149 (1991): 467–505.

207 **Perhaps the most famous example** Information about Walmart in this section and the rest of part III is drawn primarily from Harvard Business School cases: Ghemawat and Bradley, "Wal-Mart Stores in 2003"; Yoffie and Kim, "Wal-Mart Update, 2011"; Alcacer, Agrawal, and Vaish, "Walmart Around the World"; company annual reports; and public sources where listed.

207 **roughly 700 million miles** "Drive for Walmart," Walmart.com, last accessed March 30, 2016; http://careers.walmart.com/career-areas/transportation-logistics-group/drivers/.

207 **including one by the company's founder** Sam Walton and John Huey, *Sam Walton, Made in America: My Story* (New York: Doubleday, 1992).

209 **in Rogers, Arkansas** "Walmart: Our History," Walmart.com, 2016, http://corporate.walmart.com/our-story/our-history.

209 **Edward Jones** Information about Edward Jones in this section is drawn primarily from David Collis and Troy Smith, "Edward Jones in 2006: Confronting Success," HBS No. 707-497 (Boston: Harvard Business Publishing, rev. March 21, 2012); David Collis and Michael Rukstad, "Can You Say What Your Strategy Is?," *Harvard Business Review*, April 2008, pp. 1–9. I am grateful to David Collis for conversations on this topic.

210 **highest in the industry** Michael Porter and Gregory Bond, "Edward Jones," HBS No. 700-009 (Boston: Harvard Business Publishing, rev. June 15, 2000).

210 **"best places to work"** "Edward Jones Ranks No. 6 on *Fortune* Magazine's Best Companies to Work For List," Edward Jones, August 3, 2015.

213 **Reed Hastings founded Netflix** Information about Netflix in this section draws primarily from Willy Shih et al., "Netflix," HBS No. 607-138 (Boston: Harvard Business Publishing, rev. April 27, 2009), and Keating, *Netflixed.*

215 *Being Digital* Nicholas Negroponte, *Being Digital* (New York: Knopf, 1995).

215 **"out of print"** Ibid.

216 **"binge watching"** Brian Stelter, "New Way to Deliver a Drama: All 13 Episodes in One Sitting," *New York Times*, January 31, 2013. Recently, Michael Wolff has made the argument that Netflix's new model increasingly resembles, rather than replaces, traditional TV; see Michael Wolff, *Television Is the New Television: The Unexpected Triumph of Old Media in the Digital Age* (London: Portfolio, 2015).

218 **industry watchers predicted doomsday** Information about the *New York Times* paywall in this section is drawn primarily from Kumar, Anand, et al., "The *New York Times* Paywall."

218 **"Every newspaper is watching the experiment"** Tom Ashbrook, "Fees and Free-Riders: The News Content Paywall Debate," *WBUR: On Point with Tom Ashbrook*, March 28, 2011.

219 ***"The New York Times* faces are very different"** Arthur Sulzberger, interviewed for "Riptide: What Really Happened to the News Business," a project of the Shorenstein Center on Media, Politics, and Public Policy, 2013–14.

219 **"In modern media"** Jeff Roberts, "*New York Times* CEO Calls Digital Pay Model 'Most Successful' Decision in Years," Gigaom, May 20, 2013, accessed June 2016, https://gigaom.com/2013/05/20/new-york-times-ceo-calls-digital-pay-model-most-successful-decision-in-years.

220 **"Start-ups would be wise to avoid"** Peter Vogel, "3 Lessons That Startups Can Learn from Facebook's Failed Credits Experiment," *TechCrunch,* October 13, 2012, accessed June 6, 2016, http://techcrunch.com/2012/10/13/3-lessons-that-startups-can-learn-from-facebooks-failed-credits-experiment; see also Tim Peterson, "Facebook Gives Up on Facebook Credits," *Adweek*, June 20, 2012.

222 **Ask Walmart** Information in this section is drawn primarily from Alcacer et al., "Walmart Around the World," and Ghemawat and Bradley, "Walmart Stores in 2003." Pankaj Ghemawat has articulated a framework for examining how geographic distance shapes business expansion; see "Distance Still Matters: The Hard Reality of Global Expansion," *Harvard Business Review* 79, no. 8 (2001): 137–47.

222 **Canada, Mexico, and the United Kingdom** Alcacer et al., "Walmart Around the World."

223 **with strong unions** Mark Landler and Michael Barbaro, "Wal-Mart Finds That Its Formula Doesn't Fit Every Culture," *New York Times*, August 2, 2006.

223 **American footballs in soccer-crazy Brazil** Ibid.

223 **ice-fishing huts** Ian Katz, "Wal-Mart Spoken Here," *Bloomberg Business*, last modified June 23, 1997.

223 **"replication and imitation"** Jan W. Rivkin, "Reproducing Knowledge: Replication Without Information at Moderate Complexity," *Organization Science* 12, no. 3 (May–June 2001).

224 **Fresh & Easy** Tiffany Hsu, "Tesco to Pull Out of U.S. and Sell Fresh & Easy Markets," *Los Angeles Times*, April 17, 2013; Tom Geoghegan, "Why Is Tesco Struggling in the US?," *BBC News*, May 5, 2011.

224 **"was difficult to re-create"** Rivkin, "Reproducing Knowledge."

224 **Flipkart is the leading e-commerce** Information in this section draws primarily from Narayandas et al., "Flipkart: Transitioning to a Marketplace Model," HBS No. 516-017 (Boston: Harvard Business Publishing, rev. March 14, 2016) and public sources of information where listed.

224 **recently described to me** I am grateful to Binny Bansal for an interview in November 2015 (all quotes in this section are from this interview).

225 **the reasons for their success** Nivedita Bhattacharjee and Clara Ferreira-Marques, "India's E-Commerce Giant Flipkart in No Rush to Go Public," *Business Insider*, May 7, 2015.

226 **"We had a digital unit"** I am grateful to Uday Shankar for an interview in March 2015 and to Ajit Mohan for an interview in August 2015 (all quotes in this section are from these interviews).

231 **"but as integrated ones"** Framing decisions as "integrated strategic alternatives" is an approach rooted in the idea of strategic fit; see Jan Rivkin, "An Options-Led Approach to Making Strategic Choices," HBS No. 702-433 (Boston: Harvard Business Publishing, December 2001), and A. G. Lafley and Roger Martin, *Playing to Win: How Strategy Really Works* (Boston: Harvard Business Review Press, February 5, 2013).

232 **"It's not about your organization"** I am grateful to Andrew Rashbass for this interview in November 2014 (all quotes in this section are from this interview).

233 **with digital sales stabilizing at about 20 percent of the market** Andrew Nusca, "Print Books Are Far From Dead. But They're Definitely on the Decline," *Fortune*, September 24, 2015; Alexandra Alter, "The Plot Twist: E-Book Sales Slip, and Print Is Far From Dead," *New York Times*, September 22, 2015.

236 **near the top in customer satisfaction** Information about Southwest drawn primarily from James Heskett and Roger Hallowell, "Southwest Airlines—1993 (A)," HBS No. 694-023 (Boston: Harvard Business Publishing, rev. April 2, 1997), and Ramon Casadesus-Masanell et al., "Two Ways to Fly South: Lan Airlines and Southwest Airlines," HBS No. 707-414 (Boston: Harvard Business Publishing, rev. March 15, 2010).

238 **"Resisting the urge to say yes"** I am grateful to Chris Stibbs for an interview in October 2013 (all quotes in this section are from this interview).

239 **"Because newspapers were natural monopolies"** I am grateful to Clark Gilbert for an interview in October 2013 (all quotes in this section are from this interview).

242 **was in 200 syndication partnerships** *Deseret News* Staff, "*Deseret News* Leadership Recognized As Innovator of the Year," *Deseret News*, September 18, 2013.

243 **During the 1984 presidential campaign** The Stahl-Darman exchange in 1984 has been documented in various sources; see, for example, Dan Schill, *Stagecraft and Statecraft: Advance and Media Events in Political Communication* (Lanham, MD: Lexington Books, 2009).

243 **A few years ago** Bharat Anand and Rafael Di Tella, "Perceived Media Bias: Some Evidence on the Impact of Prior Beliefs and Source Awareness," working paper, 2009.

243 **between a pair of journalists** This conversation is based on an actual interchange between Bill O'Reilly and Dan Rather on Fox News' *The O'Reilly Factor* in 2002.

245 **that website loading speed** "Using Site Speed in Web Search Ranking," *Google Webmaster Central Blog*, April 9, 2010; see also Robinson Meyer, "72 Hours with Facebook Instant Articles," *Atlantic*, October 23, 2015.

245 **ease of getting a cab . . . or paying for it** Leena Rao, "UberCab Takes the Hassle Out of Booking a Car Service," *TechCrunch*, July 5, 2010; Alexia Tsotsis, "Why Use UberCab When Calling a Cab Is Cheaper?," *TechCrunch*, October 26, 2010; Michael Arrington, "What If UberCab Pulls an Airbnb? Taxi Business Could (Finally) Get Some Disruption," *TechCrunch*, August 31, 2010.

245 **Fox News decided to enter** Bharat Anand et al., "CNN and the Cable News Wars," HBS No. 707-491 (Boston: Harvard Business Publishing, rev. July 23, 2007).

245 **Differentiation was central to the Fox News strategy** See Neil Bendle and Leon Li, "Fox News: Competing to Deliver the News," Case No. 13243 (Ivey Publishing, rev. Aug 20, 2013); Stefano DellaVigna and Ethan Kaplan, "The Fox News Effect: Media Bias and Voting," *Quarterly Journal of Economics* 122 (2007): 1187–1234; and Gregory Martin and Ali Yurukoglu, "Bias in Cable News: Persuasion and Polarization," working paper, May 27, 2016.

246 **we examined differentiation** Bharat Anand and Dmitri Byzalov, "Spatial Competition in Cable News: Where Are Larry King and O'Reilly in Latent Attribute Space?," working paper, 2009.

246 **"make the interesting important and the important interesting"** Interview with retired cable executive, October 2014.

247 **the average cost of making a movie** Pamela McClintock, "$200 Million and Rising: Hollywood Struggles with Soaring Marketing Costs," *Hollywood Reporter*, July 31, 2014.

247 **studio spending increased** Eric Buchman, "Why Are Movies More Expensive to Make than Ever When Tech Makes Them Easier to Make?" *Digital Trends*, December 10,

2014, accessed June 6, 2016, http://www.digitaltrends.com/movies/why-hollywood-movies-are-more-expensive-to-make-than-ever.

247 **The result was nail-biting opening-day releases** Kirsten Acuna, "Movie Studios Are Setting Themselves Up for Huge Losses," *Business Insider*, March 6, 2013.

247 **large up-front marketing spends** Anita Elberse, *Blockbusters: Hit-Making, Risk-Taking, and the Big Business of Entertainment* (New York: Henry Holt, 2013); McClintock, "$200 Million and Rising."

247 **independents like Focus Features, Fox Searchlight** Sharon Waxman, "With Acquisition, Lions Gate Is Now Largest Indie," *New York Times*, December 16, 2003.

247 **First, they paid their stars less—up front** Quotes are from interviews with senior movie studio executives between 2013 and 2015.

249 **Few U.S. companies have matched** Information about Danaher in this section is drawn primarily from Bharat Anand, David Collis, and Sophie Hood, "Danaher Corporation," HBS No. 708-445 (Boston: Harvard Business Publishing, rev. November 30, 2015); share price information from Yahoo! Finance.

250 **"It's so easy, given how prominent DBS"** All quotes attributed to Larry Culp in this section are from interviews in November 2014 and November 2015.

252 **But let's revisit how things are** Information in this section draws from personal observations during tour of Tencent in November 2012 and November 2013; it also draws from interviews with Caitlyn Chen and Dylan Zhang in November 2014, for which I am grateful; see also Willy Shih et al., "WeChat: A Global Platform?"

Part IV

261 **"The future of advertising"** Michael Schrage, "Is Advertising Dead?," *Wired*, February 1, 1994.

261 **"I just don't know which half"** "John Wanamaker," *Advertising Age*, The Advertising Century: A Special Report, March 29, 1999.

261 **"In the one-to-one world the Net promises"** Esther Dyson, "Intellectual Value: A Radical New Way of Looking at Compensation for Owners," *Wired*, December 1994.

262 **the Internet was interactive** John Deighton et al., "The Future of Interactive Marketing," *Harvard Business Review*, November/December 1996. For an economic analysis of how online advertising is shaping the structure of the advertising market, and relevant tradeoffs such as privacy versus targeting, see David Evans, "The Online Advertising Industry: Economics, Evolution, and Privacy," *Journal of Economic Perspectives* (2009), 23, no. 3, 37–60.

262 **a whopping 88 percent** Michael Lewis, "Boom Box," *New York Times Magazine*, August 13, 2000.

262 **"If no one watches commercials"** Ibid.

262 **few companies anywhere elicited as much excitement** Caroline McCarthy, "Facebook Ads Makes a Flashy Debut in New York," *CNET*, last modified November 6, 2007, accessed March 9, 2016, http://www.cnet.com/news/facebook-ads-makes-a-flashy-debut-in-new-york/.

262 **most of this information** Vauhini Vara, "Facebook Gets Personal with Ad Targeting Plan," *Wall Street Journal*, August 23, 2007

263 **actually clicks on the ad** Dave Chaffey, "Display Advertising Clickthrough Rates," Smart Insights, April 2016, accessed June 6, 2016, http://www.smartinsights.com/internet-advertising/internet-advertising-analytics/display-advertising-clickthrough-rates.

263 **falling every year** Dan Mitchell, "Online Ad Revenues Soar, but That's No Reason to Cheer," *Fortune*, December 19, 2012; PricewaterhouseCoopers, *IAB Internet Advertis-*

ing Revenue Report: 2012 Full Year Results (Interactive Advertising Bureau (IAB), 2013).

263 **40 percent of U.S. households** *The Total Audience Report: Q4 2014* (n.p.: Nielsen, 2015).

263 **$40 billion** Nick Petrillo, *IBISWorld Industry Report 51512: Television Broadcasting in the US* (IBISWorld, 2016).

263 **households that owned a DVR and ones that did not** Bart J. Bronnenberg, Jean-Pierre Dubé, and Carl F. Mela, "Do Digital Video Recorders Influence Sales?," *Journal of Marketing Research* 47, no. 6 (December 2010): 998–1010.

263 **despite Facebook's superior user data** Jim Edwards, "DATA: Google Totally Blows Away Facebook on Ad Performance," *Business Insider,* last modified May 15, 2012, accessed March 9, 2016, http://www.businessinsider.com/data-google-totally-blows -away-facebook-on-ad-performance-2012-5. A 2013 survey of 395 large-company marketers by Forrester Research revealed that Facebook created "less business value than any other digital marketing opportunity." See Nate Elliott, "An Open Letter to Mark Zuckerberg," October 28, 2013, accessed June 6, 2016, http://blogs.forrester.com /nate_elliott/13-10-28-an_open_letter_to_mark_zuckerberg.

264 *The Affluent Society* John Kenneth Galbraith, *The Affluent Society*, 3rd ed. (Boston: Houghton Mifflin, 1976).

264 **of desirable information** One of the first papers to offer a formal theory for the informative (matching) effect of advertising is Gene Grossman and Carl Shapiro, "Informative Advertising with Differentiated Products," *The Review of Economic Studies* 51, no. 1 (1984): 63–81. For a comprehensive review of the debates in advertising, see Kyle Bagwell, *The Economics of Advertising* (2001), (Cheltenham, UK: Edward Elgar). There are other ways, too, in which advertising affects behavior that have been the focus of the marketing literature; for example, through *affect* (influencing emotions, feelings) or *identity*.

266 **Berkeley professor Steve Tadelis** I am grateful to Steve Tadelis for an interview in December 2015 (all quotes in this section are from this interview).

267 **a series of experiments** Steven Tadelis, Chris Nosko, and Thomas Blake, "Consumer Heterogeneity and Paid Search Effectiveness: A Large-Scale Field Experiment," *Econometrica* 83, no. 1 (January 2015): 155–74.

268 **its own report** David Chan et al., "Incremental Clicks Impact of Search Advertising," Google Inc. research report, accessed June 6, 2016, http://static.googleusercontent .com/media/research.google.com/en//pubs/archive/37161.pdf.

270 **promos for television programs** Bharat Anand and Ron Shachar, "Advertising the Matchmaker," *RAND Journal of Economics* 42, no. 2 (Summer 2011): 205–45. See also Daniel Ackerberg, "Empirically Distinguishing Informative and Prestige Effects of Advertising," *RAND Journal of Economics* 32, no. 2 (2001): 316–33.

271 **"as some advertisers"** "Pop-up Guidelines & Best Practices: A Discussion around our Final Recommendation," Interactive Advertising Bureau report (2004), accessed July 14, 2016, http://www2.mediamind.com/data/uploads/resourcelibrary/iab_pop-up guidelinesindustryreview.pdf.

272 **"clicking on an ad"** "Cisco Annual Security Report: Threats Step Out of the Shadows," news release, January 30, 2013.

272 **Nielsen change its approach** Jason Lynch, "A First Look at Nielsen's Total Audience Measurement and How It Will Change the Industry: Rollout Begins in December," *Adweek*, October 20, 2015; Troy Dreier, "Nielsen to Roll Out Total Audience Measurement Tool in December," streamingmedia.com, last modified October 23, 2015, accessed March 9, 2016, http://www.streamingmedia.com/Articles/News /Online-Video-News/Nielsen-to-Roll-Out-Total-Audience-Measurement-Tool-in -December-107153.aspx.

272 **Online CPMs are low and sinking** PricewaterhouseCoopers, *IAB Internet Advertising Revenue Report: 2013 Full Year Results* (Interactive Advertising Bureau (IAB), 2014).

272 **of print CPMs** Mitchell, "Online Ad Revenues Soar."

273 **on digital ads** "Digital Ad Spending Benchmarks by Industry: The Complete eMarketer Series," eMarketer.com, May 2014, accessed June 6, 2016, https://www.emarketer.com /public_media/docs/Digital_Ad_Spending_Benchmarks_by_Industry-The_Complete _eMarketer_Series-05092014-FINAL.pdf. The digital share of economy-wide advertising expenditures is greater than the share of most individual firms since the distribution of firms that spend money on digital ads is far broader than for other media such as television.

273 **will solve marketing's problems** A fascinating recent study of "dynamic retargeting" showed that since merely serving ads to people based on their browsing history does not distinguish those who have already decided whether or not to purchase the product and those who are still undecided, companies may be wasting a lot of money; specifically, the study showed that the effectiveness of personalized retargeted ads can be lower than generic brand ads. See Anja Lambrecht and Catherine Tucker, "When Does Retargeting Work? Information Specificity in Online Advertising," *Journal of Marketing Research* 50, no. 5 (2013): 561–76.

273 **"a long way to go"** Logan Koepke, "Online Ads' Black Box a Mystery, Even to Companies Themselves," EqualFuture, July 8, 2015, accessed June 6, 2016, https://www .equalfuture.us/2015/07/08/online-ads-black-box-adfisher.

274 **"The Theft of Credibility"** David Dobbs, "*The Atlantic,* Scientology, and the Theft of Credibility," *Wired,* January 16, 2013.

274 **"the *Atlantic*'s Scientology Blunder"** Dan Gillmor, "The Lessons of the Atlantic's Scientology 'Sponsor Content' Blunder," *Guardian,* January 16, 2013.

274 **"We screwed up"** Statement from *The Atlantic,* magnetmail.net, last modified January 2013, accessed March 9, 2016, https://www.magnetmail.net/actions/email_web_version .cfm?recipient_id=699462885&message_id=2459857&user_id=NJG_Atlan&group _id=0&jobid=12656579.

274 **Coke cups on *American Idol*** Theresa Howard, "Real Winner of 'American Idol': Coke," *USA Today,* September 9, 2002, MONEY, 6B.

274 **new ice cream flavor for Walgreen's store brand** Samantha Bomkamp, "Walgreen Has Starring Role in 'Celebrity Apprentice' Finale," *Chicago Tribune,* May 13, 2013.

274 **LG's home entertainment system** "LG Invites 'All-Star Celebrity Apprentice' Viewers to Chat Live with Joan Rivers," *PR Newswire,* last modified April 24, 2013, accessed March 9, 2016, http://www.prnewswire.com/news-releases/lg-invites-all-star-celebrity -apprentice-viewers-to-chat-live-with-joan-rivers-204471441.html.

275 **"In most traditional content organizations"** I am grateful to Janet Balis for an interview in May 2015 (all quotes attributed to her in this section are from this interview).

275 **"We were really the first"** I am grateful to Paul Berry for an interview in August 2015.

276 **Recall the experiment on** Anand and Rosinski, "The Impact of Brands and Advertising on Perceptions of Editorial Quality."

277 **advertising doesn't help only advertisers** In a more sophisticated randomized experiment, Stanford professors Sahni and Nair (2016) examine how native advertising on the Zomato platform (a mobile app for restaurant searches) affects both propensity-to-purchase and propensity-to-confuse. Examining data on more than 200,000 users, they find that native advertising works not by "tricking" consumers into purchase: Consumers continue to search after viewing the native ad and, if they do eventually "decide to pick the advertised option, consumers reach it through search or organic clicks,"

suggesting low support for the "naïve consumer" view. See Navdeep Sahni and Harikesh Nair, "Native Advertising, Sponsorship Disclosure, and Consumer Deception: Evidence from Mobile Search-Ad Experiments," working paper.

278 **"Newsrooms used to believe"** I am grateful to Raju Narisetti for interviews in July 2013 and September 2015.

280 **"That's how it all started"** I am grateful to John Winsor for interviews in November 2014, December 2014, and January 2015 (all quotes attributed to him in this part of the book are from these interviews).

282 *Beyond the Brand* John Winsor, *Beyond the Brand: Why Engaging The Right Customers Is Essential to Winning in Business* (Chicago: Dearborn Trade, 2004).

283 **thirteen times** See "Fruit of the Loom Names Crispin Porter + Bogusky New Ad Agency of Record," *BusinessWire,* last modified November 30, 2012, accessed March 9, 2016, http://www.businesswire.com/news/home/20121130005625/en/Fruit-Loom -Names%C2%A0Crispin-Porter-Bogusky-New%C2%A0Ad-Agency; Maureen Morrison, "A Tale of Two Crispins: Why There Won't Be Another Agency of the Decade," *Advertising Age,* February 4, 2014; "MDC Partners Congratulates Crispin Porter + Bogusky on Being Named 'Agency of the Decade,'" *PR Newswire,* last modified December 16, 2009, accessed March 9, 2016, http://www.prnewswire.com/news-releases/mdc-partners-congratulates -crispin-porter-bogusky-on-being-named-agency-of-the-decade-79410487.html.

283 *Baked In* Alex Bogusky and John Winsor, *Baked In: Creating Products and Businesses That Market Themselves* (Chicago: B2 Books/Agate, 2009).

286 **what made certain TV ads viral** Thales Teixeira, "A Consumer-Centric Model of Viral Advertising Calibrated on Face-Tracking Data," Harvard Business School Working Paper, March 2014; Thales S. Teixeira, "The New Science of Viral Ads," *Harvard Business Review,* March 2012.

286 **study on the sharing of *New York Times* articles** Jonah Berger, *Contagious: Why Things Catch On* (New York: Simon & Schuster, 2013); Katherine L. Milkman, Liz Rees-Jones, and Jonah Berger, "The Secret to Online Success: What Makes Content Go Viral," *Scientific American,* April 14, 2015; John Tierney, "Good News Beats Bad on Social Networks," *New York Times,* March 18, 2013.

286 **"engineering virality"** Thales Teixeira and Alison Caverly, "Mekanism: Engineering Viral Marketing," HBS No. 512-010 (Boston: Harvard Business Publishing, rev. April 16, 2013); Mark Borden, "The Mekanism Guarantee: They Engineer Virality," *Fast Company,* May 1, 2010; Lewis Howes, "How to Go Viral on YouTube: The Untold Truth Behind Getting Views," *Forbes,* August 9, 2012.

286 **BuzzFeed would pick up** Felix Oberholzer-Gee, "BuzzFeed—The Promise of Native Advertising," HBS No. 714-512 (Boston: Harvard Business Publishing, rev. August 15, 2014); David Rowan, "How BuzzFeed Mastered Social Sharing to Become a Media Giant for a New Era," *Wired,* January 2, 2014.

286 **"virality lift"** Sarah Kessler, "BuzzFeed's Jonah Peretti Is the Stephen Hawking of Radical Skateboarding Birds," *Fast Company,* September 14, 2012.

286 **published a paper** Duncan J. Watts and Jonah Peretti, "Viral Marketing for the Real World," *Harvard Business Review,* May 2007, 22–23.

287 **Procter & Gamble's campaign** Ibid.

287 **150 million unique visitors** Oberholzer-Gee, "BuzzFeed—The Promise of Native Advertising."

287 **humor, animals, lists, and pictures** Oberholzer-Gee, "BuzzFeed—The Promise of Native Advertising"; Andrew Rice, "Does BuzzFeed Know the Secret?," *New York* magazine, April 7, 2013; Lukas I. Alpert, "BuzzFeed Nails the 'Listicle'; What Happens Next?," *Wall Street Journal,* January 29, 2015.

287 **"turned out to be eminently sharable"** Oberholzer-Gee, "BuzzFeed—The Promise of Native Advertising."

287 **by Buzzfeed's models** Oberholzer-Gee, "Does BuzzFeed Know the Secret?" *New York*.

287 **"losers starved"** Oberholzer-Gee, "BuzzFeed—The Promise of Native Advertising."

288 **"they're kicking ass"** Oberholzer-Gee, "Does BuzzFeed Know the Secret?"

288 **"Don't Buy This Jacket"** Tim Nudd, "Ad of the Day: Patagonia," *Adweek*, November 28, 2011; "Don't Buy This Jacket," Patagonia, last modified 2011, accessed March 10, 2016, http://www.patagonia.com/email/11/112811.html.

288 **"think twice before they buy"** "Don't Buy This Jacket, Black Friday and the *New York Times*," *The Cleanest Line* (Patagonia company blog), last modified 2011, accessed March 10, 2016, http://www.thecleanestline.com/2011/11/dont-buy-this-jacket-black -friday-and-the-new-york-times.html.

289 *Worn Wear* "Worn Wear: a Film About the Stories We Wear—Presented by Patagonia," video file, 27:52, YouTube, posted by Patagonia, November 20, 2013, accessed March 10, 2016, https://www.youtube.com/watch?v=z20CjCim8DM.

289 **a series of free repair guides** "Worn Wear," Patagonia, last modified 2016, accessed March 10, 2016, http://www.patagonia.com/us/worn-wear; "Patagonia Care & Repair," iFixit, last modified 2016, accessed March 10, 2016, https://www.ifixit.com /Patagonia.

289 **founded in 1973** Forest Reinhardt et al., "Patagonia," HBS No. 711-020 (Boston: Harvard Business Publishing, rev. October 19, 2010); "Company History," Patagonia, accessed March 10, 2016, http://www.patagonia.com/us/patagonia.go?assetid=3351.

289 **could use a toll-free line** Paul B. Brown, "In 1988, Patagonia Was Full of Anti-Marketers," *Inc.*, March 1988.

289 **that lasted longer than anyone else's** Brown, "In 1988, Patagonia."

289 **exceeded 40 percent** Kyle Stock, "Patagonia's Confusing and Effective Campaign to Grudgingly Sell Stuff," *Bloomberg Business*, last modified November 25, 2013; Kyle Stock, "Patagonia's 'Buy Less' Plea Spurs More Buying," *Bloomberg Business*, August 28, 2013.

290 **"Is Giving Better Than Receiving?"** Erik Oster, "EVB, Victors & Spoils Give 'The Gift of Giving' for JCPenney," *Adweek*, December 8, 2014.

291 **one of that site's most-watched commercials** Garett Sloane, "JCPenney's 4 Cent Video Ads on Twitter Could Threaten YouTube's Longtime Dominance," *Adweek*, February 17, 2015.

291 **Think social first, product later** Mikolaj Jan Piskorski, *A Social Strategy: How We Profit from Social Media* (Princeton, NJ: Princeton University Press, 2014).

291 *Decoded* Anita Elberse and Kwame Owusu-Kesse, "Droga5: Launching Jay-Z's *Decoded*," HBS No. 513-032 (Boston: Harvard Business Publishing, July 25, 2012).

293 **to creating ad copy for clients** Lauren Johnson, "Why Facebook Is Taking More of Its Advertising Work In-House," *Adweek*, October 1, 2015; Issie Lapowsky, "Tumblr Launches Creative Agency to Connect Artists with Advertisers," *Wired*, January 22, 2015; Ava Seave, "BuzzFeed's Director of Creative: 'Authentic Content Earns the Right to go Viral,'" *Forbes*, November 26, 2013.

295 **"worst in the history of major retail"** Jim Edwards and Charlie Minato, "How Ex-CEO Ron Johnson Made JCPenney Even Worse," *Business Insider*, last modified April 8, 2013, accessed March 10, 2016, http://www.businessinsider.com/ron-johnson -disaster-timeline-apple-guru-failed-at-jcpenney-2013-4?op=1.

295 **dropped from 84 percent to 56 percent** Dominic Green, "JCPenney Redesigned Its Logo So Many Times Nearly Half of America No Longer Recognizes It," *Business Insider*, last modified May 8, 2013, accessed March 10, 2016, http://www.business insider.com/jcpenneys-new-logo-2013-5.

295 **"@jcpenney: Who kkmew theis was"** Danielle Wiener-Bronner, "JCPenney's 'Drunk' Super Bowl Tweets Were Really Just a Mitten-Selling Stunt," *Wire*, last modified February 3, 2014; Neha Prakash, "J.C. Penney Is Having a Little Too Much Fun at

the Super Bowl," *Mashable*, last modified February 2, 2014, accessed March 10, 2016, http://mashable.com/2014/02/02/jc-penny-super-bowl/#Sdo6vmbUiqqB.

296 **15 percent of the amount** Patricia Winters Lauro, *The Media Business: Advertising; New Methods of Agency Payments Drive a Stake Through the Heart of the old 15% Commission*," *New York Times*, April 2, 1999.

296 **the urge for agencies to inflate costs** Ibid.

298 **"If you aren't thinking about connecting"** "Secrets of Creative Management: Timeless Wisdom from David Ogilvy," citing quotes from *The Unpublished David Ogilvy* (New York: Crown, 1987).

299 **"A revolution has begun"** "Creative Destruction," *Economist,* June 28, 2014.

299 **whose delivery remained unchanged for nearly three centuries** Joel Rose, "How to Break Free of Our 19th-Century Factory-Model Education System," *Atlantic*, May 9, 2012.

300 **One Ivy League professor** Michael Pupin, "Professor-Inventor Predicts Radio Universities," *Popular Science Monthly,* February 1923.

300 **"The nation has become the new campus"** Susan Matt and Luke Fernandez, "Before MOOCs, 'Colleges of the Air,'" *Chronicle of Higher Education,* April 23, 2013, accessed June 9, 2016, http://chronicle.com/blogs/conversation/2013/04/23/before -moocs-colleges-of-the-air.

300 **"Will the classroom be abolished"** Ibid. The quote is attributed to Bruce Bliven, writing for *The New Republic,* 1924.

301 **Columbia, Tufts, Wisconsin, and Harvard** Matt and Fernandez, "Before MOOCs, 'Colleges of the Air.'"

301 **"Gradually problems emerged"** Ibid.

301 **or on educational institutions** Matt Novak, "Predictions for Educational TV in the 1930s," Smithsonian.com, last modified May 29, 2012, accessed March 10, 2016, http://www.smithsonianmag.com/history/predictions-for-educational-tv-in-the-1930s -107574983/?no-ist.

301 **at least one online course** "2014 Online College Students: Comprehensive Data on Demands and Preferences," Learning House, last modified 2014, accessed March 10, 2016, http://www.learninghouse.com/ocs2014-report; Carl Straumsheim, "Identifying the Online Student," *Inside Higher Ed*, last modified June 3, 2014, accessed March 10, 2016, https://www.insidehighered.com/news/2014/06/03/us-releases-data-distance -education-enrollments.

302 **its model was of a "hybrid university"** Kevin Carey, *The End of College* (New York: Riverhead Books, 2015).

302 **"all made sense—in theory"** Ibid.

302 **first expressed more than a century ago** Ibid.

302 **or more than 40 percent of all undergraduates** "Skills for America's Future Community College Facts," Aspen Institute, last modified 2016, accessed March 10, 2016, http://www.aspeninstitute.org/policy-work/economic-opportunities/skills-americas -future/what-we-do/community-college-facts.

302 **in their families to attend college** "2014 Fact Sheet," American Association of Community Colleges, last modified 2014, accessed March 10, 2016, http://www.aacc .nche.edu/AboutCC/Documents/Facts14_Data_R3.pdf.

302 **of many education reform initiatives** "Building American Skills Through Community Colleges," White House, accessed March 10, 2016, https://www.whitehouse .gov/issues/education/higher-education/building-american-skills-through-community -colleges.

302 **one hundred colleges and universities** Bureau of Labor Statistics, *The Prominence of Boston Area Colleges and Universities*, by Denis M. McSweeney and Walter J. Marshall (2009).

303 **noted in their book** Richard Arum and Josipa Roksa, *Academically Adrift: Limited Learning on College Campuses* (Chicago: University of Chicago Press, 2011).

303 **for a Silicon Valley hedge fund** Sal Khan, *The One World Schoolhouse: Education Reimagined* (New York: Twelve, 2013); Claudia Dreifus, "It All Started with a 12-Year-Old Cousin," *New York Times*, January 27, 2014; Theresa Johnston, "Salman Khan: 'Keep It Simple,'" Stanford Graduate School of Business, last modified February 22, 2012, accessed March 10, 2016, https://www.gsb.stanford.edu/insights/salman -khan-keep-it-simple; Richard Adams, "Sal Khan: The Man Who Tutored His Cousin— and Started a Revolution," *Guardian*, April 23, 2013.

303 **"The worst time to learn"** Khan, *The One World Schoolhouse*.

303 **"She said that her entire family"** Adams, "Sal Khan: The Man Who Tutored His Cousin—and Started a Revolution."

304 **"a free world-class education"** Colleen Walsh, "Education Without Limits," *Harvard Gazette*, last modified May 9, 2013.

304 **"consisted of exactly one person: me"** Khan, *The One World Schoolhouse*.

304 **"more than ten times"** Ibid.

304 **750 million times** Sally Peck, Matthew Pendergast, and Kat Hayes, "A Day in the Life of Khan Academy: The School with 15 Million Students," *Telegraph*, April 23, 2015.

304 **from Khan online** David A. Kaplan, "Innovation in Education: Bill Gates' Favorite Teacher," *Fortune*; Peck, Pendergast, and Hayes, "A Day in the Life."

304 **Google invested, too** Clive Thompson, "How Khan Academy Is Changing the Rules of Education," *Wired*, July 15, 2011.

304 *Time* **magazine's 100 Most Influential People** Bill Gates, "The World's 100 Most Influential People: 2012—Salman Khan," *Time*, April 18, 2012.

304 **a $3 million trial** "Khan Academy Resources for Maximizing Mathematics Achievement: A Postsecondary Mathematics Efficacy Study," Institute of Education Sciences, last modified 2014, accessed March 10, 2016, http://ies.ed.gov/funding/grantsearch /details.asp?ID=1521.

304 **Thrun had been a computer science professor** Steven Leckart, "The Stanford Education Experiment Could Change Higher Learning Forever," *Wired*, March 20, 2012.

305 **Google Glass** Max Chafkin, "Udacity's Sebastian Thrun, Godfather of Free Online Education, Changes Course," *Fast Company*, November 14, 2013.

305 **"It was this catalytic moment"** Ibid.

305 **at 411** Ibid.; William J. Bennett, "Is Sebastian Thrun's Udacity the Future of Higher Education?," *CNN*, last modified July 5, 2012, accessed March 10, 2016, http://www .cnn.com/2012/07/05/opinion/bennett-udacity-education/.

305 **"I can't teach at Stanford again"** Chafkin, "Udacity's Sebastian Thrun, Godfather."

305 **"edtech"** Sarah Perez, "Software Eats Education: With $15 Million in Series B Funding, Andreessen Horowitz Bets on Udacity," *TechCrunch*, last modified October 25, 2012, accessed March 10, 2016, http://techcrunch.com/2012/10/25/software-eats -education-with-15-million-in-series-b-funding-andreessen-horowitz-bets-on-udacity/; Cat Zakrzewski, "Udacity Raises $105 Million Series D, Bringing Valuation to $1 Billion," *TechCrunch*, last modified November 11, 2015, accessed March 10, 2016, http:// techcrunch.com/2015/11/11/udacity-raises-105-million-series-d-bringing-valuation-to -1-billion/.

305 **edX** Katie Koch, "Educating Harvard, MIT—and the World," *Harvard Gazette*, last modified May 2, 2012.

305 **$30 million** Ibid.

305 **for content partnerships** "EdX Announces New Membership Structure; Expands edx.org," *edx*, last modified March 6, 2014, accessed March 10, 2016, https://www.edx .org/press/edx-announces-new-membership-structure.

306 **made its courses free** Tamar Lewin, "Harvard and M.I.T. Team Up to Offer Free Online Courses," *New York Times*, May 2, 2012.

306 **"the year of the MOOC"** Laura Pappano, "The Year of the MOOC," *New York Times*, November 2, 2012.

306 **"MOOC revolution is here"** Thomas L. Friedman, "The Professors' Big Stage," *New York Times*, March 5, 2013.

306 **diving for a decade** Srikant Datar, David Garvin, and Patrick Cullen, *Rethinking the MBA: Business Education at a Crossroads* (Boston: Harvard Business Review Press, 2010).

307 **had written of a "flat world"** Thomas L. Friedman, *The World Is Flat: A Brief History of the Twenty-First Century* (New York: Farrar, Straus & Giroux, 2005).

309 *inverted classroom* Maureen J. Lage, Glenn J. Platt, and Michael Treglia, "Inverting the Classroom: A Gateway to Creating an Inclusive Learning Environment," *Journal of Economic Education* 31, no. 1 (Winter 2000): 30–43.

310 **Sal Khan recently referred to** Khan, *The One World Schoolhouse*.

311 **the havoc online education** Clayton M. Christensen, *Disrupting Class: How Disruptive Innovation Will Change the Way the World Learns*, expanded ed. (New York: McGraw-Hill, 2011).

315 **broader debates swirling around undergraduate education** For different perspectives on this debate, see Fareed Zakaria, *In Defense of a Liberal Education* (New York: Norton, 2015); Nannerl Keohane, "The Liberal Arts as Guideposts in the 21st Century," *Chronicle of Higher Education*, January 29, 2012; Scott Gerber, "How Liberal Arts Colleges Are Failing America," *Atlantic*, September 24, 2012; Victor Davis Hanson, "The Modern University Is Failing Students in Every Respect," *National Review*, April 9, 2015, accessed June 6, 2016, http://www.nationalreview.com/article/416673 /modern-university-failing-students-every-respect-victor-davis-hanson; Debra Humphreys and Patrick Kelly, "How Liberal Arts and Sciences Majors Fare in Employment," National Center for Higher Education Management Systems and the Association of American Colleges and Universities, 2014; "It Takes More than a Major: Employer Priorities for College Learning and Student Success," Hart Research Associates, April 10, 2013.

319 **"The Online Revolution Drifts Off Course"** Eric Westervelt, "The Online Education Revolution Drifts Off Course," NPR, last modified December 31, 2013, accessed March 11, 2016, http://www.npr.org/2013/12/31/258420151/the-online-education -revolution-drifts-off-course.

320 **three outstanding second-year MBA students** The team referred to here that worked together to develop the content for the Economics for Managers course was: MBA students Erin Arnold, Ben Peterson, and Carolyn Wintner; doctoral student Thomas Steenburgh; research assistants Jonathan Dahlberg and (later) Katherine Boren; and course manager Li Feng. My colleagues Jan Hammond and V. G. Narayanan had similarly outstanding teams working closely with them.

324 **"three-to-five-minute rule"** Our efforts in building the learning model for HBX centered around trying to adapt the case method approach to a digital environment; at the same time, there has been a burgeoning literature on the "science of learning." For an impressive recent treatment, see Peter Brown, Henry Roediger, and Mark McDaniel, *Make It Stick: The Science of Successful Learning* (Cambridge, MA: Belknap Press of Harvard University Press, 2014).

325 **by getting rid of them** Ramon Casadesus-Masanell and Maxime Aucoin, "Cirque du Soleil—The High Wire Act of Building Sustainable Partnerships," HBS No. 709-411 (Boston: Harvard Business Publishing, rev. February 10, 2010).

329 **many of the reasons why** Jan Rivkin provides an overview of the many reasons why firms fail in "Key Concepts in a Module on Strategic Failure," HBS No. 706-471 (Bos-

ton: Harvard Business Publishing, rev. March 21, 2006). In technological settings, Rebecca M. Henderson and Kim B. Clark describe an important reason for failure: firms' lock-in to existing product architectures. See "Architectural Innovation: The Reconfiguration of Existing Product Technologies and the Failure of Established Firms," *Administrative Science Quarterly* 35, no. 1 (1990): 9–30.

330 **in his book** Christensen, *Disrupting Class.*

330 **So was the media** "Online Education: The Disruption to Come," *Economist,* February 11, 2014; Todd Hixon, "Higher Education Is Now Ground Zero for Disruption," *Forbes,* January 6, 2014.

330 **Originally articulated in the mid-1990s** Joseph L. Bower and Clayton M. Christensen, "Disruptive Technologies: Catching the Wave," *Harvard Business Review,* January 1995; Clayton M. Christensen, *The Innovator's Dilemma: When New Technologies Cause Great Firms to Fail* (Boston: Harvard Business Publishing, 1997, 2000).

331 **far outdistanced Christensen's definition** Clayton M. Christensen, Michael E. Raynor, and Rory McDonald, "What Is Disruptive Innovation?," *Harvard Business Review,* December 2015.

331 **a law of nature** See also Joshua Gans, *The Disruption Dilemma* (Cambridge, MA: MIT Press, 2016); Joshua Gans, "The Other Disruption," *Harvard Business Review,* March 2016; Andrew King and Baljir Baatarogtokh, "How Useful Is the Theory of Disruptive Innovation?," *MIT Sloan Management Review,* Fall 2015.

336 **"I'm so excited to be starting"** Layla Siraj, email message to author, June 2014; Siraj kindly agreed to allow me to reproduce her email here.

337 **"Remember when I said"** Lucas Carvalho, "HBX CORe: Harvard Business School—Week 1," LinkedIn blog, March 3, 2015, accessed June 6, 2016, https://www.linkedin.com/pulse/hbx-harvard-business-school-week-1-lucas-carvalho.

339 **HBX Live** John A. Byrne, "Harvard Business School Really Has Created the Classroom of the Future," *Fortune,* August 25, 2015.

341 **"Will MOOCs Kill Universities?"** "Will MOOCs Kill University Degrees?," *Economist,* October 1, 2013; see also Zocalo Public Square, "Will Technology Kill Universities?," *Time,* March 18, 2015; Anne VanderMey, "Why Online Education Won't Kill Your Campus," *Fortune,* October 28, 2013.

341 **"Is online learning a fad?"** Juan Cristóbal Bonnefoy, "MOOCs in Development: Fad or Future?," *Americas Quarterly,* Summer 2014; Michael Horn, "Avoid the Hype: Online Learning's Transformational Potential," *Forbes,* June 6, 2013.

343 **Where online education** See, for example, John Hechinger, "Southern New Hampshire, A Little College That's a Giant Online," *Bloomberg,* May 9, 2013; Ilya Pozin, "Private Company Solves US Education Problem," *Forbes,* November 15, 2012; Anya Kamanetz, "Minerva Strives for Affordable Elitism," *New York Times,* November 1, 2013; and Claire Cain Miller, "Extreme Study Abroad: The World Is Their Campus," *New York Times,* October 30, 2015.

INDEX

Page numbers of figures appear in italics

About the Author

BHARAT ANAND is the Henry R. Byers Professor of Business Administration at Harvard Business School. He graduated magna cum laude with a B.A. in economics from Harvard University and received his Ph.D. in economics from Princeton University.

Professor Anand is an expert in digital and corporate strategy. He has studied how new technologies affect what we watch, read, and hear, and how companies navigate digital change. He has written more than fifty articles and case studies on economics, strategy, and marketing, received awards for both his research and case-writing, and chaired various executive education programs. He is a two-time winner of the "best teacher award" at Harvard Business School.

Anand has advised leading organizations and entrepreneurs around the world. Recently, he helped create Harvard Business School's digital learning initiative, HBX, which he now oversees as faculty chair.

@Bharat_N_Anand

About the Type

This book was set in Fairfield, the first typeface from the hand of the distinguished American artist and engraver Rudolph Ruzicka (1883–1978). Ruzicka was born in Bohemia (in the present-day Czech Republic) and came to America in 1894. He set up his own shop, devoted to wood engraving and printing, in New York in 1913 after a varied career working as a wood engraver, in photoengraving and banknote printing plants, and as an art director and freelance artist. He designed and illustrated many books, and was the creator of a considerable list of individual prints—wood engravings, line engravings on copper, and aquatints.